Come Watch The
SUN GO HOME

Come Watch The
SUN GO HOME

by Chen Chen

MARLOWE & COMPANY
NEW YORK

Marlowe & Company
841 Broadway, Fourth Floor
New York, NY   10003

Library of Congress Cataloging-in-Publication Data

Chen, Chen, 1939-
     Come watch the sun go home / Chen Chen.
          p.   cm.
     ISBN 1-56924-742-0
        1. Chen, Chen, 1939- . 2. China—Biography.   I. Title.
CT1828.C519A3   1998
     951.05'092—dc21
     [B]   98-5342
                                                                              CIP

ISBN 1-56924-742-0

Manufactured in the United States of America

*To my parents
at their final resting place in Berkeley,
overlooking the Pacific Ocean*

Contents

PART III: THE LONG NIGHTMARE (1966-)
Peking, Tientsin and the Cadre Schools

CONTENTS

PART IV: LIFE BEGINS AT FORTY (1979-)
China—U.S.—China—U.S.—China—U.S...

PROLOGUE

We lived in a modest two-story house on Scenic Avenue in Berkeley, California, during the last years of the 1940s.

Every day at sunset, Mama would call from our living room in Chinese: "Come watch the sun go home!" My brother Toto and I would drop whatever we were doing and join Papa and Mama at the westward-facing picture window.

Directly across the Bay, the Golden Gate Bridge pointed its twin towers at the sky. At this hour the rays of the setting sun would be playing harp on the bridge cables and sprinkling flecks of gold across the Pacific, all the way to where we had come from—China.

We stood in silence, "watching the sun go home." Unscientific as it may sound, we always thought of it that way: Home to light up our long-suffering motherland, home to convey our longings for everything we had left there.

We would stand at the window as the half dome of the sun lowered itself into the waters, with one last wink before it went on its way to China. Then we would return to our interrupted pursuits, only to return for the next sunset.

At the end of 1949, the Chen family of four also went home; not with the setting sun, however, but eastward, facing the sun. We went around the world, back to a motherland now at peace. Or so we believed and hoped.

Forty years later, tanks rolled and killed along the Avenue of Everlasting Peace to the Gate of Heavenly Peace—Tiananmen—in my city of Beijing. I was in the United States at the time and suddenly found myself in the position of part-time professor and part-time refugee, with all the "home" I possessed packed in three suitcases.

I live today as close to the beaches of Los Angeles as I can afford, so that

I may occasionally go to the edge of the Pacific at sunset. Both my parents are gone, and my brother Toto and his family live elsewhere in California. Save for the same old sun and the same old Pacific, I am the only one left to relive that bygone scenario, "Come Watch the Sun Go Home."

Chen Chen

PART I

THE TURBULENT YEARS OF MY CHILDHOOD (1939-1949)

Peiping—Chungking—Peiping—
Berkeley—Europe—Peking

Born Unfree

I was born in Peiping,* under Japanese occupation, but my birthplace was an American hospital, the Peiping Union Medical College (P.U.M.C.) Hospital, Room 308A. My brother would be born in the same room two years later, my daughter, twenty-five years later.

In June 1937, my parents had been on their way to the United States after their honeymoon. Mama had obtained a scholarship for M.A. studies at UC Berkeley. While they were waiting in Hong Kong for their ship to sail, they received a cable saying that my paternal grandmother was critically ill, so naturally they returned to Peiping to be at her side. A few weeks later, on the night of July 7, 1937, Japanese garrison troops conducting maneuvers at the Marco Polo Bridge outside Peiping claimed that they had been fired upon by Chinese troops. Peiping was occupied immediately by the Japanese and this incident started the all-out Sino-Japanese War. Papa and Mama were forced to stay on in this ill-fated city.

My father went back to his job as manager of a small branch office of a bank. This branch office happened to be located right in the building of the P.U.M.C. Hospital, which explains why we had doctors' families as close friends all our lives, and why I have "STAFF" stamped in English, in purple ink block letters, on my medical file at P.U.M.C.

The gravest danger of living in occupied Peiping stemmed from Mama, who had been a zealous leader of anti-Japanese activities at Tsinghua University where she graduated from the Department of English and then taught in the mid-1930s. In fact, she was the chairperson of the Anti-Japanese Invasion Committee of that reputable university, and her name and enthusiasm were both well known among her peers. The unforeseen turn of events forced her to give up both her political and professional careers; she even

* Note: Peiping, Peking, and Beijing are various English transliterations of the name for the same city.

gave up her own name and, like many married women in feudal China, was registered in official files as "Chen Chiang *shih*" (Chen *née* Chiang). Acquaintances addressed her simply as "Mrs. Chen." She was to remain anonymous for seven years—to be a housewife, to be the mother of two children, to be constantly fearful of being recognized as the one-time activist. If it hadn't been for that ill-timed cable, she would have been on the Berkeley campus, pursuing her studies and speaking out for her country.

Mama was thirty years old when I was born. In those days that was quite an advanced age by both Western and Eastern standards for giving birth to one's first child. Mama was lightly chloroformed, and the doctors and nurses attending her told her later that she kept calling out a name: "Estrelita." Afterward, Papa and Mama decided that it was too exotic to be the Western name of this baby girl. For that decision, I remain forever grateful. At any rate, P.U.M.C. was the hospital they chose and the only safe place to go to under the circumstances. At any other hospital a "Chen Chiang shih" calling out such an outlandish name under chloroform would hardly have escaped suspicion!

We Chinese are lucky in that we have two birthdays: one by the Christian calendar, one by the Chinese lunar calendar. By our calendar, I was born seven days before the Chinese New Year in February of 1939, on the day of the Lord of the Kitchen. This deity is supposed to come down to each household to verify whether it is tidy, harmonious, and respectable. He then returns to report to the Heavenly Ruler. A harmonious and clean family is rewarded with good fortune, an unclean and bickering family is punished with bad luck. Every family bribes the Lord of the Kitchen by sealing his lips with a kind of sticky white molasses candy, and asks him to report only the good things. So I was born the Lady of the Kitchen.

The doctors and nurses had a good laugh that day. A baby boy had been born fifteen minutes after I was, and they said jokingly that the Lady had been so anxious to get at the offerings she had left without the Lord, and the Lord had scurried after her to catch up fifteen minutes later. My "Lord" and I came together for our one and only reunion a couple of years later, and had our pictures taken. Mama would point to the pictures in our album and say "Here's your Lord of the Kitchen."

Because of the stringent residence regulations under Japanese occupation, Papa and Mama did not set up an independent household before I was born, for fear of betraying Mama's real identity. They lived instead in the household of an architect. It was only after I was born that my parents rented a court-yard house just south of the Gate of Earthly Peace, Di'anmen (the antipodean structure to the Gate of Heavenly Peace, or Tiananmen). Directly facing our front gate was the residence of one of China's most prominent painters, Chen Pan-ting.

Some four decades later, Deng Xiao-ping was to reside in this *hutung* (lane or alley), his residence built right on Chen Pan-ting's former property. I had an obsession for wandering around by our former abodes, but not into them. Riding my bike, I went around this old *hutung* one day in 1979, not long after the disastrous Cultural Revolution had ended and after both my parents were gone. The *hutung* was strangely quiet; all the doors were closed, no children played here, as in other *hutungs*, and stone-faced sentries stood by all along the *hutung* to guard China's so-called paramount leader. I rode away quickly, never to return again.

As the first born, I was the apple of my parents' eye. They had been edu-cated along Western lines, so it didn't make any difference to them whether I was a girl or a boy. My Chinese name was given me in memory of my pater-nal grandmother who passed away before I was born, but I also have a pet name. Mama called me *Pao Pei*, which means "precious baby." But since our domestic help could hardly use this name, I became *Hsiao Chieh*, or "Miss," almost before I opened my eyes for the first time, and that address stuck with me—at home, of course—into the late 1950s.

I was kept pretty much at home, for Mama rarely ventured out on her own. Papa and Mama cherished and spoiled me. The first time I said "Papa," he was so elated he went out and bought me a new crib. When he got home from work, he'd throw me across his shoulders and march around the house, singing "There's a Rainbow on My Shoulder," in English, and I learned to sing those verses before I knew what they meant. Then one day—according to Mama—she took me out into the *hutung* where neighborhood children were at play. Mama noticed me gazing raptly at them, and when she tugged my arm for us to go home, I paid no attention. Papa and Mama decided it was time I had a playmate, a sibling. Toto came into this world two years later.

Toto was born at the P.U.M.C. a few months before Pearl Harbor. After the Japanese attack, even this tiny haven of freedom in an unfree city was lost to the occupation authorities. The American doctors and their families packed up and left, and, gradually, quite a few prominent Chinese doctors also left the P.U.M.C., and even Peiping as well, to set up private clinics elsewhere. However, we would cross paths with these doctors again and again.

The Dread, the Threat, and Papa Goes to Jail

One of the first true memories from my childhood is of the day Papa was taken away by Japanese military police. I wasn't even three years old, but to this day I remember the shadows silhouetted against a window as he was beaten. I was clinging to Mama's winter coat, Toto was in Mama's arms, and I watched Papa being flogged on the back on the other side of the window. I heard the dull thuds of the whip, and then Papa was taken away by Japanese policemen.

Tension had been gradually building up in the months leading up to this incident. Even in our quiet courtyard tucked in an out-of-the-way alley, the winds of war were felt. An elderly British couple who lived in the walled-off front part of our courtyard left China when the mounting hostilities in Europe raised the spectre of persecution by the Japanese authorities.

In Peiping, as elsewhere in China, children had to adapt while the country was racked and raped by the Japanese invader for eight long years. Such words as "curfew," "household check," and "food rations" were among the first we kids learned. And in my conception of things, a windowpane was always vertically, horizontally, and diagonally pasted with paper strips in compliance with air-defense regulations; and both Toto and I scrambled under tables with great celerity whenever sirens announced an air-defense rehearsal.

Children born under occupation instinctively sense where danger lies, and from a very tender age we knew what could be said in public and what in private. Perhaps this instinct has become an inherent part of Chinese nature, engendered by the all-too-frequent states of apprehension and fear people have experienced over centuries. And it has made the Chinese more wary and perhaps more versatile in critical situations.

Nevertheless, before Papa's arrest life went on with some semblance of normalcy, for us children at least. I got my first doll, Tootsie, as a birthday present when I was one year old—a regular long-gowned doll that could shut her eyes and squeak "Ma———." She was with me for twenty-six years, until our home was ransacked during the Cultural Revolution. I also had a live doll in

Toto, and I was allowed to hold him after we were both dumped in a playpen.

Now that there were two children, we went out more with Mama or with our amah. Walking south led us to the Coal Hill Park; walking north brought us to the busy street on the other side of the Gate of Earthly Peace. From here, we could see the Bell Tower and Drum Tower looming in the distance. The prime interest of the northbound walk lay in the pair of enormous bright-red gourds, each as tall as a person, placed in front of a pickled-vegetable store; I loved both the pickles and their huge logos.

There was, however, one unpleasant feature to this walk: a Japanese sentry was posted at the entrance of the gate, and all Chinese had to bow to him as they passed through. My profound aversion to the Japanese uniform and to the deep Japanese bow stems partially from this childhood humiliation. This hateful impression was so deeply engraved on my mind that when I boarded a transfer flight in Tokyo in 1984, more than forty years later, I actually shuddered when I saw a Japanese airport guard who wore a similarly colored uniform. After that unexpected shock, I kept my eyes averted from anything walking about in that color until the plane lifted off into neutral skies.

On that wintry day of Papa's arrest and imprisonment, we were going out to visit the home of a close friend. The entire family, Papa, Mama, Toto, and I, left in happy anticipation. I believe we went in two rickshaws, all dressed up for the occasion. However, unbeknownst to anyone, our friend's entire family had been taken away by the Japanese military police. The arrest had been conducted in great secrecy, for they wanted to make a clean sweep of all those connected with this family. Our family innocently walked into the trap. I only knew at the time that everything was going wrong, that I was frightened, that I didn't understand what was happening. I hazily recall that we were hustled up several stone steps into the house, that Mama and Toto and I were pushed into the back room while Papa, in the front room, was beaten, interrogated, then taken away. The one thing I clearly remember from that day were the shadows jerking across the window and myself huddled close to Mama's coat.

Mama told us years later that the three of us were also detained for one night. She also told us she was still breastfeeding Toto at the time and that her milk dried up overnight.

The days after Papa's imprisonment were fraught with apprehension. Since all Chinese shared a common hatred for the invaders, everyone we knew pitched in to help the family. The Japanese police searched the desk in Papa's office, and I was told years later that the only evidence they got for their pains was a calling card. It had been given to Papa by one of his Tsinghua school-mates, who—as luck would have it—happened to be an underground Communist known to the Japanese.

Papa's bank did its best to bail him out. He returned after three months of imprisonment and torture. Sleeping on cement floors during these three winter months left him with lifelong back pains. Papa had been a soccer star in his college years, and he keenly felt his disability. But we were fortunate to have him back, and thanks to Papa's gregarious nature and optimistic outlook on life, he even befriended some Chinese wardens in the prison. One of these was to save our whole family from eventual disaster.

Someone Delivers a Message

Life went on after Papa's return, yet even we children knew it wouldn't be the same again, for we were marked, and that meant constant danger. Papa and Mama did their best to shield us from the psychological effects of enemy occupation, but the fear and hatred grew, even in our sleep. Of the only two dreams I remember from those years (I was about four then), both have to do with fear and being left on my own.

In one dream we all went to the zoo, and while Papa and Mama led tod-dler Toto between them, I loitered behind. Then a man came over and slipped a noose over my shoulders. I tried to call out but no sound came from my throat. Although I was in the middle of a milling crowd, no one took any notice. I managed to wriggle out of the noose and ran toward my family. Just at that moment, Japanese troops came marching by and blocked the way. I tried and tried to get through the columns of soldiers, but to no avail.

In the other dream I was alone on a hillside, and the setting sun cast a deep purplish hue on the rocks. Crawling on all fours, I tried again and again to climb to a house on top of the hill. Suddenly, I found myself in our house again. I wanted to tell Mama how hard I had climbed, but she told me to grab some things quickly, for we had to leave before the Japanese came.

I don't wish to sound silly, telling all about these childish dreams. I am doing so only to convey some of the stark impressions and pervasive fear that left such deep mental scars in children of the war years. We didn't know what it is to be carefree. Even our few happy memories were frequently linked to an unhappy context.

I remember I got my "Shirley Temple" doll when I was about four. I never saw a Shirley Temple film in my childhood, for Asian distribution of Hollywood films was suspended before I was born and banned in Japanese occupied areas throughout the Pacific war years. I had heard a lot about the child star from Mama, however, and I was simply thrilled by the doll. Clad in a white dress with blue polka dots, she was in a box still wrapped in cellophane. Mama told me the doll was the treasured toy of a girl whose family had to flee from Peiping, and she had left "Shirley Temple" with me for safekeeping. Mama wouldn't let me take off the cellophane wrapping because she wanted the doll to be kept as it was. The doll became legally mine only after the war, when we learned that the family had reached safety in another country—and I tore off the wrapping to hug it for the first time.

The Japanese occupation became increasingly repressive and even small children like myself heard horrible things. I remember a story about a bombed and derailed passenger train. Among the casualties scattered along the railroad tracks was a woman with both legs blown off at the thigh and bleeding profusely. When a trainload of Japanese troops and press-ganged Chinese auxiliaries passed by on another track, the woman cried out for a bullet to end her agony. The Chinese soldiers, though they wore Japanese uniforms, were stricken by the sight. Some openly wept; not one could bring himself to fire upon the dying woman. Then a Japanese soldier raised his rifle, laughed, and shot her.

Then in late 1944, a warden that Papa had befriended during his prison days sent us an urgent message. According to secret information, the enemy was losing the war in China and would try to stave off defeat by launching a big clean-up. All people on their list of suspects would be rounded up and sent to Manchurian labor camps. There would be no bail, and no return. Papa was on the list.

From that day on, we children were kept at home. We prepared to leave in great secrecy; our home with everything in it would be left as it was, and friends would attend to the house and our belongings after our departure. Mama started to coach five-year-old me and three-year-old Toto to give the correct answers on the journey. That was one of Papa and Mama's gravest concerns. We had been brought up to know who our enemy was, and one of the first things Toto learned to say was "I'll cut the heads off Japanese soldiers and feed them to our dog!" Now he would have to twist his tongue around such untruths as: "We're grateful to the Japanese for saving China!"

There was another concern. Due to daily air raids and ground action, trains were bombed or derailed almost every day and casualties among the refugees were high. My parents' greatest worry was the fate of their two babies. If either Papa or Mama were killed, one would still be left to look after us. What would happen, however, if both of them lost their lives and one or both of us children survived? In the end, they asked our cook to come along. They gave him a large sum of money and, in the event that Papa and Mama were killed, he was to take us to our relatives.

Both Toto and I were told repeatedly of this decision once we were on our way. We were instructed to hang on to the cook in the case that Papa and Mama both died. The situation must have been really grim if even small children had to be drilled in such a macabre plan.

We took a good deal of luggage with us, as we didn't know how long we would be leading a refugee existence. To the conductors on the train and to our fellow passengers, we were a family seeking new pastures in the inland regions. Papa posed as a wealthy merchant with a charming wife and two kids, while our cook passed for the old family retainer.

The Great Train Getaway

The escape route started with a journey by train from Peiping to Tai-yuan. We kept our departure as low-key as possible. The leave-taking was brief and subdued; there was no telling who would or would not survive the long war.

Our family had bought two tickets for a sleeping compartment with four berths, since Toto and I were both toddlers. Our cook's ticket was for less expensive quarters where the berths were not screened off and afforded less privacy. To our dismay, the other two berths in our compartment were taken by a Japanese officer, his wife, and their baby girl. I was physically frightened by the officer's nearness, his dark-rimmed spectacles and gold-capped teeth. He and his wife smiled a lot and offered us candy; Mama told us under her breath to accept it and smile.

Papa and Mama kept us out of the compartment as much as possible on the pretext of going to see our cook, who was not allowed to enter the better sections of the train although we could visit him. I was hastily taught how to say "thank you" in Japanese and instructed to bow deeply to the couple. The major concern was Toto, for we hadn't been taught a single Japanese word at home, even under the occupation. But all Chinese knew the Japanese imprecation ba-ge-ya-lu; and that was the sum total of my baby brother's Japanese vocabulary. Getting a three-year-old to understand what he ought say or not say is no easy matter.

As a result, Papa and I spent most of our time in the compartment to keep up appearances, while Mama went out with Toto as often as she could, with the excuse that he had to go to the bathroom or that his crying might disturb those in the compartment. She brought him back only when he was asleep. My own impression of that train ride consisted mostly of smiling gold-capped teeth, constant bowing, and offers of Japanese jellybean-like candy, which I didn't dare decline.

On top of the tension in the small compartment, there was the ever-present danger of being bombed. The trains running on this line were bombed almost every day by the Chinese air force, supported and supplied by the Allies. Japanese bombers, on the other hand, made frequent sorties against targets in Chinese areas. In any case, civilians always paid the heaviest price.

On the day we traveled, the skies were cloudless, and that increased the likelihood of air raids. The Chinese conductors on the train took perverse pleasure in relating to Chinese passengers the horrors they had seen or heard about, and Papa was regaled with the details of the bombing that had taken place the day before.

Everyone was greatly relieved when the train chugged safely into Tai-yuan. Papa and Mama took leave of the Japanese couple with barely concealed relief; we bowed many times and bade them to disembark first. Then, with the help of the conductor and porters on the platform, we piled our luggage on one side of the train.

Papa suddenly discovered we had gotten off on the wrong side of the tracks. Almost all passengers had disembarked on the right-hand side next to the station exit, whereas we were standing on the platform on the left-hand side.

The train had been vacated by now and stood motionless on the tracks. Other passengers who had landed on this side grumbled, picked up their few belongings, and crossed over. Papa thought of moving our heavy luggage through the doors of the train, so that we wouldn't have to take the crosswalk farther up ahead. Papa, and then our cook, went through the train doors to reconnoiter. They saw Japanese guards at the exit with bayonets fixed to their rifles, checking all passengers and luggage. Many people were body-searched, some were taken away. Papa and Mama were at a loss as to what to do. Several porters hovered nearby, expecting us to call upon their services.

Suddenly, there was a hiss and a clatter. The train eased forward and moved out of the station. Our family and our pile of luggage, which had been invisible to those on the other side, were now exposed to all eyes . . . . But as we stood there, paralyzed with fear, the Japanese guards shouldered their rifles, did an about face, and marched out of the station! Papa and Mama couldn't believe our good luck: since our little knot of people and luggage had been out of sight on the other side of the train, the Japanese guards had apparently assumed that they'd accomplished their task and had withdrawn, leaving the regular Chinese station staff to collect tickets from the few remaining local passengers.

Papa and Mama learned later that we had had a narrow escape, for our disguise wouldn't have held up if our luggage had been searched. The Japanese kept an especially sharp lookout for members of the Chinese intelligentsia because this part of occupied China was on the path for clandestine crossings to Free China, as the Chinese-held territories were called. Our luggage couldn't have passed for that of a merchant; both the contents and style would have looked wrong to an experienced eye. Papa and Mama would have been interrogated, at the very least, and anything could have happened. It was providence that landed us on the wrong side of the tracks, for by the time we had crossed over with the help of the porters, the weary ticket collectors were only too anxious to get rid of us so that they could take a break.

Having safely arrived at the first stopover of our journey, we set off from our hotel to get some dinner near the Drum and Bell Towers of Tai-yuan. Every ancient Chinese city has its Bell Tower and Drum Tower, and since we had lived near these towers in Peiping, to me it was almost like going home.

But this place also gave me my most vivid impression of an inland Chinese city. The restaurant where we went to eat happened to be catering to a Chinese-style wedding. A long-gowned waiter showed us to a table and, as we squeezed our way between banqueting wedding guests, I stopped briefly to gape at the bride. She was clad entirely in red, her face dark from expo-sure to sun and wind. Most of the guests, too, were suntanned, and they filled the restaurant with rowdy laughter and raucous shouting. This was a side of life my parents had secluded me from and the only weddings I had ever been to were quasi-Western. But now that we had emerged from our sheltered childhood into the heartland of China, the cruder realities of life opened up before me.

Holding On to the Mule's Tail

After a brief stay in Tai-yuan, we were on our way again. Over the next couple of months, train rides increasingly gave way to journeying by foot, on mules, and in a varied assortment of carts and wagons.

All this took place in late 1944 to early 1945 as China entered its eighth year of war. Cut off from the Western world and controlled by Japanese media, we knew next to nothing about the progress of the war in Europe and the Pacific.

A whispered name, however, instilled hope in the Chinese people in occu-pied areas, and this name was "Lo Szu Fu"—Roosevelt. We were to be grief-stricken by his untimely death shortly after we arrived in Chungking. I remember one tearful relative rushing home and announcing to the family in his Szechuanese accent, "Lo Szu Fu is gone!" We went to see if newspaper boys were out with the extras, and encountered everywhere in the city grief over the passing away of a great man, a grief we shared with the world.

I believe Papa spent his time in Tai-yuan inquiring and planning in detail our passage to freedom. I know we didn't have a guide with us, but we were passed from hand to hand along the way. It was winter, and as some sections of the Yellow River or its tributaries were frozen over, we crossed on ice at several places. Other stretches of the river consisted of leaping muddy waves, and it was frightening to look down the steep banks.

At one point, the only path over some mountains on our route was a nar-row winding trail. Surefooted mules carried all our luggage, but the muleteers told us it was too risky to ride. The only way to negotiate the path was by walking behind a mule and grasping its tail. The men said even they never ventured onto this path without a mule to hold on to.

The muleteers followed the more heavily laden animals, while we were directed to those with lighter burdens. Toto was too small to reach a tail or to walk on his own, so Papa piggybacked him. I had my own mule and was repeatedly admonished to hold onto my mule's tail for dear life.

Many years afterward, I still had a fancy for mule's tails. But while clutching that tail on those narrow slanting ledges, my sole concern at my disadvantaged height was what would happen if the mule decided to "poop." Since Japanese soldiers or air raids were nonexistent in those mountains, my worries were focused on that explicit threat two feet from my face. Others in the party must have noticed, for I had a feeling that the muleteers were cracking jokes about me.

It was also in this region that Papa woke up to a subtle danger: Toto wanted to pee and Mama had taken him to the edge of the narrow path high over the Yellow River. One of the mules passed by behind them, nearly brushing Mama. Papa observed that the muleteer eyed Mama and Toto in a strange way. It suddenly dawned on Papa that any one of us could be nudged over the edge, unintentionally or intentionally. Our luggage was heavy enough to excite cupidity, Mama was a beautiful woman, and we children could fetch good prices; child abduction was a common practice in those times.

So from that day onward, Papa and our cook were more vigilant than ever before. Because no one knew where we were. There were no post offices, no telegraphs, no telephones. We were alone in the wilds, with nothing more reassuring to entrust our lives to than a mule's tail!

As it turned out, the "mule's tail path" was, physically speaking, the most perilous part of the entire journey. But other causes for dismay were abundant throughout the trip—as abundant as the lice larvae I picked up on the way.

I had my sixth birthday during the journey, but no gifts, no birthday cake and, since we were still in enemy territory, not even a "Happy Birthday" song. Mama looked at her Precious Baby and decided to give me at least a decent wash and scrub. The tiny room of the inn we stayed at that night had a larger-than-usual oil lamp, so Mama could see my head clearly when she washed my hair. Suddenly, she gasped and hugged me, wet hair and all, and started to cry. Papa asked what was the matter. Mama pointed to my head and wailed: "*Chi tzu*, lice larvae!"

"What do you expect," said Papa, "when we're a thousand miles from civilization, with no running water and moving from one dirty inn to another?"

Mama was appalled, for she came from a small town where hygiene facilities were extremely primitive and had known lice larvae in her youth. "But I won't let my babies go through that again!" she vowed.

She boiled our clothes and, short of actually boiling us too, used the hottest water we could stand to wash Toto and me. I had a very hot birthday indeed that year.

The danger of being kidnapped or waylaid and murdered was constantly on our minds during this fearsome journey. One night we children were tucked into bed before Papa came home from his inquiries about the next day's march. I couldn't sleep, for Mama was getting more and more upset over the lateness of Papa's return. After several gunshots rang out somewhere in the vicinity, she called our cook from his quarters. But there was nothing anyone could do. Papa returned after what seemed to be ages; he said he had heard some shooting on his way back.

By then our conveyances had upgraded to covered horsecarts. Papa and our cook took turns riding a spare horse. Mama was an expert horsewoman, and she, too, had her share of cantering alongside the wagon.

But that morning after the shooting, she sat outside on the left side of the forward platform of the covered cart, while the driver sat on the right. We children "played house" inside the tentlike cover. Suddenly, agitated exclamations were heard up ahead. Between the heavily accented utterances of the local drivers and the exchanges among my family members, I made out that a dead man was lying across the road.

I scrambled as fast I could on the moving cart toward the cotton-padded door curtain, for I had never seen a dead man. But to my irritation and disappointment, Mama seated herself firmly on the flap of the curtain and prevented me from looking out. I went to the right side of the curtain, for the cart driver had jumped down to steady the skittish horses. But Mama knew her precocious Precious Baby only too well; she leaned over and with one hand pinned down that side of the curtain as well.

I fell back on my last resource and started to cry, hoping that when Mama entered the covered part I might catch a glimpse of the excitement outside. Mama, however, merely scolded me and told me to keep quiet. I looked out from a small glass pane on the side of the cart cover: Open fields stretched out on the left, low peasant huts squatted along the right, and I visualized a wide dirt road with a corpse sprawled across it. I waited and waited for the dreadful moment when our wheels would roll over something soft but resilient. However, it never happened.

Our cook accompanied us as far as the border between Japanese-occupied and Chinese-held territory. He then waited at a little village for the cross-the-border guide to return and report our safe crossing, before retracing his steps, alone, all the way back to Peiping to join his family.

Escape to Freedom Under a Starry Sky

The fugitives who made up this convoy were total strangers, grouped together solely by their choice of the same guide and the same band of rickshaw men. Papa and Mama must have had connections in selecting this point as our escape route, for on the other side of the border was the town of Hsiao Yi, and a cousin of Mama's, a follower of Generalissimo Chiang Kai-shek, was in charge there.

It was still winter, and we were warmly bundled up. The rickshaw men grumbled as they lashed on our heavy trunks and suitcases. No one in the vicinity seemed to pay any attention to this fugitive group of fourteen men, women, and children as we gathered in the deepening dusk. Soon, the guide and the rickshaw men took us out to the open countryside.

It was a windy, moonless night, which turned pitch dark as we progressed, but the rickshaw men knew every inch of the way. Papa had six-year-old me beside him on his rickshaw seat, and Mama in her rickshaw held Toto on her lap. I was wide awake, entranced by the windswept silence, the ominous darkness, and the bone-chilling atmosphere of frozen fear.

After almost fifty years, I can still see that vault of heaven, the vast barren land; I can still hear the whistling wind. As the wind cleared away the clouds, we moved on under a starry sky. Papa whispered that we were lucky again, perhaps, for the stars would illuminate our path but were not bright enough to cast shadows. That was essential, because in front of us, to the left stood the guardhouse of a Japanese border patrol, and we'd be killed if we were sighted.

Suddenly, Toto started to cry—in a way he never had before or since that night. Although Mama tried everything, he simply wouldn't stop; finally she threw a blanket over both of them to muffle the sound, but he cried even louder and put up a struggle. Our fellow travelers started to mutter about the lives of these thirty-odd people—including those of the rickshaw men. Later, Mama told me it was the most desperate moment of her life—if Toto had kept on crying, she might have had to suffocate him to save the group, as many Chinese mothers in similiar situations did when pursued by Japanese soldiers.

Toto stopped crying as abruptly as he had started, and the entire group was visibly relieved. Papa loosened his grip on my arm. By the time we approached the bridge that marked the borderline, it was in the wee hours of the morning, and the cold had driven the Japanese soldiers back into their barracks. The Chinese sentries hired by the Japanese to stand guard on the bridge had already been paid off, and they always helped the guide and the rickshaw men with their charges.

We crossed the bridge. We were in Chinese territory.

Papa picked up the exhausted Toto. Mama swept me into her arms and told me: "Now you are truly in the land of China, and you are a Chinese. And now I can have a name. I'm not only Mrs. Chen, I am also Chiang An-tao." The group started to sing Chinese songs aloud, now that we were in our own land—and I, a child born under enemy occupation, was free for the first time.

The guide and the rickshaw men came to say good-bye. They would risk the journey home before daylight and pick up another group of refugees— these men were professionals who made their living that way in those war years. They recalled the frightening moments of Toto's crying fit and won-dered why the Japanese guards hadn't even stirred; usually, when there was any noise, the Japanese would at least poke their heads out and fire off a few warning shots. Then the guide realized the wind had changed direction that night and had blown the sound of Toto's crying *away* from the guardhouse. "Heavens, you were really fortunate!"

Uncle A. K. Chiang sent his aides to meet us, and we were soon in the fam-ily bosom. We were to attend a banquet in our honor that night and Mama kept reminding me that the name of this first Free China town we had come to was Hsiao Yi—Filial Duty and Loyalty—two virtues prized by the Chinese and symbolic of the virtues she wished us to have. The wine for that banquet was Shao-hsing rice wine. Papa and Mama were both strong drinkers—they generally didn't drink, but when they did, there was no competition. Sipping my allowance of sweetened water, I watched them, fascinated, proud, and mar-veling at the way they outdrank everybody without getting tipsy themselves.

Uncle A. K. and his colleagues walked us home through the now deserted street of the small town. There was no restraint, no fear, only relief and laughter.

The Ride into Chungking

In the Chinese classic *Pilgrimage to the West*, the Buddhist monk and his three disciples, among them the mighty Monkey King, overcome eighty-one (nine times nine) perils before they accomplish their journey. Those four were on an important mission; we four were simply a family taking flight. But considering the relatively serene life we had enjoyed, on and off, prior to our escape, I flatter myself in thinking that we had to have a fair bit of pluck to have survived so much—the threat of bombings, Japanese blandishments, the train disembarkment, steep trails, lice larvae, and various other dangers and discomforts.

From Hsiao Yi onward, we went as far as the 1945 railroad tracks could take us, which was to Pao-chi. Then we became motorized; that is, we rode on some of the most notorious buslines that plied the highways in Chinese territory. They were infamous because they were unreliable, uncomfortable, unscheduled, and poorly maintained, although the drivers themselves weren't to blame. But compared to what we had been through before that, including the unforgettable mule's tail trail, riding those buses was seventh heaven. In fact, we were almost driven to seventh heaven in the literal sense, as the buses careened downhill on worn-out brakes, hairpin curves, and avalanches of loose gravel. A Chinese saying goes: "The road to Szechuan is difficult, more difficult than climbing to the sky." These lines originated four centuries ago. Colorless as it sounds in English translation, it reads poetically in Chinese.

We pushed forward on the perilous roads to Szechuan, heading for Chungking. The overworked buses had to zigzag up the mountains and zigzag down again. I couldn't conceptualize this intricate process at that age; my major preoccupation was what the bus would do after we had driven to the top of a hill on a winding road. Hop to the top of the next hill to wind down again? I thought at the time that a winding road actually went round and round a mountain like a spiral staircase!

I learned a very useful word on the Szechuan roads—*p'ao mao*. The original meaning of this word is "to cast anchor," but applied to a motor vehicle it means "to develop engine trouble and stop." The phenomenon occurred with our buses so often that I assumed *p'ao mao* was a normal function of all motor vehicles.

The term was also very handy. Any undiagnosed or undefined engine failure was referred to as *p'ao mao*. At the exclamation "*p'ao mao*" from the driver's seat, all passengers would hasten down from the bus to look for food, water, a toilet, or simply to stretch their legs. All except Papa, that is, who was an avid driver himself and invariably went to squat beside the driver and puzzle out the current *p'ao mao* with him. So readily did we accept *p'ao mao* that the term, in that specific context, became associated with a sense of convenience rather than inconvenience.

After innumerable windings and *p'ao mao*, we eventually arrived in the Chungking area. The bus gave a last gasp and we finally disassociated ourselves from the decrepit conveyance. We found our Fifth Uncle (husband of my Fifth Aunt) who had come to meet us. He helped us into a lightweight smooth-gliding landau, while our luggage was packed in a less comfortable cart.

Then we moved through paved lanes where wildflowers bloomed on the roadside. Most important of all, the horses' hooves *clicked* on the flagstones. We had been traveling for months on dirt roads, and, oh, how I had missed that clicking sound! What came to me at that particular moment was a line from a classical poem: "Exulting, the spring wind hastens the horses' hooves." And amid the delightful sound of clicking hooves, we soon arrived at the doorstep of Fifth Aunt.

Papa had six sisters and one older brother. Sixth Aunt was his only younger sister; Fifth Aunt was born before him. They all were rather close, in the way members of a large family could be. There were also quite a number of other relatives in Chungking at the time. As it turned out, almost every Chinese I knew then or met afterward, in China or in the United States, was in Chungking at one time or another during the war. But they are mostly older people; Toto and I were on the bottom rung of the "Chungking generation."

I Cry Through Two Stacks of Toilet Paper

We settled down in a small town called Ge-le-shan, the Hill of Song and Joy, not far from Chungking. Papa rented a piece of land on the hill to build a little house. I found it rather ridiculous the address should be "12 Dragon Cave Curve," for I could find neither a dragon cave nor a curve. The house was built in a short time out of bamboo, mud, and whitewash, and we moved into the humblest abode we have ever lived in. We didn't have running water and we used oil lamps. That is when I learned to trim lampwicks, a handy skill for my "Cadre School" days to come, in the 1970s.

Erected on the main road was a gate with a painted sign in black and white that stridently proclaimed the campus of the Shanghai Medical College, for it was to this remote corner of the Hill of Song and Joy that the faculty and students of that institution evacuated after Shanghai fell into enemy hands. However, the one and only neighbor we had on our hill was a gracious and elegant lady who asked to be addressed as "Grandma," in English.

She lived with her spinster daughter Mary, an accomplished nurse. Toto instilled such profound interest in Mary that she wanted to be his godmother, so the trips to Grandma's and Godma's place two hundred yards down the hill were usually rewarded with affection and confections—Western style.

Our home was built on a clearing on the otherwise rocky and uneven hill. No more than a dozen yards from our front door a precipice plunged to the foot of the hill. The normal way to get up and down that hill was to take the path that wound past Grandma's house.

Toto and I both knew the danger posed by that precipice. We seldom went toward the brink, but I sneaked out a lot and roamed the hillside by myself. I found the rock crannies on the barren hilltop most satisfactory for my obsession for playing house. I even blueprinted my house-to-be. One day I took Papa up the hill to inspect my future premises. Papa walked at a leisurely pace, so I got to the hilltop before he did. There I had a nasty shock.

I discovered a human figure wedged in a crevice which I intended as the "stream" in front of my imaginary door. The figure was inert, so I imagined it was a corpse. It was clad in locally woven and dyed blue cotton cloth; the head lolled at a strange angle and the face was hidden from me. I ran back to Papa and pointed wordlessly at the crevice. He went over, spoke a few words in Szechuanese, softly at first, and then more harshly. He sent me scuttling down for our Szechuanese amah, Ho-ma. "And you stay home," he snapped. "Don't come up again!"

When Papa and Ho-ma came back, they told us that the man was a heroin addict. Heroin was popularly called *pai mien*, white powder, in those days.

Papa pointed at the figure staggering down the hill. "He's on one of his jags, so he's very weak. Lucky for you and for us." Naturally, I had to give up my housing "plot," in both senses of the word, for after that day I was forbidden to roam the hillside on my own.

The months we stayed in that little house on the hill were to be the last of the holocaust in China—there were 36,000,000 Chinese casulties during the Sino-Japanese War. These months were also months made more complicated by the deepening rift between two antagonistic Chinese political parties, namely the ruling Nationalist Party (Kuomintang, or KMT) and its adversary, the Chinese Communist Party (CCP).

After we settled down, Papa went to look for a job in Kunming, which was where Tsinghua University evacuated to during the war years. He ended up working temporarily at a newly established United Nations agency there. Mama had been a good teacher since her teens, so she joined the staff of United School affiliated with the Shanghai Medical College. The schoolyard for the United School nestled in the lap of the next hill—in those mountain- ous areas one refers to the next hill as though it were the next block. We could see what was going on in the school from our house, and vice versa.

I turned six during our escape, so it was high time for me to go to a regu- lar school. Actually I had had tutors since I was three, for my parents would not have me go to school under Japanese occupation. There were also many teachers who preferred to "tutor around" for a living; anything was better than working under the Japanese. I had all the courses a three-year-old could han- dle: Chinese, English, arithmetic, and piano. By now, age-wise, I should have entered first grade, but with my previous education, Mama wanted me to take the entrance exams for second grade. I passed with flying colors.

When Papa came home on his monthly home leave, he flew into a rage. "She's got enough education to start in the fourth grade, how could you put her two years below her real level of knowledge?!" Mama insisted that it would not be good for me at my tender age. The final compromise was that I would try for third grade.

The United School, for children of the Medical College staff and their associates, was both dedicated to education and fairly relaxed with regard to regulations. Papa convinced the school mistress that I had to be reexamined, in a test all by myself. Since I couldn't have cared less which grade I was put into, I felt I was the victim of a between-adults issue. I wheedled, whimpered, and whined, all to no avail. Papa held me with an iron hand: Off you go to your inquisitors.

I started to cry when I sat down in front of the exam sheet, and the school mistress consoled me by handing me one stack of paper after another to dry my streaming tears. Mind you, it wasn't Kleenex; it was toilet paper Chinese-style, wartime version, yellow and coarse. It scratched my nose. I was feeling very sorry for myself. If I hadn't had the privilege of all that tutoring, I wouldn't have had to sit here for an extra exam. The damnedest question I remember from that third grade entrance sheet is: "How many pairs of feet do centipedes have?"

I got into the third grade. I was six years old, two years younger than most of my classmates, and two years is a big gap at that age. I felt displaced or misplaced, both mentally and physically, and I always pretended to be older than my years. I entered junior middle school at ten, senior middle school at thirteen, and scheduled my college freshman year for sixteen.

With Papa in Kunming, Mama teaching, and me third-grading, Toto was the only one left at home with Ho-ma. Mama taught illiterate Ho-ma how to read the clock, and asked her to bring Toto out every time there was a recess at school, so that Mama and I could wave at them from our playground on the next hill. But when Ho-ma forgot the time and they didn't show up in front of the house, Mama would rush down the school hill and up our hill to see if everything was alright. Many kidnappings were rumored among the non-Szechuanese evacuees at the time, and boys were especially prized in war-torn China.

After a few panics like these, and especially after Ho-ma's husband came to visit and they talked long and animatedly in Szechuanese, which none of us quite understood, Mama decided it would be easier on everyone's nerves to take Toto along with us. Toto ended up being the youngest pupil at school; he either sat in Mama's classroom drawing pictures, or came to mine to join our singing lessons.

Flaming Torches Wind Down the Mountain Path

President Roosevelt died, VE-Day came, Hitler committed suicide, the United Nations was established. All this took place in 1945. However, to us Chinese living in the vicinity of the provisional wartime capital Chungking, the war was still on. For those from northeast China—generally referred to in the West as Manchuria, the Japanese invasion had begun four-teen years ago, after the Mukden Incident of September 18, 1931; those from north China counted eight years after the "Seven Seven Incident"—the Marco Polo Bridge Incident of July 7, 1937. We had become so accustomed to war that we found it difficult to imagine a life of peace.

News of fighting and bombing in those last days of war was mixed with rumor when it came to our small town near Chungking; anticipation of vic-tory was mingled with fear. The tidings of the atom bomb were received with mixed feelings; while it was a major breakthrough, Japan could still take revenge on its close neighbors by means of air raids.

One night, when Papa happened to be on home leave and we kids were trying to defer bedtime, we became aware of a muffled thudding in the dis-tance. Papa listened for a while, then said, "No, it can't be thunder, the sky is too clear."

We played a little longer. Mama, preoccupied with the persistent thump-ing, wondered aloud if it could be carpet bombing. "No," Papa figured. "They don't bomb at night, and the sound has lasted too long for a bombing raid. And, anyway, we should have heard the sirens."

Even Toto and I became jumpy, for there was no doubt that something unusual, some new kind of sound, was reverberating over the mountains. This would be the first time we children, born under enemy occupation, were to hear it—the sound of gongs and drums beaten for a Chinese celebration. That sound would burst out in the silence of that night with rapturous joy.

We sat around distractedly. The sound came and went with the breeze, now weaker, now stronger, but coming ever closer, sounding ever more clear-ly. Mama began wistfully, "Could it be that . . ." She wasn't able to continue, for fear the hope would fade away. Papa couldn't stand the suspense any longer and we went out of the house. We were just in time.

After listening a couple of minutes in front of our house, we convinced our-selves that the sound held nothing ominous. We strained our ears to establish its source, but it seemed to come from all directions. Our neighbor, Mary, also came up the hill in silent anticipation, and Mama started to say, "It must be . . ."

Suddenly flecks of orange light began to come over the mountain direct-ly facing our little hill—one flame, then another flame. "Fireflies!" I exclaimed, thinking of my chief nighttime diversion. It was my last foolish remark that night.

All at once there was an explosion of sound and light. Roaring gongs and drums, pounded by students and staff of Shanghai Medical College, punctuated with the joyous clashing of cymbals, erupted at the foot of our hill. And a torrent of torches cascaded down the mountainside, tracing the undulations of the mountain path. Borne by local peasants, this moving chain of light zigzagged across the slopes, until the entire mountain was festooned in loops of flaming torches.

As more torch bearers rippled over the crest of the mountain, the leaders descended into the valley to merge with the gongs and drums in a spontaneous eruption of joy. There must have been thousands—even tens of thousands—of torches, and under each flame was an exulting heart, one of the four hundred million Chinese who had suffered and survived the war.

Up the hilly path clambered a friend, shouting breathlessly *"Sheng li le!* Victory!" He ran up to us and, gasping for air, briefed us about the unconditional surrender of Japan! It was ecstasy, it was intoxication, it was unbelievable and indescribable happiness!

We lived to see that night; many didn't, and for them, we lived through that night, too. Many years later, I was to live through another period of ecstasy, the downfall of the "Gang of Four" in 1976. My parents didn't. For the Chinese people, there will be other periods of ecstasy to come that we will live to see, if not personally, then through the lives of future generations.

The repatriations to our respective places of origin soon began, but the few airlines were so swamped with reservations that we didn't get our turn until December. Sadly, due to confusion and inexperience, many accidents occurred. Toto's Godmother Mary died in one of the plane crashes on her way home.

The Pinched and the Amah-ed

Our family returned to Peiping approximately a year after we fled the city. For the record, a round-up actually did occur shortly after we left, and the victims were never heard of again. Due to the domestic upheaval in China after World War II, the atrocities committed by the Japanese upon the Chinese people were never fully disclosed to the world, unlike the war crimes of the Nazis, or even the Japanese maltreatment of British and American war prisoners; nor did we have a Wiesenthal to hunt down the perpetrators.

A good deal of evidence was shown to the Chinese people after the 1949 Communist takeover, but China was closed to the world at the time. The facts should be made public, but little has been done, since no one wants to relive these bygone agonies after so many years. But the pain is still there, the pain of more than 30 million Chinese dead.

Papa went back to his job, and was promoted to manager of a higher branch in his bank. We rented a Western-style two-story house with a big garden and I enrolled in a private school close by. Toto was also ready to go to school by then. The school we went to was actually meant for children of the well-to-do. Most of them came from doctors', bankers', or shop-owners' families, and there were even a couple of kids whose fathers were KMT generals. There used to be a saying in Peiping that "the rich live in the East City, the distinguished in the West City, while the poor and lowly end up in the North and South." Our school was in the East City.

By then, I had seen somewhat more of the world than most of my contemporaries and should have felt confidence in myself. But with my head still in that little house on the hill, and my wardrobe yet to be upgraded after our sojourn in the boondocks of Szechuan, I was intimidated by my more urbanized, older classmates.

Two boys especially took delight in pinching me: they pinched my arms when I wore short sleeves and my legs if I wore skirts. I went home with purple and blue marks, but I merely explained I had fallen at school. To have Mama come and complain to the teacher would have been worse than being pinched. The other girls were also afraid of these bullies, so they didn't dare tell, either. It was only when I started to sob after a particularly painful pinching that another boy stood up and told the teacher I was being tormented every day.

As one can see, we were brought up to stand on our own. An outstandingly intelligent but extremely mischievous boy whom I met when we were both toddlers received almost daily a caning on the palms of his hands, but each time walked back to his desk with a smile playing on his lips. Such defiance was appreciated by his classmates, but infuriated the teacher, who vented her ire with the next caning. This boy will be referred to throughout this book as my lifelong friend.

Toto would seem to bear out the Chinese saying that "a great vessel is long in the making," for I must say that he is now definitely accomplished in his profession. But not so in his first performance at school. When he went for his entrance examinations, he suddenly forgot how to write the numeral 8. Mama was hovering around with the other mothers when she noticed his distress. She tried to tip him off by forming a pair of spectacles with her fingers. Toto took the tip but made a "sleeping eight," exactly as Mama did: ∞. This didn't bother him, however; the real humiliation came when he was "amah-ed" to school.

Our cook had returned safely from his dangerous mission and returned to our household; one of the amahs who brought up Toto also returned to us, for it was well known that Mama doted on our domestic help.

This amah still treated Toto as the baby she had nursemaided, oblivious of the fact that he had already attained the dignified status of first-grader. She insisted upon staying with Toto at school to see that he was well looked after. Imagine Toto's mortification as the amah followed him all over the playground, calling out: "Toto, don't run, you'll hurt yourself!" "Toto, careful, don't fall!" "Toto, do you want something to eat?"

Toto came home livid with rage, declaring that he refused to have amah go with him to school again. This hurt her feelings very much, for she simply couldn't understand that Toto was growing up.

Tarzan, Bambi, and the Half Peanuts

Now for the fainthearted side of the seasoned travelers we should have been: Toto and I were both afraid to go to the movies, and I actually walked out of *Bambi*, of all films! Mama had taken me to a luxurious, remodeled movie house called Sterling Light to watch the film. We even bought higher-priced balcony seats, and were all set for good entertainment. Twenty minutes later, I was snivelling and pleading to go home—at that point Bambi had only gone out to play, and nothing ominous was apparent yet. I cried "he'll get lost and won't find his way home!" Mama was terribly exasperated with her Precious Baby, but I had my way. When I learned from later accounts that Bambi's mother was killed, I secretly congratulated myself on my premature exit.

Toto's true colors were shown up when he went to see a Tarzan film. We had two favorite cousins at the time, both studying at Tsinghua University, and our home became theirs on the weekends. When a mid-1940s Tarzan film was shown at the same posh theater, Toto pestered them until they agreed to take him there. I played deaf and dumb, and anyway, after my disgraceful conduct over an animated Bambi, they preferred to leave me alone.

Off went the three musketeers, six-year-old Toto sandwiched between his cousins. Forty minutes later, one big and one small musketeer returned.

What had happened was that the threesome went into the movie house in high spirits, bought expensive balcony seats, got some nibbles, and then proceeded to go upstairs. My cousin described the scene: "Toto dragged his feet more and more slowly, and when we came to the top of the staircase, he stopped and began to whimper, and asked to go home!" The cousins looked at the entrance to the seating area, at the crowd milling through it, and then at their forlorn little cousin. The upshot—one cousin went in while the other took Toto home.

Mama treated the self-sacrificing cousin to another show the next week, just as she treated herself to another showing of *Bambi*.

For me, the four-person family was ideal: Papa, Mama, Toto, and myself. It gave our household a four-cornered symmetry, filled the four sides of the table, and was ideal for going out in our car, in pedicabs, or on trains. From early infancy, I had somehow become Papa's daughter, and Toto was always Mama's baby. It was a well-balanced situation and, despite the inevitable squabbles, there wasn't too much jealousy or contention between us siblings.

The best thing about having two children in the household is that we shared everything fifty-fifty. The concept went so deep that I divided any number by 2, automatically. Toto and I divided everything: candy, chocolates, cookies, peanuts, fruit—I divided, that is. And when I did the dividing, practically everything went into the kitty to be split into two shares, even chocolates of different shapes and candy with different colored wrappers; only the absolutely indivisible was put aside for Mama. Mama said one day she hoped shopkeepers would weigh out goodies in uneven numbers more frequently, so that she could have a taste of them too.

I knew this remark was meant as a joke, but it left me with a feeling of guilt. I talked to Toto and we agreed to leave some things undivided, to be laid aside for our parents. It never occurred to us brats that we should donate part of our own share to them. However, we could both be generous with the undivided portion, since that was no-man's-land.

However, this fifty-fifty obsession could be carried to unpleasant extremes. Toto and I had a tiff one day, and right after that were given a bag of peanuts by a visitor. I was still steaming with rage, but business is business, and we sat on the carpet to share out the peanuts. I poured them out and divided them not scoop by scoop or even one by one, but by splitting each peanut and giving half to each person. That way, the division would be really equal, even unto peanuts of different sizes. It took a long, long time, for I remember I couldn't decide what to do with the little stubs between the halves. Toto stared at me with enormous eyes. So astonished was he at the lengths to which his sister could go that all the fight went out of him.

As for me, I got a scorching reprimand from Mama, for she was distressed that I should be so fastidious over material things. She told me that if I was so mean as to insist on absolute egalitarianism, I'd often be miserable since one can't go fifty-fifty with everything in life. Besides, siblings should share, not divide. I learned a big lesson that day.

Life in the Big House

Papa and Mama had never owned a house until 1947. Papa got a further promotion and raise at his bank that year, and he also made some money on the side with friends. By then, inflation was rising at an alarming rate, and my parents thought it time to invest in some real estate. So they purchased a big house at the height of our affluence.

Papa had his eyes on an impossible piece of property—a gray-colored steel-and-cement building that had been a dairy products plant and its managing office. The location, however, was fabulous: It was one block from the Coal Hill Park and the magnificent imperial palace called the Forbidden City; it faced one of the elegant corner towers of the palace wall.

All our friends advised Papa and Mama not to buy this abandoned plant building, for it was not meant for residence. But the price was unbelievably low, and Papa closed the deal (although he later put in just as much money to have the place remodeled into a two-story residence). At any rate, we children were thrilled, for our parents promised to dig a swimming pool in the yard.

The remodeling went off remarkably well. We lived in that house for a little more than a year before going to the United States. I shared a room with Toto in the big house; despite our bickerings, we were inseparable.

In years of peace, our parents had scheduled our lives in a straight, ascending line: six years each of grade school and middle school, after which we both would enter Tsinghua University—where else, after all. When Papa and Mama took us to the alumni reunion in 1947, all guests had name tags pinned on the upper left side of their jackets or gowns. These tags were five-inch lengths of starched red silk ribbon, with the lower end cleft like a swallow's tail. The name and graduation year of the bearer was written on it with Chinese writing brush by attendants at the entrance.

When our turn came, Papa's and Mama's names were inscribed along with their respective years of graduation, 1932 and 1933. Mama was in these days her own self again, with her own name.

Then the attendant jocularly inquired if we kids should also have tags. In response to our longing looks, Papa asked him to make out two tags with our names on them, and to put down "1959" and "1963," the years he figured we ought to receive our caps and gowns at that university.

No one anticipated that our line of ascent wouldn't be a straight one, but would zigzag like the torch-lit path on that Chungking mountain. By the time we went to college, our own circumstances had changed, and even dear old Tsinghua, a multi-disciplinary university when my parents were there, had been restructured into a polytechnic institute.

So the two of us literally "tagged" after our parents at the reunion, with our future proclaimed on that five-inch strip of silk—which generated immense amusement among our parents' peers.

Tsinghua University was established with U.S. funds. Traditionally liberal and Westernized, it became one of the hotbeds of the student movements in the late 1940s. We felt particularly attached to Tsinghua: not only was it here that our parents met and married, and not only were many of its faculty our family friends—it also was the alma mater of quite a few of our favorite cousins.

Around 1947, it had become customary for a few of our first, second, and third cousins and their sweethearts to visit us over weekends. The canteen food at Tsinghua left much to be desired and, since the university was situated in

Peiping's suburbs, there were few restaurants in its vicinity. So the house of Second Uncle and Aunt (brothers and sisters are numbered separately in traditional Chinese families) became a kind of surrogate home to them.

Some cousins came mostly on polite visits and to enjoy a hearty meal, but a couple of our favorites—such as the victims of the earlier Tarzan episode, actually used our home as laundry, restaurant, and free takeout snack bar. Papa and Mama made them all feel welcome; many times I noticed Mama pressing a bit of pocket money into their hands. That, after all, is what "folks" are for.

By the end of 1947 and early 1948, the carefree visits took on a more serious tone. Some of my cousins would shut themselves up with Papa and Mama for hours at a stretch. Toto and I would sit and sulk in front of the closed door: to us, the sole purpose of their visits was to entertain their winsome young cousins! But now they even brought their schoolmates at times, and talked many long hours with them.

Several times during the frequent student demonstrations of the late 1940s, motivated by "Anti-Hunger and Anti-Civil War" demands, we felt very tense at home. Neither Papa nor Mama would go to bed before our cousins returned or phoned from Tsinghua to say they were safe and sound after the demonstrations of that particular day. Clubs and fire hoses were the only response they got from the KMT authorities, and so they came to ask for advice from old hands like Mama and Papa.

Clubs and fire hoses were anticipated again in 1989, when student demonstrators once more sought advice from today's old hands—the students in the late 1940s, now people in their sixties. Old hands and new hands all underestimated their 1989 rulers, however, and paid an immense price.

When we moved into the big house, tension in society had been mounting. One day we couldn't go to school because the streets were blocked by protestors. I was leaning against a second-floor window and watching the demonstration go by, when suddenly, two uniformed men chased a young man who looked like a student right up to our tightly shut iron gates. I was horror-stricken when the two men beat the younger one over the head and then walked off, leaving the latter to stagger away with blood streaming down his face.

Mama, grim-faced, had also watched this scene. I asked why the two had singled out that person to beat up? And then why did they let him go? Mama said the younger man must have been someone they paid to disrupt the demonstration, and he had been punished for not accomplishing what was expected of him. Mama said something like "we're particularly wary of this kind of sabotage." Those words gave me my first inkling that it isn't always a simple matter to separate the good people from the bad ones in this world.

It was only after we arrived in the United States that our parents talked openly about the doings of our cousins. Some of the quiet ones had been more influential as student leaders than the more vocal ones. Papa and Mama had known what they were up to, but hadn't inquired or tried to get involved, since the protective coloring of a rich uncle with a big house and a large domestic staff helped rather than hurt their cause.

We Leave on the President Taft

In the spring of 1948, Papa went on a prolonged business trip to Shanghai and Nanking. He came back with passports and tickets for all of us to sail on the *President Taft* in late June the same year. Toto and I were kept in the dark—which wasn't easy with such snoopy kids, for while Papa had his own passport, Mama's bore a picture of herself with Toto and me. When we had gone to take that picture, I hadn't had any idea what it was for.

The adults obviously had weighty considerations for their decision, beside which our objections sounded flat and trivial. Not that these objections lacked anything in volubility or noisiness, for now we both had big voices, both vocabulary-wise and volume-wise. We didn't want to leave Peiping again, for we'd miss a great swimming season in our pool; we'd miss the fun of spying upon our favorite cousin who had begun to date a beautiful schoolmate; we'd miss our dog, Tiger; and we'd miss our new kitten.

From what I learned later, the true reasons for our departure and eventual return were Mama's unfulfilled 1937 wish to visit the United States and pursue her studies, and our parents' desire—after their harrowing experiences during the Anti-Japanese War—to get away from the escalating civil war in China. The big cities were still in KMT hands in the spring of 1948, but the countryside was falling increasingly under the control of the Communist forces.

Our 1948 departure contrasted sharply with that of 1944. This time there was no secrecy or anxiety. And at the time we left China, people felt concern but less tension than they would a few months later. Everyone, however, expected some kind of change in a couple of years. We rented out our residence to an American couple by the name of Geddes, complete with those servants who wished to stay with the house. Everything remained in it—our furniture and books, even our pets.

We flew to Shanghai to board our ship. *President Taft* was a merchantman with limited passenger space. In addition to quarters for the officers and crew, it was equipped with four cabins that contained bunks for the ten passengers making the one month trip across the Pacific. The number of passengers in each cabin, assembled by family units, happened to be one, two, three and four; we were the four persons in one cabin.

We saw cargo being picked up and unloaded at a Japanese port, we did a lot of whale-watching on the way, I sniffed out a couple of deck romances between officers and passengers, and I suffered enough seasickness on the Pacific to preclude all forms of motion sickness—plane, ship, train, or car—for life.

Papa and Mama both spoke fluent English, but neither Toto nor I could say much in that language at the time. Toto, being only seven, could still hide behind Mama and play cute, but I was constantly encouraged or enjoined to speak in English. That, of course, had the effect of putting me off shipboard socializing during this cruise, and even on future ones.

I remember the absurd daily duty I was assigned to on the *President Taft*. One of the elderly ladies traveling with her daughter used only cigarette ash to cleanse her teeth. And since Papa still smoked a couple of cigarettes per day to look smart, he promised to provide whatever he could contribute.

I was instructed to say "Here's your cigarette ash, ma'am" in English and hand that lady a paper packet with its precious contents every morning. One of my main objections to this errand was that I couldn't understand why I had to say "ash" and not "ashes," for the stuff sure looked plural enough to me; and when one is requested *not* to say something, it often slips out spontaneously. I had to rehearse every time before putting on a dress and a smile and knocking, to make sure I was handing her ash instead of ashes.

Then we dropped anchor at the Hawaiian Islands. This was in July, 1948, before Hawaii became the fiftieth state. Honolulu was the first foreign city I set foot in, and I never forgot the fresh breeze, the swaying trees, and the beckoning flowers. I went back after thirty-five years in search of that dream, but I roamed high and low, far and near, without finding any flowers. Then I was told there are seasons, too, in this seasonless paradise.

We knocked at the Golden Gate and landed in California in late July of 1948.

Scenic Avenue, Berkeley

The *President Taft* docked in San Francisco, and we were met and taken into a Chinese-American family by the name of Lew. They lived in a sizable two-story house with a large backyard on Pine Street. There has been a friendship between the Lews and the Chens spanning three generations and going well into the fifth decade.

We met by chance.

Lew Pa and Ma were second generation immigrants from the province of Canton in south China. They had four sons and one daughter. All three grown-up sons had served in the U.S. Army during World War II, and one was killed in action. Another son, Marshall, was posted in Tientsin after the war, and this American G.I. was introduced to us when he visited Peiping.

Marshall soon returned to civilian life and college studies in California, and the visiting Chens were welcomed at his parents' house, which was also shared by his siblings. The hospitality and warmth of the Lew family encouraged the Chen brats to slide down the banisters at the first call for dinner. I blush now as I think of the impression we must have left with the Lews—these newcomers right off the ship, storming up to their room and into the shower, and then zipping down again via the banisters. However, of all the banisters I have ever slid down, I vote the Lews' the best.

Toto and I were in for a surprise: saying grace at dinner. In China we had dabbled in some aspects of Christian culture, such as learning half a dozen Christmas carols, going to church weddings, consuming quarts of ice cream at the YWCA (where I learned the word "Christian" for the first time from the letter C), and romping around the Salvation Army headquarters in Peiping where we knew a major, but we had never sat down to pray at the dinner table.

And what a table it was! To this day, I recall the aroma wafting from Lew Ma's kitchen and the sight of Cantonese-style roast chicken heaped on huge platters. After some thirty days of President Line cuisine, we simply goggled at the tantalizing food. But hold it! Lew Pa bowed his head to pray in English, while Toto and I, surreptitiously prodded by our watchful parents, folded our hands and exchanged sidelong glances of dismay. The prayer lasted an age, and I gathered from a few of the words and phrases that a section had been added about our presence in the household. Then we were poked again by our parents to lift our heads, which we did, with our chopsticks simultaneously readied for the gustatory attack. From that day until we left the Bay Area a year later, we sat down together at this table so many times that my memories of Bay Bridge are still directly linked to the Lews' table.

Then we bought a Dodge and moved to Scenic Avenue, Berkeley.

The choice of Berkeley as our home was a natural sequel to the unfulfilled trip of 1937—the one aborted by the fateful cable calling Papa and Mama back to Peiping as they were waiting in Hong Kong to board a liner bound for the United States. An eight-year war and two babies had intervened, but Mama's dream had never faded. She went now to the English Department at UC Berkeley. The fellowship, naturally, had expired, but the record was still there. Given the unusual circumstances, the department allowed Mama to audit classes and reconstruct her studies program until a formal decision was reached concerning her graduate studies or research.

That was in the autumn of 1948, and Mama was almost forty. Even with the G.I. Bill bringing older students to campuses, a forty-year-old Chinese mother of two children, striving to pick up a scholastic career interrupted by war and eight years of forced anonymity, was a rarity.

Mama threw herself into her courses after putting us kids in school, and I know those brief months at Berkeley were professionally the most joyful ones she ever experienced. Mama was a strong scholar, but as fate would have it, she never achieved her goal in her chosen field. She was to earn fame, much later, in a totally unexpected role. Well, snoopy as always and curious to know how one learns things at graduate schools, I leafed through Mama's notebooks while she was cooking dinner. She took the lectures down in fluent longhand. I read them with awe, for that was my first acquaintance with Mama's English-language capability.

Previous to our arrival, noted linguistics professor Dr. Y. R. Chao and his wife were already the natural Godfather and Godmother of the Chinese students and scholars in Berkeley by virtue of seniority, prestige, and personality.

No Chinese who had been at UC Berkeley had failed to attend Mrs. Chao's dinner parties, by choice or by obligation, as I found out many years later. Our family not only frequented their home, but also shared several memorable excursions with this remarkable and almost legendary couple.

However, Papa and Mama's easygoing ways and relative youth also attracted a small circle around Scenic Avenue. Most of them were related to Tsinghua and the P.U.M.C. Hospital, and that made them as good as relatives. Many were younger men in their thirties who had left their families behind to pursue their studies in the United States. They somehow reminded Toto and me of our cousins at Tsinghua, even if we called them "uncle." Papa and Mama could not afford to lavish hospitality on them as they did on our cousins in Peiping, but the weekend comings and goings were the same.

That Christmas of 1948 was the high point of our stay. We coordinated our Christmas agenda with the Lews and the Chaos, so that we would have the younger Chinese at our home on Christmas Day. Mama and a couple of friends cooked, Papa did the odd jobs and entertained the guests. Toto and I snared the most complaisant uncle and we sat on the stairs to sing. We went through our entire repertoire of Christmas carols, now expanded to include more than a dozen songs. The other guests got an earful as the trills and warbles drilled through the intervening doors and transcended the clatter of Chinese woks and choppers in the kitchen. Papa emerged at last to announce abruptly: "I'll pay the three of you each a penny if you'll give us some peace!" We jumped on Papa at the insulting inference and offending price. He eventually raised the payoff to a nickel.

The biggest change in our American household was that now we had to do our own domestic work. It was not uncommon in China for families with incomes of the lower-middle range and up to hire domestic help: clerks, teachers, shopkeepers could all afford servants even if the wife didn't work. We always maintained a modest staff of a cook and a maid or two, until we moved into the big house in Peiping. Mama was never the Grand Dame-type of "Tai-tai" (Mrs. or Madam) and liked to help with the cooking; Papa loved to putter around in the house and fix things—leaving, of course, a mess for someone else to clean up. The gossip in Peiping was that no family could hire servants who had left the Chen household, for Mama "spoiled" them by being too easygoing. However, the really spoiled ones were Toto and I; we had never washed so much as a dish or a pair of socks before we arrived in the United States.

Now we did the house chores ourselves: Papa took care of the car and the yard and helped with the shopping; Mama looked after the cooking, cleaning, and laundry; and Toto and I were supposed to keep our things in order. In China, we had been too young for an allowance. My only savings were from the holiday tips given to children on Chinese New Year, which depreciated to next to nothing after a few months, thanks to the horrendous inflation in China during the last years of the KMT regime.

Here, however, Papa and Mama learned from our neighbors how to make kids work the American way. Apart from a very small allowance, Toto and I were given a list of work rates. I remember clearly that dishwashing after a meal for four came to a nickel, dusting rooms other than our own earned us a dime; but the bonus job—fifteen cents—was getting on all fours to scrub the kitchen floor. That was too inconvenient for Mama who wore a Chinese cheongsam most of the time for economic reasons, and painful for Papa with his bad back. So Toto and I vied for the kitchen floor, as the pay was three times higher than for doing dishes. I figure my lifelong frugality started on that kitchen floor. But I am only frugal, not enterprising, for as I scrubbed, I kept counting up my financial gains by means of addition, not multiplication.

Since my clothes, saddle shoes, and other necessities were supplied by my parents, my only extraneous expenses were for buying toys. I pined for a big doll that cost five bucks—or one hundred nickels, which would take a long time to accumulate. To reach that goal, I did as many chores as could be allocated to me, and saved from my small allowance by giving up popsicles.

By the time we left Berkeley, I had not only bought my big doll, but had amassed a total of sixteen silver dollars. Eight of these I squandered in Europe, the rest I took back to China. But those eight coins weighed heavily on my consciousness when the new regime proclaimed it illegal for any Chinese to possess foreign currencies. I hid them in a trunk and counted them every time I went into the storage room. To me they represented not only the hard-earned fruits of much household drudgery, but also the result of painstaking piggy-banking and of squirreling away pennies, nickels, and dimes until I could exchange them for dollar coins. I vowed I would never part with them, and I didn't for as many as eighteen years.

The small bag of coins was overlooked by the Red Guards when they first ransacked our house in Tientsin in 1966. Later, when the intrusions into households became more frequent, we figured it would be safer to let the

36

coins go. I counted my eight dollars for the last time, and Papa took the small, palm-sized bag with him during a train trip and flipped it out the window when crossing a bridge near Tientsin. Those eight dollars must still be resting on the riverbed.

Toto was the first to return to that Scenic Avenue house when he came to study in the United States in the early 1980s. He was let in, and the current owner generously took him around the house—he knew Toto was no imposter when my brother pointed to the old trap door and the built-in shelves. I chose the wrong date when I went back to our old house on Thanksgiving Day of 1983. It was late afternnon when Sister Lew took me there. I told her I would like to ask permission to take a few pictures in front of the house. Lew suggested I ring the bell and see if anybody was at home.

In answer to my ring, a flowery dressing gown surmounted by a head of curlers showed up at the side window from where I used to look out at visitors. I laughed, explained the situation, and asked if I might take some pictures from the sidewalk. The lady good-naturedly pointed to her attire, and said she'd let me in if it were another day, but she and the turkey were both running late.

Toto later took my daughter to pay her respects to the house. And when the singing uncle returned to visit the Bay Area and Toto had taken him over as well, I groaned: "Do you realize this is the sixth party in ten years to visit the former residence of the Chens? Why don't you make a deal with the owner to open the house as a tourist attraction!"

But the house is always there, in my mind's eye: the street number beside the door frame, the hedge, the bay window, the garden with honeysuckle, and the sidewalk with the fallen leaves crunching underfoot. Forever.

Two Chinese Kids in Hillside School

Toto and I were rare animals in the classrooms and on the playground of Hillside School in 1948; we were the only two Chinese kids among several hundred Anglos.

Toto, having entered grade school at the normal age, got into second grade without any problems; he was seven, which was just about the right age. I had jumped classes a lot in China, and should have been in sixth grade, but being a nine-year-old and weak in English, I was put in fourth grade. That was the only year I sat in the same classroom with my peers, for I popped up to seventh grade once I had returned to China the year after.

We enjoyed and looked forward to every schoolday, birthday, and holiday. Toto, however, had to go through an initiation: two classmates insisted upon watching him pee. Toto came home quite upset. So the next time we saw puppies sniffing each other before tugging at their leashes to play together, Mama observed: "See? You and your classmates are like those puppies. Once they've satisfied their curiosity about you, they'll accept you." Those two boys, Earl and Tommy, became Toto's best friends and did much to unburden our fridge of its ample supplies of ice cream.

I was exempted from any such ritual and was quickly accepted, due partly to the fact that I excelled in two fields of study—spelling and arithmetic. I don't quite know why I was so good at spelling. One of the reasons could be that Chinese characters have to be memorized as an entity and I unconsciously applied the same method to English words. I was always at the top of the class.

I do know, however, what made me tick in math: It was the Chinese "nine-nine multiplication table" which rhymes easily since all Chinese numbers consist of a single open-ended syllable. Every Chinese can rattle the table off by heart like a nursery rhyme, and that makes mental calculation much easier. Besides, I'd already been through multiplication, division, and fractions before coming to America.

My handicap was English. I could read and recite but not relate to the text. There were also many passages and events and names which were familiar to my classmates but failed to register with me. For instance, a fascinating name has long stuck at the back of my mind, but I never knew if it belonged to a city, a person, or a building. Just last year, however, something clicked when I heard on TV that swallows were coming back to San Juan Capistrano! That name, San Juan Capistrano, was the long-buried puzzle.

Toto and I gradually caught on with American ways; Toto in the course of buying and losing eleven baseball caps, and I by learning how to tie my sweater around my hips. But we were both well behaved and diligent, prompted, perhaps, by a talk Mama had with us before we were let loose into the great land of the free.

"When either of you were naughty at home," she said, "only the misbe-having one was scolded. And when any one of you misbehaved outside our home in China, it was `the Chen kids' who were naughty. But now that we're in America, for anything you do wrong people will say, `Oh! it's those Chinese kids!' Do you get my point?"

Our exemplary behavior extended to the daily trek to school, three long blocks from home. Actually, it was Toto who was exemplary; while it had been a daily fight in China to get him ready for school, I don't recall a single instance of him being tardy in Berkeley. Every morning, Mama or Papa would walk us around the corner and up two blocks to a stairwaylike alley called Vine Lane. They'd stand at the foot of the steps while we scampered up and waved good-bye. Hillside School was only one block from the upper end of the lane. We would pass a house with the most beautiful tulips in its garden, and then be escorted across the street by older students acting as crossing guards.

We were delightfully surprised to learn that there wasn't any homework to be done; children in China were given loads of homework even in grade school. Now we could finish everything in the classroom, leave the hard-cov-ered textbooks in the desk, and simply go home! But we had other assign-ments at home; we both wanted to advance in English and Chinese, so we did a couple of hours of extra studies in the afternoons.

Equally surprising to us were the classroom parties. One day, when Toto's class had a birthday, I couldn't believe my ears when he told me they had eaten cake right in class; and I just couldn't wait for a kid in my class to have a party, too. Our own birthdays, mine in February and Toto's in April, were well down the road and we started talking about them weeks in advance. Mine was my tenth—a good round age, so my parents sent in generous pro-visions for my classroom party, and had a party at home for my closer class-mates and Toto's Earl and Tommy. I saved a couple of gifts from that birthday for more than thirty years.

When Toto's turn came, we'd already decided to go back to China, and the party in Toto's class served also as a farewell gathering. As for the birthday party at home, aside from the omnipresent Earl and Tom, Toto asked in a small voice whether he could have Sarah, too. It was not so much the roly-poly Sarah as the tone of Toto's request that provoked a round of teasing from the rest of the family. Cornered, Toto admitted, "Sure, she's quite roly-poly, but she has a good heart!" We all had a good laugh and then sent off invitations to a couple more girls to maintain the gender balance.

It was also at Hillside School that I had my first brush with puppy love. I had grown up among boys—a brother, cousins (all male in my age group), and sons of family friends. Playing and fighting with boys was a normal pastime for me. But I finally had my first puppy love. There were two boys who visited our home more often than the rest, and we went to the same parties. The brown-haired one pulled me aside when he gave me my birthday gift and asked me whom I liked better, him or the blond one? I was quite taken aback, for I had never had to consider a "like" or "don't like" question with regard to boys, either in Chinese or in English.

My ambivalent "both" did not deter brown-hair. The mere fact that his gambit had gone unrebuffed gave him enough confidence to act in a protective way toward me. I knew I would get a scolding if I asked Papa or Mama how to deal with the situation; but as it turned out, all my anxieties about my next encounter with young Michael were dispelled by my parents' decision to return to China. There, I entered a girls' high school and it was not until seven years later that I met a second, somewhat bigger pup.

Much as I loved the five-days-a-week regime, I couldn't help wondering how many school days American kids actually had. After a full year in an American school, I took a calendar and counted up the days. By my 1949 calculation, out of 365 days we had spent 186, or just about half, in school!

I sat there a long time, stunned by my discovery. In China, we went to school six days a week, had fifty days for summer vacation, three weeks for winter vacation (which incorporated the Chinese New Year holidays), one day for the then National Day, October 10th, one day for New Year's Day, and half a day for what was then Children's Day, April 4th. That was about it. How come American students got so many days off a year, and still East came to West for advanced studies?

The cogitations of a ten-year-old don't hold much water, but they were sufficient to keep me quiet whenever there have been arguments regarding the merits and demerits of educational methods, East versus West. I have always given a fifty-fifty rating to both systems, but I've witnessed the travails of my children and their endless exams, and I've often wondered what became of my classmates. Did the class taught by Miss Marliave produce any Nobel laureates, any academicians, or any poets?

Lost and Found Among the Bookshelves, I

I was born a bookworm, and my lifelong love affair has been with Books. I have almost never slept without a book by my side. In my last years in China in the 1980s, I had a twin-size bed, about four inches wider than the average Chinese single bed. I always had a stack of my current infatuations on the right side of my pillow, and when I eventually got a telephone, it lay on my left.

One day, my daughter Mimi looked at my sleeping arrangements quizzically and observed: "Do you know, Mama, your bed reminds me of Mao Tsetung's?" When I asked her why, she replied: "You sleep with books, and Mao in his later years had only books on the other half of his bed."

Mama told me I never tore a book when I was little. I started to play with characters after I was two, because Mama had just had Toto then, and sometimes I found myself with nothing better to do.

My first real recollection of The-Book-and-I relationship dated from the time I was three or four. I was taken along when my parents went visiting. At their friends' house, I found my haven among their bookshelves. Most people used open shelves, but curtains were hung over the books as protection against the dusty winds in Peiping. On this particular occasion, I ducked behind the curtains, sat on the floor and read contentedly by the light coming through the opening. Besides, I was playing house at the same time—a student studying in her tiny room. I lost track of the time, and suddenly a hand flipped open the curtains and jerked me up by the straps of my overalls. "There she is," Papa's voice said. "We should have looked here in the first place."

This became a pattern. Once I had paid my respects to the hosts, off I trotted to their bookshelves. I usually ended up among the bottom shelves where I found many banished junk treasures. My parents would fish me out when they were ready to leave.

By the time we left China for the United States in 1948, when I was nine, I believe I had finished most of the children's and young adults' books in Chinese—there weren't too many of those in the first place. And I also finished my first classical novel in Chinese, *Pilgrimage to the West*, the one about the Monkey King.

To supplement my reading needs, I began to peruse the newspapers, which made my parents uneasy. At that time, the official KMT newspapers were the only ones a person could subscribe to without risk, and a seven- or eight-year-old believes the newspapers as he or she believes books. My parents were liberal; they were critical of the KMT regime, critical of "Old Chiang." I became upset; I even cried and said they shouldn't talk like that about the Generalissimo. They exchanged a look and that topic was dropped from the dinner table, not to be resumed again until we got to the United States. However, that look made me wiser; I realized there must be something they understood that I didn't.

I started to play with English on the *President Taft*. I would write down in a row "bat" "cat" "fat" . . . all the way down to "sat," and another row with "bin" "din" "fin" . . . to "win." Then I would compare the two sides to see which was the longest, and therefore the "winner." After I had finished all the combinations and competitions for the three-letter words, I went on to the four-letter words, such as from "bead" . . . to "read."

Incidentally, I have a clear conscience to this day; I didn't play with "dirty" four-letter words. I swear that when I wrote down the row "buck" "duck" . . . to "tuck," I never made the combination with "f"—it just wasn't in my dictionary. If I had known the word then, the "-uck" row might have been a winner!

This was a game I never told anyone about, but I rather surprised my parents and myself when I, a Chinese girl, came out tops in my class at my Berkeley school not only in arithmetic, which was expected, but also in spelling. I guess the game I played with myself on the *President Taft* helped.

My English reading life commenced in those years at Berkeley, and it became a part of me which no one could take or tear away.

"Come Back to Peace"

A momentous change took place in China while Toto and I blissfully underwent our Americanization—the peaceful takeover of Peiping by the Communists at the end of January, 1949.

Apparently our family had not made any definite plans as to how long we would stay in America, and since Papa was still on the payroll of his bank in China, he spent the remaining months of 1948 looking around for investment opportunities for his bank, traveling to the Midwest and the East Coast. The proceeds from the lease of our big house in Peiping were enough to cover the expenses of our much smaller household here, so we were comfortable financially.

However, the speed with which events were taking place back in China was entirely unexpected. When we left China, everyone had reckoned that the civil war between the KMT and the CCP (Chinese Communist Party) would last about three years and end in the early 1950s, with the CCP ousting the terminally corrupt KMT. But the strategic advances of the Communist armies were rapid beyond all expectations, supported as they were by the bulk of the Chinese population—the destitute peasantry. The entire Northeast (Manchuria to the West) was taken over shortly before we settled down in Berkeley and, by the turn of the year, Communist troops were poised to take Peiping and Tientsin. How Fu Tso-yi, the KMT general in charge of Peiping, would deal with the situation weighed heavily on the minds of all Chinese students and scholars in Berkeley.

It so happened that this General Fu and his wife were friends of our family. Rather than being a warlord, Fu had risen from the rank and file. His area of authority before the Sino-Japanese War had covered the provinces that now form the Inner Mongolian Autonomous Region. Mama taught at one of the schools there after she graduated from Tsinghua University and before she returned to teach at that university and became betrothed to Papa. The General and his wife learned about the extremely attractive but single university graduate and were concerned about her safety. Mama became their protégée, and the junior officers and local officials knew better than to pester her.

The General was one of the pillars of resistance against the Japanese invasion. So when he was promoted garrison commander of Peiping after the war and our family returned to that city, the friendship between the Fus and Mama was renewed and strengthened, especially now that Mama was a married woman with two children. We kids were taken to meet Uncle and Aunty Fu when I was about seven or eight. I was quite impressed by the fact that both the Fus came out to meet us in the plain cotton-padded robes worn by ordinary northern Chinese in winter—no silks, no furs, just cotton.

So at the beginning of 1949, the fate of the several million civilians in

Peiping and the city itself—a treasure house of dynastic architecture and arti-facts—was in the hands of General Fu. As a military man, he was known to be a good commander with a well-disciplined army; but history had decided he was not to fight his last battle. During his last winter as a general, his army had been infiltrated by Communist agents and many of his officers were reluctant to see Peiping, which had never seen war within its walls, turned into a battleground. Since even the general's own daughter by his first wife was an underground Communist Party member, Fu came under tremendous pressure to surrender Peiping peacefully. He did.

We heard the news with immense relief and staged an impromptu celebra-tion with all the Chinese who came from or were connected with Peiping. As none of those present were politicians, the celebration was simply for peace and the avoidance of bloodshed. The fate of the KMT regime in Nanking and elsewhere was sealed, doomed as it was by its hopeless turpitude. It did not take a Communist to see that. For better or for worse, China needed a change.

My parents had been strongly against the Japanese invasion and greatly disillusioned with Chiang Kai-shek's ambiguous approach to that issue as far back as the early 1930s. But their major expectations were for a peaceful and democratic new China. With many of their alumni and relatives connected with the CCP, they were inclined to place greater trust in the nascent New China than in the old regime which had failed their hopes. What with General Fu—a gentleman of integrity—casting his lot with the CCP and the correspondence of many close friends describing the euphoria accompanying the takeover of Peiping—"come back to peace," they urged. Papa and Mama decided to return at once.

Toto and I raised an anguished howl. We had just adjusted to and been accepted in our new milieu; I was well on my way to Americanization via bub-ble-gumming and partygoing in my newly acquired pair of Mary Janes, and Toto was rapidly familiarizing himself with the legend of Babe Ruth (along with a souvenir cap) and all the makes and years of American cars. We could-n't go back. We couldn't miss so-and-so's party, we still had Easter to celebrate . . . . Oh, yes, I'd joined the Brownies and had new knots to learn! Toto and I became close allies in a joint campaign against going back. Between us we had a thousand reasons. But less than thirty dollars. So, well, we lost.

But in a way, we won, for our strenuous opposition put the return trip on hold for a couple of months. It was after much careful planning that our parents decided we would leave Berkeley in June at the end of the semester, and return to China by way of Europe. Papa and Mama's chief consideration was that Toto and I were at the best age to take along on such a trip: we were old enough to remember the places and things we would see, but young enough to go half-price or even less. We would very soon become teenagers, and then there'd be no way we could go along as accompanying children. As it turned out, theirs was a sagacious decision, for we would never again have the chance to travel abroad together.

Our residence in Berkeley had been brief but eventful. We had come to stay out of the war, and went back on the promise of peace. During that peri-od, Papa had joined the Masons and given speeches concerning the inevitability of change in China. Mama had a taste of academic life, closely observed the Truman-Dewey-Wallace three-way race and wrote for a Chinese journal an article entitled "Watching the American Elections in the Rain." I not only became fluent in English, but also resumed my piano lessons and joined ballet sessions at school; Toto became a favorite with his teacher and the school's principal, both of whom cried when he left.

We were told that our parents had left a sum in our Berkeley bank, which could cover a year's expenses if we ever came back to the United States for graduate studies. This deposit was frozen by the U.S. government when the Korean War broke out. It was eventually released and trickled back to us in China via our relatives in America, as Chinese were not allowed foreign assets under Communist rules.

When I bade farewell to my class, I said: "See you in ten years," not know-ing this would be the last I would ever see of them. The school generously presented Toto and me with a complete set of textbooks from grade one to six, among them *Times and Places*, *People and Progress*, and all the related work-books. Along with the books and magazines we shipped back, they provided me with ample reading material and a sense of continuity.

Pullman Pulls Us Across America

During the school year in California, we had taken advantage of weekends to go by car to see all the attractions close to Bay Area, which included Yosemite, Lake Tahoe, and Carmel. We also zipped up and down Highway

101 over one long weekend, all the way to Los Angeles, the city I now call home. Now it was time to see the rest of America.

The first leg of the long trip home consisted of crossing from the West Coast to the East Coast. However, we shipped all our belongings direct from California to China, among them books, magazines, a Singer sewing machine, an 8mm film projector, a slide projector, a portable projection screen, transformers for all the 110-watt electrical gadgets, plus one set of furniture we all loved—the red kitchen table with pull-out flaps and folding legs together with four steel-framed chairs. This table survived all the stormy years in China including several years of exile in a government warehouse. It came back to us two chairs short, but is still serving faithfully in my apartment in China. The four Chens with their summer clothes went in the other direction, to reunite with our shipment many months later.

We traveled by train, and Toto and I each shared a berth with a parent in the Pullman wagon. I have loved trains ever since. Some evenings, our parents got us ready for the night, then went to sit for a while in the dining car. Toto and I would scramble into the upper berth with the night curtains pulled together—a most ideal location to play house. The only annoyance of train rides was that American trains were never on time. In China, train schedules are strictly observed, under normal circumstances. But no one seemed to bother about schedules when we traveled across America in 1949.

We saw the great canyons of the Southwest, passed through Salt Lake City, slept in tents at Yellowstone, and saw a great number of bears. We made a good, long stop at Penn State where we had a reunion with two of my cousins—a niece my parents had doted upon during their courtship days and her brother, who came for that reunion. She eventually devoted her entire professional life to Penn State, and it was exactly forty years later to the month that I visited her again in the same city. She asked me then whether I still retained any impression of Penn State. "Sure," and I quoted a Chinese four-character idiom *Yu yu tsong tsong*, meaning lush greenery. "What an accurate description!" she exclaimed. "We call our city the Tree City."

It was on Pullman in 1949 that I got my first taste of independence, at my parents' expense. I was up and around one morning and was more than ready for breakfast. Papa said, Why don't you run along to the dining car, get a table, and wait for us? I did as was told. When the waiter came, I hemmed and hawed and said I had to wait for my parents. What with all the "miss"-ing, "ma'am"-ing and "would you like something . . .," however, I thought "what the heck, I know what I want, anyway!" So I ordered everything from orange juice, cereal, bacon and eggs to toast and the relevant fixings—one item from each section of the menu.

I was into the cereal when my family came on the scene. One look at the waiter approaching from the other end loaded with platters for this young lady told my parents by how much the family wallet would be depleted. Papa ordered the usual modest basics and declined all tantalizing suggestions from the waiter. I was not reprimanded or made fun of, but perhaps that was the beginning of my lifelong fixation for reading menus from right to left. It was only subconscious at first. But Papa noticed that trait when he took me out when I was older. "Keep your eyes on the left-hand side and tell me what you want," he commanded. "Don't look for the lowest price then check what the course actually is!"

We stopped over in Washington, D.C., and New York and went to Niagara Falls. What struck me most was the statue of a meditating Lincoln in the Lincoln Memorial. That image stayed with me all my life, for Lincoln's air of pensiveness and profundity signified greatness, and those qualities are what I've always believed a leader should have. In 1977, Mao's mausoleum on Tiananmen Square was opened for all Chinese to come and worship him after his death in 1976. I will not comment on the unnatural waxlike appearance of his mummified body; but when I walked into the hall where a post-Cultural Revolution statue of Mao Tse-tung, sitting in a marble armchair with legs jauntily crossed, stares down haughtily at the commoners below, the contrast with Lincoln's statue hit me like a physical blow. Tears welled up, not of fond memories of the so-called Great Leader of China, but of anger—my unvoiced exclamation was "Not again!"—over the arrogance and cult worship which refused to die.

So we left the United States and passed through Montreal and Quebec City to board a Cunard White Star liner for Southampton. That took place in the early summer of 1949, and it was the last farewell to the Americas for my parents.

Around the World

The short voyage across the Atlantic was uneventful, apart from the fact that Toto was the social lion of the tourist deck, particularly among the older ladies who simply adored the little Chinese boy who spoke such fluent English. I fell into disgrace because of my constant bubble-gum chomping and blowing. One disapproving British lady said to my face: "Look what the Americans have passed on to you!"

Popping a defiant last bubble, I withdrew to our cabin, thinking I now would have one more reputation to look out for, in addition to those related to myself, "the Chen kids," and "those Chinese children," as listed by Mama. Maybe that's where I started to become pro-American—right in the middle of the Atlantic Ocean, or, at least, while we were traveling around the world that summer.

Our first stop in Europe was London, where we stayed with a couple of my parents' Tsinghua University schoolmates. Their children, also a sister-and-brother team but a few years older than Toto and myself, had grown up in Britain. While the two sets of parents enjoyed each other's company, the children failed to get along. Why? All the bickering between the two pairs of Chinese siblings stemmed from British and American differences. They laughed at our American accent and we wrinkled our noses at their British boarding school English, and Toto and I suddenly turned very pro-American as we vehemently defended football versus soccer and baseball versus cricket. And most of the arguments were carried out in Chinese.

Regardless of the bickering with the Lo children, however, we immensely enjoyed our London tour complete with the Buckingham Palace and its fabulous guards, the Tussaud wax museum and the pilgrimage to Cambridge and Oxford. We were duly impressed with the one-egg-per-person-per-week regime due to shortages in postwar years, strictly observed by monarchy and civilians alike, and we learned that the Los had saved up months ahead in order to serve us eggs for breakfast.

We left London for Paris with a lighter load, for according to our itinerary we were to return to England after spending a month on the continent, pick up our luggage, and then board the *S.S. Canton*, a British ocean liner that would take us home to China. The forty-five-minute flight from London to Paris was the most enjoyable I ever experienced in my childhood. Actually, that was the last time my parents ever flew in an airplane. They would never fly on a jet, because the so-called Chinese People's Airlines were not open to ordinary Chinese people, at least during their lifetime.

In Paris we were again received by Mama's cousin, A. K. Chiang, the person who met us when we escaped from Japanese-occupied territory in early 1945. He was a ranking official in the KMT government and after the war was dispatched to Paris as Consul General. He had us comfortably accommodated in a hotel within walking distance of his residence/office and lionized us at a special reception for us on the Consulate grounds.

Versailles, Fountainbleu, the Louvre, and all the Parisian delights awaited us, and aside from several French expressions such as *"s'il-vous-plait"* and *"merci beaucoup,"* I learned to say *"Louis Quatorze"* in French because it was repeated at every palace museum. Toto and I had never been left out of anything when we were in America, but in Paris, our parents left us in the charge of the maid at the hotel and went to a topless show with Uncle and Aunty Chiang. We stayed up until they came back, not out of anxiety of being left in the hotel, but because we were curious to find out what they had seen. My parents told us in the most neutral terms how the dancers had been clad, or unclad, and we asked a round of innocent but detailed questions.

Being the relatives of the Consul General had one disastrous result. My parents asked one of Uncle's aides to book us a hotel in our next stop, Rome. Assuming we must be rich tourists from America, he made reservations at Hotel Bellini in Rome. Papa started to fidget the moment we were shown into the lobby. We were given a grand suite, and being tired out we reluctantly decided to spend the night there. We moved out the very next morning. We kids were told that suite cost a hundred dollars a night (in 1949), but I suspect it was more than that, for we counted pennies all the way through the rest of Italy and Switzerland.

Bellini or not, Rome was magnificent, the Catacombs eerie and Pompeii sad, and the lakes and mountains of Switzerland gorgeous beyond description. I still had my sixteen silver dollars, and I used about two dollars to buy a plastic tea set that served six dolls or persons. These became my most used toys well into the mid-1950s. From Peiping to Tientsin my girlfriends and I played party with them endless times. We used real food, which drove our cook crazy. I spent another three dollars for three bags each containing one thousand used stamps and another couple of dollars on embroidered Swiss handkerchiefs. There went half of my hard-earned savings.

We returned to Paris for a very brief stay and did one illegal thing there: We bought as many eggs as we could safely stuff into our suitcases and hand-carried them through British customs. This time we did the Paris-London trip by train and ferry, and since customs officers were concerned chiefly about liquor, which we didn't have, we passed through with very innocent looks on our faces. Back in London, imagine the Los' delight when each of us opened our hand-carried—hard-sided in the 1940s—suitcases and started taking out eggs! I remember there were about a hundred in all.

We were now ready for the thirty-day journey back to China, through Gibraltar, the Red Sea, and the Indian Ocean. There were many, many Chinese in tourist class returning to the new country—students, minor officials once assigned overseas by the KMT government, artists, and other professionals. We were the only complete family going home. All were filled with hope.

We saluted the Rock of Gibraltar and called in at Port Said and Ceylon (now Sri Lanka). India left me feeling sad, and Mama said she hoped to see the day when China and India would leave poverty behind and reach American and European standards of life.

That ocean voyage was really comfortable. The *President Taft*, which had taken us to America, was not a passenger ship and had been tossed about a good deal by Pacific storms; seasickness had been the major pastime. The Atlantic crossing, on the other hand, had been too short. But on the *S.S. Canton* I quickly got accustomed to the routine and made good use of my time in the cabin sorting out my three thousand newly acquired stamps.

The ship held a costume party and a gala evening shortly before we reached our destination—Hong Kong. Mama let me wear one of her smaller-sized Chinese dresses and braided my hair in a different way. Toto was put in a raincoat and a cap and held a hatchet made out of paper carton by Papa; he was supposed to be a fireman. The other passengers improvised costumes with whatever they had, and, after the screening of a new film *An Unfinished Dance*, many volunteered to perform. After a few numbers, I became sleepy. So I went back to our cabin to change and read.

Suddenly a powerful soprano resounded from the makeshift stage through all the cabins and decks, as powerful as that of the Italian opera singer in *La Traviata* we had heard in Rome on open stage. I heard the singing, and I heard feet pattering through the corridor as people hurried back to the performance. I threw on some outdoor clothing and ran back in time to hear one of the returning Chinese artists, Madame Kwan, bursting out in a magnificent aria. The audience gave her standing ovation and encored her well into the night. She was a well-known singer from China trained in Europe, and later became Associate Dean of the Central Music Conservatory I went to. Those scheduled to sing after her cancelled their numbers in deference to a true maestro.

We disembarked in Hong Kong and managed to book a cabin on a boat from Hong Kong to Tientsin. When we got back home, it was after seventeen months of absence. We came back to a different world.

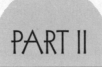

PART II

GOLDEN YEARS, GODDAMN YEARS (1949-1966)

Peking and Tientsin, China

Innocents from Abroad

We disembarked from our ship at Taku Bar (Tientsin Harbor) in the late autumn of 1949.

When we got back to our big house in our city, which reassumed its old name, Peking, Toto and I raced up and down the stairs to examine every familiar nook and cranny, with our exulting dog Tiger close on our heels.

Our ever-present cook was still with us; the amah who followed Toto all over the school playground had left Peking with her husband, but another amah stayed on. One of our favorite cousins, Ta, who had helped look after the premises while we were away, was waiting for us. We were back *home*— and there's no place like home.

My parents were open-minded and trustful by nature. And now that many of their "progressive" friends worked for the new government under Communist leadership, they looked for the best side of things. After all, China had entered a new era. There was no immediate change in our lifestyle, and no pressure, at the beginning.

Our shipment of books and household articles arrived. Soon our rooms were decked out with useful things from our Scenic Avenue house—from rosebud-shaped salt and pepper shakers, to the outsize 1949 model of a record-cutting machine. (I wonder if any Americans still remember that contraption.) We showed our 8mm home movies to friends and Papa's bank colleagues, not knowing that this constituted a self-contrived threat to Papa's political fate. We were to learn our lessons the hard way.

And there was much to learn about—such as our "family class background":

The national flag of the Republic of China is referred to as the "blue sky, white sun and red-filled earth"; its color scheme parallels that of the flags of France, Great Britain, and the United States. It was adopted after the 1911 Sun Yat-sen revolution, and still serves as the flag of the Republic of China in Taiwan. The national flag of the People's Republic of China is an all-red flag with gold-colored stars, and is known as the "Five-Star Red Flag." The big star represents the Communist Party, while the four smaller ones stand for the four social classes that supposedly make up the People's Republic, namely the workers, peasants, the petty bourgeoisie, and the so-called national bourgeoisie, meaning those who stayed on with the new government (as distinct from the iniquitous "comprador bourgeoisie"—iniquitous, because it had cooperated with the foreign imperialists and colonialists in plundering the Chinese economy).

In early 1950, when I entered the Bridgeman Academy in Peking—a well-known six-year high school for girls originally run by a Protestant church—I had to fill in a form in which one of the questions was: What is your family class background? How the heck was I to know what that was?! I went home to Mama, but nobody in our family knew, at the time. I should simply have written down Papa's occupational category—senior functionary at a bank. This would have simplified certain things for us. But not everything.

We got a copy of a current magazine and looked through it for the definition of our class background; we found an illustration purporting to show the four classes. I remember clearly that a petty bourgeois was depicted as a thin man in a Chung-shan suit (the so-called "Mao jacket" is actually a misnomer; it was copied from the uniform worn by the founder of the Republic of China—Dr. Sun Yat-sen, or Sun Chung-shan to the Chinese), while the national bourgeois was shown as a well-built man in a Western suit. We all agreed that Papa, the head of our household, seemed to fit best in this last category.

So I confidently stated in the form that my family class background was the national bourgeoisie, and Toto followed suit when he, too, started to go to high school. How innocent and naive we were, as we tried to adapt to a brand-new set of values!

I had my doubts afterward, for at the time Papa was not a stockholder, and therefore did not conform to the Marxist definition of the bourgeoisie. I asked my parents whether I should ask for clarification of our class status, but they answered staunchly that the national bourgeoisie was a part of the people — one of the four small stars on the national flag. And we belonged to that category, rather than to the schoolteacher-like petty bourgeoisie. In the Chinese context, this was the correct decision—or a very wrong one, depending on the times.

GOLDEN YEARS, GODDAMN YEARS (1949-1966)

"The Houses Get Smaller and the Cars Get Bigger"

The peaceful liberation of Peking led many well-wishing Chinese to place their trust in the new Central Government. The regime's apparent probity was demonstrated by lenient treatment toward well-to-do families; land reform, to end the feudal system inherent in China's rural regions; and, what was critical for the urban economy, the exercise of state controls to stop inflation. This was particularly important to the man in the street, who had suffered through the long war years and the ensuing civil war not only from chaos and social upheaval, but also from rampant inflation—the value of KMT paper money could deflate by the hour.

People felt greatly relieved, now that prices were low and stable, and goods which only the affluent had been able to afford became available to the average person. While this was what the new regime wanted, egalitarianism also set in, and China was to suffer the consequences in the years to come, as economic and all creative activity stagnated for lack of incentives.

We heard other home owners and car owners quipping, "our houses get smaller, and our cars get bigger." Asked what this meant, they explained that they had "voluntarily" reduced their living space and given up their own cars to take public buses. Hence, "our cars get bigger." Our turn soon came.

Our house was rather ostentatious by any standard, from its Western-style facade to the polished terrazzo floors inlaid with strips of brass; it was also located on a most desirable site. The house became an object of desire to the government, and the persistent efforts to persuade Papa and Mama to sell it reached frenetic proportions.

Anyone who has experienced such insistent and interminable pestering must take his hat off to the officials responsible in the P.R.C. government for a job well done. I suspect that from the day "Operation Chen's House" was launched, they must have had a chart or date book specifying whom to send to us at what hour each day.

Mind you, Chinese don't make appointments before they pay a visit, so we were thrown into suspense every time the doorbell rang. Those who came had one specific mission: to get my parents to say "yes, we'll sell the house to the government," for—as we were told again and again and yet again—this was the need of the people, the need of the government, the need of the country, and it would also benefit us.

Not only did those visits get on *our* nerves, they also irritated our dog. Tiger was a very friendly dog, but after a couple of months of such day-in-and-day-out visits, this "bourgeois running dog" could tell the difference between family friends and our non grata visitors. She started to growl, to bark, and even to chase these luckless callers.

Finally, my parents gave in, and sold the house "voluntarily," then rented a tiny courtyard right across the street from the schools Toto and I went to. The house, together with all the larger pieces of furniture and that cumbersome record cutter, went at a good price. We later learned that successive ambassadors of the Soviet Union were domiciled there, and they were followed by a string of high-ranking Chinese cadres.

There are three sequels to this story:

Papa eventually invested the money from the sale of the house in bonds and shares, and thus became a "national bourgeois," post-1949-style.

One of my uncles by marriage hadn't had a chance to see the house while we lived in it. Then, in the 1970s, some twenty years later, he visited one of his old friends, the father of a high-ranking cadre. The cadre's secretary met my uncle at the gate of the big house, showed him around, and then remarked: "This used to belong to your brother-in-law." My uncle was duly surprised and impressed by this Kafkaesque lack of reticence.

In the late 1970s, I came across an article released in memory of Chou En-lai. The author mentioned the late premier's consideration for the welfare and well-being of the people and quoted him as having said: "Some government officials are pressing civilians to sell their houses . . . Do not try to buy any houses while the owners still live in them." What they had put us through was precisely what Chou had told them not to do. Reading those lines after almost thirty years, I didn't know whether to feel angry, or simply laugh the whole thing off.

We Are Taught to Hate the American Imperialists

At about the time of the founding of the People's Republic, Mao Tse-tung proclaimed that China would "lean to one side," the side of the Soviet Union. So the Soviet Union became our "Big Brother."

In our geography classes, we were taught how fortunate we were in sharing our entire northern border with our Big Brother—that we had nothing to worry about from that quarter. (That is, until the 1960s, after which a twist of history turned brothers into foes.)

In our history classes, we were told that it was the Red Army of the U.S. S.R. that had not only defeated Nazi Germany, but also forced Japan to surrender by their post-A-bomb entry into the Pacific War. However, my history teacher faced students who had learned some history before the 1949 takeover and were old enough to remember the last years of World War II. To convince these skeptical students, or perhaps to convince herself, our teacher emphasized the following points:

First, the Red Army's advance into Manchuria hit the Japanese in the rear. This changed the entire military balance, something the A-bombs couldn't have done. Therefore the decisive factor in the Allies' Pacific victory was the U.S.S.R.'s participation.

Secondly, Stalin had pledged that the Red Army would enter the Far East war theater within three months after VE-Day. August 9 1945, happened to be ninety days after VE-Day. Therefore the Soviet Union had done as promised; it was a mere coincidence that the A-bomb was dropped just before the U S.S.R.'s involvement in the Pacific war.

I remember these arguments clearly; we had to memorize them for our exams, although no one really believed them. I had to repeat them to myself a dozen times to impress them firmly on my mind—in order to get a good grade. Years later, I asked my daughter, who learned her history in post-Big Brother times, what the decisive factor was in the Japanese surrender. She replied matter-of-factly, "The A-bomb, of course."

In our physics and chemistry classes, we learned that all technology of any importance had been invented by Russians. The familiar names Edison and Newton were hardly mentioned, and in their stead we heard long and unfamiliar Russian names. However, when a textbook translated from Russian proclaimed that gunpowder was invented by a Russian, we all raised our voices in anguished questions. Our teacher looked at us helplessly and said: "Let's assume they don't understand Chinese and are therefore ignorant of the earlier Chinese invention. Anyway, I won't ask who invented gunpowder in exams."

This lean-to-one-side tendency naturally extended to language studies as well. Courses in English—the "language of the imperialists"—were suspended for a period of time, and students "Rrrrr-ed" their way into foreign language classes (most Chinese, including myself, find the rolling Russian "R" hard to pronounce). Almost everyone in the cities joined the Sino-Soviet Friendship Association for a five-fen fee, and everyone learned Russian.

As Papa put it humorously a decade later: Out of respect for our Big Brother he had started to take Russian lessons no fewer than six times, only to drop out after trying to learn the alphabet. He never got beyond the third letter in it.

After the outbreak of the Korean War, a campaign was launched to wipe out pro-American sentiments. While the "fraternal affection" for the U.S.S.R. was ordained by goverment decree, the empathy between Chinese and Americans stemmed from historical facts, notably that the United States government had not made any territorial claims upon China at the turn of the century, nor had it had concessions—enclaves with extraterritorial powers—in Chinese cities, as many Western countries and Japan did. Moreover, the universities, hospitals, and even high schools set up by American foundations; the many missionaries sent to port cities and inland areas of China; and the YMCA, YWCA, and Salvation Army had sowed the seeds of goodwill.

So as tension mounted in Korea and United States forces approached the Chinese border, we were instructed to stamp out any vestiges of "pro-America," "worship-America," and "fear-America" mentality, and to replace them with hatred, scorn, and disdain for U. S. imperialism.

In my class at the Bridgeman Academy, I was "the girl who has just returned from America." Since I was a native of Peking, however, I wasn't regarded as a curiosity—except when my classmates found out that my summer shorts zipped up at the back instead of on the side. They teased me about it and would try to pull down the zipper without my knowing it.

One day our teacher said to the class that since we had an eyewitness to the decadence of United States imperialism, why didn't we ask her to describe the evils she had seen? I was taken by surprise and racked my brains for something "evil" to talk about. I started with my school: sunny California, tulips by the sidewalk, birthday parties in class, lunch in the cafeteria—all flashed across my mind's screen. I had broken an ankle when I fell from a swing, but I couldn't blame that on the "imperialists." I began by telling the class about our everyday lives in America, then two "evil" memories came to my rescue— one of a drunkard lying in a San Francisco side street and the other of the slums on both sides of the New York subway when it surfaced to the elevated tracks on the way to the Bronx Zoo.

I did my best, but I wasn't able to talk about things I couldn't have seen. My teacher cut me short when I started on my excursion to the Grand Canyon and told the class: "It's obvious she wasn't in the United States long enough to learn about the corrupt nature of imperialism, but from what she has told us we can draw the conclusion that American cities are dirtier than ours, and they have more drunkards."

When I told Mama what we were supposed to say at school, she was upset. "Ever since you were born I've been trying to teach you to love. But now they're trying to teach you how to hate!"

To the newly founded Chinese government, involvement in the Korean peninsula became inevitable, and the Chinese army, posing as a Chinese People's Volunteer Army, crossed the Yalu River on October 25, 1950. (In post-Stalin days, the CCP revealed that the pressure to do so came directly from Stalin.)

Almost at the same time I received a round-robin letter composed by my entire class at Hillside School. They had written it one year after I left them, and in it each one told me what he or she had done during the summer vacations. A long letter in exquisite handwriting from our teacher Miss Marliave accompanied the round-robin letter.

After a long and painful discussion, my parents asked me to write a heartbreaking reply: "Now that our countries are at war, I'm afraid I cannot keep up this correspondence." That was the first time I used the long word "correspondence," and it was only to "de-correspond" with my young friends. I never met or heard from any of my Dianes and Sukis and Michaels and Tommies again.

From Mary Janes to Cotton-Padded Shoes

When I was in America, I was as vain and as vogue-conscious as any ten-year-old. I must have been a real pest when I badgered my parents for a pair of Mary Janes to wear to my classmates' parties. Everyone else wore them, so I had to have them too. I begged so hard for those "party shoes"—I didn't know the name in English—that Papa and Mama finally gave in. When those ten-dollar (1949 U. S. dollars) shoes were shipped back to China with our other belongings, however, the mere thought of them gave me pangs of remorse, for they were too small for me after only six months.

By that time I was giving up my American vanities for Chinese realities. I stopped tying my sweater around my waist because I was gawked at; I rotated my skirts ninety degrees so that the zippers landed on the right—and therefore *the* right—side of my waist. And I gradually got rid of all but one pair of back-zipping shorts. That lone pair of dusty-rose back-zipping 1949-vintage shorts lay in a trunk in Peking until they once again became fashionable in China in the 1980s. My daughter put them on, proudly sporting the once-again trendy color, trendy style, and trendy back-zipper.

In the 1950s, Mama and her crowd—the "missus" bracket in the cities—dressed up and wore makeup approximately the way they did in the 1940s, only in a slightly more subdued manner. With all the political movements going on, parties became less frequent, but until the late 1950s everyone still looked dressy when they went out visiting. Papa wore Western-style suits, and warm, silk-padded Chinese robes in winter, also approximately the way he always dressed; naturally, he also got himself a couple of Chung-shan suits for etiquette's sake. Toto was dressed in anything cool enough or warm enough for the season, in a reasonable way.

Not me, but it wasn't my fault.

When I entered Bridgeman's it was in a stage of transition. The old principals were gone or had resigned and we had been given new textbooks, but the school still held to its own traditions and we wore the same old uniforms. The winter uniform was a long, shapeless Chinese gown of indigo blue, drawn on over flannels, sweaters, woolen trousers, *and* a cotton-padded jacket, for our classrooms were poorly heated. After all these items had been crammed into them, the gowns still had to "flow," so one can imagine how many sizes larger they were made for us. It goes without saying that the gowns drooped and flapped in autumn and spring when there were fewer layers of clothing under them.

Practically all my schoolmates wore parkas. The GIs sold so many of them on the Peking black market there was hardly a family that didn't possess at least one. The fashionable thing to do at the time was to mask the unfashionable olive green with black dye, resulting in an interesting brownish green.

We all wore woolen socks or stockings, which our mothers kept themselves busy knitting for us. To protect our feet from the scratchy wool and to protect the wool from the shoes, we wore cotton socks both inside and outside the woolen ones. That made three pairs of socks in winter, inside oversized cotton-padded shoes which my maternal grandmother painstakingly made and which I detested because I thought they looked like black rabbit ears.

One morning, as Mama was giving me a final inspection before sending me off to school, Papa laughed out loud: "Looking at you from behind," he said, "I can see seven bands of clothing, but hardly any colors. Even a barber's pole has more color than your get-up." He hated that long gown we had to wear.

After Papa's sarcastic remark I became self-conscious about my back view. What made it look so ridiculous was, of course, the long gown. Actually, all the girls had an aversion for these gowns, winter or summer.

We had gym outfits for our physical education classes, but at all other times we were required to wear the gowns. Girls of the 1950s, however, were more active than those studying at Bridgeman earlier when those uniforms were first designed. We rode bikes to school and ran and played during the class breaks. So the slits on either side of the indigo-blue winter gown and the light-blue summer gown split still higher. Sometimes they ripped open all the way up to the top of our thighs, and then we had to borrow safety pins to repair the damage so that we could go home in decent shape.

In 1951, Bridgeman was transformed from a private school into a public school; it was grouped with the other public middle schools and assigned the designation "No. 12 Girl's Middle School." Even with such an anonymous name it managed to achieve some distinction in the years I was there.

But, for us, the best thing about the change was that we didn't have to wear those gowns any longer. Even our amah felt relieved, for the slits were nearly beyond repair. The gowns ended up as strips for mops, and the smaller scraps went into the cloth soles of Grandmother's endless cotton-padded shoes.

Papa in Jail Again

After a few months of being cramped up in the tiny courtyard we rented after we sold our big house, we were on the move again. We bought a house in two parts, with a large garden, a pavilion, rockeries, a man-made creek, and more than a dozen date trees. House One was said to be built in Japanese style; House Two was a Chinese-style building with seven or eight rooms linked together in a straight line, railroad style. After the constraints of the little courtyard, we were quite content to settle down here.

The wedding of our favorite cousin Ta and his beautiful schoolmate took place in this house, with both families coming for the ceremony. The groom wore a natty gray Chung-shan suit, and the bride a pink Chinese *ch'i-pao* (*cheongsam* in Cantonese), white gloves, and makeup. They were both Communist party members, but they looked splendid at the wedding. All the ladies wore dresses or *ch'i-pao*; the men were in either Western outfits or Chung-shan suits. We children tied a red ribbon around Tiger's neck to mark the occasion. Since red is the color of joy to the Chinese while white is reserved for funerals, the Chinese expression "red and white occasions" translates as "weddings and funerals."

While land reform went on in the countryside, ideological reform started among the intelligentsia, especially in the universities. Called "brainwashing" in the West, it took the form of criticism and self-criticism. No one knows where or when this sadistic ritual originated, except that it was already practiced in Yen-an, the Chinese Communist home base, in the early 1940s. Such criticism and self-criticism was to strip all Chinese of their honor, dignity, self-esteem, and—most traumatically for intellectuals—their professional pride.

However, ethical problems among "Party members"—as adherents of the ruling Chinese Communist Party were simply called—began to come out in the open at a very early stage of the new regime. Corruption, particularly in the sense of appropriating public money for private use, was highly damaging to the reputation of the new government. To be fair, I should say the majority of higher party officials, influenced by the integrity of then-Premier Chou En-lai were better disciplined than, for instance, their present day successors. Those who embezzled money for their own pleasure were meted severe, and even capital, punishment in the early 1950s.

A political movement was launched in response to those problems. Known as the Three Antis—anti-corruption, anti-extravagance, and against bureaucratic practices—it was at first focused upon officials and key personnel in the new government, but soon spread to merchants, manufacturers, entrepreneurs, and bankers who dealt with the state-owned enterprises. This was followed by another movement called the Five Antis, expanded to include such economic crimes and misdemeanors as bribery and tax evasion.

Under this guise of legitimacy, the net was drawn in around the well-to-do middle class. Many businessmen were taken into custody, and employees were encouraged or even forced to inform on their superiors. Papa was taken in early 1952.

A colleague of Papa's told us afterward that a group of cadres (i.e. state-employed functionaries) were waiting for the bank staff when everybody came to work as usual that day. It was announced that all senior executives above the rank of branch director would "assemble for screening." In plain English, they were taken into custody without warning, and without warrants. Messengers sent to the houses of the detainees told their families to prepare a bundle containing towels, soap, toothbrush, toothpaste, a washbasin, toilet paper, a supply of clothing, and some cash to pay for food. Subsequently, our entire family suffered seven months of grave anxiety and frustration.

During the various political movements and campaigns in China since 1949, to be taken into custody could mean anything—detention, solitary confinement, interrogation, maltreatment, abuse, or even torture. Sometimes the family would not be notified of the whereabouts of the detainee. But since there was no official arrest and the person was not put on trial or sentenced, the authorities could simply deny that innocent people had been imprisoned. Such denials, moreover, were partially true since the victim was usually incarcerated in some unofficial place of detention, often a cellar or storeroom in his or her own place of work. It was like that then; it still is like that now. And those who were eventually released never considered seeking redress. It just wasn't done.

Mama cried when Papa's soiled winter underwear was sent home for washing; it saddened us, too, when our letters and home-cooked food were returned to us. Mama went a few times and stood in line, only to receive a bundle of dirty laundry and hand in some clean clothes. There were no letters, no visits, no explanations.

Papa's salary was suspended and our savings account frozen. We had a large household at the time, since Mama's father—a small-town teacher who had owned some land—her stepmother, and her stepsister had fled the advancing Land Reform Movement and had been living with us for some time; and we still had our cook and our amah. So we had to borrow money, and borrowing money is a deeply humiliating thing for us Chinese. Nevertheless, we had friends and relatives who were willing and able to help.

We had two smaller shocks at the time. One came from our cook—the cook who had accompanied us on the desperate flight from the Japanese and who had been in our household ever since I was born. He must have been pressured into reporting about this Western bourgeois family, for he started to check on our comings and goings. I remember one evening when Mama was worrying over household expenses with Grandma, the cook stepped in from the dark without knocking and told Mama not to go to friends to borrow money. He spoke harshly, saying things like "You have money, so don't try to blame the government for your inconveniences."

It was really sickening that someone who had our trust, who had been with us through such perils, would turn against our family in this way. But we couldn't dismiss him then, for it would have been interpreted as an "act of reprisal against the proletariat." He left of his own accord after Papa's release, eventually becoming a chef in a restaurant.

The other painful experience occurred when Mama was called in to have a talk at the Five-Antis Office in charge of Papa's case. She arrived a little too early and found my favorite cousin, her fond nephew, Ta, chatting animatedly and familiarly with the cadres in the office. Visibly embarrassed by Mama's untimely arrival, he hastily departed.

I entered senior middle school (the tenth grade) that summer. Many of my classmates had fathers in custody at the time, for Bridgeman Academy was still favored by the middle class. None of us mentioned our parents' detentions, but whenever the father of one of the girls was released the word spread quickly, and we very subtly conveyed our feelings of relief to the lucky girl. In September, 1952, in the month leading up to National Day on October 1, I noticed that such releases were increasingly frequent.

One night after a heavy rain, as Toto and I were fast asleep in Papa's bed (during those seven months Mama put us in Papa's large bed next to her own), I was awakened by a bearlike embrace from someone with a scratchy beard. I started to call "Papa, Papa!" even before I could see who it was. It was already two o'clock, but the four of us sat with our arms around one another and talked through the rest of the night.

After a warm bath and a shave, Papa told us how he happened to get home at such an hour. His fellow detainees had been released one by one during the past several days, starting from the lower-ranking executives and moving toward the top. Papa guessed that since he was the de facto president of his bank—one of the largest private banks in Peking—his turn would come toward the end of the countdown. So he wasn't exactly expecting to go home that night. He only realized such a thing might happen when half a dozen of the last detainees were summoned for a talk. They were informed that the screening had been completed and they could go home. There they should wait for instructions on how to do a "summing-up" of their period of detention.

A jeep was at the gate, ready to take them to the various city districts where each lived; those in the East City were dropped off at the white marble bridge in front of North Sea Park.

The rain had stopped by then, but left large puddles on the pavement. It was after midnight and there were no buses at that hour. Peking didn't have taxis or pay phones at the time. Papa and two other men trudged doggedly down the long, empty streets. A pedicab showed up and the driver asked if they wanted a ride. The price he asked was high—about ten times the normal daytime fare.

Papa told us he had to let the two others, who were older men, decide first whether they wanted to take the pedicab. Both refused on account of the exorbitant fare. But as Papa said: "Seven months! How could I delay my homecoming because of a mere pedicab fare!"

The next morning, at school, I mentioned to my best friend Lily Wan that I had almost been late for class because Papa had come home last night. Lily's father was a physician, one of the old P.U.M.C. gang and a close family friend. Lily went home for lunch and returned with the message that her father wanted Papa to see him as soon as possible.

When Papa went to him, Uncle Wan gave him a thorough checkup and forbade him to take too much nourishment too hastily. In fact, that had been the reason for the urgent summons: Uncle Wan knew what detention was like, and he also knew the consequences of overeating on a weakened constitution. So Papa took a prolonged but well-attended road to recovery.

Papa didn't tell us children much of what he'd been through, but we guessed his screening had centered on such hot issues as the 8-mm home-movie showings, his Masonic membership in the United States (with an impressive ring as evidence), and his participation in a club for entrepreneurs in China in the late 1940s.

To us children, Papa related only small episodes from his life in detention. One had to do with an apricot stone: Undernourished, underfed, and never getting anything tasty to brighten the monotony of his scanty diet, Papa one day found an apricot stone at the foot of a high wall when he and his fellow detainees were let out for their exercise period. Delighted, he pocketed his trove and later cracked it open with a rock. Then he remembered that bitter almonds could be poisonous, so he took only a little nibble from the almond. It was sweet. That almond lasted Papa three days.

Papa, after seven months of detention was found guilty of only one fault: it was the Five-Antis Office ruling that Papa had ripped off the government when he sold our big house. He was ordered to return what he had allegedly overcharged. This was impossible at the time, since Papa had invested all the money in a couple of large enterprises and couldn't withdraw his shares; doing so would have exposed him to the accusation of "trying to disrupt the reconstruction of New China." Meanwhile, Papa had to make a show of being grateful to the government for clearing up his case.

A few months later Papa was summoned again, to be informed curtly that after a reexamination it had been decided that the house sale had been done in a legal manner. Also, Papa had "behaved in model fashion" after his release, since he hadn't complained to anyone about his detention, and his case was dismissed.

Our Dog Tiger, and the Day Stalin Died

We always had a dog, until the fateful day in 1952 when Tiger was taken away.

Tiger came to us in 1947, when she was already four years old—all hair, all nose, and friendly enough toward Toto and me. We vied to please her, and she tolerated our excessive petting with a supercilious air. Her former owners had gone abroad and my impression was that she treated us, her adopted family, with a trace of superiority.

Then one day we became family: A couple of months after her arrival, a family friend came visiting and teased Toto on the front steps. He made a gesture as if to spank Toto, and, whoosh, Tiger leaped up to fight off the "aggressor." Our guest was both surprised and amused by Tiger's protective feeling for her young master, while Toto and I smothered Tiger with hugs and kisses.

Tiger knew who was the boss, however, and I always found myself wondering: "How do we look from a dog's point of view?" She could differentiate between parents and children, even between Papa and Mama—and she was definitely not a feminist! One pat or word of praise from Papa would send her into ecstasies. She would drop her dignified ways and race upstairs and downstairs, twirl on the carpets, jump up and down the couches, and, to Mama's utter dismay and Tiger's extreme pleasure, bounce into the bedrooms and onto each bed and perform a 360-degree pirouette on the bedspreads. Then she would scamper off in roguish retreat to the garden.

The first time it happened we thought she had gone crazy. It was only after several recurrences that the real reason dawned on us. Toto and I were green with envy, and Papa accepted this distinction with obvious pleasure.

Tiger was nine years old when the blow fell in 1952. This was during the Korean War abroad and the Three-Antis and Five-Antis Movements at home. We learned that on account of the "American imperialists' bacteriological warfare," all city dogs (but not cats) were to be exterminated.

Dogs were popular household pets in those days and the owners demanded to know the reasons behind such draconian measures, for most dogs were tied up in courtyards or gardens and seldom appeared on the street. Cats, on the other hand, could roam about freely and spread germs unchecked; so why dogs and not cats? The explanation given was that germ warfare was not the only consideration; the other reason was to save food, because dogs ate too much—a lame excuse at best, since even the tiny Pekinese was included in the extermination order.

I put more credence in a rumor whispered among dog owners at the time: The true reason for this inhumane act was that dogs interfered with the activities of plainclothes agents. Dogs bark, and so were doomed; cats don't bark, and survived.

One of the bizarre consequences of this event is that urban Chinese under forty cannot relate to dogs normally. In fact, many are terrified at the sight of one. Most have never seen a dog, let alone raised one; there are no dogs at home and none at the zoo. Dogs are too commonplace to be a zoo attraction. One visits the zoo to see pandas, monkeys, lions, and hippopotamuses, even lizards, but who'd go to a zoo to see dogs! So Chinese city kids are deprived of the pleasure, among many others, of the DOG.

The blow struck in the early summer of 1952. It was rumored that hundreds of thousands of dogs had either been taken to the high city wall and thrown down, or clubbed to death—how could our Tiger stand such horror! My heart tightened every morning when I bid her good-bye before going to school. No one knew when our turn would come; and every day there were more girls crying in the classroom for the dogs they had lost.

Lily came to school one day with her eyes all swollen from crying, and I felt the breath of doom. When I went home and opened the gate I instinctively knew Tiger was gone—she would never come to greet me anymore. This was the first of the many real pains I was to know in the years to come, the terrible feeling of inevitability, of helplessness, of utter despair. I cried, I moaned, I wailed. I remember my grandmother asking: "Why cry so much over a dog? I haven't seen you cry for your father." I was shocked. "Don't you know Papa will come back?" I retorted. "He'll definitely come back, but Tiger will never come home again."

Lily and I remained faithful to the memory of our dog friends and shared many moments of grief long after our dogs were gone. Many months later, on the cold windy day of March 5, 1953, Joseph Stalin died. Halfway through class, we were instructed to listen to the radio; we were expected to cry over the great man's death. Unfortunately, I found tears hard to summon, and during the class break I went over to Lily's desk. Pulling a long face, she whispered: "I can't cry." I had a sudden stroke of inspiration. "Let's think of our dogs!" I said. Nothing could have worked better; Lily burst into *real* tears, and I joined in with gusto.

After the break, our teacher told the class: "Some students have shown political awareness by their profound grief over Comrade Stalin's death, such as . . . All of you should take example from them." Lily and I were included in that list of names.

I didn't dare look at Lily when we were named. We never mentioned that incident afterward, but I suspect both of us had guilt twinges, for after that hearty outburst we never cried for our dogs again.

The Good Girl at School and the Tomboy at Home

I started to wear glasses when I was twelve and, outwardly, looked every inch a demure, docile Chinese schoolgirl, complete with pigtails. Although I behaved in accordance with this facade at school, at home I was my natural self—an out-and-out tomboy.

That I should be a tomboy was only to be expected, what with a younger brother close on my heels age-wise, as well as with me day in and day out, and numerous cousins, most of them male. And when I finally acquired my own set of girlfriends at school, most of them had more brothers than I did . . . . What else could I be!

Toto and I started to ride bikes at an early age. I learned to do so when I was five, wobbling up and down the *hutung* near Di'anmen, the Gate of Earthly Peace. Toto learned a couple of years later, and we both upgraded ourselves to adult-size bikes as soon as we could reach the pedals, though we had to wriggle from side to side on the saddle to do so.

We wanted the larger bikes because we aspired to become acrobats. We learned to "freeze" on our bikes—make them stand still for long periods of time; we could lie across the saddle with one hand guiding the handlebars and the other turning the pedals. But apart from our domestic help and the ubiquitous Tiger, no one watched our performances.

When I began to ride my bike to school, I considered myself the best rider in the East City's *hutungs* and streets. Imagine my chagrin when I happened to look back and saw our new cook tagging behind me! I made a U-turn in the narrow alley and asked him why he wasn't serving breakfast at home. Caught redhanded, he admitted that Papa had asked him to tail me for three days, not because he doubted my riding skills, but to make sure I had traffic sense. Putting on all the Miss-like haughtiness I could muster, I sent the cook home.

In spite of my staid and decorous behavior at school, the word spread through the interfamily grapevine that this girl was constantly in the trees and on the top of the walls, instead of on the ground or in a room, where good girls belong.

In our one-pavilion, one-creek, two-part house with its one dozen jujube-date trees, Toto and I further developed our arboreal habits. Jujube dates are almost an obsession with Peking residents; people love to have a date tree in their courtyard or garden, and a house with a dozen date trees is anybody's dream.

Toto and I each had a favorite tree, not for its dates, but to use as a perch. Every day after school, we clambered up into our respective trees and read our respective books among the branches. For me, those were the days of Fielding and Richardson, and the pocket-sized *Everyman's Library* books were very handy to carry up to my perch.

About his agile offspring's behavior Papa once commented: "I'm a lucky man. I don't have to look all over the house for my children when I come home from work. I only need to stand in the gateway, look up at trees number one and two, and identify the forms among the branches, leaves, and dates."

When the date-picking season came around in September, we both contracted an "occupational disease"—neck pain. Date-picking in Peking consisted of rapping the branches smartly with a long bamboo pole and then gathering the fallen fruit from the ground. But that was too amateurish for us. Our equipment was improved by the addition of an iron hook at one end of the bamboo pole and a tiny net painstakingly sewn on under the hook by our maternal grandmother. With this, we hooked selected dates off one by one instead of beating around at random. We knew every branch, leaf, and date on our trees.

We started to hook dates right after school and continued until dark. So during the date season we were often seen at the dinner table holding our heads really high—so high that we looked at the ceiling instead of the table—and dropping into our mouths whatever our groping chopsticks managed to snare from the dishes. Our necks usually resumed their normal angle halfway through dinner, allowing us to face our tolerant parents.

As for the jujube dates, we didn't eat them; they were all given to other households as home-grown produce. The fun for us was entirely in the picking; who cared about the dates, anyway?!

When Papa and Mama decided to move to Tientsin in 1953, Toto and I again resisted, and were again overruled. Our last bargaining chip was the date harvest. The move was to be made in August, just before all those ripening dates would be ready to be picked or hooked! Those were *our* dates, and we wouldn't leave the house until we had completed our annual date harvesting! Our parents brushed aside this impassioned argument.

Fortunately for Toto and me (and unfortunately for the new owners), our house was sold to very close friends, the Lings. We didn't plead; we simply announced we'd be back from Tientsin over a weekend to pick our dates. Tientsin is only a two-hour train ride from Peking.

The following flashback was narrated to me in animated, staccato Shanghainese some twenty years later by the old amah in the Ling household, in front of my kids:

"I'll never forget the first time I set eyes on you. We'd just moved into your house, and one day the doorbell rang, sharply and repeatedly. `Coming, coming' I said. `Don't be in such a hurry!' I opened the front gate, and there stood two kids, each with a shoulder bag and a pole. `We're the Chen family children,' you announced. `We've come for our dates!' Before I could answer, you two had already slipped past me into the yard. I followed you into the yard but, *ah-ya-ya,* you had disappeared! Then I heard this *pi-li-pa-la* (pattering sound) in the trees. There you were, both up in the trees! I chuckled and chuckled, and went about my chores. When you finally came back to me with loaded shoulder bags, you said, `Please tell Uncle and Aunty Ling we've come, but we won't come again next year. We'll let ourselves out.' And like a whirlwind, you were gone!"

Lost and Found Among the Bookshelves, II

When we returned to China in late 1949, we shipped back some books. We didn't worry about future book supplies, for no one anticipated the thirty years' cessation of normal communication with the rest of the world. Besides, Mama had a sizable library in our big house anyway—but she was soon to learn about her daughter's voraciousness.

I always tell people I was never taught English, which is true in a certain sense; because I acquired my English from books—as I did Chinese. Remember, what with hopping back and forth between school grades and sailing across oceans, I didn't get a proper grade school education. (As a Chinese, I couldn't use the abacus—a sure sign of inadequacy.)

The only time I recall actually studying English was in the early 1950s, when Mama got two renowned professors of English, a woman and a man, briefly, to teach her Precious Baby. While the one's preference for *The Knights of the Round Table* left me with a decided crush on Sir Lancelot, the other's inclination for *Heart of Darkness* enshrined it everlastingly at the top of my list of masterpieces.

By 1951, I had rounded up all the better-known Chinese classical novels and persuaded Toto to help me convince our parents we needed to buy the non-classics. We managed to obtain from the used-book stores in the Tungan Bazaar such interesting volumes as *The Seven Chivalries and the Five Faithfuls*—the Chinese "Robin Hood" tales—and its numerous sequels. Our parents disapproved of our lowbrow reading, but we had outgrown the proper children's books, and they were too few and too tame, anyhow.

As we grew up, Toto branched out toward the Chinese classics *Tales of the Three Kingdoms* and *Tales of the Rebels*, eventually finding his way to Jack London—with such devotion that he now resides in the vicinity of Jack London's burned-down Wolf House in California! I thrived on romance: On my English side with *Pride and Prejudice*, and on my Chinese side with *Dream of the Red Chamber*.

I encored *Dream of the Red Chamber* ten or twelve times, each time lavishing loud sobs on the heroine's untimely death. However, a moment of personal triumph was to come of these constant rereadings:

In the early 1960s, when I was a budding editor for a music journal, someone in the editorial staff asked about a word that means "warming somebody's hands with one's own hands." I said confidently, "Go look in chapter so-and-so in *Dream of the Red Chamber* in the bookcase." The others were skeptical, for they hadn't found the word in authoritative dictionaries.

I stood up, plucked the volume from the bookcase, and flipped it open. To my own stupefaction, the word jumped into my eyes. But I handed the open book to the others with studied nonchalance, and said: "That's your word." That was my crowning victory! I could have remembered the chapter, I could have remembered the word, but for all my genius I couldn't have known the page number in an entirely different edition. Pinpointing that single character in a book approximately the size of Galsworthy's *Forsyte Saga* was nothing less than black magic.

My readings of Shakespeare, Dickens, Scott, Fielding, Irving, Mark Twain, Austen, Richardson, Thackeray, the Brontes, and many other were amply supplied from Mama's collection, especially in 1952, during the seven months Papa was held in detention, when we had no income and I had to be content with our own bookshelves. Lacking new novels to read, I even went through the literary histories of East and West in both languages as well as selections of essays by renowned scholars and writers, among them Hu Shih and Lu Hsün.

After Papa's release, my three-yuan-a-month allowance was reinstated, and so after my temporary financial recession, I was out again in full force. At the time I already had a good-sized stamp collection—an expensive hobby as well. An inveterate collector, I continued to collect stamps on the one hand and authors on the other. By the time I started my search, English books were already hard to find in China. There were only a limited number of books in English, and these were circulated and recirculated; to me, those used books were priceless treasures.

By chance rather than by choice, my collecting-by-author started with Louisa May Alcott. Miraculously, *Little Women, Little Men, An Old-Fashioned Girl, Eight Cousins, Rose in Bloom, Under the Lilacs*—you name it—all turned up on the bookshelves of those dear old used-books stores in my favorite Tung-an Bazaar. Digging out a good edition of Alcott required patience and perseverance.

My cherished illusion that I was now acquiring books like an independent and sophisticated adult suffered a setback one day. The middle-aged sales clerk at the counter would sometimes ask the customer's last name and put it down on the receipt. But without a word, he handed me my receipt with "Chen" already written on it. I was dumbfounded: "How did you know my name is Chen?" He smiled benevolently and said: "You've been coming to this store since you were still in your parents' arms, and you started peeping at my bottom shelves before you were tall enough to reach the counter. I watched you grow up. You come here more often than your parents now."

After we moved to Tientsin, I had a large dose of translated Russian and Soviet novels. Deprived of my Peking used-book stores, I was compelled to rely on official publications for my supply of "bedtime stories." After I got over the difficulty of remembering all the forms by which Russians address themselves in public and in private, I became quite attracted to their literature as well.

I came down with rheumatic fever in my last year at senior middle school, and I was naturally quite depressed. But the illness didn't prevent me from reading, and I did a lot more of it.

At the time, Mama had volunteered to select books for the YWCA Library in Tientsin, so the Hsin Hua Bookstore, the one and only state-owned bookstore, would deliver all new social studies publications every Thurday to our house. Mama would scan through them and decide which ones to purchase for the YWCA.

These books ranged from political science and social science to literature. I am a fast reader in both languages. (Papa timed me one day with a stop watch—I went through a page of Thackeray—an *Everyman's Library* edition—in 52 seconds.) And I could usually finish an average Chinese book in one evening. So I actually read all the books the Hsin Hua Bookstore delivered to our house, and made my recommendation or damnation to Mama, who would then reexamine them briefly and do the ordering. That was when I started to consume social and political science books as I did novels.

My discovery of erotica in both languages came about accidentally, and I never confessed this to Mama, and they never entered my personal book-review notebooks. I found one volume from a four-volume edition of *The Golden Lotus*, or *Chin P'ing Mei* under a pile of old newspapers when I was twelve. What stimulated my interest was not the book itself, for this was before I had read the essays of Hu Shih and Lu Hsün who both reviewed this classic of erotica, so I was completely ignorant of that title. What triggered my curiosity was the site of discovery. Since my parents had so obviously hidden this book, I knew it was not for my consumption. But forbidden fruit tastes best.

I maneuvered the book to my room; frankly, I didn't find it any fun. I only remembered that some disgusting guy in the book tickled a girl from behind with a twig when she was peeing in a corner of a garden, and she was shocked. I put it back again, not knowing what a chance I was missing. For when high-ranking Communist cadres realized that this was the number one erotic classic of Chinese literature, they lost no time including the reading of this novel among their exclusive privileges; one had to be above a certain rank to be able to see it. I had my chance to read it again in the early 1960s when it was lent secretly to me by a friend in a library. It was then that I understood the furor and fury over that classic.

My discovery of D. H. Lawrence came about in the same way. Our bookshelves were rearranged when we moved to Tientsin, when I was fourteen; I found a copy of *Lady Chatterley's Lover* tucked behind Dickens. I read through the book quite a few times, but I didn't really understand what it was about. For instance, I was impressed by Lady Chatterley's fondling of the little chicks, but I didn't realize what that had to do with what happened afterward.

Lady Chatterley's Lover remained a whispered title in the People's Republic, even among English-reading people, and it was not until the 1980s that it was officially translated and published.

By the time the Cultural Revolution began, I had virtually exhausted the holdings of the two or three good-sized libraries near at hand, and made a clean sweep of what would soon be called "poisonous weeds": Western civilization was to be proclaimed decadent bourgeois humanism, and everything Soviet had already been labeled revisionist. That was the time I started to read works by Engels as my bedtime stories.

A Homestead in Tientsin

Papa resigned from the bank soon after he came back from his 1952 imprisonment and in 1953 joined a well-known private corporation that had factories in Peking, Shanghai, and Tientsin. My parents contemplated moving to Tientsin for good. The political atmosphere in Peking was becoming too sensitive, and since they had no political ambitions, they preferred to stay away from that nervous, uneasy city.

Tientsin, on the other hand, was relaxed and comfortable to live in. Besides, it was only a two-hour train ride or about seventy miles from Peking. We could always come back and visit. My parents purchased an English-style house in the former British concession with three bedrooms, two bathrooms, spacious living, dining, and kitchen areas as well as servant's quarters, a garage, and a very large garden.

It seems I always raised objections when our family was about to take a decisive move. Instead of offering foolish pretexts this time, however, I argued seriously and pleaded to stay in Peking, for I was doing well in my school; I had very good grades, close friends, and a growing sense of independence. I could board at school, I said. I was fourteen.

My parents made me visit Tientsin during the summer vacation before our move to give me time to adjust to the environment. A respectable but staid girls' middle school there agreed to put me in the same grade I was in at my Peking school: the second year in senior middle school in the Chinese education system, equivalent to the eleventh grade in America. As a matter of tradition, most of the better-known middle schools in China in the 1950s were still segregated by gender.

Very reluctantly, I moved to Tientsin with the family, vowing to return to Peking when I entered university in two years' time. I disliked my new school instinctively, for it was more strait-laced than the relatively liberal Bridgeman, which retained many of its old features after it became state-run in 1951. Even its students spoke, laughed, and walked in a distinctive way.

I was more of an observer and visitor than a participant or resident in Tientsin in the several years to come. I set up a strict regimen for myself: I practiced on the piano three hours a day, I read so much I had to exchange my glasses for a new pair, and I became a fervent philatelist.

To this day I can't figure out how those days were long enough for all that I had to do: I practiced on the piano for three hours after doing an average of two hours of homework, then sat down to do some reading and ended up working on my stamps until 10:30 P.M. And on my only day off, Sundays, I had to travel nearly two hours round-trip by ferry to the Central Music Conservatory across a river for my hour-long private piano lessons.

I regret to say I resented my middle school so much I stayed there as briefly as I could. It took me exactly eight minutes to ride to school on my bike at breakneck speed. I'd leave home at 7:40 A.M.., ride through the school gates at 7:48, then put up my bike and step into the classroom at 7:50, just as the preparatory bell rang for the eight o'clock class. My classmates joked that I was more punctual than the bell. I even went home for lunch, timing my dash there and back by the minute. Tomboyishness apart, I suppose I developed a very stubborn streak in those not-very-happy years in Tientsin.

Moreover, I developed a malicious pleasure in harassing our English teacher. English classes had been resumed after a few Russian-only years. I remember one of the reasons given for this resurrection was that some Chinese still had to learn English to interpret for all the American POWs in Korea and persuade them to give up their capitalist beliefs!

I got in my English teacher's hair when she tried to fault my accent. For while she *dahn*ced, I danced; and when she shopped for to*mah*toes, I preferred tomatoes. She tried to convert me, but I stood firm. Then one day I thought, what the heck. I read: "We stahted to dahnce ahfteh hahlf pahst eight . . . " in an exaggerated imitation of Oxfordian English. The class roared with laughter and she never again took exception to my California accent.

School aside, however, there were many other attractions in Tientsin that made our life quite different from the one we had led in Peking. For instance, our ties with the YWCA became closer.

We were not a religious family, but we shared with many Christians their principles, hopes, and concerns and Mama began to participate actively in the YWCA Peiping chapter in the late 1940s. We celebrated Easter and Christmas, and Toto and I were nurtured on the traditions and legends that go with them.

We also went to YWCA for their ice cream, which our parents considered safe to eat.

Back in the 1940s, Toto and I were not allowed to eat or to drink anything iced or cold anywhere else, outside of our home. The water that went into these things was often contaminated, and there was a real danger of contracting diarrhea, or even cholera.

Older people feared these diseases, partly as an aftermath of the cholera epidemics during the Japanese occupation. The Japanese authorities would cordon off whole areas and drag away anyone they suspected of having that disease, including many people who only had diarrhea. Without even attempting to verify their suspicions they would then bury these people alive in lime pits. After Chinese burial details brought back these horror stories, people would turn pale at the mere mention of *hu-lie-la* (cholera).

For this and other reasons, most Chinese have been brought up on the belief that cold beverages are unhealthy, and cold water—termed "raw water" in Chinese—in particular was, and still is, difficult for Chinese to accept. Not in my case. I had drunk tap water all my life; and that habit later proved to be a lifesaver for my baby and myself when the only source of sustenance for us was a faucet.

We also learned our first Christmas carols at the YWCA and had expanded our repertory in Berkeley. On Christmas Eve of 1949 when we had just come back to China, we sang carols all over the North Compound of the P.U.M.C. It was the first year of the founding of the People's Republic, everything looked rosy, and the YWCA had organized a children's carol-singing group. We trooped along the snow-covered paths and sang, Toto and I in English, the other children in Chinese, and I remember I was given two very big apples, red and shiny. It was the last time we celebrated Christmas that way.

As I recall, weekend parties and children's performances at the YWCA were quite frequent in its Tientsin chapter. Papa and Mama attended a costume ball one year in the mid-1950s, Papa wearing a crimson-colored fez and carrying a baton in imitation of the President of Indonesia, and Mama decked out in a gorgeously embroidered white robe dating from the Ching Dynasty.

At home, parties were frequent, and Mama invited her new acquaintances in Tientsin to tea parties. Pastries, canapés, pâté, sausages, tea, and coffee made for very Western-style tea parties on the warmer days of the year, while spicier Chinese delicacies were served on the cold winter days.

Those were the good years: the country prospered, a cease-fire was in force in Korea, and after the Five Antis campaign, there was a temporary recess in the political movements at home. Everyone was in an easier state of mind and feeling better disposed toward the new government. After all, it was trying to give the ordinary Chinese people a better life.

Food was on the whole cheap and abundant during the mid-1950s, especially seafood. Those were the days before overfishing, ocean pollution, and massive exports for dollar earnings, and piles of prawns could be seen in every marketplace. Called "twin prawns" because they were usually sold in pairs, they averaged a good six inches in length. Their price was sometimes as low as five *fen* each in Tientsin, and five *fen* in those days were equivalent to a quarter in today's U. S. currency. Any family with a wage-earner could afford prawns, which are considered quite a delicacy by the Chinese.

I remember our dilemma at home was that we did not have enough cooking oil to prepare the prawns with. Cooking oil, food grain, as well as cotton yardage had been rationed since 1953 or earlier, and although every family had a stock of oil, people used it sparingly. But cooking oil was essential for tasty prawns. So while Toto and I drooled at the prospect of fried prawns, Mama and the new cook who followed us to Tientsin fretted about the oil.

Surprisingly, I had my full share of fried prawns at no other place than my college, the Central Music Conservatory. I'd heard stories of girls from several Tientsin families not being able to stomach the miserable food served at their university canteens; imagine my surprise when we were served several times a week with fried prawns and Chinese-style beef Stroganoff! The stories I brought home with regard to college cuisine were quite different from those we had heard before.

I Mis-schedule One Exam

After less than two years in Tientsin, I was waiting for my 1955 high school graduation and all set to have a go at the college entrance exam. I was hoping at the time to get into a Peking university or college.

Then on my sixteenth birthday in February of 1955, something big got me and changed my life schedule. But I was downed, first, by German measles and had to absent myself from school for a week.

When I went back to class, I overheard a classmate telling another one in awe: "Even her measles are German!" The Chinese name for that disorder doesn't have the word "German" in it, but since our family-friend doctors had learned their profession in English at P.U.M.C., they usually diagnosed our illnesses in English. Not knowing the name in Chinese, I simply translated it literally, with the result that my classmates thought this girl back from America had contracted a German version of the disease! (I was referred to as the girl—or, later, woman—back from America during all my forty years after I returned to China, because of that twelve-month stay in the United States.)

A low fever persisted, however, after the German measles went away. I was taken to various doctors to determine the cause; it was rheumatic fever. As I only had four months to go to finish middle school, I didn't want to quit. But Uncle Wan was uncompromising. "How can you let her go to school when she's running a low fever all the time?" he said to my parents when they went to him in Peking. "Keep her at home!"

There went my "schedule"! Rheumatic fever brought me down twice and left me with a heart murmur.

After a seven-month convalescence, I recuperated from that bout of rheumatic fever and assorted pains and agues. I had been treated by numerous physicians, in both the Eastern and Western traditions, with pills, injections, and herbs. But I knew in my heart who had rid me of the fever—I, myself.

Once, because I over-ate ice popsicles or fried tofu, I ran a high 40° C (104° F) fever over and above the persistent 37.5° C low fever I'd been suffering from for seven months. During the efforts to bring down the higher fever, the rheumatic fever was forgotten; but when the 40° C fever eventually subsided, the 37.5° C fever went with it. I named this remedy "beating evil with evil."

Rheumatic fever is very boring, for one doesn't really look or feel sick; one is simply unwell. It's still possible to do a lot of things, but important things have to be sacrificed or put off, such as my college matriculation. I used up that year reading, reading and reading, both day and night. And since I always nibble while I read, I don't know how many bushels of melon seeds, peanuts and chestnuts went down with the literary fare I was ingesting.

I went back to school where I left off a year earlier, to hurl myself into the college entrance exams, a hurdle indeed for any Chinese student. My best friends in Peking had all been accepted into colleges the previous year, and were now waiting for me to return to Peking, too.

The complicated process of college entrance in China—from estimation and analysis of chances through application and exam taking to eventual acceptance—has always been a centralized process; even the current economic and administrative decentralization have failed to remove this ritual. I am ignorant of the inventors of its intricacies, but its lineage can unquestionably be traced back to the civil service examinations held by the National Academy in China's Imperial times.

When I applied and took exams in 1956, the social atmosphere was relatively calm and relaxed, and all students seemingly had equal opportunities to college entrance based on the exam scores he or she achieved. In addition to the unified national exams I had applied for, I also took separate exams for a music college, which required additional aptitude tests. So I would have two options if I passed both sets of exams.

I have to admit that I wasn't as diligent as some of my classmates were. Some girls did their homework until well after midnight, and suffered as a result from headaches and insomnia in their teens. Not me. I got rid of my homework as soon as I could, for I had so much piano-playing, book-reading, date-picking, stamp-collecting, and doll-housing to do. But I was always among the first six in a forty-student class. I had a retentive memory, and a quick scan of the textbooks when I smelled an exam brewing was enough to pull me through.

I applied the same system when preparing for the grand college entrance exams. I'd say I was fairly relaxed, for I already knew I'd passed the music conservatory exams, and I could take up music if I made up my mind to do so. However, I was aiming for the English Department at Peking University, where all the faculties of Tsinghua, Yenching, and Peking universities in this specialization had been brought together during the restructuring of these universities in the early 1950s. That would be almost as good as majoring in English at Tsinghua in the 1930s, as Mama had done. It was not to be, by a sheer stroke of fate.

I'll never know what gremlin or goblin possessed me when I copied the schedule for this chance-of-a-lifetime exam. Whatever it was, I put down "history" in the slot for "geography," and vice versa. I'm usually quite accurate in the things I do, so I never questioned my schedule. And, not having bosom friends in Tientsin, I was out of touch with my classmates after we started to prepare for the exams.

I felt no pressure at all, since my choice put me in the category of "social" rather than "science" studies, and I only needed to take exams for Chinese, politics, mathematics, history, and geography. I also needed to take one for English, but the result would only serve as reference and wouldn't affect the final score. And anyway these were all my strong courses.

But when I walked into the school to take the history exam and saw the other girls flipping through their geography textbooks for a last glance, my heart sank into my shoes. On my schedule geography was for the next day; I had boned up on history the night before, and all my geography books were lined up for this coming evening. With a sick feeling, I borrowed a book for a last-minute cram. It didn't help.

My performance was pathetic, to say the least. I remember I even counted on my stamp collection to answer one of the questions, which happened to be about Bulgaria. A Bulgarian stamp with a bunch of fruit printed on it and another one with roses came to my mind in response to my desperate search signals. They enabled me to write a few lines, but couldn't save me from disaster.

I was beaten. I imagined my score would be so abysmal I'd get a slip informing me that I'd failed to make the requisite score for any college admission. That would mean a terrible loss of face!

However, I neglected to take into account the strength of my other subjects; my other four exams turned in exceptionally good marks. They saved my bacon, so to speak. Nevertheless, my average score was still half a point on the 100-point scale below the standard needed to get into Peking University, so I was assigned to a college in Peking for Russian studies—in fact, one of the choices on my application form. I couldn't complain. After all, that college was in Peking.

I went to that college with my roll of bedding and a trunk, and after two weeks, I was having second thoughts. The music conservatory's acceptance could still be reconsidered. Besides, I faced a distinct disadvantage in regard to Russian studies: I simply couldn't "Rrrrr . . . " Well, I thought, even if I can't roll that "R", I can still roll up my bedding, then unroll it again when I enroll at the music conservatory in Tientsin. I was also encouraged by the prospect of this music college moving to Peking in about a year's time. So, good-bye to languages, and off to music at the conservatory, where I met my future husband. Whenever I look at my two children—the best albeit rather remote products of this mis-scheduling—I do not regret my decision.

Knowing that a person's destiny can be changed by a mere quirk of fate, I often made fun of myself when I told others how I ended up being a musicologist. All my listeners sympathized, for they remembered the life-or-death feeling of those exams. But not my son Deedee.

"You're talking about the difference made by a single day," he remarked. "What were you doing all the rest of those weeks you had for preparation?" I laughed and laughed, for he was the first one to mention the true reason for my erstwhile dilemma.

My Favorite Cousin Becomes a Rightist

The close communications of our family with our favorite Cousin Ta diminished after Mama's accidental encounter with him at the Five-Antis Office during Papa's imprisonment, but didn't break off. No one mentioned the encounter, however, and I believe it never went beyond the four members of our family, and him. Our move to Tientsin provided him with a good excuse not to visit us anymore, but I knew how profoundly my parents still cared for him.

In 1956, Mao Tse-tung initiated a brief period of outward liberalization, and put forward the call "Let a Hundred Flowers Bloom and a Hundred Thoughts Contend." It was met with enthusiastic albeit guarded response. Like wildflowers pushing through cracks between heavy flagstones, voices were raised, tentatively at first. But when the "Bloom and Contend" activities assumed the proportions of a full-blown campaign, everyone, or almost everyone, believed the Communist Party sincerely wanted to listen to different opinions, to candid criticism! That year, almost a third of a million people shared this erroneous perception.

Later, I tried to figure out why this time Papa wasn't roped in. Then I remembered he was visiting the Shanghai area and had taken a boat trip down the Fu-chun River with two of his old bosses from the bank. His back pains returned after he came back from the excursion, and by the time he had recovered and was itching to attend the meetings to give them a piece of his mind, the wind had turned. He stayed silent.

Cousin Ta (and a few others among our relatives) bore the full brunt of the counterblow. A Party member and an engineer, he complained about an unjustified investigation of his associations by the Party in the late 1940s, when he was a high school student. He accused his superiors of being jealous of his competitiveness, and of using the investigation as a means to push him down . . . .

Similiar grievances resonated throughout China: Professionals asked nonprofessional Party members to leave them alone or to step down from their positions of administrative leadership; many others strongly criticized the arrogance, ignorance, inefficiency, and bureaucratic ways of Communist Party members. When Mao Tse-tung had heard enough, he drew in the strings of his new "net," and launched his counterattack against the voices of dissent.

Mao cannily used the name of the masses to reinforce the counterattack when he entitled his *People's Daily* article "The Workers, Peasants and Soldiers Speak Up!" A feeble duplication of this act of imposture would take place in 1989, when the powers-that-be hired people at ten yuan a day plus a free straw hat to counterdemonstrate against the Tiananmen protestors in the name of the workers, peasants, and soldiers.

The counterattack of 1957 was conducted, at first, within the format of the "Bloom and Contend" movement; that is, by means of verbal polemics and "big character posters"—a diabolic Chinese invention used to promote political campaigns, but which in practice often harmed the author as much as it did the target.

By then, I was already in college—at the Central Music Conservatory, to be exact—but I was too unpolitical and unsophisticated in those days to voice any specific ideas of my own, so all I did was join the crowd and sign my name under big character posters with the largest number of signatures. I also signed a request that the college move to Peking as soon as possible—a genuine wish of mine. After the counterattack started, I did a self-criticism for "helping the cause of people with ulterior motives" and reproaching myself for being so naive, and was let off the hook.

At the time of the counterattack, few people foresaw what it would cost those under attack—that they'd be banished, interned, branded, that the lives of hundreds of thousands, and their families, would be afflicted for decades to come. "Criticism and self-criticism" was a common enough thing for us, and we only sensed that it might be somewhat more rigorous this time. At that last costume ball at the Conservatory before the counterattack, I danced with a criticized schoolmate; neither of us knew that his life would never be the same again.

Mao named those who criticized the Chinese Communist Party "Rightists," and requested that they be categorized as such. The most notable, or notorious (depending on which way you looked at it), were stripped of everything—job, position, titles, even residency rights—and sent, many of them, to the labor camps in the Great Northern Wasteland in far-off northeast China. Among them was a second cousin of mine, Wei. He told me, twenty years later, that he and his wife were washing the feet of their one-year-old baby girl when officials came and took him away. His wife was pressured to divorce him, to "draw a line" between them. She didn't.

Those of lesser notoriety than the first kind were also expelled from their work units—*dan wei*, but labored in reform camps closer to their places of origin. They were treated slightly better than ordinary criminals and were assigned to another work place after a few years.

A third category of "Rightists" were simply "sent down to the countryside." They were free to move about in the vicinity and worked in the fields.

However, since they were dispersed to out-of-the-way places and their destinies left to the discretion of local (county, township, or village) authorities, many never returned to their original positions.

The lightest offenders were labeled—literally "capped" in Chinese—Rightists and stayed where they were, shorn of their titles and powers (if any), often degraded in rank and salary rating, and banned from publishing articles in their own names.

All Rightists, if they were Communist Party members, were expelled from the party.

Cousin Ta belonged to the second category. He left the beautiful girl he had married under our date trees and their baby son. He was sent to a labor camp situated somewhere between Peking and Tientsin, and was expelled from the Communist Party. His wife was urged to divorce him. She didn't, at the time.

He dropped out of sight but not out of mind, for we learned of his whereabouts from his parents in Shanghai. And we heard four or five years later, in the early 1960s, that he had been "de-capped" (the absurdity of those concepts and terms!) and was a semi-free man. He stayed to work another two years as member of the labor camp's staff until the mid-sixties, when he found a *dan wei* willing to accept him as an architectural engineer.

Mama told me that one day in the early 1960s the doorbell rang at the gate of our Tientsin home; she went out to answer it. She opened the gate, and there was Cousin Ta. He asked: "Second Aunt, will you allow me to come into this home?"

Gazing at him, Mama thought of the first time he entered our home, the months he took charge of our house, his wedding in our garden, her encounter with him in that Five-Antis Office, the sufferings he had gone through. Mama said: "This house is open to you, as always." And he was in our home again.

A few months after that, at my own married home in Peking, someone clattered up the stairs and knocked at the door. I opened it and stood face to face with my favorite, favorite Cousin Ta. I had already learned of his return to our Tientsin home, so it was a happy reunion rather than a dramatic surprise.

If anyone was surprised, it was he, for as he was inquiring how to find my apartment among the look-alike buildings of the residential sector I lived in, he came upon two cute little toddlers who piped up together: "Aunty Chen is right up here!" He was astonished to hear the bratty young cousin of his memories called "Aunty." He kept shaking his head in disbelief that I was now a full-fledged adult and a married woman.

That New Year and the one following it, while he still worked at the reform camp, he sent me greeting cards. Both were handmade with clippings from cigarette packs pasted on cardboard. I cried when I saw them. In them I sensed all the pathos, all the nostalgia, of a man who had lost everything and was trying to recapture memories of better times.

He later found a job in another province with help from other cousins. His wife divorced him after he was resettled, and then married an older man who was, in fact, one of their former bosses. It would be another fifteen years before they met again.

In 1980, a film called *Legend of the Tianyun Mountain* was released. Many younger people were profoundly moved by the fate of the protagonist—a Rightist with experiences almost like my cousin's, complete with a charming wife who later married the boss. I asked my cousin what he thought of the film, and he wrote back: "To those who were lucky enough not to experience such things, the film may seem overdone; the less fortunate who went through it all probably feel that the facts are understated. But I'm happy that someone has at last realized what we suffered as human beings."

Yes, these were human beings, but when the hunt was on for Rightists they were no more than figures for meeting quotas. Every unit was given a percentage to accomplish, and had to produce the required number of Rightists or be charged with failure to complete a task. Not knowing the fate lying in store for the victims, some *dan wei* even asked people to draw lots to make up the tally!

I couldn't decide whether to curse or laugh when I heard a story from some Rightists still interned at the labor-camp site that served as our "cadre school" in the early 1970s.

These were Rightists from the army: teachers, trainers, clerks, writers. When they first came, an officer who had escorted the group to the place was mistaken by the labor camp as one of the Rightists. Despite all his statements, pleas, and protests, his case was only cleared up after thirteen years had passed.

The Gentleman Driver

Papa was a zealous driver ever since the early 1930s—quite a singular attribute for a Chinese "gentleman." To be seen as a person of rank or dignity in China, rather than drive oneself one should be chauffeured, unless of course one doesn't mind being accused of having newfangled notions. To this day most major and minor VIPs (down to township heads) in China are chauffeured.

However, Papa drove. When I visited my cousin at Penn State a few years ago, we had a hearty laugh as she told me the following story:

Papa was their daring and dashing young uncle in his bachelor days; his nieces and nephews adored him. She remembered the day Papa got his first car in Peiping in the early 1930s.

My cousin's dignified parents—one of Papa's older sisters and her husband, a Vassar-ian and a Cornell-ian from the 1910s—were not at home that day. Suddenly she and her two siblings saw this young uncle drive through the gates and into the yard in a red car. In China, owning a car, even an used one, in those days was a big deal—not to mention actually driving one. Papa asked: "Care to go for a ride?" Wow! All three kids piled in, and their uncle drove the clattering and clanking vehicle through the ancient streets of Peiping.

It was truly a used car, for the horn didn't work. And in those days, driving without a horn was inconceivable. In our Chinese way, one honked when passing people, one honked when making a turn, one honked simply to attract attention. "Now what are we going to do?" Papa inquired.

"We'll be the horn!" replied his passengers. So Papa drove on and they *honk-honked* as loud as they could. After almost sixty years, my cousin's eyes still gleam with mischievous delight when she recalls the effect of these "horns" on astonished pedestrians.

Papa managed to keep that car even during the years of Japanese occupation, though it was seldom used. We acquired a new Dodge in Peiping in post–World War II years, and Papa would drive our family of four to Tsinghua University, or to the Summer Palace Park outside Peiping. During weekdays, however, he was driven to work by our driver, as etiquette required. I can imagine what a nerve-wracking time our driver must have had with a backseat driver like Papa in the backseat.

Papa tried to persuade Mama to drive and offered himself as instructor. Mama flatly refused—not the driving, but the instructor: "You'd scare me to death with your orders and scoldings! I'll learn only if our driver teaches me."

So, one day, we children were taken to the vast empty field in the East City to watch Mama drive. That field, situated east of the former Legation Quarters had once been used by the foreign community to play polo. When we got there, Papa told us to get out. We protested: "We want to be driven by Mama!"

"No way," replied Papa. "Do you want to risk your lives?!"

So the three of us stood on the sidelines and heartlessly watched Mama "risk her life" with our driver in the passenger seat. Mama drove past us several times, very fast. But that was that. Just as Papa never got beyond the third letter in the Russian alphabet in the 1950s, Mama never got to use the reverse clutch. Having proved she could make a car run, she simply quit. So we were driven by Papa when we were in California, traveling up and down good old Highway 101.

After we returned to China in 1949, we still kept a car, and we still had a garage at the houses we lived in. But the outings became few and far between, for in addition to the changing social environment Toto and I were both going through the reorientations of adolescence, and we hated to be seen tailing our parents.

Papa had the car all to himself when we moved to Tientsin. The distances we traveled in Tientsin were much shorter than those in Peking. For instance, it was only a fifteen-minute bike ride to Nankai University from our home, and we had few places farther than that to visit. Riding a bike, it took Papa twelve minutes to get to the factory where he worked as deputy president, and Toto and me five and eight minutes to get to our respective schools. Mama hired rides on pedicabs. The car became a decoration in our closed-up garage, or maybe the justification for having a garage at all.

Toto rebelled during one of Papa's last attempts to put his car into active service. We went out to dinner one evening to the former Tientsin Racecourse Club, which was far enough for the car to roll at moderate speed for a good six or seven minutes. Toto and I were coaxed into the backseat. On the way, Toto spotted some classmates. He flipped his cap over his face and slid down almost to the floor of the car.

"What am I going to say if my classmates see me in a car?!" he moaned.

"They'll kid the life out of me. No one rides in cars!" When we got to the club, he climbed out of the car only after I made sure that the coast was clear of his classmates.

I think it was after Mama insisted on walking to a friend's place several blocks away while Papa drove the car slowly behind her, that Papa decided to sell the car to a friend in Peking. That friend kept that car a couple more years, until the post–Great Leap Forward famine in the early 1960s, when there were shortages of everything, including gasoline.

After the years of famine, when the country recovered some degree of normalcy, Papa couldn't resist getting onto motorized wheels again. So when the Red Guards came to ransack the houses on our avenue in August, 1966, the head count in our garage came to two motorcycles, four bicycles (including one for Toto and one for me), and a flatbed pedicab for occasional deliveries. Papa was the only person at home at the time who knew how to operate all seven vehicles—just as he was the only one who could use all seven cameras in our cupboard.

When Papa came to Peking for the last time in his life in late 1967, we talked about that nightmarish ransack and wondered what those Red Guards had thought at the time. I said I doubted whether they had ever come upon anyone who owned seven vehicles and seven cameras. Papa protested: "Come on, you know very well that one of the motorcycles belonged to a friend and two of the bikes belonged to you and Toto."

None of the vehicles ever came to light again, and all the compensation we got for all those cameras was a paltry forty yuan.

"On Wings of Song"

What with reading *Dream of the Red Chamber* in Chinese, and the Shakespearean plays and sonnets, the novels of Jane Austen and Louisa May Alcott in English; what with shedding all those tears over the fate of those heroes and heroines, I had become decidedly romantic, but had little practice in real life.

The junior and senior middle schools I went to were still segregated by gender, so my encounters with the opposite sex remained much the same as in my childhood days: cousins, brothers of friends, or friends of my brother. There weren't any brushes or crushes of a romantic nature until I was well over seventeen.

The first one worthy of the name was still a big pup-ish affair, even if the pup was already in his twenties. I had known him almost all my life and I believe I had just started to walk or talk when we first met, so it wasn't love at first sight.

It started out with innocent hand-touching and accidental bumping into each other, and culminated with some demure kissing. It's a little odd, though, that neither of us exchanged any endearments or lovey-dovey phrases; perhaps neither of us had prepared any lines to quote under such circumstances. Eventually, we went to our respective colleges, and neither of us ventured to resume that romance at our next meeting—which took place among a sizable group of close friends.

I met my future husband at the Central Music Conservatory during my freshman year. Ballroom dances were very popular at universities in the 1950s; the presence of visiting professors from the U. S.S.R. and other East European countries guaranteed us several grand balls each year: on March 8, International Women's Day; May 1, Labor Day; October 1, National Day; November 7, October Revolution Day; and New Year's Eve, not to mention some smaller dance parties.

I met Fan at one of these balls.

I was standing just behind a couple of rows of seats, talking and giggling with some other girls, when a smiling young man came toward the empty seats and beckoned in my direction by crooking his forefinger. I was surprised at this unceremonious gesture and looked around asking who was that guy crooking his finger at? The girls replied, "It's you, silly girl!" One girl whispered his name and pushed me forward, but I hesitated, uncertain as to whether I should dance with a stranger.

The first steps of the waltz showed the difference of our upbringing, so to speak. I had learned my steps from my Bridgeman classmates, who in turn had learned them from their older brothers; I had danced with family friends who had all been brought up in Western culture, and we circled counterclockwise whether it was a waltz, a fox-trot, or whatever. Those who had learned via "revolutionary" channels, in the military or during the Yenan revolutionary base days, turned clockwise, Russian fashion. We got jammed up with the very first steps, and I realized we were at odds as to what was the right way to circle. I mumbled I'd follow him. I was barely civil when the dance ended, first because of the finger-crooking, then for the uncomfortable turns.

Fan came from a city in a nearby province. The middle child among five siblings, he left home to join the People's Liberation Army at the age of fourteen and still in eighth grade. Those very young ones who joined up were usually assigned to headquarters, or hospitals, not to combat roles; he served in a military song-and-dance ensemble, learned to play a few instruments, and even went to the Korean front with the so-called Chinese People's Volunteer Army. A large number of military personnel were demobilized in the mid-1950s after the Korean armistice, and along with junior functionaries joined in the competition for a college education. At that time, the government correctly estimated that in order to upgrade the establishment from a rag-tag band of revolutionaries to a force for national reconstruction, it must first improve the education of its functionaries, referred to in China as "cadres." Those who entered college could either keep getting their salary if they pledged to return to the same work place; or, as in Fan's case, receive an allowance sufficient to cover minimum expenses, then once they graduated, they would be reassigned a job at their previous salary level. Students getting their first jobs after college, like myself, would get much lower, entry-level pay.

Fan excelled in his exams and had his choice of the two coveted music conservatories, one in Shanghai and the Central Music Conservatory then located in Tientsin. He chose the latter.

He was a charmer, and had quite a long list of girlfriends from his army days, according to some of his old army buddies who landed in the same conservatory. After I met him at that dance, I noticed he'd gotten himself attached to three or more girls in almost every grade in the piano studies.

As one of the advantages of socialism, university or college tuition was free. Once a college student, health care was also free. In exchange, the graduate would be assigned a job according to the needs of the country, at a work place called a *"dan wei"* (a word I'll use throughout this book).

The conservatory provided the instruments for student use, and each student was also assigned a small practicing room. Almost everyone needed pianos, so we shared the piano rooms from 7:30 A.M. to 10:30 P.M., fitting practice hours between the classes we had to attend. All students were required to live at school, and since the Chinese work and study six days a week, I would dash home in time for Saturday dinner and return Sunday evenings in order not to be late for Monday morning classes. Not many students had homes in Tientsin, and I was glad that the temporary location of my college gave me a chance to wean myself from my family in a gradual way.

To be honest, I quite enjoyed life at the conservatory. The facilities, though spartan by Western standards, were adequate. The dormitories housed four to six students per room on double-decker wooden bunks. Girls on the same floor shared a couple of washrooms and toilets. There was hot water for showers three times a week; for daily hygiene we used warm water from thermos flasks.

The only thing the students paid for was the food, and meals were provided at the canteen on an all-you-can-eat basis in normal times. During most of my college years I paid 10.50 yuan per month for food—about a quarter of an average worker's monthly wage at the time, and in the good years the menu included fried prawns.

We had approximately four hundred students and two hundred faculty and staff while the college was in Tientsin. In a sense, it was an extended family since everyone knew one another, at least by sight, and romancing between young people was a favorite topic of conversation, naturally.

Fan was popular with a number of girls, so I was surprised when he asked me to serve as accompaniment for his vocal recital as requested by his department of conducting. The college appointed accompanists for students who majored in vocal studies, but for routine courses taken by non-vocal majors, students relied on friendly exchanges of services.

I wasn't a person to say no, so we checked our schedules and started practicing together. The first piece was Mendelssohn's "On Wings of Song," in Chinese. Fan was a pretty good tenor, and I was attracted by his voice the moment he started to sing. Our collaboration went off well in both private practicing and public recitals, and we became more friendly.

It was not until a few months later that Fan started to display a definite interest in me. Once a group of us went on an excursion to Peking, and I stayed with a classmate at her Peking home. Fan came to meet us one early morning, and while waiting for the other girl, he hugged me for the first time—right in front of the mantel over the fireplace of the living room of that house. I decided I must be in love.

Further hugs and kisses were exchanged over the next few months, and they were different from those I had experienced with Big Pup. There was tenderness, excitement, caring . . . and tension—it was the last, confusing feeling I couldn't quite figure out.

So one Sunday morning I mustered enough courage to go over to Papa and Mama's bedroom. "Can I snuggle into your bed?" I asked, at the age of eighteen.

My parents each had a double-sized Simmons bed, and I crawled under Mama's quilt to confess about Fan, everything from the first waltz and the first song to the first hug in the living room of the friend's house. I didn't omit any details, for so far there had been nothing I needed to omit. Halfway through my confession, Papa started to snore! Ow—his Precious Baby was telling about her first young love and he was bored! Mama heard me through and finding nothing to worry about, merely gave me some comforting general advice.

I did not tell them, however, that my frustration stemmed primarily from what I'd already learned about Fan's past and recent encounters with girls. A classmate had told me in good faith that I was too naive to deal with someone so experienced, and I knew it was true. Still, I didn't tell my parents since it was his past and shouldn't be any concern of theirs.

Neither parent took Fan seriously, for I took other fellow students home as well. What they didn't know was that the romance would soon become very serious indeed.

One thing, perhaps, that attracted us to each other was our very different backgrounds. Fan told me he had never met a girl stuffed with so much knowledge, his own reading list being somewhat brief and limited in scope; and he had lived a kind of life I had only read about in books and newspapers. He had seen a few life-and-death situations, and he was an insider among music professionals, while I was merely a student.

By the next summer a tug-of-war had developed, and the issue was, of course, sex. Not that I didn't know what goes on between males and females. I had read all about that in a book written in English, hidden away in a drawer in our bathroom; I had skimmed through chapter after chapter whenever I'd had an excuse to use that bathroom for an extended period of time. I was not even twelve then. The book described everything, including positions, but all under the chapter titled "The Wedding Night." Being literal-minded to a fault, I thought I would defer further exploration into the matter until the Wedding Night. I wish I had.

The first argument occurred while we were watching a movie. We were holding hands, and I felt him wriggle around and then guide my hand to his open fly. I was shocked and offended. I'd never seen a grown man's thingumabob, not to mention touch one. I slapped his hand under cover of the noisy war film we were watching. When we got back to the college, we had a bitter fight in the privacy of a practicing room. I accused him of immorality and called his action an insult; Fan said that was real life and told me I had hurt his pride. That triggered in me an extended aversion to maleness—a bad beginning. He wasn't happy, either, with having to put up with a girl who knew about a lot of things, but only on paper.

Romantic romance was over, and we now had to face the real-life aspect of our make-believe. Unlike him, I didn't want to do it before marriage, and in his thinking I was supposed to submit if I loved him. To do or not to do it eclipsed other more lighthearted interludes during our days of courtship, and the continual falling out and making up was agonizing. Right then we established our negative pattern of heated bickering and sullen silence. After many disturbing scenes, I gave in with a feeling of sacrifice. I was in the last year of my teens.

We Start "Leaping . . . "

China was, and still is, a very underdeveloped country. Before coming to power, the leaders of the Chinese Communist Party struggled side by side with those who existed in poverty and had a clear understanding of how matters stood with the common people. All that changed, however, after the CCP took over the reins of government, and particularly after Mao began to regard himself as the Great Savior of China's 400 million earthly souls. The Communist leaders gradually withdrew in magisterial aloofness behind the walls of the Chung-nan Hai (Central-South Sea) compound, once an imperial park just south of North Sea Park. In so doing, they distanced themselves from the ordinary people who had helped bring them to power.

Apart from Premier Chou En-lai and his staff, who maintained concern for the interests of the populace, few if any of the leaders made any real attempt to "Serve the People," as they were exhorted to do by Mao in his extravagant and flowery calligraphy on the brick *ying pi* at the entrance of the Chung-nan Hai compound. The mental attitude of those leaders was, and still is, "I bestow" and "I instruct," as with the Emperors and Empress Dowagers who in Imperial days resided in the Forbidden City next door. While Stalin and his cohorts were sometimes called the scared men behind Kremlin walls, Mao and his associates progressively cocooned themselves behind the walls of an imperial compound with its front gate protected by the *ying pi*.

The *ying pi* is a screenlike wall erected immediately inside the front entrance to a courtyard or a compound. Its function is not so much to ward off evil spirits, as the ancient builders liked to pretend, as to conceal the goings-on in that compound when the gates are open. Ironically, this wall is intrinsic to the feudal mentality the CCP professes to oppose. Once that party's leaders became the powers-that-be, they unhesitatingly embraced many of the practices and trappings of their feudal forebears. Such protective walls, devised in the days before aircraft or satellites, provided those within with security and secrecy. And, since the post–1949 occupants of Chung-nan Hai never managed to update their concepts to include the snooping capabilities of satellites, they too felt safe as long as they had high walls around themselves.

When Mao had put out of circulation about 300,000 dissident Rightists, he felt secure enough to launch his ultra-ambitious plans for the country. He started off in 1958 with a loud propaganda fanfare proclaiming a "Great Leap Forward." This was followed by a series of calls and campaigns which, in their sheer lack of rationality, or even sanity, became a kind of sneak preview of what was to come, on a much vaster scale, during the Cultural Revolution eight years later.

The Great Leap Forward, in short, embodied Mao's dream that China, by accomplishing a series of prodigious gains in different fields—industry, agriculture, science, and even hygiene—would very soon land among the world's advanced nations. In fact, everyone in the country was set to "leaping" one way or another in those feverish days.

One of the first leaps was against sparrows, since those poor little creatures had, a few years back, been classified along with rats, flies, and mosquitoes as one of the "Four Pests." (Again those ridiculous "threes," "fours," and "fives"!) Mao had decided sparrows were "pests" because they were said to consume too much grain.

For several years before the "Leap," Peking and Tientsin had already been virtually freed of flies, and the number of mosquitoes had dropped sharply.

Even I spent a couple of hours every day during summer vacations swatting the mosquitoes lured into a vacant room by turning on a light and opening the windows. As for rats, what might be called the "Tale of Tails" is so disgusting that my genteel readers should feel free to skip the next paragraph:

All public sanitation activities were supervised by the neighborhood committees omnipresent in all Chinese communities, and they had each family report to them the statistics of the campaign against pests. Some committees requested not only the number of pests each family destroyed, but also evidence in, for instance, the form of the chopped-off tails of rats. I remember one family was unable to meet the statistical demand for rat tails and mingled among their contribution the tails of several turnips. The committee members discovered the falsification, the family was criticized for lying to the government and made to catch and chop off the tails of more rats.

Sparrows were harder to catch, however, and at the very outset of the Great Leap anyone who could leap, hop, or jump was mobilized to round up the last of the Four Pests. ("Mobilization" is another infamous example of People's Republic terminology, which means in effect persuasion by one's unit or neighborhood committee to do something generally against one's inclinations.)

A date was set up to be the Doomsday of the Sparrows; I believe it was nationwide. The entire city of Tientsin started to chase sparrows at the crack of dawn on that day: drums, gongs, clappers, even pots and pans—in short, all things that could rattle, clatter, or clang—were employed to prevent the sparrows from landing and to force them to fly until they dropped dead of exhaustion.

The music conservatory contingent proved to be the best equipped for Operation Sparrow, for with the exception of pianos, cellos, and double basses, all instruments were pressed into service. We were taken in trucks to the city suburbs to reinforce the peasants there. Those who could blow, blew; those who could sing, sang; those who couldn't do either whistled, whomped, or whooped. And we picnicked at intervals. It was quite a heroic effort—as well as a pleasurable outing for us students.

To be truthful, we didn't kill any sparrows that I know of. I don't think we even saw many of them. We were too busy with our decibel competitions at ground level to pay any attention to sparrows overhead. However, innumerable sparrows were captured and exterminated all over China, until Mao realized his mistake—sparrows ate insect pests as well—and replaced sparrows, on his list of pests, with bedbugs.

The next leap came in the shape of a campaign for thorough cleanliness, and everyone was set to scrubbing and sweeping and washing and dusting. Neighborhood committees came on weekly inspections to every home, every unit, and every school. All our music studies and practicing were laid aside, while we devoted our energies to cleansing the old campus till it was absolutely spic and span. At any rate, my only memories of that period are of scrubbing, not studying.

One of the absurd standards set for cleaniness was that all furniture should be spotless on all *six* sides. The side count included not only the four sides and top of the item in question, but the *underside* as well. I marveled at the originality of those inventive minds as I prostrated myself to wipe the bottoms of desks and bookshelves.

While we scrubbed and polished furniture and staircases, we were also required to cleanse ourselves.

The authorities had became aware of an increasing centrifugal tendency among the intellegentsia during the Bloom and Contend campaign. As they couldn't silence all voices simply by slapping a Rightist cap on all doubters and dissenters—whose growing ranks included Party members and non-Party members alike—a relatively benign subcampaign was initiated in the wake of the anti-Rightist movement. It was named "Surrendering One's Heart to the Party," meaning that people should reveal their innermost thoughts and feelings to the local Communist party organization—an echo of the "Rectification Movement" of 1944 in Yenan and the "Campaign Against Bourgeois Thinking" in universities in the early 1950s. It was solemnly promised that nothing revealed during these brainwashing "surrender" sessions would incur punishment. There wasn't any at the time; but since everything that was said was noted down and inserted into the subject's personal file, the information was there to be used on later occasions, such as during the Cultural Revolution.

And in the "voluntary" way that my parents had surrendered our house, we gullible students surrendered our hearts and souls. Many of us did it with sincerity and loyalty, since it was allegedly the need of the Party, the need of the country, that we should cleanse ourselves to be better qualified to serve the people in the years to come. We all exposed ourselves and wrote stacks of paper with self-criticisms, for we wanted to be "Chairman Mao's good students," "Chairman Mao's artists of the future." Amen.

If I was somewhat hypocritical in the process, it happened this way: I always had two streams of thoughts, as many bilingual people do, and I knew there were two me's: one who thought in Chinese, and another who read, reflected, and thought in English. I sincerely unloaded the unproletarian contents of my Chinese thoughts to the Party, but not from the English side of my mind. These English thoughts were to stay with me, probably because they were hard to translate in the first place.

The Great Leap was, of course, targeted at objectives larger than mere sparrows or spic-and-span undersides and surrendered hearts; those were the preliminaries. Its goal was to have China overtake Britain and catch up with the United States, industrially and economically, within a predetermined time. (Note the fine distinction: Mao didn't say overtake the United States.) And to this day, I can't imagine who his consultants were, or who provided him with the statistics on Britain for this monumental flight of fancy.

Once China had proclaimed its intention to overtake Britain in twelve years, the newspapers became replete with hot air. All kinds of fantasies appeared on their front pages, as incredible claims of production successes were replaced almost daily by even more incredible claims. China bounded forward—on newsprint.

We slept very little; we needed that time to overtake the Imperialists. We studied very little; we could always study after we had caught up with our opponents. As the revolutionary fever in Chinese society rose to new heights of frenetic delirium, Mao proclaimed that the entire nation should "make steel."

Makeshift steel-smelting furnaces mushroomed all over the country. Raw iron was cooked in iron pots, then the iron pots were in their turn broken up and cooked in other iron pots. I missed all the fun, however, as I was abruptly asked to join an expedition that was to conduct social and historical research among China's ethnic minorities. I left the Conservatory, I left my family, I also left Fan, for a whole year, and returned only after I had reached twenty years of age and the college had moved to Peking.

I went back to Tientsin quite often during vacations and weekends after I moved back to Peking along with the Conservatory. One day Toto and I were riding on our bikes in Tientsin when I noticed many jagged, rusty hunks of metal lining the streets. I asked Toto what they were.

"That's right," he grinned. "You were away in the sticks when all that happened. You know, we had a great time breaking up wrought-iron gates and iron cooking pots, in fact, anything made of iron. We threw the pieces into smelting furnaces in our school and that's the result!"

Those useless hunks of scrap were weighed in 1958; they helped to meet Mao's target for steel production that year, the much-publicized number of "1070" (ten million seven hundred thousand tons). Philatelists can find that number on a red-tinted Chinese stamp issued in 1958.

. . . And I Land Among Koreans

China has fifty-six identifiable ethnic groups; fifty-five of them are called "minority nationalities" as opposed to the majority Hans. These minorities make up about 5 percent of China's population, but the regions they inhabit amount to 80 percent of China's territory.

Most minorities live in the border areas, mountainous regions and grasslands, with only the Manchus and some Muslim Huis cohabiting in significant numbers with the Hans. Up to the middle of the current century, some of these minorities still existed in primitive conditions without a currency system or a written language; a few still kept serfs or slaves.

The Han Chinese (I am one of them) are typically self-centered and chauvinistic, and most of them believe they are the only true Chinese. And since all non-Chinese have traditionally been regarded as foreigners and barbarians, the Han Chinese face a certain moral ambivalence in dealing with the non-Han Chinese at home.

Ever since the Opium War and even earlier when foreign powers started to lop bits and chunks from the weakening Chinese Empire, there has been a deep-rooted nationalist obsession about keeping a tight hold on all territory regarded as Chinese. Separatist tendencies among China's own ethnic minorities have also been seen as a menace to China's territorial integrity, and have been dealt with by a combination of military suppression, political blandishments, and cultural assimilation.

After the founding of the People's Republic, on the other hand, genuine efforts were also made to improve the lot of the minorities and to prepare them economically, politically, and culturally for life in a modern society. Well-meant contacts were made, help was rendered; but so much needed to be done and so little was known about many of these peoples. The Minority Research Institute conceived a massive project to collect and compile social, cultural, and historical information about these ethnic groups. The project was all set to go with specialists on minority studies as the backbone of the project, but thousands of research assistants were needed. These were recruited from the universities.

The call for researchers on cultural history and behavior came to various arts academies. I had transferred to the Department of Musicology, which specialized in history and theory in music studies and had only four students at the time. The dean of the college wanted to know if all of us would agree to join the venture; it would count on our records. Despite the delay caused by rheumatic fever, I was still the youngest in the class. The dean joked: "Can you bear to leave your mother?"

We all committed ourselves earnestly to the mission; I with extra determination, for the dean's remark had ruffled my feathers. Looking back, I still wish to express my appreciation for being given this opportunity to acquaint myself with another culture, another group of people, another way of life. To this day I hold the Koreans in Northeast China in high esteem.

The four of us were dispersed among a number of groups to collaborate with professionals and students from other institutions and universities. When we arrived at our research sites, local professionals—if any existed—joined forces with the group sent by the central authorities. I was fortunate to be assigned to research the Korean-Chinese, for these people have a strong cultural tradition and have developed creative arts that are distinct from Han Chinese arts on one hand and from Korean arts on the other. We were sent to the Yen-pien Korean Autonomous Region, where we were cordially welcomed by our local associates—scholars and students from Yen-pien University.

On arrival in Yen-pien, we first bedded down in guest houses. But I couldn't wait to go to the villages to live with the Korean peasants. The Koreans dressed with impeccable neatness and kept their streets and houses spotlessly clean. They were also well educated; in that year, 1958, all age-eligible young people in Yen-pien were in senior middle school, which meant they would have a twelve-year civil education—much higher than the average for anywhere else in China.

After about ten days of orientation, we went to the villages to live with peasants for a couple of months to learn local history. Hans and Koreans in the research groups teamed up, with the Koreans acting as researchers and translators. Our small group was driven by jeep for fourteen hours before we got to our destination.

Living with Korean peasants, I learned to wash my face and feet in rivers and streams, and I ate with my Korean hosts. I also learned to sing their songs, beat their drums, and dance their dances; after all, I was the only girl in the group, and I was from the *wu-ma-ha-kun*—"music college" in Korean. I was well looked after by Koreans and Hans alike.

Yen-pien is quite far north—at approximately the same latitude as the U.S.-Canadian border. The first snows usually fall in early October. That year was the first year of the "People's Commune" era, and we joined the village, which had been designated a "production brigade," to harvest their rice. We had to cross a mountain ridge everyday to get to the rice paddies where we cut the rice stalks with small sickles, and one day it was so cold we were literally wading in half-melted snow. I was having my period, and sloshing around barefoot in icy water at such a time is not the best thing for a girl. The head of our group noticed my discomfort and told me to go home before the others did.

I left climbing the ridge at a leisurely pace, reflecting on how the local peasants lived with such daily crossings over the hill. I followed the winding path and suddenly found myself back in my childhood dream, the one in which I was on a hillside bathed in a deep purplish hue. I looked around in disbelief: the setting sun was at the same angle as in my dream, the hillside and rock were the same color and shape, and I was, again, all alone. I stood there for a long time, drinking in the actuality of my dream of fifteen years ago. It sounds incredible, but if I had been a painter and had made pictures of my dream vision and of the mountainside in the gathering dusk, the pictures would have been almost identical.

We went to many other villages in the vicinity on foot, and after trudging thirty-six *li*, or a good twelve miles, in a single day over punishing rocky roads, this onetime "Miss" raised a spectacular set of blisters on her feet. To me, however, the expedition was not just an adventure, it was a highly educational and inspiring experience as well. Moreover, even if my past peregrinations had tempered me physically, I hadn't been toughened up mentally, for I had always been under my parents' wing, even during my recent years of college life. In Yen-pien, I became truly independent. I grew up.

One day we trekked over rugged mountains and swift-flowing streams to the lodge of some elderly Korean laborers who had drifted logs down the Tu-men River all their lives. Lumber was a major product of Yen-pien. Our small group sat on the heated brick floor on which the occupants of the house spread their bedding and slept at night; we listened to these veteran raft-drifters tell about the life they had experienced. Their stories were told in a kind of lyric narrative, with recitation interspersed with melodious chanting to the rythmic accompaniment of a small drum.

The storytelling was in Korean, and our Korean colleagues tried, at first, to translate for the few Hans in the group. But later, there was no great need for translation, for all the feelings and emotions—agony, suspense, fear, deter-mination, exhilaration, triumph, relief—expressed by these men who had spent a lifetime negotiating the perilous Tu-men River currents could be sensed without actually having to understand the words.

We stayed over at the raft-drifters' campsite that night. I was the only female, and the old couple who took care of the dormitory loghouses put me in a small room where all the guest-house bedding was kept. They told me that it would be convenient for me, as well as warm in that small room. It was; I almost got barbecued that night.

This room straddled the main heating pipe for the floors of two or three of the houses and, prompted by their traditional hospitality toward guests from afar, our hosts threw a few more logs in the stove. I woke up in the middle of the night, feeling as though I were sleeping on a hotplate. I felt my way around but couldn't find a cool spot to lie down on. I pulled quilts down from the shelves one by one until the the quilts under me became cool enough for me to lie on.

When I woke up the next morning I found myself sleeping uncovered on top of a stack of quilts two feet high. I grumbled when I made up my bed, which meant folding each quilt back into neat squares and piling them on the shelves again. When my kind hosts inquired if I had been warm enough, I said yes, it had been *quite* warm, and left it at that.

It was only on the long walk back to our base village that I told my colleagues how I used the items in the storage room to keep from being cooked alive. They laughed, and the boys kept teasing me about the VIP treatment reserved for the lady guest.

The fervor of Great Leap Forward was felt even in this remote corner of China. In response to—or under the pressure of—Mao's ambitious plans to propel China immediately into the stage of full-fledged Communist Society, the entire country started to "enter into Communism," county by county, city by city. Almost every day the local newspapers carried banner headlines to the effect that such-and-such a county "Announces Entry into Communism Today . . ." One day the county where my village was situated also declared that it had advanced into Communist Society. I honestly believe Karl Marx turned in his grave!

At the same time, material shortages became noticeable in the border regions, long before people in the big cities sensed the threat of famine. On top of the rationing of oil and grain inherited from the mid-1950s, sugar became hard to get, and a meat shortage developed. I tasted, for the first time, venison from a local variety of deer, as efforts were made to stretch out the dwindling stocks of farm-produced meat with occasional catches of wild game. I also learned to eat raw fish, and noticed how little nutritious food the average Koreans had.

The Queen of Roses

A rose garden and a queen of roses are hardly things one associates with life in China during the days of Maoism; but the garden was actually there—for much of that time, at least—and the queen was my mother.

Mama's career had taken a good many unpredictable twists and turns, and she was still a housewife, after we had survived the initial shocks on our return to China and planned to move to Tientsin. Many educated Chinese women were starting to get out of the home to take up jobs. Mama's schoolmates taught in schools or universities, or worked in banks and other institutions, all of which were now run by the state. But neither Mama nor Papa wished to become a state employee, a cadre, so to speak.

At this juncture, a prominent physician, Dr. L. H. Wu, passed away, leaving a garden full of roses. He had no heir, so some of his old friends gathered to decide what to do with his possessions before possible government confiscation.

We were living in the House in Two Parts at the time, and aside from the space taken up by the date trees, there was lots of room in the yard. My parents assumed the legacy and, with some assistance from other friends of Dr. Wu's, transplanted his roses at our home. That was just before Papa was jailed for nine months, and during those uneasy months Mama had much to look after on a very tight budget—her aging parents, her lazy brats who kept fretting over the demise of our dog, and an informing servant, to name just a few things. And now on top of all that, there were the newcomers to our household: several hundred rose bushes. It's a miracle any of them survived.

After Papa's release, he worked around the roses a lot while he recuperated, and he and Mama's arrangements to move away from Peking included the second transplanting of those roses. A few dozen plants were left for the house's new owners, but almost five hundred bushes, representing a couple of hundred varieties, were once more uprooted, wrapped with their soil in straw bags, and loaded on a truck to be transported to Tientsin in the late autumn of 1953.

It was an anxious wait, that winter, for while Tientsin was only seventy miles away from Peking, its soil and water were substantially different. However, the majority of the plants leaved and flowered the very next spring. During the more orderly years of the mid-1950s in Tientsin, we had only a bamboo fence instead of the usual brick wall on the long side of our garden in the four-house compound, and many people came simply to enjoy the fragrance in late May; the bolder ones peeped through the interstices in the fence, and lovers lingered under the trees in front of our house at night. Friends brought friends and, finally, when we got tired of running to the door every time the bell rang, we held open house on weekends.

While peonies, plum blossoms, and chrysanthemums were regarded as native Chinese flowers, roses were decidely categorized as a Western import. And, unfortunately, the new government downplayed all influences from the West, suppressing not only individuals and their thoughts, but also clothing, furniture, and architecture—and even roses. In the minds of many, roses were bourgeois.

The generally relaxed social climate in Tientsin, however, allowed our roses to grow, and also enabled Mama to obtain through our cousins in

America books on rose growing and its history. Mama was thrilled when research into both English and ancient Chinese texts revealed that roses were actually shipped out of China on a British vessel of the East Indies Company in the late eighteenth century and hybrid in France with the Damascus rose, producing the roses we now know.

Mama felt that, by setting straight this forgotten record, roses would be placed in as prominent a position as peonies. The fact is that China, while importing much from other cultures in more ancient times—say during the Tang Dynasty in the seventh to tenth centuries—became very nationalistic and protectionistic in recent centuries, all the way up through the People's Republic.

It so happened that in the mid-1950s Premier Chou En-lai visited India. He was so enchanted by the roses lining the road from the airport into New Delhi that he asked Peking officials if our capital could also be decked out like New Delhi.

His wish became known to Mama through some of our friends, and I remember Mama took a train to Peking one morning with the most gorgeous bouquet of roses I've ever seen. The sheer size of the bouquet aroused my curiosity, for the Chinese of the 1950s were somewhat deprived when it came to flowers and beauty; you could even say no flower culture existed in China in those days. Mama, smartly dressed in a pantsuit, smiled mysteriously and told me she'd tell me all about it when she got back in the evening.

Well, the bouquet was for Premier and Madam Chou En-lai and was delivered to them in person by the Chief of Protocol, a former KMT official and a family friend. Mama also enclosed her research on the origin of roses that established roses as a Chinese flower.

Then two of the deputy mayors of Peking, one of them a college friend of Papa and Mama's, initiated with Mama the idea of cultivating a rose garden in the park of the Temple of Heaven in Peking's South City. The concept of such a garden derived from the one very close to our house in Berkeley, and Papa was invited to design it.

In the meantime, Peking was feverishly building and decorating for a display on October 1, 1959, of the nation's achievements during its first ten years. Three mammoth buildings were under construction around Tiananmen Square. On the north side of this vast square stood the Gate of Heavenly Peace (Tiananmen), the southern gate of the Forbidden City, where many years later Bernardo Bertolucci made *The Last Emperor* (1987). The towering cenotaph to the Revolutionary Martyrs was erected on the southern side of the square in 1959, and as I remember it was designed to be one meter higher than the Tiananmen, to signify the predominance of .the proletariat over feudalism. The least functional building was the Museum of History on the east side of the square; it was put to better use as a venue for sales promotions in the 1980s. And on the west side loomed the Great Hall of the People with an auditorium seating ten thousand and twenty-nine enormous rooms representing the twenty-nine provinces of China. Enormous is the only description that fits the Great Hall, for it conveys little sense of beauty or elegance in its structure and interior design.

But Chou En-lai wanted roses to be planted in the flower beds in front of the massive hall, for roses in northern China go into their second blooming period in autumn just around October 1. There was some dissent, naturally, when peony and chrysanthemum specialists cited the un-Chineseness of roses; but, thanks to Mama's research, they were silenced by the facts. Since neither of the other flowers bloom in this particular season, roses were confirmed as the honorable flower-elect.

A frantic search for blooming rose bushes got underway, Mama was invited to act as special counselor for the project, and about three hundred of our rose bushes were donated to the project. The older, well-traveled bushes remained in Tientsin; it was their offspring of the last six years that went to Peking.

This was the first time Mama worked for and with the government—literally hand-in-glove, since she particularly enjoyed working with the ordinary laborers and the trained gardeners. She also appreciated the earnest efforts put in by the officials. And so, when I got back from Yen-pien, and Toto had survived the anxieties of college entrance and enrolled in the Peking Iron and Steel Institute, Mama was totally engrossed in the rose project.

On the eve of the official ribbon-cutting ceremony of the Great Hall of the People, a huge reception was held for all who had contributed to building it. Mama was among the participants, one of the thousands of ordinary functionaries and laborers, and she was proud. As a *Tai-tai* (Missus), she found her place among the down-to-earth people she loved to be with.

Mama was then formally appointed Consultant to the Peking Parks and Afforestation Bureau and spent almost half her time in Peking, living in an office/bedroom provided by the park administration of the Temple of Heaven. By that time, our household had been joined by an uniquely precious person whom I shall call Ah Po. She stayed with us until she passed away, a total of twenty-eight years. Ah Po took charge of our housekeeping in Tientsin and, although a housekeeper, was more outspoken and in charge than any other domestics I'd ever known. She was the first of them to sit down in the presence of my parents without being asked; all the others usually stood. She behaved and thought like a peer rather than a subordinate. Anyway, our home was in good hands. My college was now in Peking, Toto's college was also in that city, and Mama would be there every other week from Monday till Saturday. Papa was the only one permanently at home in Tientsin.

The three years of famine immediately following Mama's assignment slowed down the project of creating a specially designed Rose Garden, as it did other projects throughout the country, but work picked up momentum again once famine relinquished its hold in 1962. Papa drew up the blueprints, Mama assisted the workers, and the first Rose Garden in China bloomed. A second was subsequently set up in another park in Peking, and then in Tientsin . . . .

While China had one site in Peking's suburbs and another in Shantung Province where wild roses were grown for medicinal purposes, garden roses were not popular until Mama's flowers took root in the center of Peking. And the moniker "Queen of Roses," or "The Rose Lady" (which Mama preferred) was attached to her name.

Fate took a cruel twist during the Cultural Revolution under the personal ministrations of none other than that "proletarian" virago Madame Chiang Ching—Mao's wife. She was letting off steam at somebody, presumably some Peking municipal officials, and according to the transcript handed out in the streets she ranted: "And look at what those revisionists have done! They've planted roses in front of the revolutionary Great Hall of the People! Roses! Can they uplift the revolutionary awareness of the proletariat?! Revolutionary young Red Guards, we must replace those bourgeois roses with cereals and vegetables!"

I was nervous when I first learned of the pamphlet; if Chiang Ching had mentioned the Queen of Roses, an onslaught on our home would inevitably follow. But as it turned out, the onslaught expended itself on the flower beds in front of the Great Hall. I was later told some smart folks arrived ahead of the mob and saved some of the plants by taking them home. Well, it was all over in a matter of hours; the bushes, thorns and all, were replaced with wheat and, of all vegetables, eggplants.

Years of Famine

The Central Music Conservatory had moved to Peking during my absence for the research on minorities, and all four of us who came back sun-darkened, toughened, and dried behind the ears were welcomed there by our peers. I turned twenty in Yen-pien and wrote my first major academic report—published later that year—on the state of literature and arts among the Korean-Chinese population.

That year was 1959, the tenth anniversary of the founding of the People's Republic of China. When we returned to Peking it was a transformed city, for under the diligent direction of Premier Chou En-lai, ten new construction projects were underway, among them the previously mentioned buildings on Tiananmen Square, and the new Peking Railroad Station. These buildings not only lent a new dignity to the ancient city but were also to remain as some of the best accomplishments of our ambitious new nation as well as monuments to the memory of Chou and his colleagues.

Providence gave China a bumper harvest in 1958, which seemed to justify the Great Leap; the majority of China's peasants who had hardly had a square meal of rice or flour all their lives could now dream of eating *you ping*—fried dough cakes—every day, and to them that was Communism.

Even if there were already indications of shortages, such as I had sensed in Yen-pien as the tenth anniversary of the P.R.C. approached, these were seen as mere imbalances that would be quickly adjusted by the sheer force of socialist economic principles. The feverish rhetoric of the Leap had moderated somewhat, but to celebrate the tenth anniversary all musicians in Peking, including students of music, harmonized a performance of the choral finale of Beethoven's Ninth Symphony, "Ode to Joy." To Chinese musicians nurtured in the traditions of Western music since the 1920s, this performance meant that we had reached the culmination of classical Western music; it also embodied our artistic commitment to the principle that "all men are brothers."

However, the overblown production statistics from local functionaries intended to win favor from Party leaders quickly backlashed. There were bumper harvests, even record-breaking ones, all over China in 1958, but they were exaggerated to unbelievable proportions. The most notorious instance—later verified as fraudulent—was the claim that 5,000 kilograms (11,000 lbs.) of grain had been grown on one *mu* (one-sixth of an acre) of land. After this claim was broadcast to the entire nation, reporters flocked to the site to take pictures and report the event. The truth of the matter was that all the stalks had been transplanted from other locations onto that small plot of land. The growth was so thick that when they placed a child on it, the stalks wouldn't even bend. And ventilation was so poor that the air was actually steaming between the plants.

However, these exorbitantly amplified achievements pleased Mao, and he ruthlessly silenced the voice of reason raised in a memorandum of ten thousand words by Marshal Peng De-huai, former commander-in-chief of the Chinese troops in the Korean War. Peng was cashiered by Mao after a stormy Party Central Committee meeting at Lushan in 1959. But economic plans and all budgets were based on these falsified statistics, and the real comeuppance fell on the shoulders of the populace just one year later.

The 1959 Anniversary was, in fact, the swan song of an ascending ten-year progression. That October first, I was again behind my school's banner, but not as part of the parade that marched through the Tiananmen Square; we were ushered to our assigned place on the vast square at dawn, to stand there until midday as the parade went by. Only then did I realize that the square was designed so that each slab of concrete pavement served as the standing place for one person; as long as one kept on one's individual slab, the rows would automatically look horizontally and vertically straight to the leaders standing on top of the Gate of Heavenly Peace. That would be the last time I participated in a celebration parade. None of us participants could foresee then that this square would witness so many fanatical and tragic events in the years to come.

After the anniversary celebration, the economy deteriorated so rapidly that everyone was taken by surprise. Nobody had the time or opportunity to store things up; virtually all food disappeared overnight—meat, vegetables, and other edibles. My parents came to Peking in November to celebrate Papa's birthday, and an old friend who shared the same birthday booked a Peking duck dinner for the two families through his connections. That was just one month after the decennial celebration, at the outset of the famine years, and that duck sure tasted good!

The best part of it was that Papa asked for an extra dish of stir-fried pancake shreds for me to take back to college in a box. The three girls who shared a dorm with me each had a nibble, then insisted I keep the rest for myself. I tied the box up with string and tucked it on the ledge outside our window to keep the food cool. Every day after that I ate a small portion, first warming it on the steam radiator. That "doggie bag" lasted me a whole week.

Food rations were reduced to starvation level in the cities during the three famine years of 1960–1962. Those with small children had a harrowing time. Parents sacrificed their small share of provisions for hungry children, who had to be treated equally, and after the relative abundance of the 1950s it was very sad to see some families bickering over a few mouthfuls of food.

However, the hardships were the worst in the countryside. The call had gone out in 1958 to set up People's Communes—those supposed prototypes of communist society which presumably would provide all their members with all the basic necessities of life. Millions of peasant families voluntarily— or so it was claimed—dismantled their own kitchens, sending their large farmhouse iron pots to be melted down to meet Mao's steel-making target, and went to eat for free at the commune mess room.

I was in a Yen-pien commune when this started, and it was like having a party at every meal. I too believed at the time that the free meals could be kept up; there had been good harvests and the peasants' fare was after all quite simple. The official propaganda machine asserted that the commune kitchen system would undergo "no change in twenty years"—a boast repeated ad nauseum even after it became clear that the system was cracking.

I was also in a commune when these commune kitchens were dissolved— the very next year, before twenty *months* were up. We veterans had been sent out once more, this time to a mountain village not far from Peking. Our task: to convince the peasants to accept the new decision to discontinue the commune kitchens. The peasants were left in the lurch; whatever grain they had once saved was gone, their kitchen utensils were gone, their poultry was gone, and they were left to face the impending famine on their own.

The Party's perspicacity, first in setting up the commune kitchens and then in dismantling them, was not to be questioned. No one was supposed to say "I told you so!" The appalling fact was that the famine took more than twenty million lives, directly and indirectly, in the next three years, but nobody was supposed to comment on or even know anything about it.

The Soviets withdrew their experts in China when their ideological conflict with the Chinese Communists intensified. This was an additional blow to the faltering Chinese economy, but it provided Mao with a scapegoat for his economic fiascos. This time, the hatred was projected toward the "revisionists" instead of the "imperialists." Having thus alienated the Soviet bloc countries, China began to seek moral support from developing countries, which Mao named the "Third World."

Students were encouraged to stay at school, where we received a bit more grain than the average city dweller—approximately three and half pounds more per month.

We were requested to finish our meals right in the mess room, and not to take out and waste anything. But we found a way to smuggle things out: we'd take out a handkerchief as if to wipe our mouths and use it to cover a leftover piece of bun. Then we would walk out of the mess room still "wiping" our mouths.

This little bit of leftover bun, boiled in water, provided us with a midnight snack. My classmates and I kept very late hours, maintaining that like all diligent scholars we worked best at night. We seldom went to bed before 2:00 A.M.

One night the chairman of our department, a very respectable professor, was surprised to see lights in the departmental library after midnight and came up to investigate. He got an even greater surprise when he found all his best students hunkered around a primitive cooking device among the bookshelves.

We were preparing our midnight snack with a spirit lamp and a pot containing leftover buns, water, a few cabbage leaves, and a few drops of oil floating on top. To keep the pot at the right height and angle, we had improvised a stand with a wire wastebasket turned upside down and propped on a few thick books.

Our professor took in this ingenious creation, then his eyes stopped on the books. We followed his gaze and realized to our horror that what we used as props were actually valuable and irreplaceable volumes on Chinese art theory. We had picked them simply by thickness and never bothered to verify what they were!

The professor must have sympathized with the efforts of his hungry students to make do with whatever was available. In any case, he gave another wistful look at the volumes, evidently to make sure we got the message, and simply said: "It's time you all went to bed—after you've had your snack." After that incident we replaced the art volumes with dictionaries.

Many students who were in college during the famine years remarked later that they actually had more time to study; there were no political movements and no expeditions to the countryside, as the nation concentrated on surviving. To preserve strength, we didn't dance even on New Year's eves, but only listened to live dance music in our mess hall. It was customary to wind up dances in China with "Auld Lang Syne," and we all stood up and danced to that melody played in slow waltz tempo—no one had the energy for anything faster—to welcome in the new years of 1960 and 1961.

In mid-1961 the government was able to give senior officials and professionals some extra rations such as sugar and soybeans. To my knowledge, there were no complaints of excessive official perks or corruption at the time. Mao himself did not lead an extravagant life, and Chou was an upright leader. And if some people did enjoy privileges, it was not done blatantly, as it would be in the 1980s and after. Since everyone was in it together, the Chinese people didn't blame or reproach, we only suffered and hoped.

By 1962, things had improved a bit. Limited amounts of candy and cookies had become available on the market, and with a ration coupon for half an ounce of cooking oil one could buy three *you ping*—fried dough cakes. I remember once, on the last day of the month, Toto—by now a student in a Peking college—found he had an extra half-ounce oil coupon. The two of us, along with my husband, went in search of the mouth-watering dough cakes. But it was late in the evening and all the shops were already shuttered and closed. We came back to my apartment room and sat there for a long time, contemplating that little scrap of paper, and thinking about the treat we had missed.

The Tablecloth on the Nuptial Bed

When I came back to our college, relocated to Peking during my absence, Fan and I picked up where we left off. However, I noticed a certain cattishness in a freshman's behavior toward me—for no reason that I could fathom, until I learned Fan had been seeing her while I was away. I thought of breaking up. But the nasty things that were said about several couples who called off their relationships during the same interval made me hesitate. The Chinese have no sense of privacy—we didn't even have the term "privacy" in our lexicon in those days; everything personal is public property, especially when it comes to spreading gossip. Having learned enough already about Fan's temperament, I would have done anything simply to avoid upsetting him and eliciting mindless recriminations that would only serve as grist for the gossip mill. Because of that, and my stubborn tendency to stick to things or people I was accustomed to, I simply stuck with Fan. The other girl went on to her next boyfriend.

The years of famine brought a measure of tranquility into our relationship, for our constitutions were so weakened that love-making was out of the question. Since petting and cuddling was more to my taste, we got to communicate with each other much better.

Many couples were formed during those college years, especially in a socially conservative country like China where colleges offered students the first real opportunity to associate with the opposite sex. One got to know one's counterparts better in those surroundings. I must admit both of us knew our strengths, weaknesses, and problems quite well before we embarked upon marriage.

The Chinese language traditionally uses blatantly pejorative terms when it comes to entitling women, particularly in denoting the status of wives. So when the CCP called for the emancipation of women as part of its overall revolution, it conveniently borrowed from its Russian counterpart the words "lyubovnik" and "lyubovnitsa," and translated these into "loved person" in Chinese. This was a prefeminist non-gender politically correct word, and every married person, regardless of gender, was introduced as "my loved person" or "so-and-so's loved person." Mister, Missus, and Miss vanished from the social scene as being of bourgeois provenance.

As the terms fiancé/fiancée also left the social scene for the same reason, what Fan and I had been doing for about four years was called "making friends."

Many other couples applied for marriage licenses as graduation approached, so that they could be together, or at least in the same city, when they were assigned to their future *dan wei*. Fan and I also discussed the advantages of getting married sooner rather than later, one of the issues being that if we didn't get married now, our classmates would be sent all over the country and could not attend the wedding; better to do it while they were still on campus.

I took a train to Tientsin to inform my parents. The reaction wasn't favorable. Neither of them thought Fan was the right husband for me; they had assumed we were just dating.

"Don't you realize it's been almost four years?" I asked.

"You're still too young to get married and start a family."

"I'm going on twenty-three next year," I protested. "And we won't have babies for a long time."

Mama asked me if we couldn't just have a party with our schoolmates—for whom this wedding seemed to be planned—and announce an engagement? I told her no one got engaged nowadays. I then told them a little about the realities of life they didn't quite understand. I said Fan already knew where he'd be assigned, and that his future *dan wei* had promised him a room in a new apartment building if he registered as a married person.

My second argument was that due to the lack of telephones, it would be difficult for us to meet once we left college for our respective *dan wei*. Meet at street corners? In public parks? In friend's homes? If we married and got our room, we could be together without the hassle of setting up dates and biking from one end of the sprawling city to the other.

In the end, my parents gave in very reluctantly, and I learned many years later Mama cried when she told her friends I shouldn't be marrying at such a young age—she had married at twenty-nine.

So out came my trousseau, which included two Cannon Percale bedsheets; buying new sheets required a lot of cloth coupons. We didn't use those sheets very often, however, for what with soap rationing and laundry still in the hand-rubbing-and-rinsing stage, dealing with full-sized American sheets was too much of an effort. These sheets dutifully traveled back to Tientsin a few years later when much of my parents' belongings went to serve the Revolution via the good offices of the Red Guards. The sheets came back to me after Mama passed away, for Toto's wife brought a large supply of linenware when she and Toto got married. Those sheets are still resting in my trunks in China, forty-some years after they passed through the check-out in some Berkeley store.

I also ordered my bridal outfit in Tientsin. Since the date we chose would be in the hottest part of summer, I had a dress made of pale green cotton with white ribbon patterns, and a silk skirt in white, blue, and gray. The family friend who made it for me looked at the material and protested: "The colors are all too subdued! As a bride you should wear brighter colors." But I stuck to my simple choices and my own patterns. And after purchasing a new pair of white sandals, I announced I was all set.

In those post-famine 1960s, most people had a simple "*dan wei* wedding," with refreshments confined to some beer, cigarettes, snacks, and candy. Colleagues and friends would show up with generally utilitarian gifts, such as wash basins, thermos bottles, and flower vases—there was no gift-wrapping or card-writing, so all the presents came in the raw, so to speak. There was always a family dinner before or after, as well as a visit to the so-called nuptial chamber, which custom required to be appointed with new furniture, new bedding, shiny thermos flasks, and the inevitable picture of the couple. The bed, borrowed and placed in a vacated classroom set aside for those new couples, was the piece de resistance—a showcase for all the guests to admire.

Decorating that bed became a problem. White Cannon Percale sheets were hardly decorative, and Chinese department stores didn't carry any bedcovers at the time due to the shortage of cotton. A flowery Chinese bed sheet might have served the purpose, but I'd always been using white sheets and loathed the gaudy things offered in stores, complete with frilly embroidered pillow-cases.

Then I ran into luck. I was looking for a tablecloth when I saw some sets on sale that only required one meter's worth of coupons. One of the sets was a largesize rectangular tablecloth with eight napkins, all beautifully embroidered in dark and light green at the edges and corners. I bought it and made two pillow-cases from the eight napkins, and announced to Fan we now had everything we needed. The small corner designs on that tablecloth went well with my pale green dress.

Fan eyed the tablecloth warily and asked if he would be required or allowed to sleep on *that*. I said, of course not, *that* goes on top of the Cannon sheets; it's only standing in for a bed cover which can't be obtained. The pillowcases would stay on the pillows, but we'd spread a "pillow towel" over them, as most Chinese do.

We still needed to display some new quilts, though, even if the weather would be swelteringly hot—since we were one of the last couples to decide to get married, all the earlier (and cooler) weekends had been earmarked for other wedding parties. Fan's family had long saved a green satin quilt cover for such an occasion, and I dug out a red one from my own hoard, which existed for reasons quite unrelated to my wedding. The green and red quilts looked terrible together, but they would have to do.

I wrote my parents in detail and with considerable pride about my ingenious conversion of the tablecloth and pillowcases. I declined to accept anything more from them, for I insisted that it was my wedding, and Fan and I would take care of the expenses from the monies we'd saved.

My parents racked their brains and finally came up with a practical and presumably acceptable way to subsidize their obstinate offspring and her consort. They proposed, and I accepted, a five-hundred-yuan nest egg for a honeymoon trip; it would cover train expenses to Fan's hometown to meet his family, and then to Shanghai and Hangchow and back. That five hundred yuan in the early 1960s was more than ten months of my first year's salary-to-be as a college graduate; it was a lot of money for both of us.

Naturally, I asked them what I should do with the money left over from that trip . . . . It's all yours, I was assured. I made up my mind to save enough of it for a good-sized German-made radio; and that meant the budget for the honeymoon was tightened up before we even got started.

We planned the actual wedding reception with our schoolmates. Those were the end-of-famine days; supplies of candy, popsicles, and cigarettes were available again, but at high prices and with quantity limits. So our friends made a calculation and asked us for thirty yuan in expenses for the reception. They bought the items mentioned above and volunteered to serve as M.C. and ushers. All the guests were allowed to pick one item—one candy, one popsicle, or one cigarette—at the door, handed out by the ushers. Not much, but after the privations we'd been through, everyone was happy with that meager treat. Our deans (including Madame Kwan whom I first met on the *S.S. Canton*), faculty, staff, and schoolmates flocked in. And since we'd been on this campus from the college's Tientsin days, even the doorman and chefs were our friends. Our ushers were afraid we'd run out of supplies, but I'd bought an extra bag of candy to be on the safe side. We broke even, and not one guest left empty-mouthed. The total cost, 28.50 yuan. Papa, Mama, Toto, and a few friends of mine came, including Lily and the lifelong friend I mentioned before. Lifelong, who was also at Cousin Ta's wedding, made a speech:

"I truly admire your nerve in choosing the hottest day of the year to marry. May your love be as torrid as the temperature."

Of course, Papa and Mama brought me something else; they were not going to let me marry on a 28.50 yuan budget. They bought me two necklaces, an extravagance in China in those years. One was a 24-carat gold chain with a crystal stone, costing fifty yuan, approximately an average monthly salary; the other was a silver chain with a coral-colored stone, twenty-five yuan. As I didn't know the extent of our family's wealth at the time, I was flabbergasted and said this was too much, could I return them the silver one to be saved for Toto's bride? Papa pooh-poohed my recycling proposal, but I tucked away the silver one anyway and wore the gold piece which looked splendid with my bridal outfit.

With the purse strings in my uncompromising hands during the honeymoon trip, we stayed at the student dorms of the Shanghai Music College while in Shanghai, and it cost us next to nothing. But in Hangchow we stayed in a real honeymoon chamber at a lakeside hotel—we had to present our marriage certificate to obtain that room. It was much larger and better furnished than others, and the charge was 3.50 yuan per day. In spite of the price, however, we still had to trot to the end of the corridor to find a washroom.

An obsessive pastime with police and hotel clerks in Communist China in those days was catching adulterous pairs in flagrante delicto, and to humiliate their captives in every way possible. As we were going through the registration process, I wondered aloud: "Since there are no photos on marriage licenses, anyone could bring his lover to pose as his wife, couldn't he?" The clerk told me it had happened. But the culprits were exposed when the real wife contacted the hotel after opening a parcel sent back by the hotel according to the registered address. The parcel contained a pair of shoes the mistress had left under the bed!

We returned to Tientsin and then to Peking. I reported to my parents truthfully that the entire honeymoon trip had cost us only a little over three hundred yuan, for we had bedded and eaten free in my home and his. So, I bought the much coveted ten-valve German radio from an enterpreneurial Vietnamese exchange student for 150 yuan.

That honeymoon was the only trip we ever took together.

A Promising Career Woman

After a few months of waiting, we got the room we had hoped for when we married. It was a room in a three-room apartment. The customary Chinese apartments had no living room then, just rooms, with beds in every one of them.

I'd lived in courtyard houses and Western-style houses. And I had friends who'd been given rooms in *dan wei* housing. The latter typically contained numerous rooms lined up on both sides of extra-long corridors, with latrines marked MEN and WOMEN at each end, and every family lined up their coal stoves, coal bricks (for fuel), and crude cupboards for food in the narrow corridors. All the rooms were cluttered with beds, beds, and beds, and perhaps a desk under the window; visitors sat on the beds, or maybe on a soft chair squeezed into a corner.

Aware of such conditions, I felt blessed to be sharing an apartment with only one family—a family with five children ranging from tots to teens plus an amah. They had the other two rooms and we shared the kitchen and bathroom. We were also among the first Peking residents to use natural gas from pipes in the mid-1960s. While the majority of Peking dwellers had to endure using public outhouses situated right in the *hutung*s, I've always had a private flush-toilet bathroom in the apartments I've lived in.

One major reason the Chinese could live on such low salaries in those years was that the government subsidized almost everything. The Communist-led government grew from its origins in the rural revolutionary bases set up in the 1920s. While both the times and the extent of administration have changed since then, the principle and the mentality of those who governed have not much progressed. The basic concept has always been "I control thee," all ostensibly for the good of those controlled; such basic thinking has currently been updated to include the concept that to "clothe and feed thee" is equivalent to conferring the basic human rights. But that's beside the point. As far as expenses were concerned, we paid 3.05 yuan a month for that room, and when we got a much bigger apartment five years later, we paid 5.40 each month for the next quarter of a century. Even with my salary frozen at fifty-six yuan a month for fifteen years, that kind of rent was no big deal.

We moved into that room with all the basic furniture provided by Fan's *dan wei*, also a practice that dated from the revolutionary base era. As I remember, we paid 2.40 yuan a year for the use of a double bed, a desk, a couple of chairs and, in deference to Fan's profession as a conductor, a piano. He felt comfortable with *dan wei* furniture. Having been brought up in a non-proletarian community, I was more accustomed to have my own things. I insisted on diverting part of our first salaries to buy one desk and one chest of drawers. I let him have them when we divorced.

I also obtained from my home some pieces of furniture I'd always liked, and a small rug.

The monthly allowance from my parents was doubled to forty yuan during the famine years. "Just don't starve," they had said. I now got off that parental welfare after I started to earn forty-six yuan a month. Papa and Mama tried, in vain, to get me to accept a sum of money; I told them that would upset my plans for my own savings, now at an all-time high of two hundred in my bankbook. Finally, Papa proposed to deposit a separate 1,500 yuan under my name; earmarked for my parents' use, I could draw from the deposit in case they needed anything from Peking.

However, now that we had a home, Fan and I rarely enjoyed the tranquility of our nest. His *dan wei*, being a musical ensemble, was constantly on the road; while I, as a journalist with China's most prestigious music magazine, attended concerts six evenings a week.

Although the majority of Chinese college graduates were distributed around the country according to quotas and were never consulted before their destinations were announced, like Fan, I knew where I would work before graduation day. I wrote my first publishable music review when I was seventeen, and got seven yuan for those four hundred Chinese characters. As I grew older, the assigned length of my articles grew longer, and the fees went higher.

My class in musicology studies consisted of four students, whom I shall list, the eldest first: A (female), B (male), C (male) and D (me). We'd all been to minority areas, and while both A and B were Party members and therefore politically qualified, C and D were strong and fast writers. We made a private rule among ourselves that whenever any of us earned a fee over forty yuan, the author would take the others out for a dinner at our favorite place: the Szechuan Restaurant of Peking, at just the right distance for a dinner-hour stroll. We'd tell the others in our dorms that we were holding a class meeting.

The best get-togethers were after we'd made a joint effort on a major paper; when the fee came in, we'd each take ten yuan as bonus and blow the rest on a banquet.

It's hard to say whether we made our reputations first or our money first. At any rate, I was already known as a writer before I graduated. A and B were informed they would have to take up extracurricular staff duties as they were considered trustworthy older students, but they would have to cut some of their courses and defer graduation for one year, which left only C and myself as current graduates, he in Chinese music history and I in Western music history studies. My instructor and departmental chair invited me to his home on campus one day. He told me the Dean and he had decided that both C and I would be consulted personally on our job placements, a privilege rarely accorded to graduates.

In fact, ours was the first Musicology Department ever in a Chinese music college. We were the first class and C and I would be the first fledglings hatched. The college wanted to keep both of us, since C was an exceptional scholar and I was the only student in the entire college with a working knowledge of a foreign language. But the music community at large was telling the college not to be so selfish. My professor asked me my personal choice; he told me one of us was likely to be assigned to the Chinese Musician's Association, and that *People's Music*, a highly regarded professional periodical, was after both of us. That journal had been courting us for the past couple of years, and unknowingly provided for our "class meetings" with their fees.

I looked my professor in the eye and asked him if he would mind terribly if I said "Yes, let me go!" For three reasons: first, despite the credits I received teaching music appreciation courses at a couple of art colleges in my student years, I didn't want to make a career of teaching; second, having been in school all my life, I wished to be out in the professional world, and; third—I was a little sheepish about this for Chinese were not supposed to take personal benefits into consideration—the Musician's Association was located on the same tramline as my future home and close to Peking's shopping street Wang Fu Ching. Yes, I declared, I'd like to go.

My professor told me he had had a hunch which choice I'd make. The Dean had pressured him to consider letting one of us go. His reluctance to release me stemmed from that fact that I was the only successor to the studies he had pursued. In the end he admitted my reasons for going made sense, though he avoided referring to my third consideration. Located in a building with a facade of flowered ceramic plaques, that association was the most prestigious and glamorous *dan wei* in China's music circles. All the outstanding composers, conductors, players, and singers were among its members.

Secretly, I went to that block, which was in fact just around the corner from Bridgeman Academy, and reexplored the vicinity, noting everything down to the frequency of the trolleys, the location of transfer stops, and the menu and prices at the closest eatery. The association was only steps away from the old headquarters of the Salvation Army, which had now been converted into a Young Pioneer's Palace, and half a block from one of the best theaters in Peking at the time, the Capital Theatre.

When I reported in for work in September, I was cordially received by the forty-odd staff members of the Musician's Association, which was comprised of a library, the editorial offices of the journal *People's Music*, and two other periodicals that released new music compositions, various committees on Chinese music and music theory, and the usual administrative personnel. The majority of my older colleagues came from the precursor of my college and had been classmates of many of my professors. They passed on to me anecdotes about my above-mentioned professors in their younger days, and I felt at home, instantly.

The editors-in-chief and my immediate boss, the managing editor, informed me that unlike other journals, our people were editors and reporters at the same time. I would work primarily in the field of new works in all genres of music: symphony, opera, songs, and other styles, and also report on music festivals.

The first major festival I covered was in Tientsin. As I knew half the creative artists and the organizers of the festival, I did a good job. "Staff Reporter" was appended to my name for the first time, only three months out of college. I had made a smooth takeoff.

As the concert tickets were free, I went to as many as five or six evening performances a week, partly because that was where I could meet my old faculty and alumni. The only drawback was our very punctilious staff manager, who lived across the street from the *dan wei* and didn't go to any concerts. She had the aggravating habit of checking the offices at 8:05 A.M. and noting how frequently staff members were late. I was one of the better cases, in fact, for I didn't have a family to look after, but I became annoyed with the 8:05 A.M.

poking in at the office. I made a suggestion during a meeting, that either we be given time off for the concerts we attended in the line of duty, hour for hour, or get a thirty-minute credit the next morning. Others chimed in with protests that it wasn't fair to have to be at work at eight sharp, since we weren't going to concerts for pleasure. The request was granted, and the head-poking ceased.

In less than a year I had made a name for myself, and I wrote so many articles I began using pen names. The first month that I made more from my fees than from my salary I was exultant. Using half of my extra earnings, I bought an exquisite reproduction of an ancient Chinese ink-and-brush painting of bamboo and iris for fourteen yuan, and a laundry iron for thirteen yuan. That painting is still my most treasured possession.

A few years after I started working, the Central Music Conservatory did some research on all of its graduates since its first class of 1955. The college administrators and faculty members traveled all over China to hold closed-door sessions with all the *dan wei* that had these graduates on their staffs. After accumulating all the necessary approval ratings, the searchers came up with one as the all-time best. Me. This conclusion was reached in early 1966, but before they had a chance to disclose their verdict, the Cultural Revolution started.

I was informed of the outcome through the usual grapevine. Since the findings of the committee were never officially announced, the only gratification I got was the knowledge that I hadn't let anyone down, not my family, my dean, or my professors. However, at one of the meetings held in the early 1970s to castigate me as a counterrevolutionary, one speaker mentioned that I was the undisclosed best-elect. "That just shows how closely you identified yourself with the revisionists," she declared. "That's why they think you were the best graduate! You *fan-ge-ming* (reactionary)!"

She was, like me, a graduate from the Central Music Conservatory, and I caught a note of envy in her diatribe. I raised my previously lowered head to give her a long look. She stopped short, and when she spoke again it was only to repeat: "You, you *fan-ge-ming*!" I gave her a faint but defiant nod.

My Daughter Is Born in the Same Hospital Room

During the second year of my marriage, the *baby* issue was raised, first in letters written to both of us by my in-laws. "That's none of their business," I snapped, "I'm no breeder of kids bearing your surname!" Then my solicitous uncles and aunties also started to ask if anything was on the way, averring that it took a baby to make a family. As my career kept me perpetually on the run, I had no plans for being burdened with a big tummy.

In any case, I got pregnant unexpectedly. I was furious at myself for not exercising sufficient caution. I really planned for an abortion, down to several skeins of dried noodles with which to feed myself during the two days I might have to stay at home after the event. In the 1960s, family planning was discussed but not yet enforced; following the Soviet and Eastern bloc pattern, abortion was normal practice as long as the father went along to sign an approval form. This, by the way, had nothing to do with women's rights; it was the government's way of discouraging premarital and extramarital pregnancies.

My parents had never pushed me about having a baby, but when I indicated I might get an abortion, both of them came to Peking. Knowing my propensity for doing exactly what I was told not to do if stroked the wrong way, Papa did the wheedling, and promised I wouldn't have to carry my baby to work on the tram like other young mothers; I could leave it in Tientsin and my parents would hire a nanny until Fan and I were allocated a bigger apartment. He quoted statistics on the numerous grandchildren among our Tientsin acquaintances brought up by well-to-do grandparents, while the parents pursued successful careers in their profession.

A more crucial task was reserved for Mama—taking me to see the foremost gynecological specialist if I was still unconvinced by Papa's proposal. And that's exactly what happened. We first went to Doctor Lin's home in the P.U.M.C. north compound where we had sung Christmas carols in 1949 and I had gone for piano lessons. Dr. Lin, a spinster all her life, lived with her relatives (among them one of the Berkeley crowd). She had brought both Toto and me into the world, among thousands of others, and was godmother to so many babies she remembered them only by their birth years.

When she came downstairs to meet Mama and me, she remarked, "Well, now my patients are the babies I delivered." We chatted and set up a formal office appointment at the hospital. The day we went and asked for my medical file the registration nurse insisted I was giving her the wrong number, because "nobody your age can be an in-patient with a five-digit number." Exasperated by her bullheadedness Mama finally told her I had been born here. The nurse grumblingly went to look up the file and returned with a folder stamped with the English word "STAFF" in purple ink. As the file was passed up to Dr. Lin's office, every nurse who handled it seemed to be surprised, to the puzzlement of Mama and myself.

Mama wondered, "Does that mean none of the former staff's families come to this hospital anymore?" That could well be, for there had been so much transition that the STAFF-stamped patients from that era could have either left the country or left the world.

Dr. Lin, after examining me, told me not to be swayed by government propaganda, which was primarily targeted at the peasants who made up 80 percent of the population and breed in astonishing numbers. She gently suggested that for career women like me two or three was a good number. Besides, she said, giving birth at twenty-five was an ideal time for both mother and child. I found all my arguments crumbling before her advice, and gradually accepted the fact that I was on the way to being a Mama, too.

But, I didn't feel like one; I didn't have any morning sickness, as everybody warned me to expect. Secondly, everybody told me I'd have cravings for unusual foods and tart snacks. Obediently I went to the food markets to inspire my palate, but it didn't react to anything. So, as a last resort, I went to one of Peking's old Western food restaurants, the Chi Shih Lin, and read the menu starting from the left-hand side, determined to treat myself and my baby. After a close scrutiny, I found nothing particularly tempting, so I ordered pork liver fried with onions. It was cooked to perfection, and I left feeling somewhat more motherly than before.

My prenatal checkups and the eventual delivery were all covered by state health insurance—that is, if I went to the hospital up the block that served my *dan wei*, instead of going down the block to P.U.M.C. But Dr. Lin pursuaded me to go back to where I was born, the P.U.M.C., where she could keep an eye on me. "I like to see my babies become little mamas," she said. I inquired about the charges at the admission office. Under normal circumstances, the entire cost, apart from food expenses, would amount to 23.00 yuan. My baby would be worth that, I figured.

Pregnancy did not prevent me from engaging in my normal activities, including a business trip to Shanghai to attend a major music festival, where I rubbed shoulders with elite musicians and conducted a meeting in the name of my journal. Being considered too young to preside over a meeting of such celebrities, however, I asked a Shanghai composer to act as chair. The Chinese are notoriously age-conscious; besides, I wasn't a Party member.

At about the same time, Fan was actively involved with the composing, rehearsing, and staging of a new musical, *The East Is Red*—he was also actively involved with a fatal attraction, whom I would learn about a few years later. *The East Is Red* was a gargantuan, three-hour song-and-dance number with thousands of performers, which was to be premiered on October 2 to commemorate the republic's fifteenth anniversary on October 1, 1964. As a matter of fact, it had been copied from a smaller performance in North Korea eulogizing their Benevolent Father Kim Il Sung, but blown up proportionately to fit China's larger size and the more significant "achievements" of our Great Leader Mao. But the music was good.

My parents visited Peking in late September, as Toto had graduated and was actually assigned work right in Tientsin. They were already anticipating the day when they'd become Grandpa and Grandma.

I was prepared, when my time came, to call a taxi—a rare luxury in those days—but also had in reserve the cars of several musical big shots; I got along well not only with them but also with their drivers. I felt a few twinges on September 30, a week before my term, and Fan called a cab, I thinking all the way that I could have done perfectly okay on a tram. My doctor predicted a wait of twenty-four hours or more, but with the parade on the next day— National Day—and the stoppage of all public transportation, she decided it would be safer if I stayed.

I immediately notified my parents who were staying with friends in the P.U.M.C.'s north compound and they cancelled their train trip home to Tientsin.

I didn't feel much different on the morning of October first, but was rolled into the delivery room at noon. When I looked at the room number, 308A, I suddenly realized what the 308A inscribed under our baby pictures stood for. All of us, Toto and I, and many of our friends had been born in this room.

I felt very much at home and didn't squeal even once during the delivery, which all my older acquaintances had promised me would be an excruciating experience.

That day was a national holiday, and before I went into 308A I listened to the broadcast of the entire parade, which in actuality went by not half a mile from the hospital. There were only three staff members on duty, attending to three mamas in the same stage of the maternity process. Dr. Lin strolled in, for she was concerned about me. She was like a cool breeze and swept away whatever hidden anxieties I'd had. I smiled to her gratefully but not gracefully, gave a push, and my baby girl wriggled out.

So, my baby beat the premiere performance of *The East Is Red* and was born on October first. Dr. Lin also brought the news back to Papa and Mama since she lived in the same compound and knew my parents' hosts.

My parents were overjoyed on two counts: first, a baby on October first and, secondly, a baby girl, which especially pleased Papa. Mama came with flowers, which were disallowed by the nurses on the grounds that some patients might be allergic, and since no one else had flowers, these would stand out. I comforted crestfallen Mama, saying I was really too exhausted and sleepy anyway to look at flowers. We started to plan on a name. There had been a brief cloudburst when I was struggling in 308A, and I had seen a rainbow when I was wheeled out to the ward, so "rainbow" eventually became Mimi's official name.

I told Dr. Lin, who came to visit me next day, about the flower incident. She smiled and said: "I forgot to remind your mother that the days of flowers are over. The patients who come here now are from all parts of the country, and most of them are so poor they can barely afford the cost of traveling. Flowers and the feelings they convey are too far beyond the ken of other patients."

Fan and I bought two first-class train tickets to Tientsin. The compartments would be less crowded, more comfortable, and less smoky. To my amazement, a taxi hired from the hospital maneuvered right up to the door of the train compartment.

Papa, Mama, and Toto were all at the station to welcome the first grand-baby. And when we opened the bundle at home, everyone was delighted, for Mimi, at four days old, had exquisite features, unlike the nondescript cluster of wrinkles most infants have. Ah Po, who'd never had a child herself but had brought up many, gave Mimi one look and announced authoritatively, "That'll be an easy one to bring up!" Toto, now elevated to the grand role of Uncle, kept peeping into Mimi's crib until I shooed him out. He grumbled that I was like a big cat jealously watching over its kitten.

Papa beamed with pleasure the next morning, for Mimi hadn't cried all night. He told me Mama and he had equipped themselves with ear plugs and sleeping pills in preparation for the grandbaby's presence. "I didn't even notice we had a baby at home," he declared. "I'll take care of her from now on!" Ah Po, always the practical one, knew what a mess Papa would leave if he took to baby care. "I'll supervise," she said.

She first demonstrated to all of us, including Toto, how a baby should be wrapped. "None of your fancy frills," she said. "Her fingernails could get caught in the holes." Mimi was dressed in buttonless undershirts fastened on one side with ribbons and made from old cotton shirts ("not out of frugality," explained Ah Po, "but because they must be absolutely soft.") She started cutting diapers from our old winter flannels from the time I became pregnant ("none of your cast-off American sheets; they're too cold for babies"). Mimi, clad in an undershirt and a diaper, was then placed on a small quilted pad; Ah Po had made many of these, to catch the wetness the diapers couldn't absorb. Then Mimi was wrapped diagonally in a square cotton quilt with the lower corner folded upward to close the bundle. The baby's head was framed by the triangular upper flap, which could be tucked down outdoors.

Then she tied up the whole into what she called a "candlestick bundle," for the baby lay as straight as a candlestick inside the coverings. That was the way Chinese babies were supposed to be wrapped: to keep them from scratching themselves, to keep them warm, and to make them easy to pick up for feeding or carrying. Imagine my surprise, however, when I noticed that Mimi's bundle was done up with Papa's silk ties! Ah Po beamed and said one couldn't wish for anything better, for ties were cut on a bias and remained tight after they were knotted but afforded sufficient give for the baby to move about. I eyed Papa and asked if this wasn't sacrificing too much. He replied that he didn't see much use for ties now, and besides he was tired of some of the old ones.

Knowing Mimi would be put on a bottle after my eight weeks of maternity leave, I breastfed her only occasionally, and the process was at best half-hearted on both sides.

To the Chinese, the paternal side of the family is the one that counts, and paternal grandfathers and grandmothers are informally called "*Ye-ye*" and "*Nai-nai*," whereas the maternal grandparents are entitled "*Wai-kung*" and "*Wai-po*," the "*Wai*" meaning "outside" (of the family). That's what I called my maternal grandparents; I'd never met my paternal set of grandparents. But after feeding Mimi a few times, Papa announced to Fan: "She can call your parents whatever you wish, but I'll be her `Ye-ye,' her own grandpa. I won't have that `out-' crap when it comes to this baby." Mama and Ah Po made their own choices: Mama ended up as "*Chin Po*"—my own grandma, and Ah Po as "*Hao Po*"—my good grandma.

I spent a relaxed maternity leave pretending to be a mother. But Mimi seemed to spend more of her waking hours in the arms of my parents, Ah Po, and occasionally Toto than in mine. Mama, charmed by the smiles directed at her by that little mite of a thing, whispered, as if Mimi could understand, "This little thing has what we call peach-blossom eyes. She'll be a handful when she grows up!"

I Go to Clean Up the Countryside

The years following the famine were comparatively tranquil. The frenzied rhetoric of the Great Leap Forward died down, and some attempts were made to right the wrongs to which Rightists and other doubters and dissenters had been subjected. Though crippled in life and career, some of these were decapped like my cousin Ta, and many went back to the *dan wei* they had been expelled from. But they could only hope for the best, for they were still officially regarded as having once attacked the Party.

While recovery was underway, however, and many wished for a mild policy as practiced in the mid-1950s, another sweeping political movement was brewing. As my lifelong friend remarked, "They simply won't give the ordinary people any peace. Every time there's been a couple of years of serenity and everyone has a bite to eat, the Communists think up a new movement to fix somebody up."

This time they came up with the Four Clean-Ups Movement, meant to fix up the rural bureaucracy.

The much publicized People's Commune had survived the roller-coaster ride of the Great Leap Forward and its aftermath, the famine. It emerged with its reputation sadly tarnished and its earlier utopian ideas thoroughly discredited. The commune kitchens where everyone had eaten free were long gone. The rural commune members who survived the famine were organized in military fashion and worked virtually day and night, but aside from a meager supply of grain for food were practically without income; recompense for back-breaking toil in the fields amounted to pennies per day in Chinese currency. Nor were they allowed, in many areas, to raise chickens or vegetables for sale on the tiny private plots they were allotted around their houses, since selling such produce constituted "capitalism." The peasants were grumbling.

Mao, by then, had distanced himself from administrative duties for a few years and, by doing so, managed to gain even more power, as he could disclaim responsibility for further mistakes and at the same time point an accusing finger at others from a position of almost God-like invulnerability.

Liu Shao-chi became Chairman of the State, with Chou En-lai assisting him as lifelong Premier. Thus in name, Liu's wife Wang Kwang-mei became the First Lady. Wang was from an industrialist's family. Her older siblings were my parents' schoolmates at Tsinghua, and from her eldest brother I learned the expletive "damn fool" in English even before I could speak much Chinese. Miss Wang, however, had enrolled in the Catholic university of Fujen and was spotted by high-ranking Communist Party members for her intelligence and social connections. One thing led to another, and during the 1946–1948 civil war she crossed to Communist-controlled territory. Once there, she was so closely courted by Liu Shao-chi that he actually had a unit of his cavalry surround the building Miss Wang lived in and would not lift the siege until she said yes. This tidbit, by the way, was passed on to my parents by the "damn fool" guy, who was now a reluctant brother-in-law to the Number Two man of the CCP.

It was this Madame Liu—better known as Comrade Wang Kwang-mei since women in China don't change their names after marriage—who had the dubious honor of initiating the countryside sweep. As can well be imagined, Wang was a lonely figure among the loved persons of the top leaders; the rest either came from very poor backgrounds, such as Chu Teh's last wife, or had been associated with the revolutionary forces as long as their spouses, as was Chou's very popular wife Deng Yingchao. Being a well-educated person from an immensely rich Westernized family, Wang had to prove she was something besides Liu's wife.

She went to the countryside under a pseudonym and stopped at a place called Tao Yuan (Peach Orchard), where she found the county and village leaders involved in numerous instances of misconduct. These she wrote up in a very long report, usually referred to as "The Experiences of Tao Yuan." The authenticity of her findings could not be argued, and the CCP leaders found to their dismay that many, though not all, of their rural functionaries—trusted Party members—were little better than their generally corrupt and despotic counterparts under the KMT. The Communist revolution had its roots in the rural areas, and those on top fully understood how badly it would shake their foundations if the peasants became discontented. Peasants, after all, make up 80 percent of China's population as well as the bulk of her army.

So the Party Center decided to launch the Four Clean-ups Movement, targeting the leaders of the communes, production brigades, and production teams in the rural areas. The movement itself was carried out by work teams composed of city cadres sent to the countryside with the task of rooting out delinquent local leaders, then transferring the latter to another location or simply demoting them to simple peasants—the lowest of the low in China's hierarchical society.

I wasn't recruited initially, because I was still on maternity leave in Tientsin. My colleagues wrote to tell me that five of our nine-member editorial staff were to leave for a nearby province some three hundred miles from Peking. I counted heads and realized that with me on leave, we were truly short staffed. When I went back to work in due time, the entire building looked deserted, as almost half of the cadres there had gone on that expedition.

Fan was involved in the making of the film version of *The East Is Red*. He and a veritable army of performers, conductors, and composers were being daily transported by chartered bus to a big hotel in west Peking that served as headquarters and furnished canteen facilities and rooms for catnaps. Whenever either of us managed to wangle a two-day vacation we'd go see Mimi in Tientsin.

Papa had made some renovations at home. He converted the now carless garage into living quarters for Toto, putting in a separate entrance to give him more independence and privacy. Papa had a flair for changing uninhabitable spaces into livable ones. Toto's old room adjoining the master bedroom became Mimi's nursery, and when either Fan or I visited we bunked down by her cradle. Those were the days Mimi later referred to as "the only time ever I had a room all to myself; too bad I was too young to enjoy it."

October 1, 1965, Mimi celebrated her first birthday with a cake and one candle at her Westernized grandparents' home, since her little Mama was gearing up to cleanse the countryside. The first batch of work teamers from our *dan wei* had returned after almost ten months of hardships in the poverty-stricken countryside. One third of that batch would remain with the team; the others would return to their old jobs, to be replaced by people like me.

I didn't have too far to travel. I was assigned to one of the more prosperous people's communes in Peking's suburbs; a three-hour bus ride would take me home if needed. "You're always lucky when it comes to going to the countryside," my lifelong friend commented. "For the minorities' research, you went to Yen-pien, which is better developed than most Han areas. Now when it's your turn to go cleaning up, you get assigned to Shun-yi County." In later years he would say, "See what I mean? You even landed in the best place for a cadre school." "Yeah," I retorted, "in a labor camp." But he cited other locations mutual friends of ours had been sent to, and asked me if I would have traded places. "No way!" I said.

The structure of the people's commune was something like this: each county administered several people's communes (usually founded on the basis of former *hsiang*, or townships), which in turn were subdivided into a number of production brigades, then into production teams. The leading bodies at each of the above levels were the local Party committee, which in those days combined political with administrative functions.

I'd been to the countryside quite frequently after that yearlong excursion to Yen-pien, both when in college and later at work. I had also been in the countryside for summer wheat harvesting and so was familiar with the use of sickle and pitchfork. This time around, my chief function was to read aloud to the mostly illiterate peasants the policies and decisions proclaimed by the central authorities, take notes during discussions, and occasionally write up reports that I doubt were ever read.

We were all quartered in peasants' homes. Most Chinese peasants owned their own houses after the post–1949 land reform, as opposed to most city dwellers who lived in houses or apartments rented to them by the government or by their *dan wei*. Typically, the houses of peasants in northern China consisted of two or three rows of buildings sitting in a courtyard with a couple of trees and a latrine in one corner. In poorer regions, the house might be built of mud and thatch; those in our village were constructed of brick and tile. The household head and his wife (and his elderly parents, if any) lived in the row of rooms facing south, therefore the north rooms. Side rooms facing east and/or west were generally occupied by the younger generation, single or married, and provided space for storage or for guests. The work teams were usually housed in the side rooms, for which a small compensation would be paid to the owners.

We had all brought our own bedding, and we now spread it out on the mats covering raised brick platforms, called *kang*, which took up more than half the space in the bedrooms. These *kang*, linked by flues to the cooking stove in the main room, were comfortably warm in winter, but uncomfortably so in summer, since we had to use the stove to boil water. The water came from a nearby well and was carried to the house in buckets slung at both ends of a bamboo shoulder pole. I was by now an old hand (or rather, old shoulder) at carrying water; the trick, or the fun, of getting water was lowering a pail into the well with a flip and a dip. As an old hand from my Yen-pian days, I taught the flip to the novices among us, but some just couldn't get the hang of it. We also carried water for our host families as a mark of courtesy.

We work teamers did not cook for ourselves but were assigned to "eat the rounds" of thirty-some households in the production brigade. This tradition, called *p'ai fan*, or assigned meals, dated from an egalitarian practice in the CCP's early formative years. It had enabled work team cadres to meet all the families, and every house had shared the cost of feeding them—all except the poorest households which were not requested to host. The tradition had by now been slightly modified: we each paid a monthly flat fee for food, which was evenly distributed among the families who fed us.

The food was plain but reasonably good. We usually had thick corn-grits porridge with pickles for breakfast. The mistress of the host household of the day was allowed to take a day off from field work, and she'd spread the word around as to what she'd treat her guests with for lunch. Lunch was the main meal, and we were served either steamed buns, pan-baked bread, or rice—all categorized as "principal food" since in China cereals are regarded as the basis of a person's diet. For entrees, called "subsidiary food," we would have fried tofu, greens, eggs, and occasionally a bit of meat. When and if there was soup, the mistress would bring out a bottle with a gauze-tipped chopstick in it, pull out the chopstick and swash it around in the bowl, leaving tiny sparklets of oil on the soup. "It's genuine hand-milled sesame oil," she'd proudly announce. I think of that scene every time I use sesame oil now, wondering if my former hosts can now afford to pour out sesame oil instead of dabbing it in with a chopstick. . . . Dinner, like breakfast, consisted of thick porridge and pickles and was ready at about 6:00 P.M.

We soon found out that every host family of the day actually regarded it as something of a holiday when the work team came to dinner. They'd plan a treat for themselves on that day, and on other days would go back to their normal fare of porridge and pickles. That means we were being holiday-treated every day.

We team members rose at daybreak, an hour after the womenfolk in the household, who were up and around before dawn. After breakfast at about 6:30 A.M., we and all the field laborers assembled on the threshing floor and the production team leader assigned everyone his or her work for the day. This usually took half an hour. There was a ninety-minute break for lunch and a nap at midday, and the work day closed between five and five-thirty, depending on the season.

People would assemble again in the evenings, one from each family, to assess their work points for the day. It was a nightly routine and the most boring part of collective farming. Each point or half a point (on a ten-point scale) had to be verified and often argued over. We team members also attended those meetings, and I saw many of the peasants, old and young, doze off after the day's hard labor. The meetings adjourned only after every last person's work points were settled. The only ones exempted from both the mornings assignments and the nightly work point assessments were the so-called skilled laborers—the horsecart drivers, the vegetable growers, the village blacksmiths, and so forth. These came under a fixed point system and were assigned work individually. The earnings for a day's work by those with the highest number of points came to about forty fen (roughly 20 United States cents in those days) in some of the more prosperous areas.

Among the hardest-working basic-level functionaries in China then were the production team leaders, who not only labored in the fields full-time but also had to plan the projects, evaluate the finished jobs, settle domestic and neighborhood disputes, and oversee the nightly work-point assessments. Their only compensation for such yearlong drudgery was a few hundred work points on top of those they earned by their own labor. The production brigade leaders, one rung above the production team leaders, received a higher compensation and split their time between the fields and their primitive offices. Higher than this level were the commune leaders who enjoyed better treatment since they were paid either a low salary or some monetary compensation, which made life more tolerable for them than for their brethren in the fields. Under China's authoritarian system of administration they also wielded considerable local power, and used or abused such powers depending on their circumstances and inclinations.

Mao had these commune, brigade, and team leaders in his sights, and we the work teams were supposed to discover and disclose their misdeeds, and to see that they didn't go unpunished. Many work teams succeeded in doing so, with the result that the culpable leaders were chastised; some were driven to suicide. The entire countryside was shaken up, but, with all information tightly controlled on the excuse that this was an "internal movement," very few people outside China ever heard about its existence. As with all the CCP's political and economic mass campaigns, a shocking number of injustices, false accusations, and humiliations were visited upon both the leaders and the peasants. The Four Clean-Ups Movement was followed immediately by the Cultural Revolution, and the pent-up anger and resentment generated by the Clean-Ups would eventually spill over into the Cultural Revolution era and cause unrest in certain areas of the country.

The work team I was in did not succeed, as did some of the others, in exposing any major miscreants; in fact, aside from some minor accounting discrepancies, we found almost nothing wrong in the doings of our production brigade and team chiefs. The headquarters of the overall work team began to pull some experienced members out of our team, leaving the rest to stay in the village and work with peasants.

I was never to know the outcome of my mission this time. Before we made any final summing up, all staffers from the Federation of Literature and Arts and its various associations (like mine) were summoned back to Peking. We were informed our mission in the countryside had to be cut short, because we had to go back and carry out a very important directive issued by none other than Mao Tse-tung himself.

Buses came to pick us up. We loaded our luggage and greeted colleagues. We chatted happily on the way back to the city, not knowing and not suspecting what lay in store for our *dan wei* and ourselves.

PART III

THE LONG NIGHTMARE (1966-)

Peking, Tientsin and the Cadre Schools

"They Always Start with the Artists!"

In the spring of 1984, I joined a group of American tourists on a cruise on the Yangtze River. I was to speak about Chinese culture during the tour; that was right after my first lecturing trip to the United States in 1983.

A well-known Hollywood actor-actress couple was in the group. We sat around and talked about the harsh repression of Chinese artists during the Cultural Revolution; we also talked about the witch-hunt era in Hollywood. The actress, who has since passed away, told me something that was engraved on her mind:

In the 1930s she and a few fellow artists had gathered at the New York harbor to meet a German actress who had escaped from the Nazis. After the German actress disembarked and was greeted by her American colleagues and reporters, she stood with tears streaming down her cheeks and remarked: "Whenever they start, they always start with the artists!"

My Hollywood friend told me she remembered these words when the "Hollywood Ten" affair started, and again when she read about the Cultural Revolution in China. She was glad she could pass this story on to me—to someone in another age group, another culture, another political system. It was one more confirmation of the fact that when dictators and political bigots take to ideological persecution and the suppression of free expression, "they always start with the artists," whatever the era, the country, or the guise in which such persecution takes place.

All work teamers from the Federation of Literature and Arts in the Four Clean-Ups campaign were summoned back to Peking in late May of 1966. The message was that Mao himself had issued a directive in which he charged the federation and its various associations with degenerating to the brink of revisionism—an extremely serious accusation in the mid-1960s.

We learned much later that the federation representing the artists owed its bad name partly to an informer. Earlier that year, the federation had held a costume ball in our auditorium and the Master of Ceremonies had addressed the mixed assemblage of costumed guests as "Ladies and Gentlemen." This ran counter to the proletarian code of etiquette which required that all persons who worked for and believed in the Communist cause be called "Comrades." Furthermore, there were many unusual and allegedly "outrageous" costumes at the ball as well as a number of unorthodox performances between dances. I was an avid partygoer, but it so happened that I was on home leave from the Four Clean-Ups and was staying in Tientsin with Baby Mimi and my parents when the big party was held. I remember feeling quite disappointed when my colleagues told me about all the fun I had missed.

However, the organizers had invited one guest too many—a writer from one of the army cultural ensembles. The goings-on at the costume ball deeply offended his "class sensibilities," so he wrote a report denouncing—and exaggerating—all that had happened there, and accused the organizers of giving free rein to "demons and devils." The report found its way into Mao's hands, and that self-ordained defender of Marxist orthodoxy severely condemned the federation and the various associations affiliated to it.

We, the underlings, were made to criticize the heads of our federation, and cleanse our own minds at the same time. The federation and its associations, while operating under the direct supervision of the Central Propaganda Ministry, were non-governmental bodies administered by professionals rather than by petty bureaucrats. The heads of our *dan wei* were fellow artists who had risen from the rank and file. We addressed them by their names, rather than by their titles (such as "Minister Lu" or "Bureau-chief Hu"), as was the practice in other organizations.

To see people whom one has worked with and rubbed shoulders with day in and day out humiliated and forced to criticize themselves was bad enough; on top of it all was the uncertainty in the air—it wasn't clear how far and how long this movement would extend. None of us suspected at the time that this elite group of artists and scholars would not resume their professions again until 1978—that is, those who remained after the ten-year holocaust of the Cultural Revolution. Some would not live to see that day; others would behave in such a way as to forfeit all professional and moral credibility; and many would be so disgusted with all that happened that they would turn their backs for good on their vocations or their country.

It was also in that fateful period in 1966 that the Red Guards' movement began.

When the first Red Guards started to rampage on the streets, the Federation of Literature and Arts became one of their targets. They swarmed into our building, demanding to be shown the notorious revisionists named by the Great Leader, so that they could "struggle" with these enemies of the people. Our staff tried at first to protect our own revisionists, but under the pressure of thousands of youngsters besieging and overrunning the building day after day, there was no recourse but to bring out the heads of the federation and associations and "exhibit" them every other hour.

It was indescribably painful to see these perfectly respectable people lining up and waiting in the corridor of the office building to be exhibited on an open balcony. Each had a billboard hung on his or her neck, inscribed with some degrading epithet or other before his or her name and a red cross daubed across the name—as is still done today in China on court proclamations announcing the execution of criminals. They would then step up to the balcony in single file and state their names to the crowd. The crowd would roar: "What's your role in the conspiracy against Chairman Mao?" The victims were defiant at first, but as the crowd booed and yelled and became increasingly menacing, they simply mumbled "I'm guilty" to every accusation and question hurled at them. The only exception was the M.C. of that costume ball, who refused to bow his head or utter a single word. He was pushed around a lot, but not beaten.

That was in July, the hottest time of the year, and they were taken out on the balcony rain or shine. As I learned later, however, they had a better fate than the deans and chairmen and professors of arts colleges, many of whom were shorn of their hair, kicked and severely beaten, and had ink splashed on their clothing. Often they were made to kneel and subjected to a variety of brutal and sometimes ingenious torments. One of my friends mentioned years later that he had pains in his neck "ever since the time I was made to wear that necklace of bricks."

In late July our chiefs were ordered to "assemble for screening"—the terminology used was the same as when Papa was taken away in 1952. The difference was, while Papa was a non-Party functionary at a private bank operating under a communist government, the majority of our chiefs were Communist Party members damned by their own Party chairman.

Our building became relatively calm after these main targets of attack were taken out of circulation. Although I felt sorry that they were separated from their families, it was a relief to know that they would no longer be pilloried every day.

This was, however, only the beginning. Just as the saying "they always start with the artists" implied, we were seeing only the tip of the iceberg. Everyone, including those Red Guards, would suffer in their turn, and for many the ordeal would be worse than for those who were the first "exhibits." . . . Meanwhile, among the first artists to die that summer was Lao She, the famous writer of *Rickshaw Boy* and a family friend. Unable to endure the humiliation and injustice, he committed suicide by drowning himself in a lake. Many others would also die by their own hands.

In the Wake of the First Storm

I noticed with apprehension that many Red Guards were beginning to group people by their family backgrounds. Under the post–1949 government, and according to the Chinese Constitution, all four classes represented on the national flag were regarded as being of the "people" (as opposed to being "class enemies"). While there had been discrimination, it had taken a more or less veiled form. Now, suddenly, all people of non-proletarian birth fell into disrepute, and since my family had, of our own choice, been categorized as national bourgeosie, I had sinister premonitions.

Mao gave his personal support to the young Red Guards roaming the streets of Peking. At first, these young kids were only rude, crude, and demanding, not violent; but as their numbers increased, their ferocity grew. Then on August 18, 1966, a mammoth rally was held at the Tiananmen Square, attended by a million young people, each frenziedly waving his or her "Little Red Book" of Mao's quotations and screaming slogans as Mao and his heir-designate Lin Biao waved to them from the rostrum atop the Gate of Tiananmen thousands of yards away. Mao told the Red Guards they should "sweep away" what he referred to as the "Four Olds": old ideology, old traditions, old customs, and old culture.

Immediately after the rally, the mob descended upon the households of peaceful and unsuspecting civilians.

At the time, my husband and I lived in Peking in one room of an apartment in his *dan wei*'s dormitory building, and the compound it stood in was relatively quiet. Then I started to hear stories of Red Guards ransacking private homes in the old residential areas of Peking, of people being brutalized, beaten, and killed. This was so unbelievable, so uncharacteristic of our non-violent society, that everyone assumed that these were only unfortunate, isolated occurrences. But the violence escalated by the day and I realized, finally, that our home in its genteel and patently non-proletarian residential area in Tientsin might also become a target of attack. My Mimi was also there; I hadn't brought her to Peking after being hastily summoned back from the Four Clean-Ups in the countryside.

A foreboding of disaster hung over me as I prepared to go home. Papa and Mama had a telephone then—not unusual for well-to-do households in the big cities before the Cultural Revolution—but getting a long-distance call through was a frustrating experience; it usually took the operator about two hours. Not having a private phone myself, I went to a post office and asked the clerk for our Tientsin number. She eyed me suspiciously when I said it was a home number, for now most people with private phones were becoming targets of the Cultural Revolution. Out of fear, I wrote down a false caller's name—and as I did so I realized why feelings of insecurity or dread made people lie.

No one answered the phone!

I was sweating now. I asked the operator to change the call to the Fengs, who were family friends from the old P.U.M.C. and lived only five doors away from us. Aunty Feng answered the phone. Her voice was calm as she said cautiously, "Yes, the Red Guards came to help us sweep out the oldies. Your parents and your daughter are well. Their phone may have been disconnected. Your father came and borrowed my bike today. I'll tell them you'll be coming."

Relieved that the members of my family were still there, I analyzed the message: Papa had to borrow a bike, that meant all of his numerous vehicles had become immobile; however, since he could still ride a bike, he was free and physically able to move around. But Aunty Feng's cautious tone indicated that "homecoming" would be different and might never be the same again. In fact, that day marked the beginning of the agony of losing my old home, losing my parents, losing some of the most important elements that had kept my life in China on a more or less even keel.

I asked for a day's leave to visit Mimi over the weekend. Since the Red

Guards wore random pieces of army uniforms, I wore Fan's old army top to make myself as inconspicuous as possible.

I got off the train at Tientsin and caught a bus that took me to our street in fifteen minutes. The treelined avenue was still the same, seemingly quiet and serene; it was noontime and no one was in sight. Turning into our driveway, I opened the gate and front door with my own keys. They were all in the living room—Papa, Mama, our housekeeper Ah Po, and Mimi. Papa was stretched out on the couch. He flashed a feeble smile and, in answer to my inquiries, told me that his back was troubling him.

Toto was away from home, still busy with his commitment to the Four Clean-Ups campaign. I learned later that he began to run a temperature the moment he heard what was happening at home. Unable to find an excuse to ask for leave of absence, his terrible sense of helplessness and frustration vented itself in a bout of high fever—in the Chinese explanation fever was a manifestation of the "fire" burning within a person.

Mama told me the Red Guards had come again that morning, so perhaps we would be left alone for the rest of the day. Then she told me how the trouble had started a couple of days ago:

At first, no one had paid too much attention to the blustering demagoguery and random forays by the bands of Red Guards in the neighborhood. After all, this was a peaceful city and the peaceful residential streets were inhabited by peaceful citizens, many of them professionals, or in Chinese terminology, "high-level intellectuals." An aunt and uncle of mine had been pushed around a bit because they were professors at the renowned Nankai University in Tientsin. But, well, young students are sometimes apt to go overboard. . . . That's why no one took it too seriously when the first rumors spread that Red Guards were breaking into private houses, wrecking things, and beating up people—until the evening before they actually came.

One of our old friends went on his bike from door to door to alert his friends that this time it was no joke. He specifically reminded them of the potential danger of having any Western publications and goods at home. Papa and Mama had a brief discussion and decided we had nothing to hide; all was perfectly respectable and lawful—even the 1964 vintage GE refrigerator had been imported through legal channels. The one and only thing they concealed was the big stack of *Life* magazines; this was secreted between the ceiling and the roof rafters.

Ah Po went around the neighborhood the next day to gather information. She was from a very poor family and as a "proletarian" had nothing to fear. She offered to keep Mimi in her care and see that the baby wouldn't get frightened. Papa and Mama braced themselves for the hurricane. And then the door bell rang.

It was over in about three or four hours. During that time all our good hardwood cupboards and their contents (including a complete set of newly purchased Smetana and Dvořák records and Papa's numerous cameras), the big camphor chests, hardwood desks, clothing, fabrics, and the GE refrigerator were loaded on a truck and taken away. These Red Guards had the decency to write a receipt for what they took. The reason they gave for taking these things away was that they were "oldies," representative of feudal and capitalist culture—which included even our kitchen table from Berkeley with its four steel-tube, red-upholstered chairs.

We had never had any gold ingots or jewelry, as many well-to-do families did, and I suppose the ransackers were a bit disappointed. But the most unconscionable confiscation was that of my parent's bankbook. (In China, one deposits money in a bank and is given a bankbook, with which one uses to get cash, or make deposits; personal checks haven't come into use so far.) The one-and-only bank was the state-operated People's Bank of China and the money in Papa and Mama's bankbook represented the savings of their lifetime. Yet it was taken away and Papa was to live in poverty until his untimely death four years later. Mama got five percent of our savings back before her death, and was obliged to say she was grateful. Toto and I received the remaining 95 percent in 1979.

I sat on a stool beside Papa's couch as they told me what they had gone through. They were calm, for they were convinced they had nothing to fear, and they knew it wouldn't do any good to protest. Besides, what had been taken away were *shen wai zhi wu*—literally, things apart from one's body—money, furniture, cameras, and so forth. Such things counted for nothing, so long as all members of the family remained physically unharmed.

I asked Papa, "Now that the money is gone, can you tell me how much we actually had?"

Honestly, I had never tried to find out before; my only concern had been the judicious management of my small allowance and later my small salary and earnings from my writings. I never knew or cared whether we were wealthy people. I *whew*ed when Papa told me the figure. Suddenly all the mystery and tension were gone, and we laughed about the things we could have had. Papa also told me how much each ransacked family had possessed, for there was no longer any privacy about such matters.

I'm still a saver, but the charm of material wealth faded that day with the rays of the setting sun in our living room. As soon as I could, I returned the fifteen hundred yuan Papa had given me to "buy things for him when he might need it," knowing I would be too proud to ask for money after I began earning a salary.

Mimi trotted in and cuddled up to Papa, and we sadly agreed that I would take their pet away. With the constant threat of renewed ransacking, my parents preferred not to have to worry about Mimi's safety; besides, it would look better if I took my daughter away from this "capitalist" family. Ah Po could come with me, for it would be okay for me to retain an old lady to look after the baby. As a servant in my parents' home, her presence could only aggravate their problematic circumstances.

Papa and Mama looked wistfully at my baby and told me she had the time of her life after the ransack: Papa and Mama were excellent bridge players, and they had had a few decks of good playing cards. Whenever they played bridge, twenty-two-month-old Mimi would sneak around their elbows and try to filch a card; it was simply too tempting. The other players would, of course, be alerted to the card thief, and she rarely got hold of a real "*pa-pu*"— her way of pronouncing *p'ai* or card in Chinese.

When the ransack was over, playing cards were strewn all over the floor. While the adults agonized over the wreckage, Mimi gleefully eyed the many *pa-pu* lying around, and chuckled to herself as she stealthily picked up the cards with no interruptions.

I had an encounter with the Red Guards before I left home the next day. They came in and asked who I was and what was I doing in a capitalist's home. I told them I had come to draw a clear line between my bourgeois family and myself by taking away my daughter and assuming charge over the old proletarian lady, Ah Po. They demanded that I criticize Papa to his face to show I wasn't lying.

I stood in front of Papa's couch and "criticized" him. I said something to the effect that the Japanese had given him his back trouble, and that he should be grateful that these Red Guards were so humane as to allow him to lie down when being criticized. I also said that we had all come back from a capitalist country to build a socialist society, but he had been so obsessed with amassing material wealth that he had neglected to reform his thinking. He should pay attention to that from now on . . . .

The Red Guards were satisfied with my "severe" criticism. After they had left, I knelt beside Papa and asked him if he was offended. He and I both knew that it had been an act and he said he could in fact use a couple of ideas from my remarks when he did his own self-criticism. The part about his maltreatment in Japanese prisons was good; he hoped it would save him from beatings at the hands of the Red Guards.

The Red Guards had locked up and sealed the door of the corridor leading to our three bedrooms and the storage room. I asked them to open the door so that I might take out some of Mimi's belongings. They let me in. To this day I can't bear to think of what was done to our home with all my childhood memorabilia in it. Every scrap of paper, every inch of ribbon, had been flung about, littering the floor with ankle-deep debris. Papa and Mama cleaned up the mess after many days. I never had the guts to ask them how it felt to salvage the remnants of what had been their home.

The Horrors and the Absurdities

The shock of what had happened sank in only after I returned to Peking with Ah Po and Mimi, when we were all crammed into our one little room. I corresponded with Papa and Mama regularly. The opening passages of our missives were all full of platitudes about "thought reform" and "drawing the line"—in case the letters were censored. But we got one another's messages anyway, by what I like to call "indirect communication." This function came in handy again after the 1989 Tiananmen Incident when I corresponded from the United States with my close friends in China; they would mention *Waiting for Godot*, and we understood what was meant. It's absurd for any totalitarian regime to assume that it can impose absolute controls over the communications and thoughts of the people it rules.

Our immediate clan lost more than a dozen relatives during that chaotic decade. Although some, such as my parents, died of old age or seemingly natural causes, their deaths were certainly accelerated by the unnatural circumstances into which they were thrown; the others were murdered or committed suicide. No one, not a single one, in my clan escaped completely unscathed, Party members and non-Party members alike, for we were all professionals and non-proletarians, and our turn came sooner or later.

My maternal grandfather—the schoolteacher who had had some land near Shanghai—was already a paralytic in his eighties when the Red Guards dragged him out of the courtyard where he lived with his wife and daughter. He died on the pavement in front of the gate. Grandma, Mama's stepmother, who was in her seventies at the time, was sent back to the village she came from half a century earlier, to live in poverty and disgrace. She, however, was to survive the Cultural Revolution and passed away in her nineties.

One of my uncles by marriage—the one who came to meet us with the landau near Chungking in 1945—committed suicide on the first day of the ransack. He had been labeled a "Rightist," because, unfortunately for him, his calligraphy was superb and he had been asked to write out big character posters during the Bloom and Contend period in 1957. With his calligraphy as evidence, he was "capped" and kicked out of his job at the bank. And when he was again targeted during the Red Guards' reign of terror, he hanged himself from a beam over the bed he shared with his wife.

As for being labeled "class enemies" and "reactionary academic authorities"— a term applied to intellectuals of any prominence or accomplishment—there were so many among our clan that I can hardly come up with an exception.

Back in Peking, Ah Po told me what happened in our Tientsin neighborhood during those fearful days: The housewives among our relatively well-to-do neighbors were driven out onto the streets before the actual door-to-door ransacking took place. They were accused of being "bourgeois parasites"— Mama held the position as a rose garden consultant and was spared that humiliation. Many of these well dressed and neatly coiffured ladies had the hair on one side of their head shorn off in public. In the terminology of the Cultural Revolution this was called a "yin-yang haircut." Among them was Aunty Feng who had answered my phone call so calmly.

No one was killed by this particular group of Red Guards who stormed back and forth through our avenue. But only a few blocks away, one Aunty Chu was killed when an amah in her household, who bore a grudge against her, took advantage of the ransack to tell tales about her. The Chus were beaten up in separate rooms, and when finally Dr. Chu was taken through the living room, he saw his wife of many years hanging from the ceiling with a broken arm. He was told she committed suicide. She was never given a decent funeral.

One of the most appalling stories I heard happened to Wing, a girl from a family we knew well. She had married in Peking and her baby was just two months older than Mimi. The day the nightmare occurred, she had been working late and had not yet returned to the courtyard house where she lived with her husband's family, which included a mother-in-law and a grandmother-in-law. Some evil-minded neighbors falsely informed the Red Guards that the late household head, Wing's father-in-law, who had died a few years earlier, had been a KMT agent and had kept a list of secret agents at home.

When the Red Guard didn't find any list, they beat up members of the family with steel cables encased in rubber, which caused internal bleeding but left few marks externally. The victims thirsted for water, then died soon afterward. There were five deaths in the household, including a married daughter who had dropped by for a visit that day. Wing and her infant son were the only survivors—her baby had been saved by his amah: when the Red Guards had entered the courtyard with death threats, the amah who took care of the baby sensed that something terrible was about to happen and she slipped out carrying "her" baby.

This brutal massacre outraged people in both Wing's and her late husband's *dan wei*, and their colleagues sent up appeals for an investigation to prove the victims' innocence. The object of such an investigation was to protect the surviving members of the family from further persecution, not to bring the murderers to justice. This last was impossible, since Mao's blessing was sufficient to absolve those Red Guards of any atrocity they committed in that period.

I have been asked repeatedly by Western friends in the years after the Cultural Revolution whether or not I feel bitterness toward the Red Guards. Rationally, I don't. Most of them were themselves victims of the Cultural Revolution; they lost their chances for an education, many also lost family members, and when Mao no longer needed them, they were ordered to go "to the mountains and countryside" for political reeducation. There they led a barren, miserable existence. Many lost their lives in interfactional fighting, from illness and neglect in their exile. Those who survived came back cynical, embittered, and disillusioned by their negative experiences in life. They are a lost generation, sacrifices to Mao's last machinations.

As the "Red Terror"—a term actually coined by the Red Guards themselves—continued, Mao personally kept on initiating wave after wave of frenetic anarchism, now focused, however, on his own kind—his own Party officials. The "non-proletarians" were dumped for the time being; licking their wounds, they watched in bewilderment as Mao and his Red Guards went after Mao's erstwhile comrades-in-arms.

Toto accomplished his Four Clean-Ups mission and went back to Tientsin in the autumn of 1966. By then our bedroom quarters had been unsealed and Papa, Mama, and Toto moved back to the two adjoining bedrooms; a side room was reserved for Ah Po. Three other families, among them Dr. and Mrs. Feng, had been evicted from their own houses and packed into our home. These families occupied the living-room-cum-study, the third bedroom (formerly mine), the garage-converted-bedroom, and the rest of the side rooms.

Again, we considered ourselves fortunate. Although the bulk of our more valuable possessions were gone, there were various small things left around that made life more convenient. Staying in our own home, Papa and Mama could reach into nooks and crannies for things such as a bit of wire or a ball of string. Papa's salary was cut drastically and he was only given a subsistence allowance for two people: Papa and Mama. With help from Toto's tiny salary, they managed to get along.

As the Cultural Revolution dragged into its second year, its manifestations became more and more absurd. Mao met the Red Guards umpteen times, waving from the vantage point of the Gate of Heavenly Peace as the chanting mob surged past. It was rumored that gold ingots, pieces of jade, and precious stones were found on Tiananmen Square after such gatherings, presumably fallen from the pockets of the Red Guards who had appropriated them simply as pretty baubles during the ransacking of so-called bourgeois homes. Those Red Guards, most of them ignorant of the innate value of anything or any person, swept through the country leaving death and destruction behind them. Many non-Communist statesmen who had sympathized with the post–1949 government were ruthlessly beaten, killed, or forced to suicide. Mao's lust for personal power and his obsession for mass movements unleashed forces that destroyed much of what he and his comrades had striven decades to acquire and achieve.

On top of all that, his heir-designate Lin Biao and Mao's wife Chiang Ching clambered onto the political stage and introduced some of the most comical aspects of the otherwise tragic Cultural Revolution.

During the initial fervor of the Cultural Revolution, we were expected to wave our Little Red Book à la Lin Biao, flip it backward and forward with a half-raised arm, for that sickly heir-designate was too feeble even to do a Nazi-style salute.

Many in the West assumed that most Chinese willingly became slogan-chanters and wavers of the Little Red Book. Nothing could be further from the truth. This performance was a farce, and every rational Chinese despised it.

Everyone had to buy the Little Red Book—the *Quotations from Mao Tse-tung*—as well as a four-volumes-in-one copy of the *Selected Works of Mao Tse-tung*, also in a red plastic jacket. These two "must-have" books cost me one tenth of my monthly salary, but between my husband and myself we had to have three sets: one each for the office and the third to adorn our bookshelf at home.

We even equipped semi-literate Ah Po with a Little Red Book, for she had to show it when she boarded a bus. She felt so foolish carrying it that she had Mimi hold it. A Party propagandist would have captioned this scene: "Both Young and Old Love Chairman Mao"—and would have fooled nobody. Mao's works were sold by the billions, but that doesn't mean we were one billion zombies.

Because we had to chant slogans and flip that booklet whenever a bus or a tram set out from its terminal, I preferred to walk to the next stop to avoid the ritual. We were expected to go through the same rigmarole before film screenings in movie theaters, and many people deliberately went in a few minutes late; one of my friends mentioned matter-of-factly at the time: "I never see the beginning of a movie anymore!" The chanting and waving was also a requisite when hospitals started admitting patients in the morning, so many made it a point to go in the afternoon. I believe about the only place this inane ritual couldn't be escaped was when one took a train. That was one appointment you couldn't be late for.

No less ridiculous was Chiang Ching's order to turn the entire country red. The order was literally interpreted and carried out, and walls, doors, and pillars on public buildings were smeared with sticky red paint. My colleagues and I groaned openly over the fact that we couldn't locate the stores we wanted to shop in—they all looked alike!

Red–armbands appeared everywhere, as a plethora of Red Guards and quasi–Red Guard groups mushroomed in factories and work units—more often than not as a form of self-defense against continued incursions by student Red Guards. Even Fan, then in his early thirties and quite fashion conscious, pinned one on his sleeve. I looked at the armband in disgust and implored him to take it off, at least at home. Mimi was afraid of that thing, and I abhorred it.

To me, the acme of all absurdities was the replacing of the customary *Wai!* (Hello!) in phone-calls with a ceremonious "Long live Chairman Mao!" I was stupid enough to comment in public "That's nothing new—it's like `Heil Hitler'!" That remark figured later as one of the many crimes of which I would be found guilty.

The Night of the Raid

It was 1967 and the Cultural Revolution was in its second year. According to the pattern of most political movements launched by the CCP, the climax should have passed and the fervor should have begun to subside. But this granddaddy of all movements spawned so many submovements that one had hardly ended when the next began.

While the majority of ordinary people became increasingly impatient and uneasy, Mao's wife Chiang Ching, in her bid for power, initiated the first round of factional turmoil by pitting Shanghai workers against one another. From then on, *pai*—factions—became the order of the day and hundreds of thousands were to die in China as a result of factional fighting—more than those directly killed by the Red Guards.

In artists' circles in China, Chiang Ching's rise to power sparked a spate of revulsion and speculation. A starlet in Shanghai in the 1930s, she had played two or three lead roles in mediocre films under the name Lan Ping. She was notorious at the time for being opportunistic, obnoxious, and catty, and by many accounts had slept her way into some of her film roles. Never rising above the third-rate level, she became discontented and, during the war with Japan, made her way to Yen-an, passing on her way there from one man to another, at least two of whom were known to be high-ranking cadres in the Chinese Communist Party.

Mao had a wife when Chiang Ching got to Yen-an. His first wife had been the daughter of his high school teacher. She bore him three sons, and died at the hands of Kuomintang in the late 1920s. She was enshrined among the immortals of the revolution. Mao had a couple of other women while his first wife was still alive and incarcerated in a KMT prison. Then on the Long March in the mid-1930s, Mao took as his mate a fellow revolutionary named Ho Tzu-chen. She was a tough woman who not only lived through the rigors and starvation of the Long March, but also survived a couple of miscarriages on the way. They later had a daughter.

The union was tempestuous, though, and Ho went to the U.S.S.R. for therapy in the early 1940s. That was when Lan Ping, now going under the name of Chiang Ching, stepped in. As 1942 was a relatively quiet period during the Sino-Japanese War, Mao and his comrades were able to consolidate Yen-an as a revolutionary base. They were joined by many young people, among them a large number of artists with high ideals and exuberant spirits. Mao decided to lay down his guidelines for these unruly acolytes at the Lu Hsün Arts School in Yen-an. Lu Hsün never joined the Communist Party but was highly regarded by them for his scathing indictments of the old regime. *The True Story of Ah-Q* was among his many fine works.

Chiang Ching was among the listeners. Armed with notebooks and pens, everyone sat on one's own stool in an open field while Mao gave his lectures—standing most of the time—from a desk which served as a dais. Chiang started to inch up the aisle, along with her stool. She moved closer and closer to the desk, and by the time Mao had ended his two days of lectures, they were, in a way, already acquainted. Mao was then in his forties, Chiang in her late twenties, and one thing led to another until they were shacked up together in his cave-room dug in the side of a hill. The story of how she wriggled up the aisle on her little stool became the subject of some gossip at the time.

Mao's womanizing had, however, been a controversial topic among his peers as well. His relationship with Chiang Ching even provoked the wrath of the Communist International, for Ho, a revolutionary in her own right, was recognized by that worldwide authority. Mao was severely criticized by his comrades-in-arms, but was allowed to keep the relationship on condition that Chiang would never be allowed to appear in public as Madame Mao, or intervene in politics. These regulations were instituted not only to minimize the scandal, but also for security reasons, as Chiang's background could not be thoroughly verified while Yen-an remained isolated from the rest of the country. Who was she? Was she only an ambitious third-rate actress? Or was she an enemy agent?

When the Communists came to power in 1949, Tang Na, the person she had formally married but later divorced in Shanghai, left China, not so much to distance himself from the Communist government as to avoid Chiang Ching—he knew her vengefulness all too well. Others were less well informed and therefore less fortunate. Reviewing all the political factors of the Cultural Revolution, there emerges a clear pattern of Chiang Ching's vengeance on those CCP officials who had opposed her union with Mao, on artists who held her in very low esteem during her Lan Ping days, or on people who simply knew too much about or thought too little of her.

The above is not meant to discount the political power play that fueled the so-called Great Proletarian Cultural Revolution, but to provide a clue as to why so many upper-crust Chinese were labeled *fan-ge-ming*—"counter revolutionary."

In August 1966, early on during the Cultural Revolution, Mao wrote his own big character poster "Bombard the (Bourgeois) Headquarters" initiating his offensive against Liu Shao-chi, whom he presumably regarded as a traitor to communism and a threat to his own power. Meanwhile, seeing enemies in almost all his old associates, Mao appointed Chiang Ching as a head of the "Central Cultural Revolution Group," which was given supreme authority over political events in China.

Chiang led off her vicious campaign of revenge with an attack on Wang Kwang-mei, wife of Liu Shao-chi and the First Lady of the State. Since Chiang Ching had never been allowed to flaunt herself as a "Madame" of any kind, even after Mao became China's Great Leader, one can well imagine Chiang's jealousy of Madame Liu who appeared regularly at diplomatic and state functions.

In the spring of 1967, Chiang took advantage of her newly acquired powers to have Red Guards abduct Madame Liu to the sports field of Tsinghua University and "strike her down" as a member of the capitalist class. The Red Guards humiliated Wang by forcing her to wear a necklace strung together of Ping-Pong balls—a parody of the string of pearls Madame Liu had worn during a state visit to Indonesia years earlier with her husband.

We, the staff at the various associations, were driven in buses to the site of the so-called "struggle meeting." I was disturbed by the unlimited escalation of the personal attacks that the Red Guards were mounting, but I had to raise my fist and mouth slogans with the rest of the huge crowd while Madame Liu stood on a platform about a mile away.

I never even shared the same square mile of territory with Chiang Ching, but I've heard her voice once over a broadcast, and that was enough to turn off both me and my radio. She had that quavering falsetto affected by sleazy actresses in early Chinese talkies. I heard her on tape on another occasion, addressing a group of Red Guards. "Young Red Guards!" she squawked. "I've already taken my sleeping pills and was ready for bed. Then I learned you are holding this important meeting, so I came, groggy and sleepy as I am. I've come to support you, even though I've taken sleeping pills. Our Great Leader Chairman Mao sends his greetings to you!" And the mob shouted back frenetically, "Learn from Comrade Chiang Ching!" "Salute Comrade Chiang Ching!" "Long Live Chairman Mao!" (In Chinese it was "Chairman Mao for ten thousand years"; he lived to be eighty-three.) "Forever Good Health to Vice Chairman Lin!" (Lin Biao, the heir-designate, was forever in bad health, as everybody knew.)

I guess that by 1967, the criticisms against Chiang Ching must have reached disturbing proportions, because the powers-that-were even coined the charge "Bombarding the Proletarian Headquarters" (paraphasing the title of Mao's poster), to be leveled at anyone who spoke disparagingly of that woman—a crime I must admit I committed all throughout 1967 and 1968.

My personal life, meanwhile, was proceeding more or less normally. In early 1967, a family in the building owned by my *dan wei* left Peking of their own choice to return to their native province, and their spacious three-room apartment was vacated. After some reshuffling by the *dan wei's* housing authorities, I was given a one-room apartment, and we moved out of that shared-room arrangement. We now had a very large room all to ourselves (that "we" including Ah Po and Mimi) plus our own bathroom and a good-sized kitchen by Chinese standards. A few months later, I also found out I was pregnant again.

But the situation at our Tientsin home was becoming a problem. After the first fever of the Red Guards' attacks in 1966, endorsed by Mao, had subsided, attention shifted to inner-Party power struggles, and ordinary residents were left more or less alone. However, many delinquents among the Red Guards who got their first taste of helping themselves to other people's belongings during the "official" ransacks had made a mental note of the more vulnerable households, and repeatedly returned to rob the residents and even beat them up. The police were notified and dealt with them as petty criminals, but the victims themselves were not permitted to offer any resistance. Anything mercifully left over from the 1966 ransack was taken away piecemeal and Papa suffered more slaps and punches than the several he had received in 1966.

To escape those random beatings, he came to Peking and insisted on sleeping on a foam mattress placed in a corner of our big room; Ah Po had another corner bed, and the other half of the room was occupied by Mimi's crib and the *dan wei* bed shared by Fan and myself. Papa was elated when he learned about my second pregnancy, and Ah Po started to feed me as well as our tight budget would allow—I'd never had so much broth made of beef, lamb, and pork bones, with lots of vegetables.

Despite a brief visit from Mama, Papa began to miss her after a couple of months and returned to Tientsin in spite of his apprehension of being beaten up again. I saw him off at the station. He was in good health that year and walked with almost his normal stride, but I was filled with foreboding as I held Mimi and watched Papa melt into the crowd of passengers at the station entrance. Papa did not look back. He never came to Peking again.

The baby and I grew very normally. This time I couldn't afford a self-financed delivery at the P.U.M.C., and besides, its veteran doctors and normal staff had been removed from their posts. So I entrusted my fate to my no-payment health-insurance hospital, which, if the truth be told, was not a bad one at all.

If I'd been pretty fast in delivering my first baby, I was efficiency itself for my second. The actual time of labor lasted about only one hour, and my first impression of my baby boy, Deedee, was of his very chubby hips and thighs! Fan and Mimi came to pick us up and hired a taxi—these vehicles only served hospital patients in those days. Mimi was excited about Deedee and insisted on holding the bundle, although she could hardly get her arms around it. She was fortunately diverted by the joys of her first car ride (actually her second, since the first was when she left the hospital when she was four days old), and forgot about her little brother until we got home.

I lactated abundantly, perhaps because Ah Po kept on feeding me eggs she had hoarded and all kinds of ingeniously concocted soups. There was the rationed milk supply as well, but my own milk was more than even my ravenous baby could cope with. Ah Po heated the extracted excess and fed it, with sugar added, to Mimi, jokingly telling her it was condensed milk. Condensed it was, for Mimi was sated the entire day after drinking only one glass.

We were all on the plump side in the first months after Deedee's birth—until the night of the raid.

Engrossed with my pregnancy and my baby, I had assumed everything was going normally with Fan at his *dan wei*. I was surprised but not unduly alarmed when he told me sometime in April, that there could be trouble. He told me there had been factional strife; it was now focused on him and there were signs that the other faction was planning to place him in "detention."

Such detentions had been going on for some time; the practice had actually been initiated by one of our schoolmates, an acclaimed pianist, and his wife at the time, the daughter of a very high CCP leader. They were both ultra-leftists, and daringly went to the homes of eight high CCP leaders who had been fingered by Chiang and took these men prisoners. These illegal detentions shocked many. Those who committed the act were reprimanded but not punished, and their captives were either taken into proper protective custody or sent home. But the precedent was set that it was revolutionarily correct for just anybody to storm in and carry people off from their homes.

I was surprised and somewhat concerned that such a situation could threaten us, but not overly alarmed, since Fan's only explanation was that there had been some factional conflict. He suggested that he leave town to visit his parents, taking Mimi along, for his family had never seen her. With Mimi as camouflage, his departure would look like a normal home visit. Not knowing the risk he was running, I agreed and packed Mimi a neat little bag.

One of his colleagues, concerned for our safety, came after they had left. This person cautioned me more explicitly than Fan had done. After he left, I checked our room for anything that could be used against us and conferred with Ah Po about what to say regarding Fan's departure with Mimi if the question was raised.

They came at night. Later I learned they had people watching our building to determine the best time to break in. They arrived at around 9:00 P.M. There were six or seven in all; I knew two or three of them. They announced that Fan was known to have "bombarded the proletarian headquarters" and had been criticized at his *dan wei*. They knew very well Fan had fled and wasn't away on a normal home visit. They suggested, menacingly, that I should side with the revolution instead of aiding and abetting a fugitive from revolutionary justice.

Then they conducted a thorough and systematic search of our belongings. Unlike previous ransacks when the Red Guards had their eyes on material things, these people were after material evidence of Fan's *fan-ge-ming* crimes. They scrutinized every page of our books, notebooks, and music scores, even taking out scraps of paper left innocently as bookmarks. They sifted through drawers and took away Fan's old notes and diaries from his army days.

I was first benumbed by the information that Fan was accused of a *fan-ge-ming* charge, then experienced the humiliation of seeing our private life laid completely bare. Fortunately, I had disposed of our letters to each other right after the Cultural Revolution started. I hadn't anticipated such a raid, but having heard stories of private correspondence and intimate letters being made public, I'd suggested we get rid of them, just in case. By the night of the raid, there was actually very little left that might be useful to the raiders. The leader of the group, Chao, observed dryly: "You're prepared, aren't you? Well, I don't blame you."

They left at about 2:00 or 3:00 A.M., leaving Ah Po and me with a home in shambles, and I knew instinctively what I'd have to face at my *dan wei*.

The raiders beat me to it, naturally. When I showed up at the office the next day, I was met with grim faces. Every *dan wei* was split into factions by then, usually one ultra-leftist and one middle-of-the-road. The ultras stared at me in contempt, and those in the faction I had joined looked very stern. They demanded to know why I had abetted a *fan-ge-ming*. I did my best to explain and told them I honestly had no idea Fan was being pursued under such allegations.

Nevertheless, I sensed my vulnerability. In China as I've known it, when one member of a family is denounced as a *fan-ge-ming*, the entire family falls under suspicion. They become targets of open discrimination and humiliation and can't stand up to defend a loved one, because that person is seen as having embraced the enemy's cause. Doing so would make the family member just as guilty as the accused. I had heard someone once remark: "It's easier to be a *fan-ge-ming* than the family member of one." Well, that was my experience, too, until I became both.

Eighty Days and Nights in the "Dungeon"

The night our home was raided and the censuring criticism I received in my *dan wei* were the beginning of my ordeal. From then on, I was in constant dread of what calamities the next day might bring, but I wasn't prepared for the ruthlessness of the blow.

It came at 10:00 P.M. on the night of June 10, 1968. I was in our one-room apartment on the fourth floor. Ah Po had retired to a room we'd borrowed downstairs. Deedee was just a hundred days old, an occasion to be celebrated for a Chinese baby, but we didn't even know the situation of his father and sister.

There was a soft knock on my latched screen door. I opened the wood-paneled door and saw two young women outside. They asked my name, then said they represented the revolutionary masses of the arts colleges of Peking and had come to investigate me. "Open the door!" one of them ordered. I wasn't in a position to say no.

After the women, several young men filed in, one of them obviously the leader of the group. "You know what kind of person your husband is," he said. "And how you have aided and abetted him. It's for your criminal actions that we've come today. You will come with us to undergo investigation of your crimes!" The shock of his last words rooted me to the spot.

"Didn't you understand what I said?" he asked. "Take a few things and come with us!"

I protested that I had a breastfeeding baby; no, I couldn't leave him because I didn't have the money to buy him milk.

They conferred for a moment, then announced: "You can take the baby, your confinement won't last long. All depends, of course on how you cooperate with us. And if you don't obey us now, we'll take necessary measures!" In those days, and now, the term "necessary measures" was synonymous with violence.

I asked them to allow Ah Po to come upstairs "so that I can at least hand her the keys." They brought me the dazed old lady. We gazed at each other, and I told her not to worry, Deedee would come with me. I asked her to find someone to write my parents a letter informing them that I'd be gone for some time. I'd be okay.

Deedee and I were bundled into a covered and curtained jeep. I couldn't see the streets outside, but I knew my city too well; I could guess from the distance and turns exactly where the jeep was heading. We were driven to a small street beside the P.U.M.C. Hospital, my birthplace. That hospital had been renamed "Anti-Imperialist Hospital" in the first fever of the Cultural Revolution; its counterpart, a hospital the Soviets helped to construct in the 1950s, was renamed "Anti-Revisionist Hospital."

By my calculations, the jeep turned into the compound of the College of Fine Arts, and drove to the perimeter of the campus. We were taken into a narrow passage leading to the campus cafeteria. There were padlocked studios and classrooms on both side of the passage. My captors opened the door to one room and told me I would stay here while I was being investigated.

The high-ceilinged but poorly lit room contained a wide bed with a dirty mattress, a square wooden table, a brace of chairs, and a cement sink with a faucet—I had no way of knowing then that this faucet would play a key role in ensuring our survival, that I'd depend on its water to keep myself and my baby alive.

I find it very difficult to give a suitable name to the site of my confinement. It wasn't a prison, or a cell; it was simply a vacated plastic arts studio, used to lock up a mother and her baby. I suppose I could use the word "lockup," but given the anonymous callousness of my guards, given the fact that we were immured day in and day out, that I could be interrogated or beaten any time of the day or night, and that we were not even allowed to step out into the passage until a full month later—calling it a "dungeon" better conveys my feeling about it.

My captors took some money from me for "meal tickets" and bought food for me at the cafeteria whenever they remembered to do so. My eating hours became quite erratic. I would sometimes go for a couple of days without a meal, especially during weekends when my keepers must have gone home to their parents. That summer was a particularly rainy one, and I spent several weekends watching the rain streaming down the grimy windowpanes of the one tiny window and thinking that I would be passing another day without anything to eat. To this day I have a lingering partiality for steamed cornmeal buns spread with sesame paste; that was the best-tasting thing given to me there.

Since I was determined that Deedee wouldn't go without his milk, as his uncle Toto had done when Papa was imprisoned by the Japanese, I drank from the tap when there were no meals and no hot water for me. Thank heavens I was a healthy and productive "milcher"; my son stayed chubby.

Diapers were out of the question. The cloth diapers we Chinese use wouldn't have dried in that dark, airless room, even if it hadn't been for the rainy season. So I toilet-trained him as best as I could, and my baby remained basically clean.

One night, he ran a high fever. That was during a weekend and there weren't any guards around to give me any help; besides, I didn't want to run the risk of having them take my baby away from me. I held my baby close to my body and fed him water incessantly, until his fever broke at around 4:00 A.M. Our bedding was almost dripping with his sweat and mine.

Deedee chuckled for the first time during our confinement. After a month or so in that room, I implored my captors to give us a little air and let us out into the passage. We were let out for about an hour each day, if they remembered to do so. One day, I was sitting on a stool in the passage with Deedee on my lap, when I accidentally overturned a piece of brick with my foot. Ants under it scurried around when exposed to daylight. Deedee gave a happy chuckle. I found another brick and kicked it over. Ants scampered in all directions, and my baby chuckled so much he nearly fell out of my arms. From that day on, I looked for bricks every time we were let out. Those ants were my baby's first "pets," the first moving creatures he saw other than human beings.

For allowing me to keep my baby with me, for letting us stay in a room above ground, for locking us in a room with running water—for such "revolutionary humanitarianism," as my guards more than once described their treatment of me and my baby—I repeatedly and profusely thanked them during that first month in captivity.

Then one day those who had come from Fan's *dan wei* to ransack our apartment on that fateful night in May showed up. The head of the group, Chao, actually smiled when he said: "You didn't expect to meet us here, did you?" I had to admit I even felt something akin to relief when I saw this person. All my captors during the past three weeks had been anonymous and faceless; he at least had a name and a face and a place of origin I knew. He told me they had brought Fan back from his hometown and were now holding him in detention, pending investigation into his "attacks upon the headquarters of the proletariat."

The head of the Public Security Ministry had sent around a directive decreeing that anyone who uttered even a single sentence against "our leaders" should be arrested and imprisoned. I had heard of that directive before I was taken away from home, and that was what I feared more than anything else. Even if I had expressed my antagonism against Chiang Ching at home, with Fan joining in at times, I never expected the time bomb to explode in that quarter. And it could mean death, for I had learned earlier that year that an orchestra conductor in Shanghai had been sentenced and shot in Shanghai for being too outspoken.

My feelings about Chiang Ching and her associates had been unambivalent, and I knew how much I'd said. Everything depended now on how much Fan remembered and how much had already leaked out. I felt a constant, gnawing fear about what he might tell his inquisitors under torture.

I was not particularly afraid when my captors came two times during the night to beat me up. They took me to another room for interrogation and I was slapped or punched on the least pretext, mostly by a young fellow who seemed to be their professional thug. As I said, I didn't fear these beatings, since the questions that went with them didn't concern anything really critical; besides, my parents and Toto had been beaten so many times already, it was only fair that I should take a turn.

During those anxiety-filled nights in the dungeon, I often lullabied my baby to sleep. One particular song I sang was "My Old Kentucky Home," especially the sad and poignant line "then one night come a knocking at the door, and my old Kentucky home, good-bye." What was happening to my own home, to my family? Since that knock at my door, I hadn't heard a single word about Papa, Mama, and Toto; my captors had mentioned off-handedly that Mimi was with Ah Po when they went to fetch more food money and clothing for us, but I didn't know where Fan was. At times it all seemed so unreal. Was I having a nightmare and trying to wake up? Or was my past life only a dream—something that had never existed?

The most unbearable part of dungeon life was the thought that I might really be saying good-bye to my old home, my old life. For some reason I had visions of an empty lot across the street from our Scenic Avenue home where, twenty years earlier, I had played tag and played ball. I found myself thinking: Oh, give me some place, even if only that empty lot, where I can be free, where my dear ones can come together to start life anew. . . . Every night my mind drifted back to that empty lot—a vacant piece of land, deserted and overgrown with grass, but able to hold all my dreams of the past, the present, and the future, if there still was any future for me.

I made a special effort to return to Berkeley in 1983, during my first lecturing trip in the United States. I went in search of our old home on Scenic Avenue. After taking pictures of the house, a thought suddenly struck me. I turned and walked on a few steps: There was the lot, still vacant after thirty-five years. I looked at it a long time. Yes, it was there, still available to a dream from the depths of a "dungeon."

The Reason of No Reason

Apart from the realization that I'd become vulnerable after Fan's flight, I'd honestly had no idea why was I taken from my home. I obeyed my abductors because I had to avoid violence and because I knew I wasn't in a position to fight back. I never got to know the full story of my abduction. I could only make guesses at the conflicting forces at work in that period and put the puzzle together piece by piece as these came to light.

On the second day of my captivity, I gained my first inkling as to where my abductors were from. The young ruffians came to my dungeon and, after the usual political diatribe, commenced their interrogation with questions about Fan's flight. I soon guessed that this was not their affair; their questions were perfunctory, and they were not really that interested in my answers.

This knowledge only made me more perturbed and apprehensive; aside from the concerns of our immediate physical survival, I had to learn why these people wanted me so badly—abducting mothers and babies wasn't a common practice even in those anarchic days. Then the young man who acted as leader of this group disclosed a few days later that they belonged to one faction in the Central Music Conservatory—my own alma mater; the selection of the College of Fine Arts as my detention site was merely opportune. That faction was notorious for being ultra-leftist, and was surprisingly headed by my former classmates and snackmates—from the midnight cooking over upside-down wire wastebaskets—A, B (now married to each other), and C. Another key person in this faction was someone we used to call "Doggie."

In the course of a meandering series of interrogations, my captors mentioned the name of a leader of a powerful middle-of-the-road faction that was then in serious conflict with those ultra-leftists. This leader was also from the Music Conservatory, before he joined the Central Philharmonic as a cellist. I knew "Cello," as I shall call him, pretty well because we lived in the same neighborhood, and he and other young string instrumentalists were in the habit of dropping by for casual visits.

I learned that Cello became very active after the Cultural Revolution started, but he was non-violent, and wangled himself an important position in 1967. I wrote him a letter at the time in an almost motherly tone, half-congratulatory but also half-chiding him for certain things he had said and done. Cello was later ousted from his post and taken somewhere by force, and his office was repeatedly searched by rival factions.

During further interrogations, I realized my captors must have gotten hold of my letter to Cello. While I regretted Cello hadn't thrown away that letter, I was also secretly relieved, since it was merely an impartial personal letter and contained nothing political or factional.

After the interrogations, my captors told me to put down in writing what I had told them regarding the content and purpose of the letter. I worded my deposition with as much dignity as I could muster under those demeaning circumstances. I knew those young scoundrels were only cat's-paws for their masters, A, B, and C, who would eventually read what I was writing, and I wouldn't plead with *them* to set me and my baby free.

As I mentioned earlier, three persons from my husband's *dan wei* showed up just before July and were ushered in by my keeper, who stayed on to take notes. I had known the man, Chao, in more normal times. He seemed to be an old hand at grilling people, or perhaps he had been grilled himself, for he knew exactly which nerve to hit without even being rude. He never raised his voice at me, but had a knack for putting butterflies in the pit of my stomach. He was a decisive factor in the afflictions I suffered, but, oddly enough, after my eight-year ordeal that lasted till the end of the Cultural Revolution, I found I did not hate him.

Chao told me how people from their group had gone to hunt Fan down in his hometown and that he was guilty of the crime of "attacking the headquarters of the proletariat." Fan had given me an evasive explanation for his flight. He told me he'd switched to an opposing faction and a woman from the old faction had reported what he'd said to her about Chiang Ching. I had met that shortish young singer once before and couldn't believe she was so vicious. "Jealousy," Fan had explained. I failed to understand how jealousy could apply in a change of factions, and asked repeatedly what he'd actually said to her. He claimed the only thing he'd said was that Chiang Ching had been a *"hsi tzu,"* a derogatory Chinese term for an actor or actress.

That was all I knew, and Chao's insistent interrogation brought out nothing new. He indicated things were much more complicated than Fan had led me to believe. "Perhaps there's a lot you don't know," Chao said. "And I'm not in a position to tell you."

The beatings at night occurred just about the time Chao's group came. My captors were evidently getting impatient with me, for there was little I could divulge, voluntarily or otherwise, regarding Cello. However, I spent each day in apprehension, waiting to be called out for a beating or for further interrogations.

Suddenly, for reasons I could not fathom at the time, I sensed my captors were no longer pressuring me; but the pressure from Fan's *dan wei* had increased and visits by that group were becoming more ominous, as was the nature of the questions. They were thorough, and it seemed they were well informed about the comings and goings of some of our friends, mostly mine; they knew the length of their visits and their circumstances in their respective *dan wei*.

I felt the net drawing closer and closer, on me in particular. For while I couldn't know what Fan had said to others, I most certainly knew what I'd said to him. And as with all familial conversations, however, I couldn't know what he had or hadn't heard or remembered. I'd summed up all my aversion for Chiang Ching in a four-character Chinese idiom: *huo guo yang min;* it means "a scourge on the country and its people" and is used only for the worst scoundrels. I had applied that epithet to Chiang Ching in the summer of 1967, in the presence of Fan who was reading a newspaper. I don't know if he heard me that time, but once I'd pronounced those words, there were no more bounds to my condemnation of that woman—all in the privacy of our home, of course.

What I feared was that Fan had carelessly passed on some of my observations to his acquaintances. I also knew I was quite probably the author of most, if not all, of his seditious utterances, since I was politically more articulate and better informed than he was. How I wished Fan had told me truthfully what had been going on at his *dan wei*, and to what extent! I could, at least, have known a bit better what to expect.

At this point I'd been kept in solitary confinement for almost two months. I had no access to any information until someone installed a loudspeaker in a neighboring yard, and I could hear snatches of news broadcasts. That's how I learned about the sequel to the May '68 movement in France and, later, the entry of Soviet tanks into Prague.

In August 1968, three young art students were confined in a bigger room across the passage from mine. They enjoyed some measure of freedom since they could get their own meals at the cafeteria and use a normal toilet—but not go home or meet anyone. We exchanged the merest of acknowledgments, but we had a tacit understanding that they would talk loudly among themselves so as indirectly to pass on information to me.

I learned from their conversations that the escalating chaos in colleges and universities across China had prompted Mao to dispatch what were known as "propaganda teams" to all educational institutions in the country. Those teams, comprised of factory workers and, in most cases, unarmed military personnel, were restoring some measure of order. Later, similiar teams were assigned to take charge of every *dan wei* where anarchism held sway, and this included mine, the Musician's Association.

One day, one of the young men across the passage told me a frightening story he overheard in the cafeteria: A propaganda team had moved into one of the arts colleges, he said, and they found it deserted, but then heard desperate rapping on a locked basement trapdoor. The army men pried open the trapdoor and found themselves staring into faces of a group of ghostlike figures.

These people turned out to be some well-known painters who had been missing for several months. They had been put in this real dungeon by an ultraleftist group connected with my captors. They hadn't once been let out since they were locked up there; water and food had been lowered to them. Their captors presumably fled upon learning that the propaganda team was taking over, and those painters hadn't had anything to eat or drink for several days.

The young man was wide-eyed with horror when he told me this story; one of the survivors had been his instructor. "Those men couldn't open their eyes when they were helped out of that dark hole," he said. "And many were hardly able to walk. Even their hair has turned white!" He looked at me and remarked at least we were kept above ground. "Yes, we are more fortunate," I agreed softly, looking down at my bouncing, sturdy Deedee and at my now very, very loose shirt.

That was our private holocaust—a saga of suffering and death that, like the casualty figures of other CCP-engineered political campaigns and later the 1976 earthquake that took a quarter of a million lives—something the world was not supposed to know about.

The months of solitary confinement had taken their toll on me, and Deedee now needed more nourishment than I could provide. He had started to grab pieces of steamed bun or cornbread from my meager meals. Perhaps it was time to set him free. Besides, as I was the person who'd "bombarded the headquarters of the proletariat," maybe it was time to end this tortuous guessing game and shoulder my share of the blame.

The "confessions" the other set of interrogators brought from Fan were becoming more and more ominous. Apparently he had gossiped with people, though I didn't know what he had said. After almost two months of interrogations as to who said what on such and such a day, I knew Chao and company had really gotten hold of some hard evidence on me. They, too, were shrewd enough to notice I was weakening. Whatever the case, they came on two successive days to ask me some innocuous questions, but made a point of telling me that they'd be back the third day for an important session.

That was two days before Deedee turned six months old. I knew I'd reached the breaking point and I had better wean Deedee and let him go. I watched my chubby son all night, reluctant to part with him. But nothing in the world was worth more to me than the assurance that my baby would stay as healthy and sturdy as he was today. I personally was ready to accept any fate assigned to me.

When Chao and company arrived, I was desperately resolute. Chao initiated the interrogation by saying, "I believe you weren't misled by the fact that we talked about irrelevant issues for the past two days."

I agreed I had no illusions on that score, but before I could take the plunge, Chao asked very quietly: "Would you like to tell us what you've said concerning Comrade Chiang Ching, or do you want us to tell you?" Disconcerted, I asked for a break. That was only five minutes after their arrival. We then actually played briefly with Deedee and even talked about the weather!

Then I was ready. "No," I said, "you don't have to work on me anymore. I planned to tell you today anyway. Deedee will be six months old tomorrow, and it's time I let him go . . . "

Chao made a show of being alarmed, or perhaps it was genuine: "Heavens! Are you contemplating . . . ?" He meant suicide.

I understood what he was driving at and laughed to his face: "Hardly! I'd never do anything like that!"

Then I continued, "I've no idea how you got it, but I did say a lot about Chiang Ching. Do you want me to tell you right now or would you prefer that I reported it some other way?" At the time all pronouncements against the "Proletarian Headquarters" were considered contaminating and any form of "dissemination" was prohibited.

Chao waved his hands and said I would do best to save them for someone authorized to attend to such sensitive matters. I said, "Let me say this. I still can't see anything wrong with what I've said or thought, even though it's supposed to be a crime. At any rate she's Chairman Mao's wife, and attacking her verbally, even in private, is tantamount to attacking Mao. So, she wins, whatever the rights and wrongs. If you ask me, I'll admit I've lost, but I'm not guilty." (All this will make little sense, perhaps, to my Western readers, but that's the way it is under any totalitarian regime, East or West.)

"Will I be executed?" I asked. "I've been out of touch with the outside for almost three months." Chao emphatically negated that possibility and promised to update me on current policies the next day. He cautioned me once more against contemplating suicide. "I have no such intention," I replied.

I felt a strange serenity come over me, even as I wondered why they had saved that crucial question for this day. Was it another bluff? And how odd the timing! Well, there was no way out now, and I was prepared to be carted off to prison. I didn't know at the time how close I was to that fate.

Chao and company returned rather late the next day, and told me I could leave this place now and go home with Deedee, under one condition: I would be kept under twenty-four-hour surveillance by two women in his entourage. They would stay in our apartment but eat their own food. That was a rather singular form of house arrest, but no more unusual than the times. I accepted their conditions.

I asked Chao if I would be sent to prison afterward; I wanted to know what lay ahead for me. He smiled faintly and informed me of Mao's recent decision not to imprison offenders in word only. The order had been issued less than a month ago and was made known to functionaries only the preceding week. The timing was most fortunate for me, he said.

So, Deedee and I could go home for the time being. I still had my keys, and the two women went home with us that evening. Ah Po wasn't in the apartment, neither was Mimi. I decided to go to the rooftop balcony to see if they were there.

As I stepped out of the doorway opening on our flight of stairs, I beheld the stout figure of Ah Po ambling from the doorway to another staircase and holding a little girl by the hand. I walked quickly toward them, placed Deedee in Ah Po's arms, and picked up the dainty girl I hadn't seen for almost four months. The homecoming was strained, however, for my custodians were there listening to everything we said.

I must now draw the curtain, however, on a sad story, the details of which I found out much later. As related earlier I had sensed my captors suddenly lose interest in my connections with Cello after the nocturnal beatings. I expected more trouble in that respect, but they rarely bothered me again. Years later, one of my young violin-playing friends met me in our neighborhood and asked me where I was when Cello died. I was stunned; Cello's death was news to me. He then told me that Cello had leapt from the roof of the building where he was incarcerated, killing himself instantly. Still shaken, I asked if he remembered the date of that incident. He reflected a moment and said it must have been around July tenth of 1968. I was beaten on the night of July fourth. With Cello dead, his case had been closed and my captors had no more need for me.

A Crack in the Mirror

No, this title has nothing to do with Agatha Christie's; her title is *A Mirror Cracked*. Mine derives from an ancient Chinese idiom that implies a rift in a couple's relationship. In one version of that idiom the mirror is mended. In another, the damage to it is irreparable. Mine finally broke.

I had no illusions that I'd be out of trouble once I left the dungeon; in fact, that was only the beginning of my long ordeal as a *fan-ge-ming*. The CCP differentiates counterrevolutionaries with past offenses, such as those who had collaborated with the Japanese invaders, from those currently guilty of transgressions. The former are called "historical *fan-ge-ming*"; the latter "active *fan-ge-ming*." I belonged to the second category, and it was frightening to hear crowds everywhere shouting "Down with the active *fan-ge-ming*!"

I couldn't speak freely to Ah Po with my custodians constantly around. But we did it in snatches and managed to pass to each other some news. From home it was all bad.

Papa started an insistent cough after a long talk with Toto on a damp night; Toto was also being screened at his *dan wei*—for being my brother. Papa and Mama were investigated by the neighborhood committee for the same reason. Papa's cough, when examined, proved to be a symptom of lung cancer. To this day I blame myself for Papa's untimely death, and for all the pains and sorrow suffered by my dear ones, young and old.

I was allowed to write very brief letters home that were openly censored by my custodians—"for your own good." I also had to write confessions with regard to that four-character idiom I had applied to Chiang Ching. These they did not censor, but sealed up with gingerly caution as though the words on those sheets of paper were deadly viruses. They told me only authorized persons were permitted to read what I put down; people who lacked cast-iron convictions were likely to be infected by my reactionary thoughts.

I also had to write frequent thought reports on how much headway I had made toward repudiating my own sins. Very little, I'm afraid, since I still insisted I didn't know how I'd been been wrong. She'd won, and I'd lost, and that was that.

There was no news of Fan, but Chao told me he was being kept under surveillance at their *dan wei*. Fan's salary had been suspended; mine had also been withheld for a few months.

With four mouths to feed, I was at my wits' end while waiting for the first repayment. I resolved to sell some books. I picked out a complete set of the Chinese Materia Medica. It had been painstakingly transferred from Tientsin for safekeeping, but it would have to go. Ah Po took the books over to a neighbor, and their teenage son was entrusted with the mission of taking them to the used-book store. I remember this set brought in twice the price of a complete set of Lenin's works in Chinese that we'd sold earlier. Mao's works wouldn't even fetch the price of scrap paper.

The next day the youngster galloped into our apartment and, right in front of my custodians, dived for Deedee. With one hand he surreptitiously thrust some money under Deedee's bedding. He played boisterously with Deedee and crowed: "You're worth twice as much as the other set of stupid books!" My heart leapt—that was enough to keep us in food for two weeks!

By now I had realized that Chao and company were using me in an unexpected way. Their faction had been infamous for their brutality, and with propaganda teams coming to every *dan wei*, they needed a witness who could testify that they'd been non-violent. I had no choice but to play along.

I had been at home for about a month, when my custodians hinted that I could be transferred again, this time to an office building in their music ensemble. Knowing that the propaganda team would take over my own *dan wei* in a few days, I inquired why they bothered to transfer me. Chao replied that was precisely the reason for the transfer; I'd be safer with them, since the incoming team knew nothing about my circumstances and it was hard to predict how they would react when they found they had an active *fan-ge-ming* on their hands. "It's for your own good," they kept parroting.

Resistance would have been futile. I asked and was allowed to have a few words with Ah Po in private. We discussed what to do with Deedee, whom I still breastfed. She suggested I take him along, not because she couldn't take care of both children, but because Deedee would be a safeguard for me—as he had to a certain extent been during that trying dungeon experience. I agreed, reflecting that having Deedee with me would also give me more excuses to contact Ah Po. She also observed that, as much as she loathed the presence of my custodians, she knew they were not evil people. They would not harm Deedee.

We pooled some money so that once Deedee and I had left, Ah Po could take Mimi on a short trip to Tientsin. Ah Po had now become the only adult in the household able to move around freely, and I needed her to tell my folks in her own words that we were physically sound, and I, mentally sane. I believe that was the time I took a picture with my children; they were plump and sturdy, while I appeared older than I do now, thirty years later. My eyes, especially, looked weary—even a forced smile could not disguise the misery in them.

Deedee and I were unhurriedly transported to the building they'd mentioned. I had of course visited it several times before, in the capacity of Fan's loved person, to pick up his salary while he was out of town. This time I came as a prisoner, or almost.

I was told I could buy my own meals at the canteen if I wanted to. No way! I shuddered at the thought, for how would I know which people had sold out my husband or were holding him in captivity? I told the women how much I could afford for food and what my preferences were. I found out they actually took pains to line up early, and were very pleased when they managed to get me the top choice of the day. Deedee was now eating more solids, so they even bought him snacks for the fun of watching the seven-month-old baby eagerly exploring every new kind of food.

One evening those two women took Deedee in their arms and went out for a stroll. I grabbed the chance to clean up some of the disorder a baby usually creates. They came back all smiles and asked me: "Guess whom we took him to see?!" I suddenly realized with a pang that Fan could be in the vicinity and I stared at them expectantly. "We took Deedee to see his father," they announced, evidently pleased with themselves. "He's on a different floor. He was astonished how well Deedee has turned out."

For the entire duration of Fan's flight and detention, a matter of more than six months, that was the only time he saw his infant son. In the days that followed, he and I never talked about this surprise visit and the torment it must have caused him afterward. Perhaps it's not in the nature of Chinese to talk about their trials and tribulations; we learn more from onlookers about certain personal events than from those who were involved.

The days of captivity in that office room were brief, lasting just two or three weeks. One day I was politely asked to the next room, where a man in uniform, a man in overalls, and the omnipresent Chao were waiting. The two strangers introduced themselves as members of the propaganda team assigned to my *dan wei*—the Chinese Musician's Association. They had learned about me and contacted my custodians; it was time I returned to my own colleagues.

I'd been in absentia from my normal life at this point since the June 10 abduction, passing from captor to captor and from one lockup to another for almost five months; I left my *dan wei* accused of abetting my fugitive husband, and returned an active *fan-ge-ming* guilty of unmentionable sins.

How was I to face the crowd, or, as we say in China, the masses? I asked the propaganda team members. They promised I would not be abused or humiliated, but told me candidly I'd have a hard time. Some in the rival faction were jubilant that I must now eat humble pie; others in my own moderate faction were angry that I'd let them down. They told me they'd anticipated my anxiety and tried to neutralize some of the extremists. "Try to keep a low profile," they advised. "We'll help to ease the tension."

It had to be done, sooner or later. I braced myself for the uncertain encounter with my colleagues and took the plunge. I was presented as a person who had repented and turned over a new leaf. The moral was that anyone who had similiar problems should place their trust in the propaganda team and be as free to come and go as I now was.

In the meantime, my entire *dan wei* had fallen from grace along with the Federation of Literature and Arts and other artists' associations on account of Mao's pronouncement that they had slid to the brink of revisionism. All had been evicted from that prestigious building around the corner of old Bridgeman, never to return again. All our association's staffers were now stationed in an arts' college. Now that I had returned, only three others were missing. These were former chiefs of the Musician's Association who had been placed in confinement by the CCP's Central Special Cases Committee because of past associations with people who had personal knowledge of Chiang Ching. No one ever knew what the charges against them were.

It was a most difficult reintegration for me. I encountered hostility, both genuine and phony, as well as sympathy, also real or pretended. I could also sense much nervousness, which was in fact normal under those circumstances. After sitting quietly in the meeting room for a couple of weeks, I realized that, branded though I was, I could still find relative tranquility. Not all attention was focused on me all the time; everyone had their own worries. I was simply banished to a limbo, temporarily at least.

It was then that I found a mental haven in window shopping. I'd go out during the long lunch break and rove from store to store, sizing up the goods or inspecting the food. I rarely bought anything; I didn't have the money. More important was the fact that I could melt into the crowd and find freedom and anonymity among strangers—nobody there would know I was a *fan-ge-ming*.

Winter was approaching when a propaganda team took over Fan's *dan wei*. I was apprised of the development by Chao, who visited me at home. He reminded me that he and his group had made good on their word; that they hadn't mistreated me, or so he claimed, and that they'd handled my case properly. I knew he needed my testimony, for they'd be questioned too. I promised I'd tell the facts, no more, no less.

Chao predicted Fan would be allowed to come home very soon after the propaganda team settled in at his *dan wei*. He also admitted Fan had become a hot potato for his faction; they were unwilling to let him go now, but worried that the entire abduction affair (including the holding of Deedee and myself up in a room on the third floor) would be used against them by their opponents.

One evening, Fan came home after more than six months' absence—ever since the day Mimi followed him in happy innocence onto the train. Now Mimi shrank back from him; Deedee didn't know him anyway; I behaved unnaturally—I didn't know whether to comfort him or to break down crying. The practical Ah Po busied herself laying out some food and making him comfortable. He was exhausted, naturally, and had been granted a couple of days off to recuperate.

We didn't have our talk until about a week later, after Ah Po and the children were fast asleep. I gave him an outline of my experiences and what I'd confessed; he told me where he had been kept and how he had been beaten. Fan hated Chao, for Chao had always sat there smoking, looking on as others in the group worked him over, and eventually calling a halt to the inquisition and playing the good guy. Chao's composure unnerved Fan, who named Chao the most evil of them all.

I asked Fan about what was to me an unsolved puzzle: Exactly what had gone wrong, who had sold him out, and on what grounds? I told him if I'd known the seriousness of the situation we wouldn't have fallen into the trap in such a brainless way. There was no way out now, but I wanted to know what actually had happened.

Fan said it was simply a matter of the woman in the chorus snitching on what he'd told her.

"Why did you talk to her about such confidential matters, and why would she tell on you?" I still didn't get it.

Fan hesitated. "Because she was jealous of the girls in the opposing faction."

"You mentioned jealousy before; why should she be jealous?" I asked in all innocence.

Fan didn't answer that question. Instead, he said: "I was afraid she'd blackmail me. She still can."

"About what?" I asked.

"About the baby," he said.

"What baby?"

"Her daughter. She's only a few months younger than Mimi."

"What has her daughter got to do with it? She has a husband, hasn't she?" I was totally confused.

"Well, it's hard to say whose . . . "

I still didn't get it. We only had a night lamp on, and in its dim light I saw an inexplicable expression on his face. . . . Suddenly, everything clicked, and I exclaimed "*What?!*"

He shushed me. I gaped at him, unable to believe the inevitable conclusion.

"Are you saying her daughter could be yours?"

"It's hard to say, but her husband apparently hasn't noticed anything."

"How did the kid get to be yours?" (The usual way, stupid!)

Silence.

"You mean you *slept* with *her?!*"

Again silence.

It was beyond belief: "How could you sleep with someone who's in the same *dan wei* as you?" (As if it made any difference.) "How could you sleep with someone whose husband you've met?" (The ultimate betrayal!) I heaved a big sigh. "You mean when you told me about your friends you were actually sleeping with them or one of them?" (My friends were just friends; friends were not to sleep with!) "You said her daughter was only a few months younger than Mimi. You mean you did it when I was . . . "

He admitted it had happened when I'd gone to Shanghai during my pregnancy, and when he was supposed to be actively involved in the rehearsal of *The East Is Red*. That woman was newly married at the time. (Ugh!)

"Was it on our bed in the old apartment?" (As if it mattered.)

"No, it was at her home when her husband was at work." (That was better.)

I was more surprised than angered, for there were countless descriptions of adultery in the books I'd read. But that was fiction; and when it happened to people I knew, that was gossip. I had never imagined it could happen to me, and when we were both facing an uncertain fate. The timing couldn't have been worse.

However, for Fan, the timing couldn't have been better. I was exhausted mentally and physically by our political ordeal and the last thing I wanted now was a domestic scene. I told him that since he'd told me about this affair of his own volition, I would not fight with him over it. I kept my part of the bargain and never mentioned this affair again, even when we quarrelled. But the big chill had set in. It couldn't be helped.

I saw Chao one more time. It was ten years later, after the downfall of Chiang Ching. I was back at work and my *fan-ge-ming* case had been overturned. I was on my bike speeding along on a willow-lined lakeside street when Chao rode past me, going in the opposite direction. I braked and looked back, and noticed he not only hopped off his bike but turned back, pushing the bike by hand. In our bike culture that indicates great sincerity and deference.

I got off, too, and waited for him to come over. We went through some preliminary inquiries about our respective health and my children. Then he started to talk about the Cultural Revolution years in an apologetic way and indicated I now had every right to rebuke him to his face. I stopped him, saying it was over and done with. "However," I added, "isn't it good I can say openly now that Chiang Ching is a vile *huo guo yang min* creature?"

He looked at me quizzically.

"Don't tell me you didn't read my confessions!" I exclaimed.

Chao admitted he had really taken the sealed envelopes to people in charge of such cases, and was shown a few lines afterward only to impress upon him the sensitivity of my case.

On impulse I told Chao things weren't well between Fan and myself; he knew about Fan's past and present affairs anyway. He took the opportunity to ask if I remembered that he had refrained from telling me about that part of Fan's state of things. I said I did and thought it best that Fan had told me himself.

"It wasn't fair to you," he stated. "You know, I was strongly criticized for taking you and Deedee up to the third floor. I hope you don't hate me for that."

"No, why should I? It's all finished anyhow, and we're all wiser now."

A few years later, I learned Chao had gotten cancer and passed away. By then Fan had moved out, so I only had Ah Po to tell. She gave a slight shudder. "I was really afraid of him," she said, "even if he was always the quiet one. Just sitting there he gave me the creeps."

It's strange that I don't hate this tormentor; perhaps, as in all witch hunts, there are ultimately only victims, no heroes and no villains.

Before the Big Deportation

The year 1969 marked the twentieth anniversary of the founding of the People's Republic. Many were secretly hoping that our leaders would show signs of relenting and bring a little peace of mind to the weary and wary civilians.

Our battered family also hoped for some respite from the constant pressure. As I recall, my own family of four, Fan, Mimi, Deedee, and I, went together for only two outings, ever. Once was when we took Mimi and Deedee, now more than a year old, on their first visit to the Summer Palace in Peking's suburbs. The young neighbor who had helped me sell books for food also went along; he was a favorite with both children. Mimi ran joyfully along the Long Corridor—a work of art, as its beams and ceilings were painted with flowers, birds, human figures, and scenery along its entire length, so that it looked almost like a picture gallery.

Deedee showed little interest until we rented a rowboat, then he got all excited, especially when we sculled out onto the lake.

Encouraged by the success of this outing, we sallied forth again a few weeks later, opting, however, for a less expensive excursion. We went to the Tiananmen Square to see the lights on May Day evening. Both children sported the Mao button fashionable at the time—hardly buttons, actually, since they were four inches in diameter and looked like saucers. In my young, young Bridgeman days, I had come here with my school every International Labor Day (May Day) and October first to dance on the square. We had done the "collective dances" of those days, then watched the fireworks with innocent rapture.

This time, Mimi behaved out of character. She took one look at the immense, vacant square in the twilight and piped "I want to roll!" Without warning, she lay down on the flagstones and rolled over and over, short hair, short coat, dangling Mao button, and all. Deedee scrambled out of his father's arms and followed suit. Being basically shaped like a melon in those days, he could hardly get himself to roll. We laughed and hugged each other on the square. Then strings of light bulbs blazed on all sides—on the Great Hall of the People, the Historical Museum, the Cenotaph to the People's Revolutionary Martyrs, and on Tiananmen itself.

The two *fan-ge-ming* parents and the two babies who had accompanied them through flight and abduction walked around together, basking briefly in the tenuous tranquility. Then it was time to go home. That was on May 1, 1969, and I now realize with a shiver that twenty years later to the day, both my children and possibly their father were on that square again in the earlier stages of the fateful 1989 students' demonstration.

Papa's cancerous growth had stablized somewhat, but I was still not allowed to visit him, since I was under "mass surveillance"—meaning anyone could report on what I did, and I had to stay around to be surveyed.

Six days a week, I had to be in my *dan wei* at 8:00 A.M. sharp (Fan's *dan wei* decreed live-in studies for everyone, and were only allowed to go home over weekends). There was one phase of the campaign called "Purging the Class Ranks." Hour after hour, people at my *dan wei* sat together, drilling and grilling each other one by one. Everyone had to divulge to the entire group of professional acquaintances every detail of his or her private life.

I was let off easily, for I was now firmly classified as a *fan-ge-ming;* whether or not I had committed other petty sins was of little interest. I was already an open book, or in the political vernacular of the times, a dead tiger.

But one woman was interrogated in a sickening way. She had gone to Taiwan briefly with her husband and her newborn baby in early 1949. For whatever reasons, they returned to mainland China soon afterward, and unfortunately, the infant child died on the way. Some of my overzealous colleagues started questioning every detail of the baby's death, how the body was transported, how it had been wrapped and buried. The now-aging mother's reluctance to reply only incited those ghouls to greater insistence. How callous could people get, I thought. This went on until a propaganda team member stepped in to stop this senseless interrogation.

During breaks we were expected to do the "Loyalty Dance," which consisted of singing a childishly simple song "Dear Chairman Mao, the red sun of our hearts . . . " and doing dance steps fit only for kindergarten toddlers. No one objected when this *fan-ge-ming* chose the last row where she only needed to move her lips in sync and do a halfhearted stomp and shuffle.

The most nauseating ritual of all was the periodic celebration of "Our

Great Leader's Newest Instruction." By now, Mao Tse-tung had been elevated by Lin Biao—his heir-designate—to the status of "Great Leader, Great Commander, Great Instructor, and Great Helmsman," and Mao's pronouncements were glorified as the "Highest Instructions." Since Lin was of dubious literary cultivation, his exaggerated encomiums to Mao's greatness usually ran into a string of "-ests" and sounded like a broken gramophone record.

Whenever the Great One issued some directive or other during this era of insanity, it was instantly touted as opening up a new frontier of Marxism-Leninism. We were expected to rally on the streets, beating drums and gongs and waving paper flags pasted onto little bamboo sticks. Everything was fine as long as He released His Newest Highest Instruction in time for the morning news; we'd all dash to our *dan wei* and spend the first hour or so listening to the broadcast and scrawling slogans on strips of colored paper, which were then affixed to the recyclable bamboo sticks. We'd usually set out on foot by 10:00 A.M. and walk, shout and wave our little flags for an hour. On luckier days we were allowed to break ranks on the streets nearby, and we usually dispersed into the shops, for a longer-than-usual lunch break.

By some sadistic whim, however, the authorities were more likely to release His Instruction at 8:00 P.M. than at 6:30 A.M.

My heart sank every time the radio announced there'd be important news on the evening broadcast. I was usually exhausted after coping with the day's political tensions and after pedaling my bike thirty minutes to get home, and was grateful to sit down to a frugal but always filling meal prepared by Ah Po. Then I would play with my kids for a short time before tucking them in bed. It meant a couple of hours of peace, if there weren't any Highest Instructions; if there were, the entire neighborhood spewed into the streets as everyone rushed back to their respective *dan wei* to parade late into the night (however, we skipped the flag-making for the evening rallies; no one could see them anyway). I'd get home around midnight, but couldn't afford not to show up back at my *dan wei* the next day at 8:00 A.M. sharp.

A few days after Mimi and Deedee's romp on Tiananmen Square, we were made to march through the streets again for what was to become known as the "May 7th Directive." That directive would cost me more than six years of my life and many years from millions of other lives.

The directive was based on an annotation Mao had made on May 7, 1969, on a report submitted by some county authorities in a certain province. All the county's cadres had been concentrated in a rural district, and these civil servants reportedly became quite skilled at farm labor. They were said to have enjoyed their life so much that they brought their entire families from the towns to the farms. Mao took a fancy to this idea and proposed that all unoccupied people in the cities should go and work in the countryside. The rationale was: "We also have two hands, so we shouldn't live idly in the cities."

We had premonitions when we rallied in the evening of May 7, 1969. We could tell the new directive would in some way affect our fate, though it would be some time before we felt the full effects of this latest caprice of Mao's.

All of us who had been staffers at that building with the flowered-ceramic-plaqued facade were soon facing mass deportation. The entire federation and the associations affiliated with it had not been functioning for three years. All our publications had been suspended, all our professional members were in political trouble, and all our superiors were being shunted from one special investigative committee to another.

By early September, we of the arts associations were the first to go. But by going first, we had the pick of the work sites, and despite three moves within the next fourteen months, we never left Hopei Province, where both Peking and Tientsin are located. Another advantage of being the first to leave was that we didn't have to give up our apartments, so we had homes to come back to during vacations. Those who left a couple of months later were sent to much more remote places and were ordered to give up their Peking homes—sometimes even while parents or children still lived in them. Told to "pull up their roots," entire families packed up and departed, many uncertain of where they would be going and none knowing if and when they would ever come back.

Our first site was a group of villages around the Kuanting Reservoir, just north of Peking proper and not far from the Great Wall. The reservoir was a product of Sino-Soviet cooperation, but the site had been poorly chosen, for the lake behind the dam dried up before the relationship did. When we arrived there in early autumn, it looked more like a puddle than a lake.

We were given little time to pack heavy clothing for the notoriously bitter winters around the reservoir. I figured that after living in Yen-pien, latitudinally much further north, I should do all right with the coats I possessed. I was wrong.

While Yen-pien was nestled in a mountainous region, the reservoir area was situated just south of a barren plain, across which freezing winds from Siberia swept after funneling through a pass in the mountain range to the north. We had a taste of those winds when our newly formed "May 7th Cadre School of the Federation of Literature and Arts" held a schoolwide meeting on October 1, 1969. Although it was only a three-mile walk to the meeting place, every step forward was a struggle. The more slightly built women crouched in the lee of some of the bigger men to avoid being blown off their feet.

This windy October first was an unforgettable day—just as unforgettable as October 1, 1959, ten years earlier, when I wore a cream-colored gown for the chorale in Beethoven's Ninth Symphony, performed to honor the Tenth Annniversary of the founding of the People's Republic of China, and the day exactly five years ago when I gave birth to Mimi in the room where I myself was born. But all I could think of at the time was whether my winter clothing would be adequate over the next couple of months.

For the next six years, we were to exist as members of companies and platoons. We no longer belonged to a *dan wei*, for ours had ceased to exist. We were still paid the same salary, however, and were allowed to keep the only I.D. we Chinese had at the time—a work I.D. card. It enabled us to purchase train tickets to Peking, but served little other purpose.

All those from the now deflowered building (no pun intended, since its ceramic plaques had been pried off as "oldies") went to the same cadre school, along with people from some disbanded *dan wei* such as the Music Research Institute and the Music Publishing House. Each former *dan wei* made up platoons of thirty to forty people; three platoons in turn formed a company.

We were separated into groups of threes and fours to take up lodgings at peasants' homes, which were not too different from those in Peking's suburbs. Our former *dan wei* had two or three couples who now had to live apart, each with others of their own gender. I always felt sorry for them when one came to the other to ask for some toothpaste or soap. On the other hand, they knew where their spouses were. Many of us didn't know even that much.

We set up our own kitchen and canteen, and the school planned to build dorms for us. The hardest work in those months was making mud bricks for our future housing. We mixed tons of clay with straw and water, shaped the muck in rectangular molds, and left the blocks to dry on the ground, to be stacked up later for construction. Mud-pies would be a better name for them. We made thousands upon thousands of these bricks before the cadre school abandoned the site for good three months later.

As winter approached, one of our main concerns was warm clothing. Some bought goatskin overcoats at forty yuan apiece, which, despite the rank odor of the poorly cured pelts, really kept out wind and cold. I couldn't afford one, so I had to rely on the G.I. parka made over by Papa, of all people. He had become curiously addicted to sewing in 1965. After making over the uphol-stery of four of our padded armchairs, he had discovered to his delight that the cover of our cherished G.I. parka consisted of two layers of cloth. He carefully took apart the two layers and made a new cover from the better parts of both. Those armchairs, along with other furniture, were taken away in August 1966, "to join the Revolution," as people jokingly referred to the Red Guards' expropriations, but the parka remained, and became my best protec-tion against cold weather for the next few years.

I huddled in my parka and moved around constantly to keep from freez-ing. My goatskin-clad colleagues probably felt warmer than I did, but they were quite a sight: someone had the bright idea of tying shoelaces around all jacket and trouser cuffs to preserve warmth and keep out the cold. All shoelaces quickly disappeared from the shelves of the village store. We were also inspired to gird up the waists of our jackets and coats, which some did with extra-long belts, other with lengths of twine, and many with bits of straw rope.

I recall how, as the winter deepened, the local peasants looked on with amazement and hilarity at the fashion show presented by us cadres every morning. We wore fur caps which had seen better days (women tied a woolen scarf over the cap or hat), surgical-type face masks, strings and ropes every-where they could be tied, a motley assortment of old boots and padded shoes, topped off by huge and shapeless goatskin coats.

As for me, after being teased by Papa long ago for wearing a cotton-padded hat, I never put one on again. I protected my head with two layers of scarves, one a knitted two-yard-long affair to wrap around my neck, and over that a store-bought head square tied under my chin. I also had a straw rope around my midriff. It was hard work in the morning, getting geared up like that.

One day during a meeting, a woman suddenly remarked: "You know, I looked around this morning, and saw us looking no better than a pack of beggars." She ticked off our trendy trappings as listed above and complained, "Can't we at least get rid of those straw ropes? It isn't as though any of us can't afford to buy a belt or some twine!" She added lugubriously, "Where I come from, straw ropes are worn only at funerals!" (The traditional mourning garb in many parts of China was, and still is, a gown made of coarse, undyed off-white cloth, gathered in at the waist with a length of hemp or straw rope.)

We looked at each other, then nearly raised the roof with laughter. The next day, the village store was emptied of twine and belts.

I managed to survive with my parka, partly because we were on the road again before the coldest weather set in. Sino-Soviet relations had been strained for some years and border clashes had repeatedly broken out. In the late autumn of 1969, Mao's heir-designate Lin Piao issued his "Order Number One," citing the immediate danger of a full-blown Soviet invasion. We were solemnly informed that the plains just north of us were honeycombed with tunnels wide enough for two trucks driving abreast. There were reports that tanks and artillery had been emplaced in caverns in the mountains, which would become a forward defense line should the Soviets cross the frontier. We were told each to prepare a white sheet for camouflage (in winter) or as protection against nuclear radiation, and the men were assigned to stand guard at strategic spots, such as on the villages' main road, in the village store, and at our canteen, when or if the expected invasion began.

The rumors became wilder and wilder. We were told that the Soviets had pinpointed our area as the swiftest shortcut to Peking; they foresaw Soviet tanks simply bucketing across the plain and sweeping into the Chinese capital. The local peasants would evacuate or stay on to wage guerrilla warfare. As for us three hundred or so cadres, we would be better out of the way. Accordingly, we were hastily relocated to a county between Peking and Tientsin—and mercifully allowed to stay in Peking for one day.

By then, people throughout the city were evacuating in response to Lin's order. Since those who left now were doing so as part of a military operation, they were simply uprooted and shipped out. Fan's *dan wei* departed for a site close to Tientsin, and that left only Ah Po and the children at home. Ah Po hung on in the Peking apartment as long as she could, on account of the central heating, then took the children to join my family in Tientsin.

She told me much later that the city's population had been noticeably depleted by the time she left. Apartment buildings echoed with vacancies. Peking was fast becoming a ghost town.

Cadre School I, II, III

The dam-site village was the first address of our Cadre School. The local postman must have heaved a sigh of relief after we were gone; the village people hardly ever wrote or received letters, and his daily deliveries consisted largely of two to three copies of the *People's Daily* for the school and the office of the Production Brigade. Even though the mail volume of Chinese city people was quite low by Western standards, ours created a hefty load for the village postman who did his rounds on foot.

For us, however, moving to School II was hardly a reprieve. While we were spared the arctic chill of School I, we found ourselves stuck in a mudhole. This spot, in Pao-ti County, Hopei Province, was better off financially and geographically than the place we had just left and, at first, everybody felt reasonably happy. But we were burdened with many more chattels and goods than before. When we had left the city for Cadre School, no one had suspected our departure would be permanent in any sense. So much of our *dan wei's* property—vehicles, office furniture and supplies, and many other items—had been placed in warehouses. The office building itself was first used by a military unit, then was snatched up by a publishing house that appropriated the premises.

After "Order Number One" was issued, even the warehouses had to be vacated, so we were saddled not only with our own personal luggage, but also with whatever we could salvage from our institutional property. The Military District of Hopei Province had taken this cadre school under its wing, which was the reason all three sites of our own school were situated in Hopei. They found places to store much of our office property, but some of it had to be stacked in our crowded living quarters in peasant homes.

Although we were still under the guidance of Mao's all-powerful propaganda teams, the teamers themselves had changed. Those from factories had gone back to their *dan wei* and families when we were sent to the first cadre school, and military personnel took over. Quite frankly, these soldiers weren't bad guys; they'd been assigned a job and they just did what was required of them. Dealing with us cadres from the arts profession was for them an eye-opening experience, and provided them with a few titillating moments further down the road.

We were again grouped in threes and fours and put into peasant's homes. It was in the early months of 1970 when we arrived at Cadre School II, but the weather was mild compared to the early winter we endured at Cadre School I. The ground was semi-frozen, so transportation and communications weren't initially a problem, but as spring advanced, all roads and paths turned into quagmires and even the much looked-forward-to walks to meals became a squelching drudgery. On top of that, food supplies were getting scarce on account of the bad roads, and we were fed sorghum, boiled cabbage (napa), and some pickled *hsueh-li-hung* (*brassica cernua*, a leafy green plant) morning, noon, and night; even cornmeal was regarded as a treat.

Our company of musical professionals soon found an application for our talents. We did a song when we lined up for chow; the men would chant "boiled cabbage" as a bass accompaniment, the women trilled "sorghum," and all chorused "*hsueh-li-hung*" as the cadenza ending the performance. I was the author of the cadenza. We told the kitchen staff no offense was intended; we only sang the song to fortify our spirits and our appetites.

That this county was at all willing to accept more than three hundred house guests—who brought their own board—was because it had a relatively small population due to the marshy farmland, of which there was much to spare. We planted and harvested one crop before moving on to Cadre School III.

What did one do in a cadre school? We got up at daybreak and took turns toting water for ourselves, and for our host family as a token of appreciation for their hospitality. Then we usually went from our canteen after breakfast straight to the fields. Lunch was sent to us in the fields several miles away, and considering the Chinese fixation for hot food, the kitchen staff did wonders getting it there while it was still warm. If nothing particular came up that day, we were usually left to our own devices in the evenings after a day of hard manual labor.

However, to make the reports to the Military District look better, we still held criticism meetings. People in the ultra-left factions were criticized one month, while the moderates might be criticized the next. It all depended on the political climate. I was singled out for another round of criticism, and it wasn't a surprise attack, for the propaganda team members coached me beforehand on how should I play my part.

I knew my colleagues had boned up for the meeting, as we did for the others, culling sentences and paragraphs from newspaper articles. About eight or nine people delivered their prepared speeches while I sat with pad and pen and pretended to take notes. Next, I gave a "speech of acceptance"—accepting all the criticisms and pledging to reform myself. But after I'd read a page or so, also copied from newspapers, I ended it with my I-admit-to-losing-but-not-to-being-guilty conclusion. I said something to the following effect: "While I've carefully listened to and taken note of all your criticisms, I'm sorry none of them apply to my heinous sins. How I wish I could impart to you my reactionary utterances [here the teamer, who must have reviewed my files, gave a warning cough], so that you could tell me exactly where I've been wrong. I can't figure it out myself since I'm still so reactionary. I hope one day to rise to a level of class consciousness where I'll not only admit I've lost, but also that I'm wrong."

I was never called up for criticism again, nor did I ever admit to being wrong.

We plowed and sowed under the tutelage of a local peasant—he earned his work points by instructing us how to farm. One of my colleagues, a stickler for detail, insisted on sowing beans at exactly the same distance, running back and forth to compare the rows. He should have brought a ruler. And when it came to weeding the rows, no one knows how many seedlings were pulled out as weeds and how many weeds were preserved as productive plants. These were minor drawbacks, however, in the worthy cause of reeducating us ignorant city people—which was the reason for setting up cadre schools in the first place.

The revolutionary masses began to get a few days of home leave after a few months, though all persons currently under surveillance were denied that privilege. There was nothing I could say. But I found some slight solace in the tribulations of the lucky home-goers. All had to walk some five miles to meet the local bus, and if they came back on a rainy day they were really stuck. Either the bus wouldn't run or it got bogged down in deep mud; and when it did arrive, the passengers were faced with a squishy five-mile trek, carrying a bulky bag of provisions from the city.

The most exhausting manual job we did that year was harrowing, or "dragging," the muddy paddies after the harvest. I had already learned to push a loaded one-wheel cart and pedal tricycle carts, and had stood hours on end in knee-deep water planting rice seedlings—all considered heavy labor. However, those were nothing compared with dragging, a job usually assigned to oxen and the most able-bodied men. Our platoon, having less men than other platoons, had to put any woman weighing over 120 pounds to playing tug-o'-war with that drag. It was excruciatingly hard labor, pulling that toothed contraption with a man standing on it making it comb deep through the thick mud. After hauling that drag for a few hours, one didn't have the strength left even to talk.

Our male colleagues had been forewarned not to wear shorts—a taboo in that part of the countryside. But while they cursed the prudishness of the local peasantry, they were treated to an unusual spectacle. Nobody had told us that both men and women here went topless in summer! By women, I mean all those who were married and had children, not the presumably virgin girls and the new brides. The older women all wore long trousers, but nothing above that.

At first, all our cadre school inmates, whether male or female, kept their eyes averted from the village matrons. Finally, a male colleague broke the embarrassed silence, since educated Chinese rarely talk about physical nudity in public. "Of course," he acknowledged, "I was as curious as everyone else to see half-nude females. But after the last couple of weeks, I must admit they're not the visual feast I'd imagined they would be."

Feast or no feast, that was the last summer for free ogling of semi-naked women. After the women had covered themselves up once again, and after we'd coaxed a meager harvest of sorghum from the soggy fields and dragged the rice paddies, we were slated for another move.

The move was partly an economic solution, for to keep three-hundred-some cadres—scattered among approximately a dozen villages—fed, clothed, and otherwise provisioned was a herculean task and transportation vehicles were overburdened. The other reason was that morale had become very low; there had even been a suicide in another company in another village. While the cause of that suicide was primarily a love affair gone wrong, the political implications were bad.

As a result, the Hopei Military District offered our cadre school a corner in a long-established prison camp, and the offer was accepted. The artists' associations totaling three-hundred-odd people were now joined by the Writer's Association staff, which had been sent to another site a year ago. We now became an army of some five hundred cadres, augmented by a number of family members who had no other place to go. Eventually some sons and daughters also joined their parents here as more and more young students were sent to remote parts of the country; it was better to be with family, even if home happened to be on the margin of a forced-labor camp.

I was grateful for that change, since Cadre School III was much closer to Tientsin. A bus ran daily from the labor camp to the city, and once I arrived in the city limits a five-cent ride got me home. Papa's condition had worsened, so while others had almost a week's furlough in Peking during the transition, I spent most of that week in Tientsin.

When we were driven to the new school site in our own buses and trucks, we were elated by the sight of the open expanses of good land and the wide smooth-flowing canal in front of the main gate. But we also observed the embrasured pillbox at the entrance and the armed guards. For most of us, it was the first encounter with a labor camp inside the People's Republic.

We were somewhat subdued as we drove through the gates, but perked up again when we learned our company had been given the most livable quarters on the site. I believe this was done in consideration of the fact that almost 40 percent of our company were females. We slept in classroomlike dorms in a large two-story building with running water and normal indoor toilets. Life was basically civilized, and reminded me of my college days. Oh, yes, there was reliable electricity. I've forgotten to mention that while we used oil lamps in School I, School II had had electricity, although the supply was weak and erratic.

The cadre school authorities consisted of mostly new propaganda team members who had been with us from Cadre School II days. They warned us not to venture outside our perimeters after dark, because the guards were unused to seeing people roaming around at will and had been authorized to shoot on sight anyone who didn't carry a pass. Many ex-convicts and their families also lived within the campgrounds, because they preferred to be free people in this semi-free environment rather than go back to their hometowns to face discrimination and humiliation. These people were accustomed to camp regulations and observed them out of habit, whereas there was no telling how we newcomers would react if a guard challenged us. Several months later the curfew was cancelled, when the guards had learned to identify the cadres. "They're not dressed fancy," the guards concluded. "They're just dressed different, and they walk different, too."

We had almost no opportunity to meet the convicts, however, because their living quarters were in another part of the vast camp and our fields were not adjacent to theirs. Occasionally, I'd see a couple dozen of them filing past the far end of a field; all men, cropped and clean-shaven, wearing black cotton-padded jackets and trousers. The sharp-eyed among us told me they had the name of the labor camp printed across the back of their jackets. We were informed these were mainly petty thieves and burglars plus a few rapists. Their sentences were considered light, so escape attempts were rare.

This was the late autumn of 1970. We'd started out from Peking from the dam-site school in September of 1969, and in less than fourteen months had stopped in two counties before finally landing in a labor camp—formally named the "Labor Reform Farm of the Tuan-po Marshlands."

On the first Sunday at the camp, a few of us walked a few hundred feet to the dike that doubled as a highway, and we gazed downstream to where the wide river swept into the Yellow Sea; a brace of water fowl flapped out of the reeds growing along the banks. Ever intellectuals, we were simultaneously reminded of the lines from an ancient Chinese writer: "Sunset clouds soar with a lone bird, autumn water blends with the horizon."

I was to learn a great deal by these autumn waters over the next five years.

The Last Words Between Papa and Me

During the move from School II to School III, as I mentioned earlier, everyone was given a week's vacation—revolutionaries and counterrevolutionaries alike—and I spent mine mostly in Tientsin. I knew Papa's condition was critical when I saw that his once bold and flowing handwriting had become a shaky, fumbling scrawl.

I wasn't as shocked by the change in Papa's appearance. He was tall for a Chinese and had sired a five-foot-eleven son and a five-foot-six daughter. A former soccer star, he had remained athletic in his movements despite his back pains. And although not particularly handsome, he had attracted people with his striking personality and wit. When I saw him this time he was very thin, but he looked better than the walking skeletons I've known some cancer patients to become.

But I was not prepared for the groans of agony I heard throughout the night—the groans of a strong man who could no longer bear the pain. He was injected with analgesics by Toto, who had learned the technique, although only at reasonable intervals. Between injections the pain must have been excruciating. I couldn't sleep. I listened to the groans in the next room and cried in my pillow—cried for Papa's pain and for the ordeal Mama and Toto went through daily. I suffered as much as Papa did, but the pain was in my heart.

Papa didn't enter a hospital; no one, not even our doctor friends, advised him to do that. At the time of his illness and eventual death all qualified doctors and specialists had been ousted from their jobs. The capable middle-aged doctors had been dispatched to the countryside, not to practice medicine but to raise ducks and pigs; the more elderly physicians were made to scrub floors and clean toilets in their own hospitals or write self-denunciations. All the doctors we knew in Peking and Tientsin were labeled "reactionary academic authorities." When a surgeon we had known quite well vomited blood and died in a matter of hours from an undiagnosed stomach cancer, going to a hospital was, to say the least, futile.

The other reason was the humiliation. In those insane years, one had to declare one's class background when registering for hospital admittance, and with the "capitalist" yoke we had put on our own necks, Papa would, at best, be assigned to a pallet in some corridor and given the minimum attention or none at all. At home, he could at least be among his loved ones, minus myself. Meanwhile, as Papa, capitalist or not, was well liked in his factory, the medics there wrote out prescriptions recommended by specialists in cancer treatment among our friends, and helped us procure the medicine.

Papa retained his mental acuity to the last day. He had a diary in which he recorded all symptoms and medications, and even the intervals between pain attacks. The last entry was written the day before he died.

Even in his condition he tried to keep abreast of developments in the outside world. He advised me to sell an old-fashioned Grundig tape recorder I had bought for music research; he told me cassettes were coming in and the old-fashioned recorder would soon be replaced. That was in 1970 when no one else I knew in China was yet aware of cassette recorders. The first person to tell me that such a device existed was a dying man.

I noticed Papa fretted every time Mama fed him. He preferred Mimi, for he said she was more light-handed. I watched my six-year-old daughter seat herself at her Grandpapa's bedside and feed him deftly from a bowl, like an old hand. I knew that was something I should be doing, if I were a free person; I felt a bit of solace in the fact that I had given him this granddaughter to comfort him in his last days.

And his last days passed in poverty. I used two days of my precious one-week leave to return to Peking to get things I needed and straighten up my uninhabited home. I found a few things I could sell for cash to buy something useful for Papa. I took out the gold necklace my parents had given me for my wedding, but put away the silver chain for Toto who was still single. I figured no one could afford now to buy his bride a silver chain. I also took a small carpet as well as the only heirloom I had—a twenty-four-carat gold bracelet presented by my paternal grandmother to one of her daughters, who in turn passed it on to me, as a daughter of the Chen family.

I went to the jewelry and antique store that had been reopened recently on a corner of Peking's "Fifth Avenue"—Wang Fu Ching Street. The clerk gave me a better-than-expected price for the moth-eaten carpet, thirteen yuan to be exact; and a fair enough price for the gold necklace—twenty-five yuan, or half the original price. When I showed him the bracelet and asked what he would give for it, I could see he was really interested. The offer was sixteen yuan. I smiled grimly and took it back. He told me that was the best price for old jewelry and tried to persuade me to sell the bracelet, saying that the country needed gold. I pocketed the thirty-eight yuan for the other two items and told him: "You realize, I wasn't going to sell this in the first place. That's all I have left. I was simply curious to know the price of keeping a memory."

I crossed the street and bought an ounce of ginseng for Papa. I also got some little things worth one or two yuan each for everyone else at home, happily parting with the proceeds from my carpet and gold chain.

I felt a little guilty when I told Papa how I'd gotten the ginseng, for I felt I should have given up everything to help, but hadn't. "I thought I'd keep the silver chain for my future sister-in-law," I explained, "and the bracelet for Mimi or Toto's future daughter." Papa told me that even ginseng wouldn't help him now. He died before he had finished taking that ginseng.

I left for the cadre school when my time was up. Papa and I didn't know whether we would ever see each other again.

One month before he died, I pleaded for a two-day home visit. At the time the teamer in our "company" was a fairly decent man. He was intrigued by my heinous crime and had questioned me about it—not censoriously, yet with care to show no sympathy, if indeed he felt any for me. He told me the majority of the revolutionary masses were to have their quarterly home leave the following week. "I'll let you go after they leave," he said, "but be sure to get back before they do. No one will miss you, and I won't be accused of being too lenient with you."

And so I had an unexpected chance to see Papa again. He still looked all right, as cancer patients go, but was much weaker. He needed a haircut badly, so I volunteered, kneeling beside him on the bed since he was unable to sit up in a chair. Aside from one or two complaints when the crude shears I used tweaked a tuft of his hair, he was quite pleased with the effect.

As we sat facing each other perhaps for the last time, I hesitated, then asked:

"Papa, I've always wanted to ask you one thing . . . "

"Yes?"

"Have you ever regretted . . . that we came back?"

He must have thought about it a thousand times, for his reply was firm and clear:

"No, I do not regret it. Many unexpected things have happened since we came back, but until the last few years it wasn't all that bad. I've been thinking, what would I have decided at the time if I had known the consequences? Given the times and our ideals, I think we'd still have come back to China."

I was suddenly flooded with a sense of relief; perhaps that was what I had hoped he would say.

Then he continued, emphasizing the words: "Whatever the circumstances, don't regret what you've decided to do in your right senses."

That was the best advice Papa ever gave me. I still face many predicaments and many crucial decisions, and I can only rely on my own judgment. Looking back, certain things could have been handled in a wiser fashion, but since I take responsibility for my own decisions, I don't regret them.

That was the last time we saw each other. Mama told me that Papa insisted that she take down the calendar for the incoming year, 1971. "I won't live to see that year," he asserted. He died on December 28, 1970; he was only sixty-three.

I knew the end was coming and kept a small bag packed at all times so I could catch the one-run-per-day bus service. Two cables arrived at the same time; one said he was dying, the other said he was dead. I asked for, and was granted, permission to leave. The "bus" that day was an open truck. I sat in a corner of the truck and wept into my long scarf all the way home. What with the wind and the tears, my face was all puffed up the next day at the funeral parlor, and remained swollen the next three days.

The fire was out in our rooms; so was the fire in our lives. Papa was laid out and Mama, Toto, and I sat through the customary night-long wake. The balance was broken, the symmetry was gone. I felt very lonely, very small.

A group of friends and relatives accompanied Papa from the house to the funeral van waiting in the street. Toto told me afterward that the spectators were much better behaved than a couple years ago when an old family friend died—street children had hissed and booed and thrown stones at the funeral procession of a "class enemy." Now they watched the proceedings in awed silence. Toto and I mutely thanked all who had come, then accompanied Mama in the hearse to the crematorium. It was the last time the four of us rode together.

Swing Left, Swing Right

The year 1971 began ominously. The class struggle was intensifying and more and more counterrevolutionaries were being uncovered. With Mama and Ah Po in sound health at home in Tientsin along with Toto and my children, I found no excuse to ask for a leave of absence. I didn't go home until another twelve months or more had elapsed, and in later years my heart tightened every time Deedee referred to these years as "the time you were never, never at home." I was deprived of my children's early years, for I was a *fan-ge-ming*.

Even as I had been penalized for belonging to the political right, a curious blow was dealt later to the so-called ultra-left. It had to do with a submovement against a so-called "May 16 Group." Reversals in political fashions brought under scrutiny those who had been inordinately active in the early years of the Cultural Revolution. This new phase in the series of movements was more involved with factional affiliations than with individual connections, so the numbers of people affected were larger.

It was also at about the same time that the former heads of the arts associations who'd been taken into custody by the Central Special Cases Committee were sent back to their former *dan wei*. These men and women had not been mistreated, but they had been isolated for two to three years, and it was more intimidating for them to reenter the perilous vagaries of the political scene than it had been for me after only a five-month absence.

The upshot was that with the addition of newly uncovered "problem" people and the recently returned Special Cases, the once relatively minor contingent of *fan-ge-ming* like myself became larger than ever before. And since none of us were permitted home leave, we left-behinds found ourselves in vastly increased and, for the most part, convivial company.

The teamers were not allowed to leave so many problem people to their own devices for any length of time, such as during the Chinese New Year. So some dedicated activists in our company gave up this favorite family-reunion season in order to watch over us, and the teamers took turns going on home leave. Apart from the inborn Communist anxiety that problem people might conspire to sabotage and sedition, there was also the innate Chinese suspicion that *hu kao*—sexual "fooling around"—would become rampant if so many single males and females were left unsupervised.

This last was, in truth, a realistic concern—if our supervisors believed it were any of their business, which many apparently did. What with hundreds of non-senile men and women kept apart from their spouses for years on end, and what with the collective labor that daily brought them in close contact, things were bound to happen. Pairs had been discovered under stacks of sorghum stalks and underground in cabbage cellars.

The teamers were not being overly zealous; they were simply doing things the Chinese way. According to an ancient Chinese saying, "Thieves must be caught with the booty, and adulterers by the pair." And they caught the offenders in very compromising situations. Moreover, those teamers were, most of them, semi-literate low-and-middle-ranking military officers with less than refined inclinations, and while they felt flattered to be acquainting themselves firsthand with China's most outstanding poets, writers, musicians, dancers, and dramatists, they relished even more the prospect of bragging that they'd seen with their own eyes so-and-so crawling out of wherever-it-was with his or her pants down. It was probably such humiliation, more than any political persecution, that deterred me from indulging in any relationships during those long and lonesome years.

I was naturally denied home leave, so I waited anxiously for those who were able to leave to clear out. After living in crowded conditions for a couple of years, I was only too glad to have the big room all to myself. I also asked all who were leaving to lend me their books during their absence. With a pile of books, an empty room, and my own bedtime hours, I was as happy as could be expected under the circumstances.

Possibly it was then that I became used to a solitary existence, and there would be many more solitary phases in my life, by option or obligation, after that. But I've never felt lonely when I've been alone; perhaps I am too often reminded of the title of Hardy's book, *Far from the Madding Crowd*.

However, I still had a husband to think about. Our last meeting had been in late 1969, when my Cadre School moved from site I to site II, just before Fan's *dan wei* left for the countryside.

One day I received a very unexpected letter from Fan. He wanted to discuss getting a divorce, he wrote, and cited couples we knew who had terminated their marriages. By chance, I'd written him at almost the same time and our letters crossed. I didn't reply to that letter of his, for I wanted to see first how he'd answer my normal letter. An uneasy silence ensued, and abruptly as he'd raised the issue, he dropped it again.

That letter came in October of 1970. In later years, my lifelong friend, who knew more than I did about Fan's philandering, compared dates with me. He told me that letter had apparently been written when the teamers at Fan's *dan wei*, ignorant of his earlier liaison with the singer who betrayed him, put the two in the same platoon. It was soon rumored that they had "rekindled the cold ashes," which could have been why he wrote me that letter.

Fan once asked if he could come and visit at Cadre School III, which was out of the question since there was no place for him (or us) to stay. Apart from the lack of accommodations, there was also the humiliation. It was bad enough being denied home leave; asking one's spouse to come visit would have been tantamount to admitting one was no longer a normal and free person. Bad as our position was, we weren't ready to regard ourselves—and have others regard us—as convicts pleading for visiting privileges. As far as I know, not one of us "problem people" asked our spouses to come and visit. It was, for us, a matter of pride and self-respect, and we stuck to our self-abnegation with all the fortitude we could muster. Fan did not comprehend my reasons for not welcoming him, and he concluded I must be having an affair. I found it increasingly difficult to communicate with him.

Meanwhile, in addition to the normal routine including the daily labor we were now accustomed to, cadre school inmates were made to continue the search for hidden *fan-ge-ming*. Everything one had done during the first years of the Cultural Revolution was placed under scrutiny. Being a dead tiger myself, I felt totally at ease as I watched the once active ultra-leftists being grilled.

I got an unexpected jolt, however, while one of our former drivers in the Musician's Association was elaborating on the activities of the faction he belonged to. It was an ultra-left group, but I held no grudge against him personally; and since he was more of a clown than an activist, my mind was wandering elsewhere, when something he said jerked me back to the meeting proceedings.

The driver, Li, had mentioned my name. "I feel pangs of conscience every time I see her," he was saying. "And if I ever meet her son again and he calls me 'Uncle Li,' I'll die of shame. I want to get this thing off my chest. Besides, the whole business was a bore. It was hot as hell, sitting on the straw behind the matting screen, and I felt like sneezing half the time we were holed up there."

While I sat motionless with astonishment, a commotion arose. The majority of those in the room looked puzzled. Others asked: "What straw?," "Why a screen?," "Where was that, and when?" Meanwhile, two women who had been core members of the driver's faction and, unfortunately, also alumnae of mine, hissed at him: "Why mention this? That was a one-hundred-percent revolutionary action! We haven't given you permission to talk about such things!" The two motioned in my direction saying, "Anything we did with regard to her was correct, since she's a verified *fan-ge-ming*."

The teamer presiding over our usually languid meetings was very stern as he called the room to order. "I hope you all realize this was no small matter," he snapped. "And I commmend Li for his revelation. I'm surprised some of you are still trying to exert control over your past factions, which means you're still exercising your factional powers. Now let's start from the beginning, and let Li explain what happened."

My two alumnae were still reluctant to let go; one commented, "I wouldn't say or own up to anything in the presence of Chen."

Then one of my former chief editors blew up. Throwing up his hands with agitation and getting to his feet, he roared: "The abduction of one of our colleagues and her baby is the most unconscionable act in our *dan wei* since the Cultural Revolution began. I've always suspected there was a conspiracy behind it. It's time now to get to the bottom of it." He turned to the teamer: "As for the abducted person, I don't care what the charges against her are now. Since she was the victim of this despicable act, she shouldn't be excluded from this meeting."

Before my alumnae could protest, the teamer announced, "I chair this meeting, and I have no objection to Chen's presence."

An usually quiet woman, Fong, also a former member of the ultra-left faction, raised a hand. "Since this thing has come out," she said, "and since Li's account is rather disjointed, I think it's time I should speak up and try to clear things up. Li may interrupt me any time he wishes, but the crux of the matter lies with Han and Bing, those two from the Music Conservatory."

She told the listeners that Han and Bing had become very excited one day and told their fellow faction members that they now had a good way to find out the secrets of the opposing faction. They gleefully announced that their former schoolmates, A, B, and Doggie at the Music Conservatory had me in custody. "If we apply enough pressure, she'll spill everything she knows about her faction," they said.

Fong, the quiet woman, went on to say: "I'm not trying to distance myself from this incident. We were in this together. However, we had a serious disagreement that day. Chen had been missing for two days and most of us were most disturbed about the snatching away of a mother and her baby." Fong broke down and said to me, "I didn't go on that mission, because I couldn't bear to see you under those conditions, and I could never face your children again if I went."

I was still bewildered, but I gave the group an account of a mystifying interrogation during my eighty-day abduction: About a month after I was taken into that dungeon, my abductors showed up one day and asked me to go to another room. I felt a twinge of fear because I was taken to other rooms to be beaten. But they looked relaxed that day and said I could bring Deedee along.

My abductors sat behind a desk, three in a row and one of them taking notes. I sat facing them. A section of the room was partitioned off with some large mats strung up on poles.

To my utter surprise, the questions asked were about the activities of the faction I was associated with in my *dan wei*. The interrogation was so detailed that only an insider could have asked those questions. I became less tense, because my faction, being moderate, was more involved with research into musical policy issues than with investigating people; we weren't conspirators.

I remember bouncing Deedee on my knees, and he, with total lack of restraint, peed right in front of my interrogators. I asked to wash him, but they took us back to our room and locked us up for the break. After some twenty minutes they came for us again and I was asked more questions in that partitioned room.

As I recounted that incident as I knew it, to the now rather upset audience, I told them I had no idea it was a setup, but was suspicious on account of its unusual nature and unconventional format. I surmised, at the time, that another member of my faction had also been abducted, and they wanted to verify his or her statements.

The driver, Li, feeling relieved, gave the names of those concealed behind the mats: himself, Bing, and a former janitor at our *dan wei*. He said they came out from behind the mats during the break and he had a good sneeze in the passage while Bing consulted with the "front men" about what other questions to ask.

Han and Bing, now truly on the hot seat, reluctantly admitted that A, B, and Doggie (C was in hiding then) had contacted them before they abducted me and inquired which apartment I lived in at the time. Han and Bing swore they hadn't participated in the abduction itself, but only wanted to take advantage of my vulnerability to gain points in the interfactional struggle.

Ever since my abduction, I had wondered about the role played by A and B in that affair, but it had been a mere guess and never verified until this surprise disclosure. It was very disquieting to know that one's closest schoolmates—while not actually bosom friends, young people who had gone through formative experiences—would have the heart to incarcerate a schoolmate and her baby.

I bore no grudge against people who erred from poor judgment or lack of information; the driver, Li, and the quiet woman, Fong, figured among my friends even after we had all left the Cadre School and returned to normal life—and, of course, my children knew them well. Deedee particularly liked the dumplings Li made, and that gave him a good deal of pleasure.

Han took this exposure to heart, and I learned she was shaken by the strong censure voiced by the meeting participants that day. In fact, she took the first opportunity to leave the entire community—meaning our *dan wei*, her profession as a folk-music scholar, her colleagues and all. She applied to go with her husband to work at a county cultural center. Her request was granted, and she quite literally vanished from sight.

I met Han by accident at a bus stop in the early 1980s. She covered her face with one hand. "I'm so embarrassed, I'm so embarrassed," she kept saying. "I've been hating myself all those years for what I did. I must have been crazy to do those things. I left quietly, for I couldn't even face you to ask for your forgiveness."

I truly didn't expect such deep remorse, for Bing, her associate in the matter, had always tried to dismiss the whole thing lightly. I told Han I wasn't trying to comfort her, but to please believe that I held nothing against her. A, B, C, and Doggie, those opportunists and manipulators, were our mutual problems. Please, I said, I want you to forget it. She hesitantly put out a hand, which I took. We would have hugged if that were a Chinese gesture. She turned to go, saying, "It's good of you to forgive, but I still feel so ashamed when I think of it."

Prelude to Richard Nixon's Visit

I was in the Cadre School the day Henry Kissinger came to China. It was a big event in Chinese politics. After more than two decades of propagandized hostility toward American imperialism, we were now instructed on how to regard the Kissinger visit in the "correct" way.

The prelude reached back a long way: Edgar Snow's presence next to Mao Tse-tung on the Gate of Heavenly Peace (Tiananmen) was highlighted, and an ultra-thin booklet titled "Dialogue Between Chairman Mao and Snow" was published in the millions. We were each given a free copy for our own edification during study sessions. The American table-tennis team's visit to China was also given prominence, and so were Premier Chou En-lai's talks with the team. I'm ready to bet the only thing anyone remembers today about that much-touted instance of Ping-Pong Diplomacy was Chou's comment about the long hair worn by one guy in the group.

We had all known something was up, what with all the "frequent sending of beguiling glances," as the deprecatory Chinese saying goes. Now we were apprised that something real was about to happen—and that something was Henry Kissinger's not-so-secret visit to China.

If Kissinger, then National Security Advisor, had learned about the flurry-scurry that took place in a corner of a labor camp one hundred miles' distance from Peking, he would have been astounded by the chain of effects of his historical visit. Chinese authorities sent out strict orders—as they usually did when anything big was happening—forbidding non-Peking residents to enter Peking, the capital of the People's Republic of China.

A few days before Kissinger's arrival, a directive was passed down from "above" (no one ever knew from where), that all members of the May 7th Cadre School were to spend the three days of the emissary's visit studying political tracts instead of working in the fields, ostensibly to enhance their understanding of this momentous event in history. As I recall, Kissinger chose the hottest days in July to come. So all of us at the Cadre School welcomed his visit, if not from the bottom of our hearts, then at least from the soles of our feet, since we wouldn't have to hoof it to the fields for three whole days. Hurrah!

However, we counterrevolutionaries were not to be so lucky, for just as I was calculating how many inches' progress I could make in my never-ending knitting during those three days, the platoon head informed me I was to work the next day. He noticed how my face fell and, being a friend and swimming pal, added quickly that I wouldn't have to do field labor. All I would do was some indoor work around the barracks, "and you can still go swimming during the lunch break." It was kindly meant, but being a man, he couldn't make the connection between studying and knitting.

When I reported for work the day Kissinger arrived, I found to my delight that we were to pound the earthen floor of three lean-tos built for the kitchen staff, who worked irregular hours and got little sleep in the large common dormitories. They were nice people—I was to join them after a short time. So I anticipated not only light indoor work, but also a constant flow of refreshments from the kitchen staff in the form of mung-bean soup, a drink which has both cooling and tonic effects. After all, we were working on the floor of their future quarters.

The "pounding" needs some explanation: the *hon*, or ram, consisted of a heavy log of wood with four handles hollowed out on the upper section, which also made the lower part heavier than the upper. Two people would grasp the handles, lift the device and let it drop to pack down loose dirt. A layer of brick would then be laid on top of the earth.

On that particular day, those counterrevolutionaries chosen to pound the floor were my best buddies—in fact, we had been schoolmates at the Music Conservatory. We were ready to have a pleasant day by ourselves, free from the presence of the revolutionary masses. But our optimistic anticipation of doing some relaxed indoor work soon melted into dismay; not a breath of wind stirred in the stuffy little rooms, and that was worse than working in the open. The men could strip down to their shorts, but I had to swelter in my long pants and shirt, which soon became drenched with perspiration. We all had a towel called a "steel-smelters' scarf," a reminder of the iron-cooking days during the Great Leap Forward. These scarfs were longer than regular hand towels and could be draped conveniently over one's shoulders to catch the streams of sweat. I remember one of the men had to wring it out every five minutes.

Because we counterrevolutionaries were left on our own that day, we took a lot of breaks and a lot of mung-bean soup. We felt less grateful to Kissinger for his visit, having been barred from sitting in the cool, breezy barracks with the revolutionary masses. We conjectured about the true reasons for keeping everyone—revos and counterrevos alike—within eyesight. One of us remarked that this was apparently to prevent anyone from sneaking off to Peking, which wasn't impossible since we all had I.D.'s issued in that city. "What for?" another queried sarcastically. "To shake hands with Kissinger?" Others guessed the authorities were afraid someone would try to submit an appeal or make clandestine contacts. One joked mirthlessly: "One of us might be sighted walking out of the Peking Railroad Station. What a disgrace to our country to be seen dressed like we are!"

After we had exhausted this subject, we parodied a well-known ancient Chinese poem. The original poem was about farmers hoeing crops at high noon, their sweat dripping on the ground, and each grain they produced was the result of back-breaking work. We rephrased it to describe ourselves ramming earth at high noon, sweat dripping on the floor of the little room, and us welcoming Kissinger with gruelling labor—all of it perfectly rhymed. We pounded away cheerfully to the cadence of the lines and felt a lot better.

During another mung-bean soup break, one of the guys said: "All this fuss over Kissinger is simply to get the American president to come and pay tribute to China. By the way, what was this *Nee-ke-soong* before he became president?"

They eyed me for an answer. Lord knows why I remembered the Alger Hiss case so well; I had read about it way back in my high school days. I admit my recital wasn't flattering to Richard Nixon, and I provided some details of the witch-hunt with more than a trace of malicious allusion to our own state of persecution.

My listeners, none of whom were Party members, looked puzzled. "How come our leaders are going out of their way to impress an overt enemy of Communism?" someone asked. "Don't they know about the Chambers-Hiss case?"

"No questions, please," I replied. "Remember, Chairman Mao says it's better for us to deal with the Republicans than with the Democrats. It doesn't make sense to me, Communists associating with Republicans . . . quite an interesting mixture."

Richard Nixon came and went with greater fanfare than accorded to his advisor. It was winter when Nixon arrived; no one had to work in the fields, and in this sense his visit was less memorable to us than Kissinger's.

The Chinese leaders assumed they had a friend in Nixon. So for the sake of consistency in its diplomatic policies, China eventually downplayed Watergate and most Chinese people remained blissfully ignorant of the incident. According to a skimpy tiny column given to Nixon's demise by China's *People's Daily*, President *Nee-ke-soong* inexplicably resigned. To this day, the Chinese media pictures him as a staunch old friend of the Chinese people.

But for me, the prelude of a visit that was hailed as a great diplomatic breakthrough has always been associated with earth-pounding, floor-laying, poetic parody, and profuse perspiration in those stuffy little shacks. I guess my attitude toward an event of such historic significance shows I have a small person's mean little heart.

History is full of ironic little twists. About fifteen years later, when I was no longer a counterrevolutionary and had become an established scholar in both

China and America, Henry Kissinger came to China for the umpteenth time, with his bills footed this time by the Chase Manhattan Bank. Nancy Kissinger was with him.

The U.S. Ambassador's wife gave the customary all-ladies' lunch in honor of the wives of the bankers in the visiting group. English-speaking Chinese professional women were also present on the occasion. During a lull in the proceedings, I went to the ladies room, and there came across Nancy Kissinger who was also taking a break. After the usual who-are-you-and-how-come-you-speak-English-without-an-accent questions, to which I gave my stock I-never-really-learned-it-but-picked-it-up-in-a-California-grade-school answer, she made an astute observation. She said, "Young as you were then, it must have been difficult for people like you who have had special encounters with Americans. I do believe the reestablishing of U.S.–China ties has been a great relief to you."

I confirmed her speculations with the simple statement, "Ten years back, it would have been unimaginable for me to meet someone like you in circumstances such as these." I hesitated a moment, for inevitably my mind went back to the days of her husband's first publicized visit to China, and to my unorthodox personal memories of that visit. She was still looking at me, so I added affirmatively, "Yes, it was a relief. And for the positive changes in our countries' relations since then, please convey my appreciation to Mr. Kissinger."

From White Chef to Red Chef

In Chinese kitchens, I was told, the counter reserved for all flour-and-rice-related operations is called "the white board," and the one for cutting and slicing meat, "the red board." During my senior years of advanced studies in the cadre school, I graduated to the kitchen.

Before that, I had performed all imaginable and unimaginable types of manual labor. In addition to the normal field work related to rice, wheat, corn, and sorghum crops, I'd also been engaged in the planting and harvesting of cotton, potato, peanut, and hemp. The best part of the latter was that after the hemp had been fermented, the fiber needed to be washed. I'd wade into the wide canal with my male colleagues and rub, slap, and twirl the hemp fiber until it became squeaky clean. Some non-swimmers would pile the hemp in carts to be taken back to the campgrounds and hung up to dry, while we the swimming aficionados would make a round trip or two across the half-mile-wide canal—all on "company time."

I'd never been that close to the earth, or down-to-earth, in all my life, and it did me a world of good, physically. I was becoming a farm person. Then, during one of my home visits to Tientsin in the early 1970s, I noticed we had acquired a newly published book in English, *T'ien-kung K'ai-wu: Chinese Technology in the Seventeenth Century*, translated by my cousin and her husband at Penn State. A unique book compiled some three centuries ago, it dealt with methods, vehicles, and tools used in all forms of manual labor. The English version was meticulously reproduced in both its verbal and visual aspects, and autographed by the translators to their beloved aunt, my mother. I eagerly read a dozen pages, then dropped the book and stood up. Mama looked at me in surprise: "It's a great book, in either language. Aren't you going to read it?" I replied, first, that I was astounded to learn that every farm vehicle and tool used today remains the same as those depicted in this three-hundred-year-old book; and secondly, the only difference I could see was that while the ancient farmers used beasts of burden, their modern counterparts often harnessed themselves to the agricultural implements. I picked the book up again and found the page with the plow on it. I pointed to Mama how the ropes were attached to the ox: "I know how to do these knots. I first used them to hitch the guys to the plow, and now that I've risen to the status of top-ranking laborer, I use them to harness myself!"

I'd also taken care of chickens, ducks, and pigs. The only creatures I hadn't fed at the cadre school yet were my fellow human beings.

All had to take turns helping in the kitchen, and after three years of haphazard cuisine, the canteen needed a steady staff to rekindle some gastronomic interest among its long-suffering habitués. The cooks were an all-male group, and they hoped to have a woman join them.

My platoon leader, who was my former managing editor, came to my dorm with a long face and asked me to go with him to the common room. "More bad news," I thought, bracing myself for the worst. Instead he told me the company kitchen wanted me and he was mad because that meant his platoon would be short of an able–.bodied worker, but there wasn't anything he could do about it.

I was so surprised I agreed on spot. Then I realized I was still a *fan-ge-ming* of undetermined fate. I chased after him and asked him if he'd obtained authorization from, say, the teamers. "They know," he said.

"Do you realize the risk of putting a *fan-ge-ming* in the kitchen? You could get criticized for lack of class awareness."

"I know what I'm doing," he replied.

I stopped short: "What if I decided to poison the food?"—a standard practice attributed to the Chinese steoreotype of the *fan-ge-ming*.

"Don't be nuts!" he flung back peevishly as he walked away.

My tenure on the permanent kitchen staff would last as long as the cadre school itself. Throughout all the time I was there, our company kitchen was managed by a direct descendant of Confucius, an authentic one. I'll call him Confu for convenience's sake. Confu's father was the younger brother of their generation's Saint—as the eldest direct-line progeny of the clan was called. My friend Confu might be called the Stand-by. He had left that rigid feudal household in the mid-1940s when he was in his late teens and became first a student and then an archivist of music.

Confu had been put in charge of kitchen management after the initial sorghum-and-boiled-cabbage days and, after the change in school sites, was able to build up a network of connections, to the advantage of those hundred-odd souls whose sustenance depended on the canteen of Company Four.

I started at the entry level, which consisted of keeping the coal stove stoked at the right temperature. Whenever high flames were required to stir-fry enough vegetables or meat for a hundred-odd servings, I had to have the fire roaring within a minute, but when the chef wanted the food to simmer, the heat had to come down instantly. To complicate matters, there were two fires to attend to, one for the red chef and one for the white. For someone who had spent two frustrating hours lighting up her small stove at home when she first married, acquiring such skill was some feat.

After a couple of months I was transferred to the white board to help make fancy steamed rolls and buns. I loved fancy steamed rolls, but I had never figured out how the rolls got fashioned into such delicate arabesques. I confessed that to Confu before going on the job. "I was a Young Master," he replied, "just as you were a Miss. I'm still trying to figure out how the family cook made some of those delicious courses I had at home as a child."

Needless to say, few of us cadres felt any enthusiasm for work at the cadre school. "Why should I be doing this?" we wondered, as our reeducation entered the fourth year. So in most cadre school canteens, the buns were either under- or overleavened, and no one bothered to knead the buns one by one; the dough was simply sliced into squares and thrown in the steamer.

This was also the first time I ever made round buns, and I was curious to find out whether I could make those perfect hemispheres. I learned the technique and practiced repeatedly. As a result, we had handkneaded buns at almost every meal, which meant kneading some four hundred of them daily.

Gradually, bun-making became a competition between the various companies; sometimes other company canteens would come to borrow a few dozen if they had underestimated the appetites of their hungry charges. They'd bring miserable-looking, overleavened replacements the next day. Soon word went around that even the buns at Company Four were the best.

Confu's local renown rose like buns in a steamer. Going with him to the county town one day, I noticed every single store manager and clerk plus half the population knew Confu on a backslapping basis. We brought with us rolls of something that looked like large sheets of paper, and Confu took one to every store he did business with. After a series of trips among those stores, our truck was well-loaded and we ate a bountiful lunch before driving back on the long dike highway.

I asked if he could enlighten me just a little about how his network worked. "No way," he said. "Some bastards are trying to bust me on my dealings. These heartless s.o.b.'s always come back for a third helping whenever I wangle up something good to eat, but they still want to put me down. You just wait, I'm going to chew them out tomorrow, in public."

He did just that. He made a statement during the noon meal and challenged whoever was spreading rumors about his management to come out in the open if he had the guts to do so. No one did.

However, Confu did tell me about the rolls of paper. These were movie posters once printed by the China Film Press; all had been discarded and stacked in a warehouse after Chiang Ching denounced those films as poisonous weeds. Confu discovered the abandoned posters and brought down a load everytime he spied an empty return-trip vehicle. Chinese peasants have always loved colored pictures, and poisonous weeds or not, those old movie posters were well-suited for papering their drab rooms. The township's residents, largely of peasant stock, clamored for them, and one roll of those old posters could open the doors and storerooms of any commercial establishment. Confu said, "I haven't done anything illegal, not even marginally so. A friendly smile, a sincere plea, and a roll of posters are all I need to keep our canteen well provisioned. Have no fear."

I read *Catch-22* after that discourse and suddenly found a benign Milo Minderbinder in Confu.

Yang, one of my earth-ramming buddies from the time of Kissinger's visit, joined our kitchen staff soon after. Because of his strength, he was ideal for the position of white chef to which I'd already acceded. So I started to edge toward the red board.

We did what we could to stretch out our meager meat supplies. One way was by making meat patties, mixing the ground pork with a lot of chopped scallions and carrots to make the patties bigger. Once, when we were all set to deep-fry a batch of patties, Confu came into the kitchen and yelled in mock anger: "So you're wasting my precious oil supplies again! Cadre school inmates don't deserve fried meat patties!" Then he poked at the raw patties and asked if we had any leftover rice. "Mix in the rice to make them even bigger, and add some starch to make them hold together like all-meat patties."

"That rice will soak up a lot of oil," I warned.

"So what?" he said. "I'll just go scrounging for more."

Then he lowered his voice and told another kitchen staffer: "When some of the older guys just back from the Central Special Cases Committee line up for meals, always give them a bigger serving than the others. They've been locked up a long time and are afraid to ask for more. Besides, they aren't allowed to go home, so our kitchen is all they have."

My friendship with Confu was strengthened by a natural empathy. It was well into 1973 and the political witch-hunt had relaxed, but my case was still unresolved. One day, Confu followed me as I went back to my dorm.

Confu said: "Tell me how serious your case really is." I replied I wasn't allowed to discuss that with anyone. He then told me that while he was doing his accounts that day, he had overheard people in charge of my case in the next room saying they had decided to pass the following verdict on me: "An antagonistic contradiction but to be regarded as a contradiction within the people." In other words, I was a counterrevolutionary, but to be dealt with as an ordinary offender.

My knees weakened. After all those years of persecution, was I still an enemy of the people, to be treated merely with a bit of leniency? Confu asked me if I understood the gravity of the situation. I told him I certainly did, and I also appreciated the danger to which he had exposed himself by telling me this. "Do you think I'd withhold information like that from you?" he asked.

Confu's tip gave me time to think out my strategy. In line with the conventions of Chinese politics, condemned persons were given little opportunity to speak for themselves. One simply accepted the fate handed down to one; any appeal was considered "not having a correct attitude" and, under adverse circumstances, would only make matters worse. Nonetheless, I wasn't going to take anything lying down.

I was summoned for a talk a couple of days later. The people handling my case—including a teamer and a couple of politically correct colleagues—were all smiles; they assumed they'd made a fair estimation and a benign verdict. I heard them out and asked to read the document.

Then I firmly and rationally rejected their conclusion. First, I said, now that Mao's heir-designate Lin Biao, who fled the country and died in a plane crash in Mongolia, had been shown to be a counterrevolutionary, any criticism I had leveled at him should be stricken from the record; secondly, also deleted should be a few items for which there had been no evidence in the first place but were attributed to me purely by inference. Those would not be acceptable in a serious, formal political conclusion.

I could tell my reaction caught them by surprise. However, my determination must have made an impression since they agreed to review the issue. As I left, I said, "Take your time, it's been so long I'm not in a hurry anymore. I can hang on here until you reach an acceptable conclusion."

Years later in Peking, I ran into one of the more sensible members of my "special case group." That was after the downfall of Chiang Ching and her cohorts and the termination of all my problems. This person and I had had many intelligent talks during my *fan-ge-ming* years, and I now told him that my most difficult task was to get them to overturn that first conclusion. He said, "We were impressed by your reasoning. I even thought we should leave you to draw up the conclusion yourself. Your case had been classified as an antagonistic contradiction from the beginning, and I'm ashamed to say nobody even thought of looking at it from another perspective. We even thought we'd done a good job by giving you the most lenient treatment prescribed for your category."

I knew the case group had taken my objections seriously, for one of its members actually postponed his home leave. I provided Confu with some feedback on what had happened at the meeting, and we both kept mum on the subject. The revised conclusion came back a couple of months later, with all references to antagonistic contradictions dropped entirely. I was simply branded as someone who had committed "grave political errors." I stared at the term "grave" for a long time and played in my mind with alternative terms. But then I reflected that my description of Chiang Ching as a *"huo guo yang min"* creature was a pretty grave accusation and I'd have a hard time wriggling out of that. I signed the conclusion, indicating my agreement. I learned later that two of the ultra-leftists among my colleagues were dissatisfied because I hadn't been declared an enemy of the people, and one of the teamers gave a talk to bring them around.

Confu asked me to his room that evening, on the pretext of discussing the next week's menu. I found several of the kitchen staff and a couple of my buddies gathered there. We had a very warm albeit subdued celebration to mark the fact that I now formally belonged among "the people." When I told them I still had reservations about the word "grave," one of them, a former Rightist, said: "Don't fret over minor things. Think of all the freedom you've gained; you've even released your children from bondage."

I went on to become quite a competent chef, both white board and red board. With more time on our hands and fewer mouths to feed as the years went by, I even had time to practice with one of the most dependable cookbooks I've ever come across, salvaged from the detritus of a family who had left Peking. Dependable, because when I followed the author's instructions step by step, even the most ordinary beef broth turned out as delectable as a gourmet course.

One day, Fong—the quiet woman who had now become a fellow cook—and I decided to work overtime after we'd finished our early dinner, and armed with that book, we tried out a new type of stew. I was at the large cauldron, holding a yard-long ladle and waiting for her to throw in the ingredients.

"Hi, there, where's the ginger?" I called without turning my head. "It should go in right after the leek!"

"Uh-uh, you've got to wait," she replied. "There's a full stop between them, so the ginger belongs in the next sentence."

I yelled to the stove-handler in the back room: "Lower the heat, will you? We have to check out a punctuation mark."

We both examined the page, and she conceded that it was indeed a smudged comma, not a full stop. I asked for more fire and the ginger followed the leek.

When we had finished, the unfortunate fellow in the back room covered up the fire and came up front. "What in heaven's name have you been doing here?" he inquired. We let him look at the savory contents of the cauldron, and he remarked, "I thought you girls were writing love letters, what with all those dots and commas!"

The stew, by the way, was a lip-smacking success.

Babes in the Cadre School

My children went through a great deal during the long nightmare. My family and I shielded them from traumatic experiences as best we could, but we were not always successful.

When I let Mimi go off with her father to Chi-nan, I had no idea of the risks to which I was exposing her. It was only several years later that Toto had a chance to tell me how he'd rescued my little darling. He went posthaste to Chi-nan after learning that Fan had been taken by force from his parents' home and found that Mimi had been left there with virtual strangers. I don't remember if it was before or after my abduction, but I wasn't able to go.

Toto found his way to Fan's home, and while Fan's parents were going through the formalities of meeting an unknown in-law, a little human fireball streaked out of the inner room right into Toto's arms. Three-and-a-half-year-old Mimi was running a high fever from bewilderment, fear, and the sudden change in her young life. Her uncle was the only person she could identify with in this alien place; she clung to his neck and refused to let go. Conscious of how much our little princess had endured, Toto didn't leave her alone for a single moment until he got her safely home to Tientsin.

When I tried to ask Mimi later about what had happened, she said she didn't remember anything. I asked her again when she was in her late teens. I told her Toto's version of the incident. Mimi shuddered and told me she truly had no recollection; all she could remember was that from the time she was very young she'd decided never to go to Chi-nan again.

Deedee has no memory of what he went through, naturally. I took the brunt of our dungeon sojourn. All those days of malnutrition took their toll on me; the calcium was drained from my teeth. I lost seven of them as the price for having a healthy baby. I can't explain the mechanics, but feeding a ravenous infant for three months with very little input at my end made my teeth (the upper front ones, of all teeth) brittle. They became thinner and as transparent as what we Chinese call "window paper." It wasn't funny when a piece of front tooth broke off from eating porridge, not spareribs. All my previously neat and even incisors, a legacy of California's milk and orange juice, were pulled out when I was still in my early thirties. Confu, an excellent photographer, took pictures of me and Fong in front of the cadre school's pigsty. One would never have guessed we were in close vicinity to our porcine charges what with all the greenery around and our broad smiles. When he brought us the developed prints, however, I observed drily: "All those splendid teeth—none of them mine."

I was not allowed any home leave for years on end, so I missed my folks very much. After a round of correspondence, Mama agreed to let Mimi come to visit me all by herself. She was not yet seven, so we did what we could to make the trip safe for her. Mama put her on the direct bus to the farm and repeatedly instructed the driver not to let her off until I came to claim her.

My little girl slept on my bed and I held her all night. When we went into the fields, she was placed on a two-wheeled pushcart and rode all the way. She was better than most of us when it came to weeding the cornfields because she was closer to the ground.

Since the canteen was short of stools and benches, many ate standing up. I appropriated a stool and we worked out a system: I sat on the stool and stuck my left leg out at an angle. Mimi perched on my knee, which served her as a bench. An elderly man standing next to us, also a "special case," admired the sight so much he quoted a Chinese idiom, meaning "lovely and pliant like a little bird."

I left her in the barracks another day to follow the aunties and uncles around as they fed the chickens and pigs and prepared our dinner. She was thrilled to find eggs galore in the coops, was all hands and feet in the kitchen, and picked up all kinds of odds and ends treasurable only to a little girl. I was grateful for the fact that while I was regarded as a *fan-ge-ming*, no one gave my little girl any trouble. We arranged things so that Confu could take her all the way home during one of his errands to Tientsin a couple of weeks later. Mimi informed her little brother and the rest of the family that a cadre school is somewhere one can have all kinds of fun not allowed in the city, such as raising chickens and collecting eggs.

Meanwhile, after the conclusion of my case, I was granted home leave like everyone else. Finally Fan and I had the opportunity of seeing each other in Tientsin with both the children and my family around, or just by ourselves in Peking. The relationship had soured to such an extent that my mother observed to me in private: "How come the two of you always pick on each other? I can't recall ever teaching anything that would make you so quarrelsome." I told her I was sorry to bring discord to this house, but it was becoming ever more difficult to talk sense with him.

Having been forced to spend the last few years mostly apart from each other, and with that crack-in-the-mirror we never talked about again, I was painfully aware of a mounting alienation. He wouldn't mention any of his new friends at his *dan wei*, but he'd fly into a jealous rage when I brought up the names of men (plenty) I had contact with. All right, so I'd talk about the women I got on well with. And even then it seemed he took pains to check them out. "All your friends are either widows or divorcées!" he once yelled at me. Which, incidentally, was largely true, but so what! I associated with people according to their intrinsic worth, not in line with ridiculous social prejudices and marital categories.

Like an ostrich, I buried myself in the now familiar environment of the cadre school, and let fate decide whither my marriage went.

I now had a room all to myself, and my children visited the school frequently. Preschooler Deedee visited longer, and he attached himself to two little girls also staying at the cadre school. One of the mothers and I suddenly realized one day, however, that neither of us had seen the three kids for more than an hour. We searched their usual haunts without success before we went to the dike.

Three tiny dots were visible on the other bank of the half-mile-wide ice-covered canal, particularly as the girls wore red. It was early March, the ice was thinning and had melted in some places. Light as the children were, a playful jump could plunge them into an ice hole. If called, they might run so as to avoid a scolding for their truancy and get themselves drowned; if we didn't call, they would go on having a good time oblivious of the danger they were in.

The other mother started to cajole them in a mild voice, telling them we had a treat waiting for them, while I rushed back for help. Several men, including my loyal kitchen colleagues, came running with bamboo poles, but stopped on the slope of the dike so as not to alarm the little pranksters.

With forced calm but rapidly beating hearts, we watched the three naughty dots resolve into our respective offspring. We shushed the father of the other little girl, who had just learned that his precious daughter was cavorting on melting ice! He stood there muttering and smoking. I whispered prayers and imprecations. Mentally I slapped, spanked, and whipped Deedee as I watched his progress across the thin ice with a little girl on each side.

Only when the trio nonchalantly jumped from the ice onto the dike did we two mothers rush down the slope and grab up our babies. The father simply flopped down on the slope, emotionally exhausted.

The truants were surprised to see so many uncles and aunties standing on the dike with poles, ropes, and wooden planks. They were made to look back over the ice and were told how dangerous it could have been. "Did we go that far?!" They seemed to be more thrilled than chilled.

Their playtime was suspended for a few days, and, having no better pastime to assign to Deedee, I sent him along with two uncles to have a hog slaughtered. The elderly uncle, the former chairman of my association and a renown composer, promised he would keep Deedee far away from the butcher's knife.

"Hey, they're back!" someone called in the late afternoon. I hurried out from behind my red board just in time to see a stout figure pulling the shafts of a two-wheeled cart, a shorter figure hauling on a towline, and between them a tiny figure also pulling a towline—all in silhouette against the dimming sky. Deedee didn't rush up to me, but walked in step with the others, a big man five years old, and gravely announced that he and the two uncles had got the pig slaughtered. The elderly uncle gave me a wink and later told me that by the time he'd allowed Deedee into the slaughterhouse, the hog had already been killed and washed, and all Deedee saw was the carcass being quartered.

Coming to their unfortunate mother's cadre school gave my children a rare chance to learn something about life on the land. They became tougher and rougher after a few trips, and acquired firsthand knowledge about many animals. They even brought home several chicks of the best breed and Ah Po, who had always loved chickens, raised them to lay eggs.

One of the little-girls-on-the-ice was asked what she wanted to do when she grew up. She declared: "I'll also go to the cadre school. There's so much fun here. It the best place in the world!"

Her mother and I exchanged glances. "Oh, God!" she whispered. "If anything like a cadre school still exists when she grows up, I'd rather die!"

Mama Leaves Us Orphans

It shouldn't have happened, it didn't make sense, everything went wrong. While Papa's death had been accepted as inevitable, Mama's was totally unexpected. Papa was buried with great sorrow; Mama's passing away left us feeling bewildered, incredulous. It was as though she were still alive, existing in a state of suspension somewhere between earth and sky. Years after Mama died, I would still find myself thinking "Oh, Mama will like this . . . " and then suddenly realize that she wasn't there anymore.

Five years after Papa's death, in 1975, Mama found a lump in her breast and went to the right specialist—by now we always went to see doctors at their home, not at the hospital. The diagnosis was unequivocal: breast cancer, and in a fairly advanced stage. However, nobody dies of a mastectomy, and after the initial shock we made the necessary arrangements for hospitalization and subsequent recuperation.

That was in 1975, a relatively calm year during the Cultural Revolution. The other families had moved back to their original abodes. I was still doing time at the cadre school, but there were breaks in the clouds: A small portion of our savings was returned to us, with the bulk and interest promised, so that we were much better off than during Papa's last days. And Toto had returned to his job and was dating a very attractive girl, Bella, who was to become his wife.

We discussed a "worst case" scenario: If Mama had to go through a long course of therapy, we would look for extra domestic help to take care of her. Ah Po would look after the house, my children, and the cooking and oversee things in general. Mama wanted to give us a list of the family's savings accounts, "just in case," for she knew none of us had ever inquired into such matters. Toto and I brushed the suggestion aside as irrelevant, and Mama put the list back in a locked drawer.

Since the atmosphere was fairly relaxed at the cadre school for the time being, I planned to stay at home throughout Mama's operation and convalescence. Mama planned the entire project in the future tense; no one anticipated that, for Mama, the future would end within a week.

I shared a last joke with Mama in the kitchen, as we privately commented upon my Mimi's extraordinarily good looks. I recalled a Chinese joke about a sage, his good-for-nothing son, and his talented grandson. One day the son became defensive about his shortcomings and said to his father: "So what if I'm a boob? My son is better than your son!" Then he turned to his own son, and said "Don't you get fresh, my father is better than your father!"

It was generally acknowledged that I was the ugly duckling in the family. I didn't mind the distinction, however, and told Mama that day: "You know, I can co-opt that old joke, I can say to you: `My daughter is prettier than yours,' and I can tell Mimi, `My Mama is certainly more beautiful than yours!'" Mama rather relished the joke.

Mama walked out of the house, with Toto carrying her bag of toilet articles and clothing as listed by the hospital. I held a thermos, its electroplated cap gleaming in the sunlight as Mama waved to the neighbors who came by to wish her good luck. Mama called cheerfully: "See you when I get back!" She stepped out of our home, never to return.

Toto, his girl friend Bella, and I waited outside the operating room. The surgeon was a competent practitioner recommended by old family friends. Mama was sent to her ward after the operation.

As the old saw goes: "The operation was a success, but the patient died." Mama felt fine the next day, but something was definitely wrong toward nighttime; her stomach swelled up and she became delirious. The remaining sixty hours were a blur of anxiety, helplessness, and desperation.

Bella and I were at Mama's bedside on her last night—in China family members are expected to take care of in-patients. Mama went in and out of a coma. Her condition didn't seem to be worsening in the morning when Toto took over, so I went home to catch some sleep. But soon a friend brought a message: "Go to the hospital. Urgent." Mama had gone without regaining consciousness.

Suddenly I was all alone with her; in that gray hospital ward the only occupants were Mama and I. Our mutual acquaintance had commenced thirty-six years ago in a hospital room in happy anticipation of a fulfilling future; it came to an end in another hospital room with my world crumbling both within and without. I knelt beside her bed—something I had never done before my parents, since we had been a more or less Westernized family. I knelt down, for I could find no other way to express my bottomless sorrow, my endless grief.

When Papa died there had still been Mama; when Mama died there was only Toto and myself. We did all the proper things. We arranged for a solemn memorial service and Mama was laid out with all the roses that could be cut from two Tientsin parks to honor the former "Lady of the Roses," and everyone said we were models of filial behavior. But we did everything mechanically, for we were still in shock. Everything was done right, but everything was wrong; the heart of the family was gone.

Mama died of an intestinal obstruction as a result of intestinal volulus. She could have been saved by another operation, but the condition was not detected until it was too late, and the timing for surgery was lost. This was confirmed by autopsy. The Chinese don't like autopsies, but we insisted on having one done because we wanted to know what had gone wrong. In China there are no malpractice suits, and it would have been useless anyway. We had lost her, and nothing would have brought her back.

Ah Po was inconsolable; we were the only family she had. With Mama gone, she didn't know what would become of her. We promised her then and there that we'd take care of her to her very last day; which we did, for thirteen years.

Toto and I didn't divide up the family property, as most siblings do after their parents pass away. Toto was as yet unmarried, and I was in a jam, domestically, politically, and professionally. We left the family property as it was, with Ah Po taking charge of the home, which now consisted of Toto and my children. I would be staying at the cadre school, but could now come back to visit from time to time.

Fan was in Tientsin during all this painful period, and he was an immense help in many things that needed to be taken care of. But I believe he felt left out when it came to deciding certain intimate matters that could only be handled by Toto and me; he started a row the very first day after Mama died. I'm sorry to say that something else also died within me that day, because from then on I stopped being my husband's wife except in name.

What saved me from going to pieces during those darkest hours of our family life was a book I found by the side of Mama's bed at home: James Michener's *Hawaii*. I was surprised to find American writer Anna Louise Strong's signature on the fly leaf, for I knew Mama didn't know her personally. It was *Hawaii* that saved me; it was the blue lagoons, the brutal sacrificial offerings, and the cultivation and development of the islands of my dreams that carried me through those nerve-trying nights. In Mama's bed, after Mama's death, I continued what must have been her reverie with the last book she read.

Curiously enough, people said that I began to look more like Mama right after she died. My godmother in Peking was the first to notice this, and she asked me if I knew I looked very much like my mother. I replied that she must be mistaken because I resembled my aunts. No, she insisted, and told me I was becoming as striking as my mother had been.

When, in 1983, I went to Tsinghua University in the stead of my deceased parents to attend the 50th Anniversary of Mama's graduation, I was again given a five-inch-long red silk tag, bearing the names of my parents and myself. I walked into the hall packed with silver-haired septuagenarians, and hesitated. Then, one elderly man stopped me, saying: "You don't have to introduce yourself, you are An-tao's daughter. The same features, the same smile, and the same way of holding one's head high."

Snack at Eight

Deprived of the right to live a normal, purposeful, and productive life, many of us at the cadre school fell into a style of life best described by the Chinese expression *hun*, which translates loosely as "getting along in an aimless fashion." Another way of putting it is, again in Chinese, "knocking the bell day after day like a monk." This folksy idiom was, in fact, used by an army teamer at a school-wide meeting at which he lectured us on what he saw as our slothful, apathetic behavior. Perhaps he was somewhat flustered, however, by the sight of so many intellectuals staring at him with notebooks open and pens poised, for he garbled the words and said, "knocking on the monk day after day like a bell." That really made our day.

In those five summers I spent at Cadre School III, I resumed my teenage hobby of swimming and lapped the mile-long round-trip across the canal and back, every day.

Those were peaceful waters, and I swam at an unhurried pace, feeling the gentle swell rising and falling with me. These swimming breaks were one of the few real pleasures I had. There were only about a dozen of us marathon swimmers, including another woman, in the entire group of perhaps five hundred cadres, but plenty of dippers, as we called them. These would paddle around along the bank of the canal. We all kept an eye on one another, but it's a miracle no one was drowned during those five summers.

It was in the course of hard labor and the swimming sessions that Yang, one of my fellow earth-rammers during Kissinger's visit and later a fellow chef, became closer to me. We had already known each other for umpteen years, for he was a sophomore when I entered the Music Conservatory. We knew our respective spouses, and so in my way of thinking our relationship should-n't go beyond a certain point. What drew us together was chiefly a feeling of mutual compassion, since Yang had also been put under surveillance when all those submovements broadsided most of us. His wife, too, was under surveillance wherever she was. They had not met for two years, and as Yang told me later, they hardly know what to say to each other when they eventually had their reunion.

We were both sufficiently controlled, or timid, to keep our friendship platonic, but to have someone care for you made life a little easier under those harsh circumstances. I could expect a helping hand when lifting heavy objects; and when he returned from some hot, exhausting assignment I'd say gruffly, so as not to reveal any sentiment in public, "You'll find some cool refreshments on the kitchen counter." In spite of the non-romantic, almost internment-camp setting of our non-affair, it gave us some sense of being still human in those dehumanizing times. We talked a lot, even cuddled a bit when doing so was safe. Our secret joke was we'd visit each other when we were old and gray. "I'll get a cane to lean on," Yang said, "and go to see you."

In the autumn of 1971, some enigmatic developments relieved the humdrum nature of cadre school life. Security suddenly became very tight, and those who returned from home leave spoke of unusual vibrations in the capital. Something had happened, but no one could put a finger on what it was.

More than a month later, the country's cadres, meaning all those employed by the state (which I still was), were informed about the mysterious

September 13 plane crash in Mongolia that incinerated Mao's heir-designate, Lin Biao.

That day, all cadre school inmates were notified to gather in the largest room for a reading of the latest "Central Document." We were all nervous because of the uncertainty of our own fate. Then someone whispered to me: "It's Lin. He's had it!" I looked at him incredulously.

As the reader of the Central Document droned on, giving us the official version of Lin's "treasonous flight" and death, I felt what can only be described as a sense of fierce vindication. This Lin, who is unworthy of taking up any space in this writing, was, as I see it, a miserable snake and sycophant. He was hated and despised by everyone I knew, but any disparaging comments about him had been taboo, because the Great Leader had handpicked him to be his successor! In fact, half of my own *fan-ge-ming* utterances had been directed at him.

So it was good riddance to bad rubbish. That portentous incident brought some hope, some light into our dismal existence. Perhaps Heaven had some sense of justice after all, I thought.

Heaven also sent me a divertissement in the form of a second cousin: Cousin Wei, more than twenty years my senior, was one of China's outstanding playwrights. Protégé of my Fourth Uncle, a dramatist and founder of China's first national drama school, he was acclaimed a child prodigy with the release of his first play. Wei, cynically witty, was the youngest among the artists who had congregated in Chungking during the anti-Japanese war. He later returned from Hong Kong to Peking after the 1949 takeover, and his marriage to one of China's most popular traditional opera stars enhanced his colorful career and profile. In 1957, however, his outspokenness and his scathing comments about the Communist Party's misdoings earned him the title Big Rightist. It was he who was taken away to a remote farm when he and his wife were washing the feet of their newborn baby girl.

Wei was sent home after his term at the labor farm. He was becoming popular again just before the Cultural Revolution, when he and almost all established and renowned artists and/or heads of the various artists' associations were taken into custody by the CCP's Central Special Cases Committee for reasons or treasons unknown. By the time Lin Biao's mysterious plane crash took place, many had been released by that committee and sent back to their original *dan wei*, most of which were at cadre schools, without being granted even a single home visit.

As I explained earlier, these men and women were relegated to my level as "people with problems" and we often labored side by side in the cadre school. Wei was in another work brigade, with his former *dan wei* of dramatists. I toyed with the notion of accosting him and telling him I was one of his second cousins from the Chen clan. Being much older than I was, he might have some interesting tales to tell about my uncles and aunts.

Before I'd resolved to make this move, however, one of my former bosses, the Executive Director of the Musician's Association told me in private, "Someone in another brigade has been making inquiries about you."

"Oh, what kind of inquiries?"

"Well," he answered, "the funny thing is the way he put the matter. He must have seen you either at meetings or working in the fields. He described your appearance and asked me if your last name was Wu. I told him there's someone who fits that description, but her family name is Chen. And here comes the bizarre part. Guess what he answered. 'Chen will do, too'!"

I'd already half-guessed who it was, but had to confirm: "Who's the person?"

He looked around before mentioning Wei's notorious name.

I chuckled. I was still minus my front teeth and hadn't been fitted yet with a dental plate, so I rarely laughed. I told my former boss, "I knew he was around and we'd meet some day. You see, we are second cousins of the same generation even if he's twenty years my senior. I used to tag along when my father, his uncle, visited him. But I was only a teenager at the time, and you know how little heed adults pay to teenagers."

I said I was surprised Wei had recognized me, a thirtyish woman in a nondescript outfit and with hair bobbed like all the two hundred other women at the cadre school. I explained to my go-between that I bore a strong resemblance to my aunts and one of them married a Wu, and Wei may have thought I was her daughter; if, however, I came from the male side of the family my name should be Chen.

I asked my go-between to tell Wei, with whom he had long been professionally acquainted, that "Chen will do, too" was indeed his cousin, daughter of his Second Uncle, but that I'd wait a couple of months before approaching him in person. "I must get some false teeth first," I explained. "What'll he think if he meets a younger cousin looking more like his grandmother!"

Thereafter, Wei and I acknowledged each other with a nod when our respective companies crossed paths going to the fields or to meetings. Then one day, I heard our store had shipped in some milk powder, which would be sold two bags per person as long as supplies lasted. We all hurried to the store and I found myself lined up right behind Cousin Wei. "Will you have a bag to spare?" I asked, for I saw him holding cash enough for only one bag.

Those were the first words we exchanged, and he answered, "I'll buy the second one, too, and you can have it." After I'd thrust the money in his hands, we started to inquire about our respective circumstances and families. We had a good laugh over our Chen-will-do-too acquaintanceship. And during the rest of our stay at the cadre school as well as in ensuing years, I would benefit a great deal from his extraordinary perception and acuity.

As many of the "revolutionary masses" gradually left the cadre school for good—either sent to some *dan wei* or other in Peking or back to their provinces of origin—most of us who remained were the hard-nut cases, so to speak. We were either historical *fan-ge-ming*, active *fan-ge-ming*, or high-level Rightists. Finding slots for us was difficult since class struggle was still the order of the day and we were enemies of the revolution, regardless of the lenient treatment accorded us.

As our numbers continued to decline, several brigades, companies, and platoons were combined. Cousin Wei and I found ourselves in the same company, bountifully fed under the management of Confu, and I continued to be a bossy chef.

Since we had decided to keep country hours, dinner was over by 5:30 P.M., giving us hardworking chefs a long evening rest. No one else was even pretending to look busy anymore, so why shouldn't we give ourselves a break?!

That was when we initiated our "Snacks at Eight," although we never actually referred to them as such. Under the CCP, even purely social gatherings such as the "Thursday Dinner Club" of the early 1950s had been condemned as reactionary clique activities. We simply told each other 8:00 P.M. at so-and-so's place, as each one of us took turns hosting a small group of friends. We picked mushrooms, saved eggs laid by our personal pet hens, hoarded goodies brought back from home leaves, or simply bought canned meat from the school store. At the risk of offending the sensibilities of my Western readers, I admit there was no shortage of roast sparrows, sauteed frog legs, and other exotic delicacies at these meals. The only time I drew the line was when someone served up stewed weasel. Drinks were also available as Confu would provide anyone who asked with a bottle of real top-grade sorghum liquor.

Those 8:00 P.M. snacks around a crackling stove or over smoking coils of mosquito repellant taught me more about the lives of China's cultural figures than I could have learned from any number of art history courses. Cousin Wei and his buddies had constituted the elite of China's art circles for almost forty years, starting from before the Sino-Japanese War, and he recounted the personal stories and romances of many well-known painters, musicians, actors, and writers. No one, however, talked about Chiang Ching; not while we were eating, anyway. We didn't want our appetites spoiled by any mention of "that woman."

Joking apart, one of the greatest revelations to me at those snack sessions was the plight of the so-called historical *fan-ge-ming*. Most of them minor functionaries under the defeated KMT regime, they had been singled out for repression early on after the founding of the People's Republic, and although some had been officially de-capped and rehabilitated in succeeding years, they were never treated as equal citizens. Their position was more difficult than that of the Rightists; at least it was known what the latter were accused of. But many of the historical *fan-ge-ming* had been branded as such at closed, case-by-case reviews, and most people shunned or avoided them, not knowing the exact nature of their sins.

This was the first opportunity I had to listen to their side of the story. We were equal now, so to speak, and they had no qualms about opening their hearts to a few latecomers to the ranks of the *fan-ge-ming*. As each told their story, the stigma attached to their status faded, and I realized I was actually among many of the most intelligent and enduring people in China—people who had survived injustices for dozens of years.

In spite of our aversion to discussing Chiang Ching and the continued danger of doing so, we couldn't help commenting at times on her revolting behavior. Once that happened when cousin Wei was allowed to go on his first home leave six years after he was taken in custody.

He came back from his first home leave with details of an interview Chiang Ching had accorded to an American professor, who had asked to write Chiang Ching's biography. As an extra tidbit, the newspapers even reported that "Comrade Chiang Ching received Professor So-and-so in a dress she designed herself." Wei had also read excerpts of that biography in some Hong Kong newspapers.

"That woman has no shame," Wei declared. "She's a liar from beginning to end. I'm not surprised she'd need a foreigner to write her biography. No self-respecting Chinese writer would do it for her."

I told Wei to pipe down. "No wonder they don't want you to go home," I added facetiously. "The first time you do, you come back loaded up with *fan-ge-ming* gossip."

The Chinese media at the time had made a big to-do about the dress Chiang Ching wore during her meetings with that professor, saying it symbolized Chiang Ching's spirit of "reform" and "innovation."

That dress had a bodice with three or four pleats, as Chiang Ching had no bustline, and an extra-wide mid-calf skirt, which of course put a big strain on the cloth coupon allocations of fashion-conscious copycats.

Later, *The Dress* was recommended by official edict to women who still worked in cities and towns, the government subsidizing purchases with cloth coupons. The price per dress amounted to twenty-four yuan, more than half the monthly pay of an entry-level worker. Long sweeping skirts, mind you, were hardly suited for most work places, and mounting men's bikes with their high crossbars—the sole means of transportation for many women—in such skirts was downright dangerous.

As could be expected, the authorities' sycophantic decision to promote *The Dress* generated a good deal of popular sarcasm. A friend told Toto, "You know what, we've finally found a good use for that dress. Our coal stove started to die out yesterday and my wife tried to fan it up again. She was sitting on a stool in front of the grate and started to flap her skirt to keep cool. Whoosh! the fire flared up. We agreed that was all thanks to Chiang Ching!"

Many absurd and even laughable things happened during those years, but I felt utterly miserable as I lay on my bunk bed at night in the cadre school. Doubts and anxieties kept me awake. Would I be able to survive many more years of such an existence? Could one ever expect a turn for the better? Even if there was such a turn, what kind of future was in store for me?

I'd been a journalist, and I understood the political subtleties of that profession in China; I knew my career in that field was over, for I would never be trusted again.

I assumed I would be assigned some kind of work in the coming years, and I considered the possibility of becoming a translator. Even prison inmates were allowed to do that kind of work. I knew I was qualified, not only because I wrote well in Chinese, but I'd also read perhaps as many classics and contemporary books in English as anyone in China.

Indeed, a surprising number of English-language books found their way to my pillow at the cadre school by various clandestine and circuitous routes. And so, after the eight o'clock revelries with roast sparrows, frog legs, and sorghum spirits, I would retire in Jekyll-and-Hyde fashion to the world of Bellow, Heller, Mailer, and Michener.

Lost and Found Among the Bookshelves, III

The years of the Cultural Revolution not only buried my parents, my marriage, and my innocence, they also took away most of my books. After those years of turmoil, the only books in English left over from the old days were the *Complete Works of Shakespeare* in one volume, and the last volume of Galsworthy's *Forsythe Saga*, "Swan Song"—which seems rather ironic, seeing that this title is in a way symbolic of what those chaotic years did to Mao's China.

We still had the *Encyclopaedia Britannica*, 1949 edition, but my prize trophy *Pride and Prejudice*, which I actually knew even better than *Dream of the Red Chamber*, was gone. Some of the books had been flung around and destroyed during the 1966 ransack; the rest had simply been burned later as fuel by Papa and Mama. When one's life is *alles kaput*, the fate of a book is of little consequence, particularly when the possession of that book and others like it imperils its owners.

I have often wondered what the outcome was of the following anecdote: One of the professors in the music college told his students in the 1950s when the good old Schirmer's music scores were becoming hard to get: "If there's a fire, I'll escape with only two books. The first one will be *Beethoven Sonatas, Volume One*, the second one will be *Beethoven Sonatas, Volume Two*." He survived the Cultural Revolution, but I doubt that his Beethovens did.

I was with Mama when she put the O'Henrys in the stove—I had put much effort into collecting them, and the set was still incomplete. When I started to object Mama looked at me and said: "Papa's gone, but if we live through all this, we'll get the books again." As I stared at the flames licking at the pages, I promised to myself that I'd rebuild my O'Henry collection some day.

However, as destiny closed a door, it opened a window, for the cremation of my conventional collection led me to seek the contemporary. Mama's library and my contributions to it had been chiefly in the order of classics, with very few specimens of modern literature. So it was actually during the adverse and harsh circumstances of the Cultural Revolution, during my years as a *fan-ge-ming*, that I first encountered Western literature of the 1950s and 1960s.

It is still an enigma to me, as well as to others, how those books got passed around during that period of cultural persecution. But I swear it was during the years between 1966 and 1976 that Saul Bellow, Nabokov, Mailer, and Michener found their way to me at the cadre school. I remember because *Herzog* stunned me and *Augie March* shocked me but vastly expanded my vocabulary. (I simply reveled in the fact that in *Herzog* Marx's writings became post-sex reading!) I wondered about *Lolita* when I fed the chickens and mused about *The Naked and the Dead* as I hoed a corn patch. I have an acute memory that sometimes embarrassed and infuriated my interrogators, but for some unaccountable reason a lacuna exists where the source of those books is concerned.

The only one I can account for is James Michener's *Hawaii*, which I found on Mama's bed after her unexpected death, the one with Anna Louise Strong's signature in it. The secret channels by which all the Mailers and Micheners made the rounds during those years in China may have been more devious and labyrinthine than Harriet Tubman's underground railroad, but they all landed in the right hands. By the way, that *Hawaii* was later returned to the lady who acquired the book legally from Madame Strong.

Such works of contemporary literature lit up my way and gave me more spiritual support than all my past reading. In Martin Esslin's essay "The Absurdity of the Absurd," he recounted how the inmates of San Quentin responded and related themselves to *Waiting for Godot*. In my own case, the staid old Victorian works I had read couldn't help me any longer—the times had changed so much there just weren't any more common denominators. I still remembered and savored every passage in *Pride and Prejudice*, but when one is dragged through the mud every day, politically and physically, Elizabeth's mortification over her soiled petticoats—a situation that had aroused commiseration in me when I was a girl—becomes trivial and insipid to say the least.

I found out, the hard way, how to deal with the intricate and often bewildering situations that faced me in that jungle of political intrigue and barbarity known as the "Cultural Revolution." My new reading in this period helped. The cynical, critical, and often aberrant attitudes to phenomena in life found in contemporary literature opened up facets of reality I had never been exposed to in the course of my "correct" upbringing and education. I began to see things in a new light and with new understanding, and I became stronger and tougher. What with my old world crumbling and my future uncertain, I had to be strong.

It was at this time that I came in contact with the highly informative and entertaining *The Rise and Fall of the Third Reich*.

I wonder if its author, William L. Shirer, ever learned that this book, in its Chinese translation, became the hottest book in China in the mid-1970s. In fact, it was so sought after that the one copy in four volumes Toto and I had between us was tattered by constant reading and lending. Each of us eventually bought another copy.

To understand historical issues, one often needs temporal insight; contemporary issues, on the other hand, are often seen most clearly in the light of history. By the years 1974 and 1975, all my friends, including some Party members, were audibly questioning the Cultural Revolution. *The Rise and Fall of the Third Reich* gave its Chinese readers much historical insight and inspiration as they inevitably compared the physical and mental peculiarities of the Third Reich with those of the Cultural Revolution.

There was a short paragraph about weddings under the Nazis where the newlyweds got copies of *Mein Kampf* for presents. We couldn't but laugh over that paragraph. There was a time in China, too, when newlyweds were given the *Selected Works of Mao Tse-tung* (four yuan per set) by friends, and *Quotations from Mao Tse-tung*—the "Little Red Book" (one yuan per copy) by mere acquaintances. The dilemma created for the young couple was that all the books were inscribed with the names of the well-wishers and recipients, and throwing away any works of Mao was a serious political crime! As for Hitler's "one nation, one leader, one thought" formula, we had had it with the "Generalissimo," and we had it again under Mao.

I was, of course, not alone in this search for new windows and for new knowledge. We Chinese had had a long history of reading only what was approved, required, or provided. Now, people were on their own in a chaotic political jungle, and for many the hunt for literary provender became a matter of intellectual and spiritual survival. Any publication was pounced upon and avidly read, so long as it wasn't produced by the official Chinese propaganda machine.

In the late 1970s, I visited an old family friend—one of the best-known writers in China. She was around eighty at the time, so I was surprised to see a paperback copy of *Jaws* in English on her desk. "You read *that?*" I asked impulsively, for it was definitely unorthodox and out of character. "One has to know what's going on in the world," she said simply. "Or one will suffocate behind these closed doors."

Those were the pioneers, those who rebelliously indulged in searching for and reading contemporary literature before the government gave its grudging and hesitant permission to "open up." When a limited opening finally did take place, not all of us Chinese were as ignorant or as naive as some in China and in the West imagined we would be.

1976, Tiananmen Square

Tiananmen, the Gate of Heavenly Peace, has witnessed many antiestablishment demonstrations in recent Chinese history, one of the most notable being the May 4th Movement of 1919—midwife to the birth of the Chinese Communist Party. Thus, it was logical that Mao Tse-tung should stand on the wide balcony of the gate, flanked by his peers and comrades-in-arms, to announce the founding of the People's Republic of China in 1949, and that the square in front of the gate should be used thereafter for government-sponsored political demonstrations. Pro-establishment rallies on this square reached their climax when millions after millions of hysterical Red Guards surged through it, waving their little red books at the distant uniform-clad figure of the Great Leader.

The irony is, however, that this sacred symbol of China's modern revolution apparently has a life of its own; the revolutionary spirit lives on, but has been redirected against the party it once spawned. This reversal in allegiance—if we may call it that—was first openly displayed by the 1976 Tiananmen Incident, the occurrence of which the establishment at the time did its best to cover up. Those sentiments culminated in the 1989 Tiananmen Incident, which the current establishment has tried hard to misrepresent, since international media coverage made concealment impossible. It was the 1989 incident that chiseled the name of this once sacred square deep in the consciousness of the world.

By 1976, the Cultural Revolution had dragged on into its tenth year. Except for the few who had benefited from the decade of turmoil, people in all of walks of society were sick and tired of the continuous chaos and disruption it was causing. Aware of the resentment, the authorities went through the motions of rectifying some of the most glaring excesses Mao had instigated or condoned. "Policy implementation" was more and more frequently mentioned in the news. The implication of this term, in the context of those times, was that the central authorities had always been correct and prudent in their handling of such issues as personal security, private property, banks savings, and so forth, and that the violations were merely a result of ignorance and of lower-level officials not acting as instructed. The hypocrisy of these insinuations was self-evident; the more often the slogan "implement the Party's policies" was repeated, the clearer it became how little such policies were worth, since they could be made, and discarded, at the whim of even a single man.

Tientsin was turned into a model for implementing the policies regarding private property. Many houses around our home were returned to their original owners. Some lucky families recovered their old homes in excellent condition; more had to pay for extensive repairs. The two families still residing in our house moved out accordingly, and we had the house to ourselves again in 1973. That was approximately two years before Mama died.

But there was little happening in other cities around the country, and even in Peking, restoring homes to their rightful owners was extremely difficult, since many of the better private houses had been taken over by high-ranking cadres, mostly from among the military, who arrogantly refused to give up their share of the spoils of the Cultural Revolution.

Antiques, jewelry, and furniture taken away by the Red Guards during the first ransacks—or at least those items that hadn't been stolen or that simply disappeared—had been stored in government warehouses and were now painstakingly identified and returned to their lawful owners. It was pure havoc, and rather than gratitude, there was much bitter feeling. Many of the owners had died of natural and unnatural causes in the meantime, and many of the objects were misidentified or had been badly damaged. Confiscated bank savings were also given back as part of the "policy implementation." But people only wondered at the cruelty and cynicism that permitted taking away even old people's life savings for years on end, leaving them to survive the best they could, and then expecting them to thank the Party for its "consistent attention" to policy implementation.

To make a long story short, the Chen family, minus Papa and Mama, found themselves back in possession of the Tientsin house, occupied now by Ah Po, Toto, Mimi, and Deedee.

Bella had become closer to us during and after Mama's unexpected death. In fact, she had given Toto immense physical and spiritual support in those trying times. Their marriage would probably be the best thing that could happen to this stricken and crippled family. So preparations for the wedding proceeded apace.

In northern China, it is customary for the groom's family to furnish practically everything, from housing to the bride's wardrobe, whereas in southern regions, such as Shanghai, the groom is expected to provide the housing (which we already had) while the bride's family sees to the rest. Since my own wedding conformed to neither regional custom, I was surprised at the size of Bella's trousseau. Her family sent her two sets of everything: pillows, pillowcases, quilts, blankets, coverlets, curtains, and much more. I forgave Toto for the smug look on his face; after all, he was getting lots of perks along with an attractive bride.

The wedding took place at her parents' house in Shanghai, where they honeymooned before returning to Tientsin to a homecoming celebration. We gave a big dinner, partly to celebrate the marriage, and partly to thank all those who had helped us when Mama died. We should have expressed our gratitude earlier, but we'd been too devastated at the time.

I then returned to the cadre school for the last time, for instructions had been given for the remaining cadres to pull out and report back in Peking. Yang and other of my friends had already left; Confu had generously distributed what was left of his movie posters as a farewell gift to his local contacts. I got back in time to help load the school's chattels onto trucks. After that was done, buses bore us away for good from the labor camp and the canal flowing before it.

We former cadre school members returned to Peking, but were still not assigned work; we were told to assemble six days a week, eight hours per day, at a place not too far from my apartment. The purpose: to study. (What was there to study?) Our seasoned army teamers returned to their *dan wei*, and they later wrote a collective report on how they accomplished their task of riding herd over some four hundred cadres for six years. We were assigned another group of "instructors," ostensibly because we intellectuals needed them to help us comprehend the newspaper articles we were studying.

This time, we leftovers were regrouped with some colleagues who had been too old or fragile to go to the countryside, as well as with a dozen people recently released from solitary confinement in state prisons. Our numbers again soared to some four hundred people. Those recent releases had been the elite, the cream of the cream, among China's artists, accused of crimes serious enough to warrant their being locked up for eight whole years.

It wasn't an easy homecoming for me. At the cadre school, age or status had not mattered—we were all in the same boat. But after I returned to Peking, being in my thirties and not having any work made me painfully conspicuous. Sometimes I found myself explaining to relative strangers that I had a *fan-ge-ming* problem and was awaiting policy implementation on my case— the feeling I had was that of a criminal waiting for amnesty.

The children stayed on in Tientsin, as it was uncertain where I'd be assigned work, although Fan and I, now estranged, still had to share the same one-room apartment. The atmosphere between us was excruciating. New aggravations had been added to the old ones. People told me about Fan's continued philandering, and it was like rubbing salt into a wound. Divorce was constantly on Fan's lips now. I asked him to put it off until next summer, a year after Mama's death; I would by then have recovered enough strength to go through with it, I hoped.

Fan slept in the double bed, while I retired to a corner of the room on a makeshift bed with a draw curtain—my "hands off" sign. Laid out beside my pillow were a few books, my reading light, and a transistor radio.

In the early morning of January 8, 1976, the news broadcast started with a dirge, followed by an announcement read by one of China's best veteran announcers; his normally well-modulated voice was now cracked with emotion. I at once sat up in bed and called out to Fan. Before the announcer had pronounced the name of the deceased, I knew that Chou En-lai had left us— only his death could have evoked such genuine emotion in the announcer.

I hastily pulled on some clothes and ran to the apartment of some very close neighbors. Knocking until the family opened the door, I told them the bad news and we all cried together. The old man, an active do-gooder, had met Chou many times during theater performances and had taken pictures of him. Chou called him familiarly "Whiskers." I went out that morning, aimlessly, driven by an urge to find someone, somewhere, to share our sorrow. The entire country was in mourning, spontaneous, heartfelt mourning—not grief by decree. The overwhelming feeling was that, with Chou gone, we had no one left to place our hopes upon.

That Sunday, Chou's funeral cortege passed Chang An Chieh, the Avenue of Everlasting Peace, to the center of the city, Tiananmen Square, then further west to the Pa Pao Shan cemetery where the body would be cremated. I stood with my bike at the western section of that avenue, which was lined dozens deep with spectators frozen in grief, and watched the last public appearance of Chou En-lai, China's one truly great statesman, a great human being, whose untiring efforts had touched the lives of so many people.

That grief did not die down over the weeks and months. It lingered, converged, and merged with the general resentment and anger felt by the populace. Then, in the early days of April, it erupted on the Tiananmen Square in the largest spontaneous demonstration of public discontent since the founding of the People's Republic.

Chinese tradition calls for paying respects to the dead during the Ching Ming season, which usually falls on the fifth or sixth of April. Since 1959, the goverment had used the occasion to organize on Tiananmen Square rituals commemorating the martyrs who died during years of revolutionary warfare. Wreaths of flowers handmade from white paper would be ceremoniously laid at the foot of the Cenotaph to the People's Heroes on a designated date.

Despite the solemn official obsequies for Chou organized by the authorities, despite the countless newspaper articles and pictorials published to remember Chou's life and works, and despite the innumerable photographs sold after his death, which now hung in almost every home I visited, popular feeling was not assuaged. At the end of March, one single paper flower was tied during the night to the marble balustrade encircling the cenotaph. No dedication was attached to this simple offering, but people who saw the flower knew who it was for, and what it represented. The news spread and grew. The first wreaths were laid in secrecy.

Why did such caution accompany the popular commemoration of a Communist Party leader in a communist country? Many from the West failed to comprehend at first that the flowers weren't simply a thumbs-up sign for Chou; the subtlety of the gesture was typically Chinese. Chou was loved by the people not as a communist, but because he was a sagacious, humane, and upright administrator. Now, the grief over his death held powerful overtones of regret and despair that he had left the people to face—without his efforts at moderation—the strife and insanity created by an obviously paranoid and senile leader, Mao, still alive at the time. Every word of praise for Chou's qualities as a man and a politician were pointed indictments of the lack of such qualities in his peers. Each new flower became, increasingly, a personal expression of anger and defiance. The authorities, ever suspicious and wary of spontaneous popular demonstrations, understood these things as clearly as the ordinary citizen. They sent in street cleaners, at night, to trash and cart away the offending and inflammatory flowers and wreaths. But these attempts failed after a day or two when the mourners posted pickets, mostly college students and young workers, to prevent further removals.

When I first went to the square, a week before Ching Ming, it was only sparsely adorned with flowers. I didn't linger, because orders had already been issued at every *dan wei* to keep away; there could be trouble. By the weekend, however, I could no longer hold myself back and went with my neighbor, old man Whiskers. The entire area around the cenotaph was a solid mass of millions of paper flowers. Even the tall lampposts were covered with them.

The two of us squeezed our way up to the marble balustrade and found places to tie our white flowers—on top of other flowers. I had made one for each member of my family, including my deceased parents. Whiskers and I read all the dedications within sight; thousand of poems, messages, and single characters like "forever," "love," "mourn." There was a commotion behind us, and I turned to see a group of factory workers carrying on their shoulders an enormous placard bearing one single character, *Hsiang*. It means "miss (you)," "longing (for you)," "remember," "think," "reflect"—a word of many interpretations, but which summed up the feelings of all who were there that day.

By the time we turned to go, the huge square was almost impassable. The day we went to Tiananmen Square, it must have held more than a million people, coming and going. I told Whiskers I wished I could have brought Mimi and Deedee from Tientsin just to be here. Seeing this massive manifestation of the people's true sentiments was the lesson of a lifetime.

No newspapers, however, made any mention of the ordinary citizens' actions at Tiananmen; the powers were biding their time.

The crackdown took place in the night of April 5, the date for Ching Ming that year. Night was the preferred time for such operations, both in 1976 and in 1989.

There was never any public record or account of what actually happened. The policemen and thugs used for the job, as later in 1989, were not local men. After broadcasting an ultimatum to people keeping vigil at the cenotaph, ordering them to leave the area, they swept through the square, smashing wreaths, ripping up flowers, and arresting everyone in sight. Brutality and violence was committed on the mourners, reportedly with clubs and iron chains. People who passed by Tiananmen on their way to work early the next morning were stunned to see that everything was gone, as if nothing had ever happened there. Traffic, however, was redirected, and the square itself was sealed off. An informed friend told me it took three days to hose away the blood.

A vicious witch-hunt ensued. Every resident in Peking was compelled to state whether he or she had gone to the Tiananmen Square in these critical days from the end of March to Ching Ming. Everyone denied being there. All my acquaintances gave the following statement, as if on cue: "I was on my way by bus (or bike) to the West (or East) City to visit relatives, and I happened to pass the square. That's all." Nobody had stopped, or entered the square, it seemed, although only a few days ago, all had been excitedly exchanging eyewitness accounts.

There were informers in some factories, we learned, and the police put out a wanted notice for one man: male, medium height, with a crewcut. I wonder if they ever got their man. There also were executions, not based on this incident alone, but with other accusations thrown in for good measure.

The 1989 Tiananmen demonstration was in many respects a repetition of this little-publicized tragedy, only now the world knew.

The Tangshan Earthquake, and Mimi Acts as Sentinel

The most lethal but least reported seismic catastrophe in human history is the Tangshan earthquake of 1976. The death toll of this quake may never be known, but estimates of the casualties range between one quarter to one third of a million, out of a population of a million inhabitants in that city.

After so many years, I still recall the eerie silence and unbearable heat that preceded the quake. On the night of July 27–28, 1976, I was at home all by myself in our fourth floor apartment in Peking. My children were still living in Tientsin; Fan was out of town. It was so hot I slept in nothing but my undies. Not a single leaf rustled and not a breath stirred the air. There was only the oppressive silence and intense heat.

I fell asleep in the wee hours of the morning, only to be jolted awake by violent shaking and bouncing. My bed skittered backward and forward, and everything in the room rattled. But the most terrifying sound came from the window; it was as though a thousand freight trains were clanging and rumbling into the city.

I managed to scramble out of the rocking bed. Slipping into some clothes and grabbing my handbag with my keys in it, I ran down the swaying concrete slabs of the stairway and joined the cluster of neighbors under the trees between the buildings. All were in a state of shock and bewilderment. Very few families had TVs in 1976, and there were no programs on at that hour anyway, either on TV or on the radio. Nor did China have any emergency phone numbers, so there was no way of obtaining any information.

The only thing we did know at the time was that the quake had started around 3:42 A.M. It was days later before we learned that the city of Tangshan, three hundred miles from Peking as the crow flies, had been flattened by an 8.2 degree quake on the Richter scale and that hundreds of thousands had been killed instantly.

Dawn came amid general confusion and indecision. Then relatives started to trickle in on bikes: sons, daughters, or siblings living in other parts of the city. Very few families had phones in those years, and we learned by word of mouth about crumbled walls in the *hutungs*, sleeping families smothered in their ramshackle courtyard houses, asphalt roads ripped open . . . yet daily newspapers carried not a single line on the terrible earthquake.

I went up to the fourth floor a couple of times for more clothes, some food, and the bankbook with our meager savings. Then it started to rain, and what a downpour it was! For hours, people in the entire neighborhood stood or sat under umbrellas in the deluge, waiting for something to come, or to end.

We all assumed that the quake had occurred only in Peking, and since I was okay, I saw no reason to needlessly alarm my folks in Tientsin by phoning them. It was not until late afternoon that I heard, again by word of mouth, that the epicenter had been at Tangshan and that Tientsin, being nearer to Tangshan, had been hit much harder than Peking.

I went into a panic, realizing that while I had stood in relative safety under the trees, my dear ones in Tientsin might have been injured or killed. I tried to call the post office nearest to our Tientsin home. The Peking operator told me the phone line still worked but that no one was answering at the other end. I tried the Peking train station, and after many attempts finally got through. Yes, there would be trains to Tientsin, though only the next morning as all power was out and no night trains were running.

I spent the second night in agony, huddled sleeplessly under the trees. At the crack of dawn I picked up a few things and left for the train station after entrusting the apartment to the care of neighbors. Pedaling to the station on my bike, I lined up to get onto any train for Tientsin. My train arrived in that city around noon, moving cautiously over juddering, quake-warped sections of rail. All during the trip I heard nothing but wild rumors and conjectures.

I came to a changed city. There were no buses; I had to walk the five or six miles home. And it was when I had crossed the iron bascule bridge over the Hai River and was passing through the former British Concession that the power of the shocks became evident: blocks of marble had fallen from the facades of commercial and bank buildings, cracked pillars leaned drunkenly over the sidewalks, large chunks of cement littered the boulevards. It was high noon, but the streets were empty. As I approached the shopping and residential area farther south, I saw the walls of a familiar four-story apartment building split from roof to basement.

This was the second time in ten years I had come home in fear, not knowing what had happened to my loved ones. On both occasions—August 1966 and July 1976—it was noon time when I arrived.

All along our block people of all ages were lying or sitting on the street and pavements. The city authorities had sent out orders that people should stay in their houses as little as possible in case further shocks occurred. I recognized neighbors and friends; they waved and told me this neighborhood had been spared by the first shocks, and that several families were now quartered in our house.

I quickened my steps and came home to what seemed almost like a garden party, as my Mimi and Deedee flew into my arms and I was surrounded by a small crowd of older acquaintances whom I dutifully uncled and auntied. After the hubbub quieted down I learned Toto had offered accommodations in our house to several families whose homes had been damaged or destroyed, and that he had gone to see heavily pregnant Bella off to Shanghai for her safety. None of us suspected at the time that, for some of these families, this invitation would extend to almost seven years—the time it would take the city authorities to render their houses habitable again.

Our house, a one-story building, had not suffered any damage, thanks to some seismic caprice. It so happened that the first major tremor had "rippled" through Tientsin, smashing some districts and sparing others. Our home was in one of the two avenues left completely unscathed by the quake, and Toto had at the crack of dawn asked some old friends of our parents to come and share our place, including our own aunt and uncle from Nankai University.

Tientsin is in fact one of China's largest commercial and industrial cities. The death toll here during the first tremor is said to have exceeded 50,000, another figure that has never been officially released or verified.

Many of the casualties were caused by walls of two- and three-story houses simply collapsing onto their lower neighbors and burying entire families. Buildings with their sides stripped off stood like stage props with their interiors exposed. In one of these I saw a chest of drawers teetering precariously on the edge of one of the floors, undecided as to which way to fall.

One of our friends escaped from such a house, leaving her savings booklet in her room on the second floor. A neighbor's son volunteered to retrieve it for her. He climbed into a tree growing next to the house and crawled along a branch to get into her room where he found the savings booklet in a drawer. Then he jumped down to street level onto a stack of quilts placed below by others.

When I arrived in Tientsin, initial news from Tangshan at the epicenter still consisted mainly of unconfirmed reports that roads had been severed and most buildings destroyed, and that troops—the People's Liberation Army (PLA)—had been sent into the region to carry out rescue operations. But as more and more injured were trucked out and as refugees sought relatives in other cities, details became available about the devastation of the city.

Tangshan, a major coal mining and industrial city in north China, had grown rapidly in the three previous decades. Hundreds of new factories and apartment blocks had gone up. Many of the more recent buildings had been put together with prefabricated concrete slabs, stacked up like houses of cards. Those situated at or near the epicenter collapsed accordion-like, crushing the inhabitants in their sleep. The first troops on the scene were not equipped with machinery or lifting equipment, and although they labored valiantly to extricate those trapped alive under the heavy slabs, their efforts were largely futile. Casualties were also very heavy in the surface facilities of the mines, but, strangely enough, few miners underground died.

One of Toto's former schoolmates had been assigned work in Tangshan after graduating from college. During the quake her entire family—she, her husband, and two young boys—were buried under a pile of slabs. Pinned down and unable to move, she could just manage to touch her boys' hands. Cries of agony rose all around, then gradually died away as the hours passed. Her boys had only the strength to whimper, "Mama, it hurts," "Mama, I can't breathe." Immobilized from the waist down by those slabs, both parents listened helplessly to their sons' last gasps. The adults were dug out after a couple of days; both survived, crippled, the mother unable ever to have children again.

Many families lost both parents, and thousands of "Tangshan orphans," as they became known, were sent to cities around the country to be taken care of. Rescuers paid a heavy price in life and limb as they dug for survivors or bodies among the piles of masonry which continued to collapse with each aftershock. Stocks of plastic body bags ran out, and disposing of the rapidly decomposing corpses was a particularly onerous task. The survivors could be thankful, however, that no epidemics occurred, despite the unsanitary conditions and the summer heat. Nor were there any major fires of the kind that often break out after an earthquake. The victims were at least spared these added afflictions.

It was the immediate decision of the Central Committee of the CCP to rigidly control all press releases about the quake. The rare releases in the first days after the quake were curt and vague, and tried to play down the extent of the disaster. A few days later, reports appeared that praised the heroism of the soldiers and survivors; one particularly dramatic story was about a dozen or so miners who emerged after being trapped for nineteen days underground.

But there were few damage descriptions and no casualty estimates. The 8.2-degree quake was reported as being of 7.9-degree magnitude, for, as we learned later, all areas hit by earthquakes above 8.0-degree magnitude automatically qualified for international relief and assistance. This meant that international relief workers and foreign observers would be able to enter the area and see things with their own eyes.

Nobody fully understood at the time, or even many years later, why the Central Committee felt it had to hide information about the quake from the outside world. Indeed, there has been much bitterness among the survivors about the CCP's refusal of international aid, which could have mitigated their sufferings and reduced the number of post-quake deaths. Did the CCP feel they would somehow lose face by admitting that such an appalling disaster could take place in their "superior" socialist society? Was it a xenophobic fear of snooping outsiders seeing embarrassing negative aspects of Chinese society? Or was it simply the instinctive secretiveness of a totalitarian regime? Whatever the reason or reasons, the code of silence prevailed for almost ten years, and never has any authoritative data been made public about casualties and damage resulting from the Tangshan quake.

The terror inspired by the quake predictably gave rise to superstitious conjectures. Older people observed that earthquakes had often preceded the deaths of kings and emperors in ancient times; that Chou En-lai and Marshal Chu Teh had both died in 1976 and such things usually come in threes. So, many prophesied darkly that "He" (Mao Tse-tung) would soon die, and like the ancient tyrants, was taking along hundreds of thousands of sacrificial victims into the grave. Mao did indeed die forty days later.

Everyday life in Tientsin took on a wartime aspect on account of the frequent quakes and the crowded living accommodations. All who had spare rooms shared them with those less fortunate, and many took temporary refuge in safer houses whenever a major aftershock was predicted. One night, we put up nineteen people in all.

The more permanent guests at our house brought their own stoves and fuel as well as couponed rice, beans, flour, and other food from their vacated homes. For a couple of months, we organized our daily life like that in a commune. The older women cooked while their menfolk lined up at grocery stores to snap up whatever happened to be available. The younger people worked at reinforcing the house against further quakes and took turns standing guard at night to warn others in case of a major aftershock.

I asked for an extension to my leave of absence from the study session in Peking, and since everyone else was earthquake-vacationing anyway, I was grudgingly allowed to stay away. Toto had to go to work every day while I enjoyed a good share of communal life at our once-again crowded homestead in Tientsin.

Our menu consisted mainly of bean sprouts and easy-to-make Chinese ravioli. Vegetables and meat were hard to find, so the three or four families all pooled their mung beans and soy beans and raised bean sprouts. To relieve the monotony of our diet, we tried all kinds of ingredients for ravioli stuffing. One stove was kept burning day and night to heat water for the numerous thermos flasks needed by Chinese families. The yard served as a parking lot for bicycles, our chief means of transportation. The bikes were purposely left in the open in case the house collapsed during a quake.

For the quake sentinels, we put up a tent by attaching a now-precious plastic sheet to a framework of long bamboo canes. Toto and I contributed Papa's favorite *tsung-peng*—a bed made of coir rope stretched tautly over wooden supports—as it was resistant to rain and damp. Ah Po sniffled a bit over that bed, for it had been promised to her for her remaining years. But she gave it up for the cause with good grace.

The able-bodied took turns lying awake at night in the mosquito-netted tent and watching a pail of water placed beside the bed. When the water's surface began to rock, the sentinel would go to the entrance of the house and yell: "Tremor! Wake up!" Or, "Earthquake! Get out!" when the rocking became violent.

Mimi begged for permission to join us on these nocturnal exercises. She was nearly twelve and considered herself equal to the grown-ups; she was also duty-conscious and serious by nature. So she was allowed to serve as co-sentinel with me and Toto. That is, for as long as she managed to stay awake.

I treasured those intimate moments that Mimi and I shared, alone with heaven and earth and that pail of water. As we lay on Papa's bed I told her stories about our family, and she in turn told me about her life when I wasn't around.

One stormy night, rainwater rose almost level with the low bed. We felt chilly, and I held Mimi close. "Come on, let's go in!" I said finally. "The earth won't shake when there's such a storm!" But Mimi refused, saying: "What if the water in the pail starts to rock and there's no one here to raise the alarm?" And she added stubbornly: "Go in if you want to. I'll sit here until the next person comes to relieve me!"

We laughed and sat huddled together in the makeshift tent. I realized then that my baby daughter had grown up so quickly that I'd missed out on much of her childhood. Most parents like to shield their young from the vicissitudes of the outside world, but my Mimi had been through the ransacks in both Tientsin and Peking, had taken trips alone by bus and train since she was six, and now was already assuming the responsibilities of a young adult. I observed her with mixed feelings as she gravely assisted in her first major assignment—watching over a pail of water for signs of more earthquakes.

The next quake, however, was to be of an entirely different nature.

Cry for Joy

The Tangshan earthquake crisis subsided somewhat and we were summoned back to the "Office of Those-to-Be-Reassigned-Work" to resume our studies. Among the four hundred or more candidates for work assignments were quite a number of well-known cultural figures, and after having spent some time on their home turf in Peking, most were quite well informed about the goings-on in the capital. However, we did all our gossiping and rumor-swapping outside the meeting rooms, and behaved like idiots and zombies during the study sessions.

One afternoon in early September 1976, agitated instructors came to the meeting rooms and ordered everybody to gather in the auditorium for an emergency meeting. Tension rose immediately, triggering speculation as to whether we would be sent off again to some remote labor camp. But the signs seemed to tell a different story. We spotted some of the instructors looking somber and tearful. I exchanged a glance with one of my buddies, and I could tell that he and I shared the same hunch: that He had died—the He being, of course, Mao.

When we were assembled, the head of the current instructors made the announcement, chokingly, that our Great Leader had passed away, that the news would be broadcast the same evening, and that the entire country would then go into official mourning. We stood with bowed heads and all around me there was loud sobbing, real or simulated, but I found it impossible to summon tears. Out of the corner of my eye I noticed that my cousin Wei, who happened to be standing next to me, was glancing around with airy nonchalance. I groaned inwardly: "Come on, at least bow your head, so you won't be so conspicuous!" But to poke him or hiss at him would only make things worse.

Fortunately, at this juncture there was a loud crash and a commotion at the other side of the auditorium. A man had fainted and all attention was focused on him! He was quickly taken away for medical care. I was really tickled when I found out the fainter was a pal of mine; I couldn't for the world believe he was so attached to Mao as to be that grief-stricken! Years later, I asked him about that incident, and he admitted sheepishly that he did suffer from rare attacks of epilepsy, but it was pure coincidence that an attack should have occurred right then and there. At any rate, it proved to be providential for him, for he was subsequently cited for displaying deep affection for the Great Leader!

I was not entirely unaffected by Mao's death. Mao was an idealist and a tyrant with absolutely no regard for the value of human life; he had his weaknesses and a destructive obsession for class struggle. But he also achieved certain of his ambitions for China. History will be his judge. In September 1976, however, we were more concerned and apprehensive about what would happen after Mao's death and what our own fate would be.

As we anticipated, the screws were tightened again. The instructors began a new campaign to trace the authors and disseminators of a spate of rumors concerning the Communist Party leadership. We were informed that the campaign would be carried out nationwide, and in view of the past political records of many of us to-be-reassigned reactionaries, we were again to become the focus of a witch-hunt. "Those who are exposed as rumormongers will be sent away, for life," we were warned. "The only way out for you is to confess."

Knowing what could lie in store for most of us, we tried to evade, to stall; we had been dragged through the mud once—some of us twice—in our lifetime, and that was enough. I was ordered to turn in a "thought report." But Cousin Wei was under the greatest pressure, for he had talked too freely about Chiang Ching with his old pals. Wei told me he might have to come clean any day; the pressure was becoming unbearable.

It was a Thursday evening and I was feeling so dejected that instead of going home after the study session, I decided to pop over to my lifelong friend's home just to kill time. My friend, who was in the navy, wasn't home, but his wife pulled me through the door and said excitedly: "Those four, they're all gone!"

"What are you talking about?" I asked.

"It's all over navy headquarters. When people meet they stick out four fingers and then make a grabbing gesture. The four have been taken into custody."

"Which four?"

"Can't you guess?!"

"Chiang Ching?"

"Yes," she affirmed emphatically.

"Yao? Chang?"

"Yes, yes!"

"Oh, God, has it really happened?! Who's the fourth?"

"Wang Hongwen, the Vice President of the State."

"Well, it serves him right. Now, tell me how it happened and who took them in?"

She told me what she had learned from her husband who was out again information-gathering. I bade her repeat the news once, then again; only then was I able to accept the fact that it was "all over" now. That was the first time any of us heard of the term "Gang of Four."

She suggested we do something to celebrate and we decided to walk a couple of blocks to Wang Fu Ching Street, one of Peking's main shopping areas. We strolled in the gathering dusk, looking around at everything and everyone. It seemed strange that after such a momentous event the city still looked the same as ever.

"How wonderful it feels!" remarked my companion. "We alone know something nobody else knows. What would happen if I were to yell out the news?"

I said I was bursting with joy, too. Indeed, I wanted to laugh, to cry, to shout, but all I could do was revel silently in the foreknowledge of a return to sanity in our lives.

As we sauntered on blissfully, we spotted a small group of people clustered around an automobile, listening to something. We crossed the street and pushed close to listen. It was only the evening news on the car radio. We walked away, commenting pointedly: "That's no news!"

Lifelong hadn't come back yet from his scouting, and his wife joked: "Now he's got a good excuse to stay out late and get plastered!"

On my way home I stopped at Cousin Wei's place to share the as yet forbidden tidings.

"They got that woman!" were his first words on opening the door.

I was crestfallen. "Oh, come on, I was supposed to tell you the news!"

We exchanged information and I observed that Wei didn't look particularly happy. "Damn it," he said. "Why didn't I get the news earlier! I went to `fess up' today and came home to learn that the Gang was gone. Now I've made a fool of myself."

I remembered that I had been told to hand in a report on my political thinking, and I asked Wei if I should still do it. He said: "Why not? And be sure to mark the date. It'll make a good joke, you reporting to a regime that is no longer in existence."

I spread the news around as much as I dared in the apartment building I lived in. Fan came home rather late, as usual, and when I told him, he wouldn't believe me. So he went out again to check with reliable neighbors. If it were true, he said, it would be like another earthquake!

The next few days were like playing cat and mouse. The instructors were as strident as ever about class enemies doing the wisest thing by giving themselves up. Those among us who knew the truth spoke in riddles, voicing ardent support for the gone regime with barely concealed sarcasm in the meeting rooms, and whispering news to each other during breaks; those who hadn't heard the news were obviously mystified and asked what was going on.

When I had collected a good stock of information, I went all the way to Peking's West City that Sunday afternoon to visit another cousin. I rattled into her courtyard on my ancient Raleigh bike and found her alone at home and in a very depressed mood. "I feel so listless," she said. "Even the sky looks sad today."

I beamed and said: "C'mon, I'm here to cheer you up!" I made that four-fingers-and-grab gesture, then told her everything I knew. She made me repeat all I said over and over.

She, too, wanted to celebrate. So she dug out from her precious hoard of provisions a can of stewed beef. That was a real feast in those days. To this day I am reminded of the Gang of Four whenever I see a can of stewed beef at the supermarket.

Naturally, the first person I wanted to share the news with was Toto. But with no access to a telephone at home, and no guarantee that a letter would not be checked, how could I tell him? I finally wrote a letter full of riddles and allegories and hoped he would understand that something tremendously good had happened.

I remembered we had sworn the previous year that if ever the tide turned, we'd tell our parents in heaven. So I ended my letter with two lines from a classical Chinese poem: "The day our enemies are brought to justice, do not forget to tell your ancestors at the memorial rites." I hoped he would get the message.

I couldn't control myself any longer when it became evident that more and more people had learned about the Gang's demise. I spent a precious five yuan on a two-way train ticket to Tientsin the next weekend. Toto and I hugged each other and I asked him how he had reacted to my letter.

He told me he was at first bewildered by the enigmatic phrases I had written. Then he realized I was trying to tell him something important. He finally deciphered my message. He could hardly contain himself. But he had no one to confide in at the moment: Bella was having their baby in Shanghai, my children were too young, and he didn't dare be the first to spread the news in Tientsin. So he picked up a chair and whirled around the room in an impromptu waltz of celebration!

By the time I got to Tientsin the news was all over the country—spread by word of mouth. I was at last able to face the truth with my babies. Deedee climbed into my lap and asked: "Uncle told me I'm a victim of the Gang of Four, too, 'cause I was locked up in a prison. Am I?" Laughing, I gathered both my children in my arms. Then a lump rose in my throat as I realized that I would now be able to go back to work like a normal person and have my children with me again.

And I cried, for everything I had lost during this insane nightmare, and for all the pain and grief and misery these years had witnessed. I could cry at last, and cry for joy.

PART IV

LIFE BEGINS AT FORTY (1979-)

China—U.S.—China—U.S.—China—U.S . . .

The Pathos of Atonement

After ten years of the nightmare, I now walked on a cloud, finding it hard to believe I had become, once again, a normal person. But I was not quite the same person as before, not anymore.

Unlike Americans, the Chinese rarely took matters into their own hands in those days; we waited for orders and arrangements. The instructors placed in charge of us in the last months of the Cultural Revolution were hastily summoned back to where they came from, and our group of cadres-in-waiting took care of ourselves. We watched the antics of opportunists who had profited from the Cultural Revolution, who now began to say that *they* had opposed the Gang of Four all the time. But we leftovers from the cadre school shared pride in the fact that, for whatever reasons, we and we only had remained defiant to the end—the end of the Gang of Four.

I now acknowledged to those who were still in my study group that I'd said Jiang Qing* was "*huo guo yang min,*" a term now applied officially to the gang. Someone gasped, "You really did say that? No wonder the teamers refused to let you tell us about your case!" I reminded them that I'd never admitted to being wrong; I had simply said I'd lost, since I hadn't anticipated such a total turnabout. Now history had vindicated me.

Vindication came at a very heavy price. The biggest loser was the Chinese Communist Party itself, but most of the suffering fell to the lot of countless ordinary people.

In the last months of our waiting-for-work phase I met, through Cousin Wei, a film writer who had been held in the Qin Cheng State Prison near Beijing for eight long years. "When it comes to doing time in prison," commented Wei wryly, "I'm no competition for him. I've only been to various labor camps, detention sites, and quasi-labor camps like our cadre school. He

---

* Starting in Part IV, I will be using the *pinyin* romanization system for the names of Chinese people and places.

qualifies as a state prisoner!" This writer, Chi, had authored books on Chinese films, and, purely as a record of historical fact, made references to Lan Ping, alias Jiang Qing, and her roles in the several films she played in. For whatever reason, Jiang Qing's past life was taboo and her wrath crashed down on his head.

That happened in 1967. Police came to the China Film Association, handcuffed Chi, led him through two rows of his colleagues summoned to line up and watch, and took him away in a jeep. He was delivered to Qin Cheng, China's only state-of-the-art, escape-proof prison. It was not until ten years later, after the downfall of the Gang, that he learned the reason for his imprisonment. A slip of paper (a *slip!*) was discovered among the files of the already deceased Minister of Public Security bearing Chi's name and *dan wei* in Jiang Qing's handwriting with the instruction "put him in prison." The minister carried out her order, and Chi spent three thousand days and nights in solitary confinement.

Chi was not tortured or even interrogated; he was only requested to write thought reports. His family—his wife, then in her thirties, and two young sons—were not told what had happened to him; he simply vanished. For five years, his wife didn't know whether she was a wife or a widow. It was in the fifth year of his confinement that his eldest son was first allowed to visit him. He didn't recognize the boy, now a teenager. Other than his bunk, the only thing in his rubber-lined cell was a bucket; and the sole source of light was a bulb outside that was kept on permanently. His only suit of clothes gradually frayed to shreds and he knotted the loose ends to keep it in one piece. Only in the fifth year were state prisoners given some meat to eat once a week and allowed to read the official newspaper, the *People's Daily*.

I asked how he had managed to stay sane and in good health. He said he made a point of talking to himself to keep his tongue limber and his ears attuned to hearing a human voice, and he exercised regularly with a set of head-neck-and-limb movements he devised himself. Chi was released in 1975 without a word of explanation.

Chi eventually had the satisfaction of personally witnessing the sentencing of Jiang Qing. He was notified to attend the trial and had a seat next to the former First Lady, Wang Guangmei, now a widow. "One could almost feel waves of hatred pulsing from the spectators' stands," Chi said afterward. "Despite the judge's orders to the contrary, we applauded wildly when Jiang

Qing was sentenced to life in prison." Jiang Qing was committed to that very same prison Chi was held in, and stayed there until she hanged herself some fifteen years later.

As stories of persecution and torture came to light I heard the story of a woman whose circumstances were so similar to mine that her fate, too, could have been my own. Her story was one of the few that were officially acknowledged in reports transmitted to government functionaries.

She had been a few years older than I, married, with two children, and served as a minor functionary in one of the northeastern provinces. An energetic and outspoken person, she had been a Party member since her late teens. She criticized Jiang Qing's speeches and actions at approximately the same time as I did, and the charges leveled at both of us were very much the same. She was thrown in prison for her remarks but she never recanted. The prison warders and some male prisoners gang-raped her before she was executed. As she kept cursing Jiang Qing at the top of her lungs, the executioners slashed her vocal cords before dragging her out to be shot in the back of the head.

She came from a family in Tianjin, had played the violin when she was young, and two of her younger sisters had also been students at the Central Music Conservatory. Her husband was pressured into divorcing her; he took the children. Many people wept when her story was made known. Her warders and torturers were eventually punished as a result of massive popular protest, but that was only one drop in the bucket; many thousands of innocent people had been killed hideously and ignominiously in those years of darkness while their tormentors got off scot-free.

I shuddered uncontrollably when I first heard that story, and I refused to listen to it again, for I knew then what a narrow escape I had in 1968.

The Office of Those-to-Be-Reassigned-Work was now on the eve of being disbanded, for the entire nation was trying to pull together to return to normalcy. But none of the associations we'd come from had yet been reestablished. Where were we to go, some four hundred top professionals, including almost all the surviving former chairmen and directors of the Federation of Literature and Arts and its various associations?

The older ones refused to retire; they still wanted to have a go at their careers to make up for the ten years they'd lost. Not many were under forty, like myself, since most of the younger cadres had been sent back to work a couple of years earlier. Because I was a "case," half resolved but hard to wrap up, I remained in this limbo until the downfall of the Gang.

I was given a choice this time: I could name any institution in the music field as my future *dan wei*. Three things helped me make up my mind.

I had earned some fame as a journalist despite my tender years. But after the things I'd been through, I knew the penalty for expecting freedom of speech (or thought) in a totalitarian state, so I vetoed that alternative. I still wrote as a hobby in later years, and won acclaim for my articles as well as for the titles I crowned them with.

I had also tried translating, English to Chinese, in the last and mostly inactive years of cadre school, and I realized I had great potential in that field.

The third reason was probably the decisive one. I was thoroughly sickened by the inhumane and odious roles played in my abduction by my former schoolmates A, B, and C. Another behind-the-scenes person was "Doggie," a younger student who had concluded that A, B, C, and D (the four classmates are listed by age; D represents me) were the prime movers in the student body, and so had followed us around like his namesake. The nickname also referred to his reputation for having an extraordinary nose for what would serve him best. His actions during the Cultural Revolution categorized him as an extreme leftist and he had participated in many abductions. I'd once spotted Doggie strutting around through the small window of my lockup.

After the downfall of the Gang, Doggie suddenly made out as though he'd been politically correct all those years, and that he had been against the Gang. He piped down somewhat after his victims warned him they knew about his little game. (The last time I noticed his existence was in 1989, somewhere in the United States. He's probably still here, an abductor, an extremist, and an opportunist. Good people beware, for he can still fool those who don't know his true colors.)

A, B, C, and Doggie all belonged at that time to the Music Conservatory, but the music studies' world is small, and I'd still have to put up with their hostility as well as their hypocrisy. I now chose to leave the music milieu and told those in charge of our job placements that I wished to be put in the translating section instead of the music section of the Arts Research Academy where most of us appeared to be going.

I had no intention of settling accounts with A, B, C, or Doggie, but, Fate hath its ways. I came upon A and B one day in the mess hall of my temporary new *dan wei.* My hands were full with my bowl and plate, so I didn't have to shake hands—which, in any case, I had no intention whatsoever of doing. They acted as though they were my chums, and even had the gall to ask about my children. I remained deliberately cool and distant while they informed me cheerfully they were attending a three-day conference at the arts academy, and proposed that we meet again the next day.

I was taken aback by their unabashedness and nonchalance, until I realized that A and B didn't know I had learned about their role in my abduction through our good-natured driver's unexpected confession. In any event, the game was between A, B, and myself now.

They came to me again the next day and asked me to visit them, which in Chinese is "come play." I looked at them squarely and replied, "Now look, I believe certain things need explaining before I `go play.' You know exactly what I mean. It's not over until everything has been clarified."

That triggered a long letter written by B, the husband. He was usually a henpecked type of person, and the assertive tone in which the letter was written was more like that of his wife. B wrote in effect: Yeah, we did it, so what? He claimed it was their belief at the time that I was abetting the wrong faction, and they did not learn I had been beaten until much later. B had the nerve to state that their faction had been humane to me—probably meaning that I was still alive. But the most aggravating remark was the suggestion that I should "take a correct attitude toward revolutionary mass movements."

I was furious and tore the letter in half. Then I thought better of it and did not shred the pages. I called a confab of my closest buddies, Yang and others who pounded the ground with me on the day of Henry Kissinger's visit. They were now all assigned to teaching jobs at the Music Conservatory, their alma mater, and thus new colleagues of A, B, and Doggie. C had left this profession.

I gave the torn letter to my buddies to read and asked them to brief me on A, B, and Doggie's circumstances. They told me Doggie was talking about joining the CCP, and A was aiming for the vacant Deputy Chair seat, assuming that nobody was aware of her underhanded dealings.

I decided to write them a long letter, stating that I knew about their role in my abduction, including Doggie's showing up in the dungeon lane; I told them about the treatment I had been subjected to and how I lost my teeth. I told them while I wasn't able to forgive, I could forget.

"Judging from your letter," I concluded, "there is little we can communicate on. This letter and yours will be transmitted to you by hand in an open envelope; those who choose to read them are welcome to do so. There is no need for any further explanation."

My letter and theirs were handed to them by the last person on the list of names I jotted down on the envelope. That person later told me the stratagem had worked, for the two abandoned politics and any executive ambitions they'd harbored and turned to more academic pursuits.

One day, I was asked to an office to sign a document on the official overturn of my "case." The person in charge of the office, whom I knew, gave me a notification concerning the dismissal of all charges against me and guaranteeing that everything on the case would be taken out of my personal file. (I looked at him and asked, "You expect me to believe that?!") After I had signed, he continued to look at me expectantly.

"Are you waiting for me to make a statement of thanks?" I asked.

"Not exactly," he replied.

"Well, I thank you personally for going to the trouble, but the whole thing is about righting a wrong that shouldn't have been committed in the first place. You can report that I showed no sign of being grateful. I've only come to end a chapter, a long one."

He half-smiled and remarked, "No wonder they damned you as a *fan-ge-ming!*"

On my way home, I dropped by at the office of the old emcee of the 1966 costume party that triggered all those happenings, whom I got to know well during our cadre school years. I told him I had just signed my rehabilitation documents; then I told him, as a friend, about the recent encounters I had with A and B, and what I learned about Doggie. My friend, the old emcee, was now director of the educational bureau in charge of all arts colleges. All of these people I mentioned were under his authority now.

I said I felt disturbed and asked him if there was any way to get to the bottom of the abductions, torture, and murders perpetrated in the earlier phases of the Cultural Revolution, all in the name of the revolutionary masses. I listed a dozen people we both knew had committed crimes but against whom there was no evidence.

My friend gave a long sigh and said, "I never told you my own younger brother was beaten to death under a battery of spotlights, also by that ultra-left faction. Another victim who survived told me this. But he couldn't identify any of the thugs because of the lights. Can you imagine how excruciating it is to preside over meetings with people who could have been the killers of one's brother but pass themselves off today as good guys—just like those who hurt you? I'm not sure we'll ever be avenged. These are factors which, hidden in our community, could eventually spell danger for all of us."

The above events are drawn from only the comparatively small arts world. No one knows how many unknown killers are riding in government limos or sitting behind administrative desks in China today.

In the early 1980s I went to a symposium in Nanning, a peaceful "city of flowers and fruit" in the south. A woman who acted as hostess for the symposium was a native of Beijing, and I spotted her as a Bridgeman alumna by the way she spoke.

As she took us sightseeing along the banks of the Yong River that runs through the city, she suddenly said to me: "I'm getting out of here, whatever it takes. I hate it here." She then told me most people were armed with guns when interfactional fighting was at its height during the Cultural Revolution. One faction would capture people from the other, line them up on the riverbank and gun them down; on the next day, the other faction would do the same to their opponents. The killing cycle went on and on, while the river flowed reddish brown.

"Even though much time has passed," she said, "I still can't come to the riverbank on my own. I brought you here so that you can see for yourselves where hundreds upon hundreds of human beings were simply slaughtered. I imagine you too went through a great deal, but you were in the nation's capital. How much do you know about what happened in the rest of China? One thing is certain —many people with innocent blood on their hands are occupying leading positions today."

She managed to get herself transferred back to Beijing some four years later.

Peiping-Peking-Beijing—It's the Same Thing

I was born and raised and then lived most of my life in one city, known variously as Peiping, Peking, and Beijing, although I have to call it Beijing now, even if it is best known to the West as Peking.

Pei, pe, and *bei* are different transliterations of the Chinese character for "north," *ping* signifies "peace" or "calm," and *king* or *jing* means "capital." Beijing has been the capital or second capital of successive dynasties since the twelfth century, and for the last five hundred years Peking has served as the capital of the Middle Kingdom except during a twenty-year period in recent history when the capital of the Republic of China was situated at Nanking (Nanjing), meaning the "southern capital." Thus from 1929 to 1949, the name of the city was changed from Peking to Peiping, or "northern calm." I was born in the Peiping era of my city.

When the People's Republic set up its central administration in Peiping, its name was switched back to Peking, both in Chinese and English.

The Chinese language consists largely of image characters, or ideograms, which are not phonetically spelled out words. There have been various methods and attempts at using the Latin alphabet to help with the pronunciation of Chinese characters. One of them, Wade's Romanization, was the most widely used and produced the name "Peiping." "Peking" stems from an earlier transliteration.

In 1958, however, the P.R.C. government issued a new system of romanization called *pinyin*. Since it started out as an experiment and left much to be desired, it made slow headway.

Peking became Beijing in the early 1970s. I don't remember the exact date, but believe that happened around the time China was admitted by the United Nations. I was in cadre school at the time, and among the "Central documents" we were made to study was a sternly worded declaration that all friendly foreign countries must spell Chinese names and places the way the Chinese government wanted them spelled. The terms were mandatory, something like "failure to use *pinyin* will be regarded as an unfriendly or disrespectful act toward the Chinese people."

Thus I found many friendly and respectful people doing their best to curl their tongues around the *jing* in Beijing and wondering why the old Peking had to go. World War II veterans remember Chungking, not Chongqing, and feel sorry that Guangzhou took the place of Canton. Fortunately, Shanghai is still there, but whether post–1997 Hong Kong will have to change to Xiang Gang is anybody's guess. God save Hong Kong.

My fellow conservatives or reactionaries often joke about *pinyin* partly because the government has been so peremptory about its use. Should the

U.S. government not officially demand, by the same token, that Iowa not be transliterated as *Yi A Hua* and that Chinese stop referring to San Francisco as *Jiujinshan* (Old Gold Mountain)? I wonder if Ronald Reagan ever objected to being addressed as "President *Ligen*." But dealing with the Chinese authorities is like driving down a one-way street: "You do it my way, and I do it my way." It may have something to do with small spirits and big egos.

One of the most hilarious stories I've heard about the name game was when a new hotel was erected—no pun connected to the following fact—on the west side of Beijing, near the old site of the old Fu-hsing Gate. Following the new *pinyin*, the hotel was named the Fuxing Hotel. Made for it were Fuxing towels, Fuxing bedcovers, Fuxing sheets, Fuxing pillowcases, and Fuxing plates, you name it. Everyone was happy until, just before the official opening date, a dirty-minded foreigner informed his horrified hosts about the close resemblance of Fuxing to the gerund of a familiar four-letter English word.

Whether the story is true or made up, all the Fuxing towels and Fuxing plates suddenly disappeared, and the hotel's name now stands as Yanjing.

I realize, despite my irreverent merriment, the difficulty of coming up with a viable romanization of the Chinese language. How, for instance, can anyone differentiate between *Power* and *Rights*, both identically pronounced and *pinyin*ed as *quan li*? The difference becomes crucial when one considers that what the Chinese authorities want is power while the ordinary people are more concerned about rights. Yet few people—including the powers-that-be, I suspect—are quite clear about the difference between power and rights (*quan li* and *quan li*, in *pinyin* and especially in speech). Perhaps the confusion started with the first translations of the French word *droit*, which means both. And that may very well be the reason China's gerontocrats today balk at requests for human rights. "What's that? They want power?!"

But, to come back to *pinyin*, I'm glad that my name, Chen, remains unchanged. At least I'm not affiliated with some unpronounceable (to Westerners) moniker like Cai, Cao, Cui, Ju, Qiu, Qian, Xi, Xiao, Xie or Xu. Imagine the annoyance of a portly Chinese matron surnamed Cao (pronounced Tsao) being addressed as Madame Cow!

Levity aside, I'm sure there are better alternatives.

Sole Spectator of a Drama

Amid the much-publicized and over-touted efforts by the leaders of post-Mao China, the CCP, under its then Secretary General Hu Yaobang, ordered the rehabilitation of all former Rightists at the end of the 1970s.

In Chinese political terms, "rehabilitation" indicates that the person was never a Rightist in the first place. This order came twenty years after hundreds of thousands of men and women perished, either physically or intellectually. It came too late for many, such as my Fifth Uncle who hanged himself in the first days of the Red Guards' rampage; and too late to resuscitate many truncated careers and dismembered families. A fragmentary account of the life of a forgotten man has haunted me ever since I heard it:

A friend went to a remote region in northwest China on a temporary project in the mid-1960s, along with others from his *dan wei*. They frequented the local wine parlor to kill time during the evenings. Gradually, they noticed that a lone figure would come and squat under the papered window of the ramshackle building when they were there. And one night, when the group found the man weeping silently out in the dark, they inquired what he was doing here.

The man told them he was once a teacher in Shanghai but had been sent to a labor reform camp in this province after being capped a "Rightist." He had already been de-capped, so to speak, but no *dan wei* in Shanghai wanted him and so he had stayed on at the labor camp as a member of its permanent population.

"But there is no one with whom I can conduct an intelligent conversation," he said. "I spotted you people, and I come here just to hear you talk. I'm not eavesdropping, I only want to hear the kind of conversation I used to engage in."

After my cousin Ta was rehabilitated, he made a trip to Beijing in 1979 from the Yangtze Dam, where he was serving as chief engineer. He came, first, to have his case officially overturned, and second, to treat forty of his relatives and friends, all of whom had openly or covertly supported him after he was made a Rightist. That banquet cost him a month's salary, but he insisted that was nothing compared to his pleasure at bringing together all those who had remembered him when he was down and out.

He and I had dinner again the next day. At the end of the meal, he told me only one more matter remained for him to settle before he returned to the south, and he chose me to accompany him on this mission. From the play of emotions on his face, I suddenly guessed who the object of his visit was to be: his ex-wife.

This was the beautiful girl Ta had married under our date trees back in 1951. When Ta was labeled a Rightist in 1957, the two had a young son. Huang stayed married to Ta while he was sent from Beijing to a nearby labor camp. But just when his ordeal seemed to be over and he reappeared in our lives, she divorced him.

Huang sent their young son to Ta's parents in Shanghai and married an older man who was a former boss to both Huang and Ta. Ta held a grudge against her, not so much on account of the divorce and remarriage as for her marrying the very person who had condemned him to the labor camps— with, perhaps, an eye to the attractive wife Ta must leave behind.

I was intrigued but also intimidated by the possible impact of this encounter. I asked: "Can't you just forgive her and let her be? It wasn't easy and she didn't let you down that badly."

Ta promised he'd be civil and explained that was why he wanted a third party to be present at the meeting. He had to see her one last time, he said.

So the two of us planned the visit. Ta had already done some reconnoitering at his former *dan wei* and learned that Huang's husband was presently away on a business trip. We planned for Ta to go as my husband in case the stepson, who lived with them but had never met Ta, was at home.

Having been to Huang's present home, I led the way. I parked my bike, went upstairs and knocked on the door. A young man opened up, and I asked for Big Sister Huang. She came out from the kitchen and greeted me warmly, asking if I'd eaten. I told her—in front of her stepson—that my husband and I were visiting close-by and had wanted to drop in to say hello. He was downstairs watching the bikes and waiting to hear whether she was home.

With a brief word to her stepson who was already dressed to go out, Huang cordially accompanied me down the stairway to welcome my "husband." I stopped her before we reached the ground floor.

"Big Sister Huang," I said. "It isn't my husband. It's Ta. Are you willing to see him, as a guest?"

Huang leaned for a brief moment against the wall in the dim light and closed her eyes. Then she collected herself. "Yes," she said. "I would like to see him. I'll wait here."

I went out of the building and told Ta. He locked our bikes and entered the hallway. Huang led us upstairs in silence.

Once in the apartment, Huang played the part of the hostess and showed us into a small sitting room. She went to fetch tea from the kitchen, and the stepson left with a polite nod to me from the doorway. There were only the three of us now.

We sat down, but apart from a few polite glances at me, Huang's gaze never left Ta. I followed her line of vision and noticed Ta was still in his street wear—an shapeless cotton-padded jacket suitable for pedaling around Beijing in late autumn.

I had taken off my coat as I came in the apartment, so I said, "Hey, Ta, it's warm in here. Why don't you take off your jacket?" I wanted him to present himself in his well-tailored pure-wool Chung-shan suit. Ta stood up, slipped out of the clumsy outfit, laid it down on a nearby chair and returned to his seat.

From the corner of my eye I saw Huang taking in Ta's athletic physique and nimble movements. They were then both in their early fifties, but Ta looked fit and trim, while the once attractive young woman had developed a decidedly middle-age look and figure. Her former sparkle had faded into an expression of sluggish boredom, and her speech showed she was no longer leading an intellectually challenging life.

My unspoken approval of Ta's appearance somehow communicated itself to him; he sensed he'd done something right, and he became more self-assured and relaxed.

Ta told Huang the purpose of his visit was to formally notify her that he had never been a Rightist in the first place. All charges against him had now been overturned; he'd done or said nothing wrong. Huang answered that she was very happy for him, and for their son, who would no longer be stigmatized as the offspring of a Rightist.

Haltingly, she admitted that she had been expecting him, for she had also learned that Ta was in Beijing to finalize his case. She somehow knew they would meet after all these years. She just had no idea when, where, and how this meeting would take place.

Then she turned to me and said: "I expected Ta to ask one of his older cousins to be the go-between. I never thought our little cousin would be chosen!" This broke the tension. We all laughed, and I asked if she had suspected anything before I told her the truth.

She smiled. "Yes, when you said so emphatically that you had come with your husband, whom I have never met."

She and Ta then talked more lightly about old times and acquaintances. Watching them from my position, I also sensed an undercurrent between them, charged with strong emotions of reprehension and of love which had to be suppressed, for she was now someone else's wife.

During a brief moment of eloquent silence, I looked at Ta and he understood it was time to leave. Huang's eyes stayed fixed on him as we stood up. With a display of bravado Ta made a sweeping gesture and announced: "By the way, I'd also like to tell you in person that I've met a woman in her forties in Shanghai. We plan to marry when my job transfer to Shanghai is approved."

Huang wilted against the doorjamb and, as Ta drew on his outer jacket, said meekly: "I wish you both happiness."

It's customary among Chinese to see one's guests out all the way, so Huang walked us down the stairs. They shook hands for the last time. Ta looked particularly dashing as he vaulted onto his bike. He didn't look back.

We rode in silence for some time. Then I started to appraise his performance from the angle of a spectator. I commented especially on his deft movements when he took off his coat and the springy agility with which he had walked back and forth, so different from her current husband's ungainly shuffle. "I prompted you to take off the jacket because it irked me to see you looking like a bum."

Ta admitted he hadn't been able to be completely forgiving. "You all say she at least stood by me in my most difficult hours," he said. "But you'll never know what I felt when she left me and went for that man."

Ta had subsequently worked hard to regain his professional prominence and, in that respect, had risen from the ashes, only to face a woman not really worthy any longer of his love, or hate.

Ta cautioned me again: "Now don't you forget you're the only spectator of today's drama. If any of our aunts or cousins learn about it, I'll hold you accountable."

"Alright, I promise!" I kept my word until Ta's untimely death about seven years later.

Ta was transferred in due time to Shanghai where he filled the post of chief engineer at an oil refinery construction site and married the woman he mentioned that evening. For a few years Ta led an uneventful life, spending time also with his aging mother and the son he hardly knew during those twenty-some years.

Ta was in his late fifties when cancer of the pancreas devoured him in five months.

I went to Shanghai on business during his last months and visited him at the oil company hospital where he was given the best medical care obtainable. Warned as I was of how Ta had changed, I didn't recognize my cousin in the shriveled and darkened skeleton of a figure lying on the sickbed. The pain glazed his sunken eyes, and he spoke in a rasping whisper.

We talked about whatever topic we could touch upon without breaking down altogether. The Chinese very rarely hug, but when it was time to leave I hugged him for the first and last time.

I kept my promise of secrecy until Ta passed away, then I related the entire melodrama to another cousin—the one I had gone to on a bike to tell about the downfall of the Gang of Four. She let out a sigh when I told her they had met, after all. "It hurt so much to see two loving persons torn apart by political turmoil," she said. "At least they had a chance to end, together, this chapter in their lives."

At Professional Crossroads

It took the post-Mao administration almost two years, after the end of the Cultural Revolution, to get around to looking into the fate of the Federation of Literature and Arts and all its associations. These had been completely wiped out during the ten previous years; even the building with the flower plaques, which had formerly housed those *dan wei*, had been taken over by a publishing house, which had no intention of returning the building to its previous occupants on account of the desirable location.

In the meantime, all the former cadres had been placed in other cultural institutions, such as the Arts Research Academy I worked at. But pressure to restore the federation and associations was strong among writers and artists who wanted a home base of their own. At an elaborate conference of elected and selected representatives of writers' and artists' circles, the numerous deceased colleagues were deeply mourned, the Gang of Four forcefully denounced, and by unanimous appeal a decision was made that preparations should start as soon as possible to reestablish all artists' organizations.

A skeleton staff consisting of former chiefs and some administrative personnel was called in to restore the *dan wei*, and rank-and-file recruitment followed immediately. One morning as I left for work, one of my neighbors, the former Executive Director of the Musicians' Association—the man who was the go-between in bringing Cousin Wei and myself together in cadre school—was waiting in front of the building we both lived in. Now once more the Executive Director of that association, he asked me if I could spare a moment.

He told me he and the chairman of that association—the very man who took Deedee along to get a pig slaughtered—wanted to know if I would consider returning to the Musician's Association. "You realize we're asking you this as friends," he said. "Having been through adverse times with us, you can understand why we both wish to have you working with us again."

I told him I'd give him a well-considered reply, and whatever my decision, I appreciated their sincere invitation.

I was flattered, honored, and moved by their offer; I also knew that I'd be given a good position and trusted not only for my professionality but for my political integrity as well. I'd be among friends. But I would be moving backward, toward nostalgic memories, whereas my mind and activities were already oriented toward translation in literature, theater, and cinema.

After some reflection, I chose not to look back.

I went to my former boss at his apartment that evening. I asked him to convey my heartfelt thanks to the chairman, but I was not going back. His wife beamed at me, "I told him you won't go back," she said. "I know you're the kind of person who doesn't waver once you've made up your mind. I'd do the same, because the fun and pleasure are gone. It's best to go on to fresh pastures."

My former boss protested, "We wouldn't have given up on her without even trying, you know that." Turning to me, he continued: "I understand you completely, and so will the chairman." Our families remain the best of friends.

I closed this door softly but firmly behind me, and looked toward my future, which at that time happened to take the form of a film institute that had expressed a definite interest in me.

Actually, my experience with films, both Chinese and American, was quite limited. My parents hadn't taken us to many movies in the United States in those double-feature years, and I didn't care much for the films that were being shown in China when we returned in 1949. My primary interest had always been books.

After the outbreak of the Korean War in 1950, all American film distributors were forced to close their offices in China, and their holdings were confiscated and moved into the vaults of the newly established Chinese Film Archive. These films, along with many pre-1949 Chinese films in black and white, were off-limits to the general public.

But since films, as well as all other art forms, were regarded as an important means of class education (proletarian class, not school class), we students under Maoism were exposed to heavy doses of domestic and politically correct imported films whether we liked them or not. Prominent among the imported ones were Soviet and East European bloc films, all dubbed in Chinese, and I grew up watching sabre-waving Cossacks and kolkhoznik babushkas conversing in fluent Mandarin on the screen. As a consequence of such political selectivity, the general audience of those days were also familiar with many classic Italian neo-realistic and French films, such as those played by Gérard Philipe, a onetime French Communist. Some British films were also available; Chaplin's *A King in New York* was released as such.

The only American-made film shown to the general audience was the independent *Salt of the Earth*, translated into Chinese as *The Main Force of Society*. I saw the film, also dubbed in Mandarin, when in high school, and all students were subsequently organized into earnest and serious discussions on the evils of capitalism.

I had the opportunity, however, to watch a Hollywood movie in the early 1960s when I was a music journalist. I'd just returned from a business trip, and when I stepped into the office one of my associates said, "Quick, go to the personnel office to get your ticket for this afternoon's screening. You've already missed one while you were away."

The afternoon screening, I was told when I got my ticket, would be *Spring Rain*, an American film. I was also told that the federation and its associations had been instructed to watch this Hollywood film in order to criticize a certain "-ism" manifested in it—exactly which -ism I have no recollection of now. When I sat in the specially arranged screening and the title rolled out on a magnificent technicolor background, I learned that the film was actually *April Showers*, played by Ann Sothern. *April Showers* or *Spring Rain*, it was perfect, and it wasn't dubbed. The music was such a departure from what I'd heard all these years in China, that I felt grateful to whoever conceived the idea of running Hollywood movies to enhance our political awareness.

The print of *April Showers* came from the confidential holdings of the Chinese Film Archive—confidential, because SECRET was stamped on the covers of its foreign film inventories.

But after the Cultural Revolution, tickets to "internal" showings of Hollywood films from the archival holdings became one of the hottest items on the entertainment scene, at least in big cities. Behind this craving was a pendulum effect building from nearly three decades of deprivation of American films. Anyone can trash Hollywood movies, but live thirty years without them, and, well, as an old filmmaker put it: "I'm starved."

The fever for old Hollywood films was fueled unintentionally by none other than Jiang Qing—Madame Mao herself. Her followers were in the habit of noting down her sayings and later transcribing them into unofficial publications called "Instructions by Central Leaders." After she succeeded in arrogating to herself power over the film world, she started by criticizing black-and-white Chinese films of the 1930s, the classics of Chinese filmmaking. Most directors of that era had turned Jiang Qing down as both actress and mistress despite all her maneuverings, and she found sweet revenge in denouncing almost all Chinese films up to the mid-1960s as poisonous weeds. Among the few that passed her critical inspection were *Tunnel Warfare* and *Landmine Warfare*, both feature films as dull as their titles.

As for the handful of films she played in, they became top-secret items. Whoever even mentioned them was accused of "accumulating black information on the Central Leaders," and would perhaps spend years in prison.

Jiang Qing also gained unlimited access to the archival holdings, and when it pleased her to see foreign films, she had interpreters summoned regardless of the time of day or night. We learned from the "Instructions by Central Leaders" that the holdings included *Queen Christina* and *Waterloo Bridge*, among many others. She also obtained a copy of *The Dove*, but her disparaging comments about a nude diving scene in that film and her largely banal and negative comments on all Hollywood films she was privileged to see whetted enormous curiosity among filmgoers.

The films were shown, "internally," in theaters packing 1,300 or more spectators, and were supplied with simultaneous interpretation broadcast over loudspeakers. Amid all this clamor and demeaned glamour I contemplated my career switch to the cinema/film/movie world.

No longer a starry-eyed do-gooder, I would look for a situation that I would benefit from. I knew too much about the music community to remain politically neutral, and a transfer to a relatively unfamiliar group would allow me to take an impartial and detached approach; I'd had enough politics for a lifetime. I was confident in my background knowledge and analytical methods as a professional. I was also confident in my writing skills and style, which had even made my written self-criticisms quite readable during my *fan-ge-ming* period. And at the age of forty I left my transitional post at the Arts Research Academy and embarked on my second career at a film institution.

I came into the Chinese film world essentially as a journal editor, translator, and as sometimes writer. To make a long story short, within three years I became a pro, specializing in American films and history. I was the first person to introduce to a devoted readership of fifty thousand students, scholars, and even soldiers the lives and works of Orson Welles, Francis Ford Coppola, Billy Wilder, and many others. During the nine years I worked in the film institution, I published about three million Chinese characters (the equivalent of five thousand pages in English,) under my real name and half a dozen pseudonyms, and corrected a similar quantity of translations.

Giving up my former career as a journalist under a totalitarian system relieved me of an onerous burden, for I had enough of being used as a mouthpiece for the Party, even if only in a small way. No matter how the authorities feigned openness and reform, media control remained unchanged. Sleazy tabloids were more tolerated than any form of printed dissent, however mild. I felt my decision to become a translator was a valid one, for I now had a wide spectrum of essays to select from, and the end product was often more scholarly and insightful than anything else in the field written at that time in China.

"Does Your Country Love You?"
—— and a Party in 1984

Patriotism is one of the strongest traditions in Chinese culture, one that has been carried down through thousands of years. For the majority Han race, patriotism extended to loyalty to one's race and defiance to non-Han rulers, such as to the Mongols of the Yuan Dynasty (1271–1368) and the Manchus of the Qing Dynasty (1644–1911). It was this strong centripetal force that drew many fine Chinese students and scholars back to the People's Republic of China after 1949. None that I knew were politically persuaded or coerced into returning; what brought them back was love of their motherland, the promise of internal peace, and an administration not as blatantly corrupt as that of the Kuomintang government.

But, as demonstrated in episodes herein, once a person returned to the embrace of the great ancestral land, he or she went back to being a subject of authoritarian rule. In the P.R.C., all were supposed to be Chairman Mao's good children, good students, good cadres, good soldiers, or one of many other good whatnots—in other words, to serve as nuts and bolts in the omnipotent state mechanism. We became anything but individuals. Individuality leads directly to individualism, and that was taboo. Moreover, all Chinese underwent persecution in one way or another and at one time or another. It was simply a way of life, a rap on the knuckles, a time-honored means of maintaining control over a generally submissive but potentially fractious population.

For one fraction of the population, however, this way of life was applied with special rigor. On top of being intellectuals whose thoughts were supposedly more complicated than those of the workers, peasants, and soldiers, those Chinese who had lived abroad and then returned to the motherland were also considered to carry within themselves more political viruses than homegrown Chinese.

As these returnees meekly adjusted to a low-profile life and tried not to display any trouble-provoking traits, they became a self-effacing but oft-targeted group of people who nevertheless persistently and unwaveringly loved their country as all good Chinese were expected to do.

Public recognition of the plight of this fraction of the Chinese people was part of the backlash against the excesses of the Cultural Revolution. When the predominant image of the Chinese as a solid mass of slogan-shouting fanatics began to recede somewhat, human drama came to the fore. "Wound literature," works laced with pain and bitterness, became the norm for a few years from the late 1970s to the early 1980s, before cynicism set in. Protagonists other than furnace-stoking steel workers, harvesting peasants, and stern-visaged soldiers emerged in books and on stage and screen. For some time, Eurasians, Japanese orphans abandoned in China, returned overseas Chinese, and rehabilitated Rightists—all atypical outside protagonists— were presented on the screen.

Among the films was an unusual one entitled *The Sun and the Man*—the "Sun" being an allegorical reference to Mao Zedong, then already dead. The film, made in 1980, is based on the more-or-less true life story of a Chinese painter whom I had once met in Cousin Wei's home. The character in the film, a young man of humble beginnings, arrives in the United States some way or another and becomes a rich painter by the end of World War II. The Chinese girl he loved in his youth shows up when he is being honored at an art gallery. They are reunited and return to a liberated motherland by ocean liner in 1949. The painter goes on to become a famous professor and artist until he is predictably zapped during the Cultural Revolution. That's as far as the real-life part of the painter's story goes.

The unusual part is the ending of the film when the victimized painter flees the city and holes up in China's northern marshlands. When all is done and over with the Cultural Revolution, a high-angle shot shows the dying painter crawling in a circle, his tracks in the snow forming the upper part of a question mark. He dies at the spot where the dot should be—an allegorical reference to a piece of prose entitled "Questioning Heaven," written by a famous Chinese poet who drowned himself in 290 B.C., brokenhearted over his country's political decline.

The present episode isn't about the film; it's about China's so-called paramount leader Deng Xiaoping who personally banned this film. That happened not long after *Time* selected him as "Man of the Year," an event trumpeted throughout China.

The two creators of the film were an unlikely pair. Unlikely, because the writer was an outspoken and well-established man of letters enlisted in the army, and the director an extremist and thug during the earlier years of the Cultural Revolution. It seems that the latter had a change of heart when he teamed up with the writer. After the film was completed, the word spread that it could face problems, and people who had a chance to see it packed the screening halls.

Despite my skepticism about the director, I found *The Sun and the Man* exceptionally powerful in its audiovisual presentation. In the film, the painter's daughter confronts her ever-so-patriotic father. "You love your country, despite everything?" she asks. "But does your country love you?!"

These lines left a deep impression on the spectators—after the screening, many jokingly called out to each other: "Does your country love you?" "Not that I know of!"—and incurred the undying wrath of Deng and company.

Even internal screenings were stopped soon after the one I went to, and the film was proscribed upon orders from the very top. Deng demanded a self-criticism from the writer, and the Central Committee of the CCP (or one of its executive organs) blocked all attempts to have the film revised or remade. Official newspapers carried articles criticizing a film that had never been released or seen by the general public.

No one I knew took such criticism seriously at the time; the euphoria accompanying the downfall of the Gang of Four had not yet faded and the assurances of reform and modernization gave hope of better times to come. Everyone was confident that at least some freedom of artistic expression was in the offing. Besides, what was wrong with asking the question "Does your country love you?" The question had been raised by so many loyal Chinese in private in the wake of so much persecution that it no longer sounded quite so blasphemous. *Unrequited Love* was the original title of the screenplay, and it expressed feelings fairly widespread among intellectuals. But we still loved, in spite of everything.

I suspect this was also the writer's estimation of the situation when he wrote his self-criticisms—many times, for they just didn't pass official review. Many informed people felt frustrated; this was the first case after the Cultural Revolution of a film being banned. So often had openness and freedom been promised that we couldn't believe Deng would take a hard-line approach so soon.

After the writer had made repeated and invariably unsuccessful attempts to revise his self-criticism to official satisfaction, he was left alone for the time being. We figured it was all over; Deng's attention span was spent. Besides, it was now vacation time at Bei Dai He, the seaside resort where most of the CCP aristocracy and their families (grandparents, grandchildren, uncles, aunts, cousins, in-laws, and secretaries) went to escape the summer heat. Beijing was more peaceful when they were gone, and we thought all would be forgotten when the sun-tanned VIPs returned.

We underestimated Deng's unforgivingness. He inquired in midsummer why the army writer had not yet come up with a statement of deep remorse. The tenor was stern and threatening. I recall I heard the reading of Deng's instructions with a leaden heart. I was thoroughly disillusioned. Deng was simply another Mao, only more harsh. Mao had had the cunning of a politician; Deng acted with the ruthlessness of a military man.

The writer, wiser now to Deng's temperament, produced a penitent self-examination with help from fellow artists. The case was dropped without disciplinary action against the writer, such as kicking him out of the Party. Deng and the CCP hard-liners believed they had won the encounter; they had lost many hearts instead. Blinded by power, they can never understand, or care.

So, very early on, I realized this much-heralded reformer was a totalitarian at heart. This conviction was reconfirmed by the remarks of a close friend and old army veteran. He told me in private that some of his comrades who had served under Deng when he was an army commissioner used to quake in their shoes whenever their diminutive boss showed up. The worst thing about his unpredictable temper was that while hot-tempered people usually blow up over something and then forget, Deng never let an offender off the hook until the latter was totally crushed. He could never forgive.

"Too bad I didn't know the writer of *The Sun and the Man* very well," my friend said. "I could have told him a thing or two. There's no easy way out once Deng starts digging at you."

A few years later, in 1984, there was a big parade for the 25th Anniversary of the founding of the People's Republic. A marching university student pulled out from under her jacket a cloth banner that bore large characters saying: "Hi, Xiaoping!" Deng was, at the time, a hero to those students. It's perfectly natural to "hi" any George or Bill in America, but in China leaders must be respectfully addressed by their official titles. Moreover, there's the generation gap which dictates that young people may not address elders by their given names. That student had overstepped two boundaries with those few characters.

"Uh-oh," was the reaction of many who were concerned about whether Deng would tolerate this display of familiarity.

However, it seemed he wasn't offended by this incident, and quite a torrent of adulatory articles subsequently appeared in various journals and newspapers. These made a big to-do over how "democratic" Deng was to allow a mere student some sixty years younger than himself to address him by his given name; how fortunate we were, how heartwarming it all was, how inspiring to have such a leader . . . all those fawning phrases.

It so happened I attended a get-together in October of 1984 at the home of some friends. The conversation naturally gravitated to current events and the student who hi-ed Deng was mentioned. "In spite of all that fancy talk about the Four Modernizations," one guest said, "they won't allow anyone to mention the fifth and most important one—the modernization of concepts. If they could break away from their feudal lord-and-liege mentality, we wouldn't have to listen to all that brouhaha about someone addressing Deng by his given name."

We were all aware of the overheated state of the economy and we all felt a hastiness in the air, a sense of impatience somewhere. "Why all the hurry?!" we wanted to know.

"My guess is," another guest offered. "Deng is going to turn eighty and he wants to see something accomplished."

"Everyone knows Deng has accomplished nothing since the founding of the P R C ," remarked a soft-spoken person. "He was on the sidelines when Zhou Enlai and his close associates were building up the post–1949 economy. Deng, however, had done nothing to boast about, aside from winning some battles in the late 1940s. Now he wants to go down in history as a great achiever. That's why he's impatient about Taiwan and Hong Kong. He wants these territories brought back into a united China during his lifetime."

I observed that Deng wasn't famous for his diplomatic finesse. "Wasn't it Deng who headed the CCP delegation to Moscow in the early 1960s? He exchanged harsh words with the Russians and embittered the entire relationship."

"That's true," agreed the host. "The CCP had to send Zhou posthaste to Moscow to tone down the conflict and bring it within the framework of acceptable diplomatic exchanges."

"If so," I said, "then Deng also aspires to become the person not only to bring back Taiwan and Hong Kong, but also to patch up relations with the Soviets. He'd want to be the person to shake hands with them when they come to make up."

That surmise, incidentally, came true. Deng, who was long overdue to retire, hung on to a no-title post until after he had shaken hands with Gorbachev in May of 1989. Ironically, it was to report on that fateful handshake that so many Western correspondents were in China at the time of the Tiananmen Incident. They provided the world with many authentic details of a tragedy that would otherwise have been given very limited and distorted news coverage, if any at all. It was also because Deng hung on until that handshake that he bears responsibility for the tragedy; without his approval, no one would have dared to give orders to move heavily armed troops into the capital.

"The Americans are Coming . . . " "The Chinese are Coming . . . "

Americans have always been attracted by China, it is said, because they have been told since childhood that if they dig a hole deep enough, they will come out in China. On the other hand, the Chinese have also been captivated by the land called *Mei Guo*, the "Beautiful Country," the land of opportunity and of generous and big people. No matter how stern or hostile the rhetoric employed by Chinese leaders from time to time, the Chinese people's fascination has never faded, and I believe it's the same with Americans.

The first Americans, including Chinese-Americans, to visit post–1949 China started to trickle in during the early 1970s, thanks in part to the diplomatic efforts of Messrs. Nixon and Kissinger. Papa passed away without knowing there might be a reunion with relatives and friends from abroad, though Mama lived to meet a few, among them Lew Pa and Ma from San Francisco, Dr. and Mrs. Chao, the legendary couple from Berkeley, and my cousin from Penn State.

But after China's prolonged closure to the Western world, the Chinese authorities, who were accustomed to ordering every aspect of their subjects' lives, had to make major readjustments, which wasn't easy for them. Even small things bothered them: how, for instance, should former Chinese citizens who are now Americans be defined? Traditionally, anyone born a Chinese was forever a Chinese, but the changes in U.S.immigration and naturalization policy and the cataclysmic shifts in the Chinese situation over the past several decades had resulted in many Chinese immigrants becoming U.S. citizens. They were, at first, called in Chinese "Chinese-descended" scientists, professors, etc., with no mention of nationality, and in later years, "Americans of Chinese origin."

Since our friends and relatives had chosen to become foreigners, we, as Chinese, had to comply with a set of regulations before we were allowed to meet them. The "we" included Mama while she was alive, and later Toto and myself and our respective families. To meet a cousin or friend from abroad we had to apply for permission and wait for authorization; in some cases we were expected to make reports afterward. Whatever the case, we'd become so accustomed to being regulated that I hardly thought it pertinent to mention to visitors what we local Chinese had to go through before riding up the hotel elevators and knocking on their doors with smiles on our faces.

Visitors were only visitors, who came and went. But when growing numbers of people from the West came to China to settle down for work or research for a couple of years, the situation became less easy for China's security officials and increasingly frustrating for the new residents. Most of the latter understood Chinese, which made things even more complicated for they were finding out too much for their own good.

When one of my friends, Barry, reacted strongly to what he saw as the now-open, now-closed political atmosphere in Beijing, I told him about the four-character Chinese dictum *wai song nei jin*, or "relax externally and tighten internally." This was the standing principle decreed by the authorities for encounters between Chinese and non-Chinese, one which I kept violating unintentionally. Regardless of the times or the degree of openness—whether in the 1970s, 1980s, or 1990s—as long as China remains under authoritarian control and non-Chinese are seen as a potential threat to the regime, surveillance will never be relaxed, although efforts may be made to render it less blatant and conspicuous.

The same years saw the beginning of an exodus of Chinese to America. It was quite a revelation to learn that so many Chinese had rich uncles and aunts in the United States and that they had to leave China to become heirs and heiresses.

The Chinese diaspora to America beginning in the late 1970s went through two channels, both legal. One was the official channel; the other consisted of private pipelines.

On the official side, mainland Chinese students started to reappear on American campuses after the Cultural Revolution. These were rigorously screened and selected, as the P.R.C. had previously done when sending students to the Soviet bloc countries.

The selection of students for graduate studies was based on four principles: political reliability, professional excellence, linguistic fluency, and good health. These were the so-called "four legs" on which all candidates had to stand. And, in the Chinese preoccupation with numbers, the first group of Chinese students sent to the United States by the Chinese government consisted of forty persons.

The Chinese authorities had been most cautious about this project. One of China's outstanding physicists, himself a student in the United States during the World War II years, was dispatched beforehand to investigate the campuses that would host the coming Chinese grad students. This investigator was an old Tsinghua friend who had dined at our Berkeley table in the 1940s. I visited him after he came back from his reconnaissance missions and he received me warmly, not only for old times' sake but also because he was working closely on the overseas student project with one of my first cousins. So this uncle of sorts gave me a fulfilling firsthand account of current developments in major United States universities.

While we sat and talked, the forty candidates were probably sweating over their English textbooks. They had been strictly examined in their own fields of expertise and the physicist seemed to be confident about their qualifications. The first group, as I remember, consisted mostly of students in the basic sciences, and we talked about the pressing need for eventually sending abroad scholars in the applied sciences. The majority of those forty students were successful in their studies. Not as much could be said for subsequent "publicly funded" students. Many returned to China with not much more to show for their two-year jaunt than some home electronics and household appliances.

Other than these publicly funded overseas students, there were also privately funded individuals. Many came as the under-the-table price of a deal: their parents had approved a contract or established a lucrative connection and, in exchange, the son or daughter came to the United States.

Our family's pilgrimage back to the country we'd once visited was led by Toto in 1980. His story started with a chance meeting, and by last count encompasses three new U. S. citizens—Toto, Bella, and their daughter Mary, two houses in the San Francisco Bay area, one dog, and one cat.

In 1980, a professor, F. Wills, was giving training courses for management personnel in a Chinese port city when Toto was introduced to him. Professor Wills had been trying, through interpreters, to teach the intricacies of capitalist finances to a bunch of trainees who knew little more than some Marxist economic dogma and not a single word of English.

So Toto must have seemed like a breath of fresh air. He had a solid education in metallurgy and more than fifteen years of experience both as an engineer or hands-on worker, depending on the times. He also had a working vocabulary in English which, together with his other attributes, made him something of a rarity at the time.

Toto did not enjoy the blessing of the motherland in the form of public funding for studies abroad, nor had he established connections—by for instance facilitating a weapons deal—with affluent American businessmen who could foot the bill. Professor Wills' interest in him opened the door to opportunities.

The interest, in fact, was so great that Professor Wills came to take a look at his potential protégé's home. I was in Tianjin that day when the guest came. While he was shown around we must have mentioned "our house" in passing, for he inquired whether this house was really ours. "Sure," Toto replied. "It belonged to our parents and was passed on to us after they died."

Having had a house in China almost all our lives and thinking nothing of it, we didn't notice our guest's rising excitement. "This house was never public property," I explained. "You see, in this compound there are four . . . " But before I could go on about the four houses belonging to four brothers, Professor Wills stood up, stamped on the floor, and exclaimed: "Am I standing on private property?!" I realized the impact this single fact had made on him and laughed: "Yes, you *are* standing on one hundred percent private property in a socialist state."

Toto was in his late thirties when he left his wife and young daughter to go to the United States. He studied and toiled for three years, during which he did any work permissible under his student visa, until he had saved enough to go on a home visit. Another two years would pass before his wife and daughter could join him. We all pay taxes now to the Golden State.

"I've Never Had Enough of You, Ma Ma!"

My children called me "Ma Ma," pronounced as two equally stressed words, which is slightly different from the way most Chinese moms are called. Mimi started this way of addressing me, and Deedee followed suit. And whenever they were peeved by my nagging or joking, I became "stinky Ma Ma!" Mimi grew up largely under the influence of my parents, and in the years after my father passed away Mimi became my mother's constant companion, following her around on her visits and running errands for her.

She also acquired from my mother an engaging speech pattern and an upright carriage when standing or walking. This last distinguished her from the slouching girls of her generation; so much so that her classmates could spot her from a distance by the way she walked, even in the days when everyone wore shapeless blue and gray jackets and pants.

Mimi spent three years of her young life in Beijing, roughly from age two to five. She went back to Tianjin with Ah Po and Deedee when both Fan and I were sent to the countryside, staying there for the next eight years and coming occasionally to my cadre school and Beijing to visit. She returned to our one-room apartment to live only after the downfall of the Gang of Four and when I had started working again.

Mimi was almost thirteen, and started going to middle school in Beijing at a time when rehabilitation of schooling and teaching was high on the nation's agenda after ten years of devastation.

She had been a top student in grade school, conscientious in every way. After the transfer to Beijing, she was soon accepted by a group of children who had known one another since they were toddlers. There being few home phones in those years, people contacted each other simply by dropping in. Since we lived on the fourth floor, much of the communication was conducted by yelling up four floors from below and yelling back from our window. I knew Mimi's popularity was rising when her name was yelled more often than her father's. In fact, she was the most yelled-for person in our building until her brother Deedee moved in. Deedee's classmates never came up, even if he was at home; they preferred to carry on their window-to-ground conversation in front of all the thirty-some families living in our building.

By then Mimi was allowed to go around town with girls of her own age, although she and I still liked to go shopping together. I learned then that Mimi possessed skills in some quite unexpected fields:

Chinese buses are frequently crowded to the point that passengers can hardly breathe, providing opportunities for harassing acts such as rubbing and pinching. One day while Mimi and I were on a bus, a man pressed up against me. The bus was so packed I couldn't move away or around to get rid of him. Mimi noticed my discomfiture and when we got off the bus, she said matter-of-factly, "You got jabbed, didn't you?" I sheepishly admitted that was so.

"You're no good on buses," Mimi observed. "You ride your bike too much. Do you know what to do if someone pinches your butt?"

"No. What?" I was scandalized by my baby girl's worldliness.

"Reach for his hand. He'll be both surprised and eager. Then get hold of a finger, just one finger, and bend and twist it until he turns green."

"My God, have you really done that?"

"Not yet, but I've seen my classmates do it."

I told her I'd never even heard of such things in my days.

"Well," she said. "That was in your time."

I was quite easygoing on my kids. Most of the time, anyway, for I remembered what I'd wanted or hadn't wanted when I was their age. In fact, I was easygoing to such a point that my children treated me with very un-Chinese familiarity. Mimi and I went shopping one day when the weather was shilly-shallying between rain and no rain. I had neglected to bring an umbrella and kept bemoaning this oversight, until Mimi stomped one foot on the terrazzo floor in a large department store.

"If you mention that umbrella again," she scolded, "I won't take you out with me next time!"

I was flabbergasted, and so was she. We looked around us, then I said: "Did anyone overhear you? That's precisely what a mother says to a daughter, not the other way around!"

Around that time, we were planning to have Mimi's little buddy Deedee join us from Tianjin. That would mean having a family of four in a room measuring approximately twenty-five square yards (quite adequate according to Chinese housing regulations), plus kitchen and bathroom. My two children were very close to each other in spite of living in different cities, I'd noticed the two shared some mysterious way of communication. It always gave me a thrill to see them together, Mimi looking down slightly and Deedee looking up to her. Sometimes I dropped behind on purpose to watch them walking off together after we'd met one or the other at the train station. It was only a short distance to the bus stop, but in those few minutes they would already have told each other all there was to tell about either our Beijing home or the Tianjin homestead. I guess they were like ants, who with a quick touch of their antennae can pass on all the news, good and bad, and indicate where all the cookies and candies are stored.

After Deedee moved to Beijing, and before Mimi went to college and Fan left, we had a semblance of foursome family life for several years. Prominent in the family's routine were Mimi's never-ending exams in her tenth to twelfth years of school. Senior middle school years in the Chinese education system are a nerve-wracking obstacle course of exams, big and little.

The P.R.C. implements a unified middle school standard, and college entrance exams—the "unified exams for higher education"—are centrally controlled. These entrance exams are regarded as a matter of life or death. During Mimi's generation, the competition had become more fierce than ever before, mostly because of the uncontrolled population explosion in her age group. In my time, parents did little information-gathering and prognosticating with regard to the exams, but by the time Mimi was to take them, it seemed almost as if the parents were to be examined instead of their children.

When examination day rolled around in early July, I was told that many parents had taken the day off. They stood outside the exam halls equipped with water bottles, hard-boiled eggs (supposedly beneficial to the brain), and homemade goodies. Ice popsicle peddlars clustered around, since the first thing many nervous parents did on seeing their flushed and perspiring off-spring was to buy them refreshments.

I remembered my own excruciating experience, and felt the last thing I'd want to see as I staggered out after four hours of exams would be my parents. I asked Mimi what she wanted. She preferred not to have either of us waiting outside, she said, but hoped one of us would be at home when she returned.

Later, she told me she felt very independent as she walked out; after all, it was her exam. Instead of being fussed over by parents ("the poor kids looked furious at being cosseted like that"), she bought herself a popsicle and calmly came home.

The news was good and bad. Fan got someone at the admissions end to watch out for Mimi's number. The watcher saw Mimi's star flash up many times during the college selection process, but was invariably turned down for her top choice. She finally went to a reputable college in urban Beijing and moved to its dorms. That was before her father moved out for good.

Actually, apart from three years when Mimi was a child, I'd only had five years of living with her. When she was fifteen, some of her classmates had contemplated going to boarding schools for their senior middle years, mostly to escape the pressures of living at home. When Mimi had mentioned her classmates' intentions to me, I'd joked: "Do you want to get away from me, too?" Her answer had been music to my ears; she snuggled up to me and said: "I've never had enough of you, Ma Ma." We still haven't had enough of each other.

Mimi did not cost me much during her college years; tuition was free, and she received a government subsidy for living expenses. Her entry level salary, after she graduated four years later, was the same as mine had been a quarter of a century earlier, despite the inflation. I kept asking her to accept some money from me. Toto and I were relatively wealthy then—Ah Po called us "millionaires"—since our parents' savings had by now been returned to us. But Mimi, as I had done before, insisted on living on her own salary.

One so far untold aspect of Mimi's life concerns, of course, boys. In her middle school years, her girlfriends would yell from downstairs, while boys would clatter up the flights of stairs. If I happened to be at home when Mimi was out, the stock name given by male callers was "Classmate." Mimi would ask for a description, but I usually got features, clothes, and heights mixed up and earned for my pains a "stinky Ma Ma." I finally learned the name of one affable boy and pinned it onto all her callers; that at least sounded better than just Classmate.

Mimi was puzzled. Then she met the boy-with-a-name one day and asked how come he'd dropped by so many times. She came home in high dudgeon. "Never heard of a mother like that," she charged. "You aren't even fit to be a doorman!"

I still don't know the names of the other callers.

Mimi began to date seriously in college and consulted me very early on. But I'd already guessed what the subject would be before she even started.

"How did you guess?" she asked.

Well, which mother wouldn't? I'm only happy to report that I didn't snore during her briefings, as my father once did during mine.

Deedee the Quiz Kid

Deedee was born and raised under such chaotic circumstances that decisions on where he should stay were dictated by the times rather than made by his parents. He was placed in Tianjin from the time he was eighteen months old until he turned ten, under the supervision of my parents when they were alive and the sedulous surveillance of Ah Po who regarded males as a more important species than females. Fan and I were not always around; sometimes Deedee got to see us, more often he did not. But he was as strong and sturdy as any homegrown boy, and he read a good deal.

Deedee's literary enlightenment should be ascribed to his sister Mimi. By the time Deedee was three, Mimi had already put him in "school." She had a classmate who lived close by but had no place to go after school because both parents worked full-time. So the little girl stayed at our home until one of her parents came to pick her up.

Having nothing better to do after they'd finished their homework, Mimi and her friend played school. They actually had a name for it, Hallway School, since it was tucked between the infrequently used front entrance of our house and two swinging doors inside. It even had a small blackboard complete with chalk and eraser. Deedee was the school's one and only pupil.

The first time I was home on leave I noticed this rather unusual school. I had spent half an hour in the main hall fixing something and heard the girls speaking in stern and measured tones. Curious as to what they were doing, I walked to the glass swinging doors and looked in. Deedee was sitting attentively on a stool against the wall with both arms folded behind his back. Mimi held a pointer; it looked like a cue used to poke at wooden counters in a billiard-like game. She spoke in a flat, impersonal voice and was teaching her little brother Chinese characters, which he meekly repeated after her. Then the other girl started to give Deedee a lesson in arithmetic, also speaking with the same monotonous pitch. Occasionally Deedee raised a hand to ask a question. I had never seen him so obedient.

Mimi caught sight of me and gave me a dour look, as though I were a

Peeping Tom or some other interloper. Chastened, I retired to my adult world.

After another half hour of blessed quietude, the three kids whooped out of their enclosure and roughhoused their way into the yard. Leading the pack was, of course, Deedee.

I later asked Mimi where she and her friend had learned that didactic tone of speech. "From our teacher, of course," she replied matter-of-factly. "All teachers talk like that."

"The way Deedee was sitting, is that how you sit at school?" I asked.

"Sure, we all do. Didn't they teach you to do that at school?"

I was greatly amused by what I'd seen, but both the teachers and the lone student took their roles very seriously.

So seriously, in fact, that during the several years the Hallway School lasted, Deedee learned all he would have learned in the first three years of regular school. After other families who shared accommodations with us during the Cultural Revolution returned to their own houses, the school was moved to more spacious quarters, but its spirit remained unchanged. By then, I noticed official first-grader Deedee was even helping both girls with multiplication and fractions.

Learning characters in this "play school" manner made Deedee a zealous collector of words. He read anything and everything, from the periodically changing political slogans on street-corner billboards to the scraps of newspaper we Chinese used to wrap groceries with, craning his neck to see the characters better if the writing happened be upside down. When riding a bus or train, Deedee would pipe up at unexpected moments with tentative enunciations of new characters he'd caught sight of, much to the amusement of literate fellow passengers.

Deedee was much fussed over when he first entered school, because he was Mimi's younger brother; the teachers expected him to turn into another model student. What they got was a grab bag. He was bright. He was not intimidated by classroom questions—he'd gone through it for years. He was such a favorite among the girls that Mimi once scolded *me*: "Look at that son of yours! He's so pink and chubby girls carry him around during recess like a baby!" But he was also bored with learning things he already knew, and the imbalance became more and more difficult to handle. His teachers complained about his disregard and almost disdain for curricular studies, but couldn't put a finger on his problem.

Deedee moved to Beijing and entered the first year of middle school—seventh grade, that is—in a school adjacent to our apartment building. My son was growing up. While I still cuddled him like a baby at home (until an agreed-upon date, his twelfth birthday), I sidled to the other side of the sidewalk every time he warned: "Classmates!" It was okay for us to be affectionate at home, but for a boy to been seen walking beside his mom was a slur upon his forthcoming manhood.

Deedee was in his second year of middle school when his fate took an upward (or downward?) turn. Chinese TV had started what was called an "Intelligence Contest." Only eighth-graders were chosen for the school teams and Deedee was selected to represent his school in a team of six or seven.

To ready this group of students for the contest, they were exempted from other school activities. Supervision was provided by a few teachers who borrowed books and crammed the youngsters with as much information as they could absorb. Deedee's schedule became erratic, but we didn't worry because his school was so close. The team went through a series of preliminary competitions from which they emerged as front runners for the citywide on-screen test.

I happened to be visiting when Deedee's team went on the air. My friend's TV was on, and the name of Deedee's school caught my attention. Rows of cleanly scrubbed, white-shirted youngsters were shown seated behind two facing desks. A pudgy anchor moderated the competition, firing random questions at the competitors from a list he was holding. Deedee's team bungled the question: "Why are coal cinders strewn on the city streets after a winter snow?" All five of them failed to come up with an answer.

Deedee was flummoxed. "Who the heck has ever seen cinders thrown onto the streets?" he later remarked. "What a stupid question!" I suddenly realized that our part of Beijing used piped natural gas and coal stoves had been replaced before this group of local kids were born! Their opponents, on the other hand, were inner-city kids where residents still used coal stoves and scattered the ash on snow-packed streets and *hutung*s to prevent pedestrians from slipping. The opposing team got that one.

Deedee's most memorable answer was to a question related to World War II. "What was the turning point on the eastern front in that war?" "The battle of Stalingrad!" came from Deedee before the moderator had even concluded his question. Deedee's team placed second in the municipal contest.

I may be unfair when I claim this quiz formed or finished off my son. But from then on, it was no longer possible to bring him down to everyday class studies. His probing strayed so far it was hard to fathom the extent of his knowledge, or ignorance. I chided him, saying he was trying to turn himself into an encyclopedist; I pleaded with him to catch up in some basic studies, before he felt himself too old to acknowledge his obvious deficiencies in certain elementary fields of knowledge. He ayed to everything I said, but went his own way.

Once, when I took Deedee to a friend's home, he disappeared while we adults were talking. I eventually found him ensconced on a stool between two bookshelves with a two-inch-thick encyclopedia resting on his lap. Maybe he expected me to be annoyed, but my only thought at the time was that this scene seemed all too familiar: a child cached among the bookshelves in someone else's home.

I had begged Deedee, for the sake of the family and his teacher, to buckle down for once and make some grades good enough to get him into one of the so-called pilot-project senior middle schools. He did, to the enormous relief of his harassed teacher, with three points to spare.

That "Intelligence Contest" should have been named "Jeopardy" like its American counterpart.

Return to California at UCLA

I joined the film institute in 1979. Starting in the early 1980s, my *dan wei* cautiously and reluctantly agreed to let me meet English-speaking Westerners, including representatives from several embassies. Through my contacts I brought about film events welcomed by both sides, such as the screening of *Breaker Morant* at the Australian Embassy, an event attended by forty well-briefed, -disciplined, and -behaved Chinese filmmakers. The arrangements with the culture section of the U.S. Embassy were even more rewarding: a steady stream of professionals who understood enough English were able to view untranslated American films. They were given permission to go on a monthly basis to see Hollywood films not accessible to most Chinese. That was where I first watched such films as *One Flew Over the Cuckoo's Nest*.

On the other hand, I was also watched by the controlling powers. I learned of at least one incident involving me that was the cause of a couple of meetings to resolve the problem.

I had gone with a colleague to watch videos with an American couple who were newly assigned to Beijing—so newly that they had to stay in a hotel until their residence would be vacated for them. My colleague, being my superior, knew he should request permission for the visit beforehand. He had made a few halfhearted tries to reach the person in charge, but to no avail; he planned to defend himself by stating "don't say I haven't tried" should an issue be made of the matter.

We went to the hotel, signed in with our real names and *dan wei*, went up to the couple's room, and parked ourselves in front of the TV and chatted amicably while watching a documentary on tape. The floor steward knocked and came in twice while we were there. The excuse was delivering laundry and laundry bills, but all four of us understood he'd come to check on us. We shrugged it off since we were doing nothing wrong.

Nevertheless, the person-in-charge of our *dan wei*—the one my co-culprit had tried to reach—was notified of our escapade even before we left the hotel premises. Neither my colleague nor I were reprimanded at the time, for we were not to know we had been informed upon. It was only years later, after that person-in-charge and I had entered into an alliance of sorts, that he confided a few of the facts to me.

"You don't know what a mess you caused," he said. "The public security (police) called me while you were still in the hotel, to verify if we had two such persons on our staff and if you had asked for permission to visit foreign diplomats and watch videotapes. I shielded you two as best as I could, chiefly because I didn't know whether you'd been cleared by another boss, and we had instructions not to criticize intellectuals too much. I reported the matter to the secretariat the next day, and since the *dan wei* didn't want to be criticized for slack security, the report we sent in covered up for you two by saying you had reported beforehand, but the appointment had been rescheduled and there was some miscommunication. Nothing but headaches when dealing with foreign diplomats. Don't you ever learn?"

Well, my case was merely one of being very headstrong, and it actually did get me somewhere, quite unexpectedly.

Soon after the above incident (but before I learned of what had happened behind the scenes), I accepted another invitation from a departing Australian embassy couple. We were all very pleased with the outcome of the *Breaker Morant* screening, and they asked me to come to a farewell dinner at their home and bring a guest. It so happened I couldn't find an English-speaking person to bring that day, so I planned to go by myself. In compliance with instructions from an interoffice notice passed around after the hotel videotape watching, I left a note saying I'd be at a diplomat's residence for a family dinner that evening.

I immediately received a very stern call from someone in the foreign liaison section, telling me either to make an excuse for not showing up, or to take the caller himself as my guest. "No one is allowed to attend such functions alone. That's a standing order." I was defiant. "I'll do neither, and I don't think I am violating any orders. Who gave the orders, anyway? The person in charge of protocol is out of town." He gave me the name of a nosy, officious woman. "You can argue the matter with her, if you wish"—which I didn't.

I was furious for being saddled with such undesirable choices. To be on the safe side, I didn't go, and made a call at 6:30 P.M. to decline that 8:00 P.M. dinner invitation. I actually told my hosts the truth—that I had been forbidden to go without a companion or watchdog!

When the person-in-charge returned, I sought him out and told him about my displeasure over the farewell party invitation. I strongly objected to individuals not being allowed to associate with diplomats. "Those I've met are human beings, too!" I argued. "Besides, what top secrets do you expect *me* to leak? I'm no Party member, I don't get to see any of your secret documents, I don't even know *your* home phone number!" Home phone numbers of VIPs, even minor ones, are regarded as state secrets in China.

The person-in-charge actually knew how my previous contacts with the Australian couple had come about. "Sure," I said, "I was introduced to them by your liaison people when I escorted the director of the Australian Film School. Now they only wish to say good-bye to me instead of others. That's not my fault!"

I'm glad to report that I went to the departing couple's home, after they'd packed up and sent off all their belongings.

What mystified me was why, after this matter had been cleared up, that person-in-charge had me in for two prolonged sessions. One had to do with what I really think about dealing with "foreigners," and the other with my future career plans. "I haven't been in this *dan wei* long enough for either a transfer or a promotion," I pondered. "Why all this interest from someone who had considered me basically a 'headache'?" I nevertheless told him a bit about my career ambitions and about my determination to catch up in performance with colleagues who had seniority over me. I tossed in a few comments on some gross misinterpretations of foreign film titles which had gone undetected for decades. I made no effort to paint myself as the obedient, prudent functionary I had once been—my experiences as a *fan-ge-ming* had made me a much tougher person.

A few weeks later, however, to my vast astonishment I was called to the personnel office and informed that the secretariat had decided I was a candidate to accompany the authoratative film historian Chi to the United States on a lecturing trip. I was to see that "person-in-charge" and Chi for details. I went first to the person-in-charge.

He was all smiles and told me he strongly backed my candidacy. "Why?" I asked. "I break rules all the time, you know that." He said the Australian episode made him think differently of my headstrong straits. "Despite your objections," he said, "you actually followed orders and declined the invitation in time. You can stick to principles when necessary." In a word, if handled the right way, I could be the partner of choice for a professional mission.

I politely went to Chi—the selfsame writer jailed for eight years on order from Jiang Qing—as I only knew him slightly. Chi showed me the letter from UCLA inviting him to give the first overseas seminar ever on Chinese films. He was asked to be accompanied by, "if possible, a scholar on American films," acting as translator so that the trip would benefit both sides. But no one in the secretariat was quite certain what UCLA really was, I told him as much as I knew or had read about the University of California and its nine campuses. He was still waiting to hear if I'd accept the task.

I told him I was elated; who wouldn't be? But I had to clear up a few points: "I'm not a Party member, so will I be basically trusted while in America, or will restraints be placed on me?"

Chi answered that naming me as the candidate placed that trust. He suggested that the relationship established between us would be one of professional partners, one senior, one junior. We were both to observe the standing regulations at the time that we operate as a "delegation" and be responsible for each other's safety. I accepted the appointment.

For this mission, we were granted a substantial sum of money from the government, with which we made prints of classic Chinese films, acquired three fifty-pound boxes of film books, and bought a suitcaseful of presents. Among the latter were ten special made-to-order lacquered boxes which now rest on shelves in various homes and offices in the United States.

Meanwhile, it suddenly dawned on me that all I knew about seminars (*xi mi na er* in Chinese, as translated from the Russian) was what the Soviets had taught. I hadn't the faintest notion about how a seminar should be conducted in American universities. I frantically called up an American professor I knew well and asked him if he could please gave me a two-hour session on how to teach a graduate seminar in an American university. He laughed and laughed at the thoroughness of our preparations, and gave me a long lecture beginning with how to bargain for the most desirable time slot and then proceeding to the syllabus, the T.A., the office hours, the group size, exams, and grading. Yes, and even how to organize a party at the end of the quarter. This crash course on "How to teach a seminar in America" served me in good stead during all nine seminars I was to teach in subsequent years.

That professor also cautioned me not to take it as a personal offense if the students whispered, yawned, propped up their feet, or went out for coffee. "Don't be bothered at all," he advised. Curiously enough, though, of the ten or twelve dozen students I had the pleasure to associate with in later years, none behaved as he'd predicted.

I gave Chi a detailed report of what I'd learned from my American friend. Only one thing bothered Chi: the smallness of the seminar. To the Chinese mind, the bigger the better, and he was used to lecturing to outsize classes, whereas I had been spoiled by the one-on-one or -two or -four teaching sessions conducted at the music conservatory. He finally accepted the professor's advice to keep attendance at ten to twelve persons, and actually ended up having sixteen.

Armed to the teeth with information, advice, films, books, and gifts, we set out for our new frontier and arrived at UCLA's campus amid the wonder of its beauty on a September day in 1983. Our team teaching turned out to be a success and was repeated in 1986. We had, in all, thirty-two students at UCLA from ten countries and regions, and many among those former students of ours have remained our friends.

As I'll deal with the interesting aspects of my return to the Golden State in other episodes, I shall only describe an amusing sequel to our first seminar trip.

It had been a successful mission, executed in goodwill and good taste. Neither Chi nor I sought publicity or fanfare, and there was little of it apart from a well-written story in the *Los Angeles Times* <u>after</u> the seminar. We decided to keep the same low profile back in China and only consented to a minimum of factual accounts in film journals.

However, a Chinese newspaper published in English asked me to write an article for them, which I did. I sent them the article in February 1984, and didn't hear anymore about it for over a month. Then I got a call from an editor in early April, informing me that the editorial board was highly pleased with my article and would save it for the upcoming state visit of Ronald Reagan.

"What for?" I asked. "He certainly won't have the time to read your paper!" The editor argued that someone in the President's entourage, at least, might notice it. I replied drily that I felt honored, then hung up.

That article about the UCLA seminar was released, as promised, on the day Ronald Reagan arrived. I got my close to thirty U.S. dollars fee for writing it, but wondered whether anyone in the American president's group noticed the Chinese media's coy little message!

Where Worlds Meet

On our first trip to UCLA, Chi and I were invited to Palm Springs as houseguests of my filmmaker friends Danny and Sheri. I had met them when they visited China a couple years back, and we hit it off well because we shared, to a large extent, a common outlook on life. This, however, was the first time my associate Chi met them.

We were taken by our hosts to the Hungry Tiger for dinner—that restaurant chain had been founded by Flying Tigers veterans who had flown missions in China under Claire Chennault during the World War II.

We were seated around a square table with the men and women facing each other respectively. Chi mentioned in passing that he, like Danny, had gone into films from theater. I was translating.

During a slight pause, Danny asked, out of the blue: "Has he ever been to Burma?"

Being only professionally acquainted with Chi, I honestly didn't know and asked Danny: "I'm not familiar with his life story. Why do you ask?"

Danny was becoming excited and insisted: "Ask him! Ask him!" He'd noticed a faint reaction from Chi to the word Burma in English.

I turned to Chi and told him: "Danny wants to know if you've been in Burma (using the Chinese appellation *Mian Dian*). Why—"

Chi was nodding vigorously and saying "Yes" in English before I'd finished my sentence, and the two of them were suddenly quite agitated.

"*Ba mo*," Chi blurted out an un-Chinese word. I was about to ask what that meant, but Danny answered gleefully, "Yes, Bhamo. And, and, Myitkyina."

"Yes, yes, *Mi zhi na!*" responded Chi.

Sheri and I sat speechless, and our heads turned from one to the other in unison as the two men who didn't understand each other's language rapidly exchanged exotic place names. They reached out over the table for a handshake.

Danny asked me to tell Chi that his troop unit had gone into Bhamo when the airfield was still burning. Chi said his had entered on foot just as the fire was being extinguished. Neither of them had been enlisted men or officers; they were both with theatrical groups attached to the regular troops. That operation took place toward the end of World War II. Danny was a few years older than Chi.

"We were allies, we were army buddies," Danny exclaimed to the waiter who came to our table. When the general astonishment had subsided, it was established that their respective units had been stationed one on each side of the main road leading to the airport. Both had lived in tents provided by American troops, one red, one blue. Chi recalled having had a meal consisting of some American canned food presented as a gift to the Chinese Army. Some Chinese soldiers had not found the foreign food much to their taste, but Chi had liked it.

"That's why you came to America to have dinner with us," quipped Sheri.

Danny was so pleased with his discovery he started to boast. "I had a hunch our roads must have crossed somewhere. I felt a certain empathy even though we couldn't talk directly. He's slightly younger than I am, but old enough to have been involved in the war. It suddenly came to me when he said he came from a theatrical background. I'd seen Chinese performances in Bhamo."

After I'd translated Danny's encomiums to his own senses, sixth or whatever, Chi asked: "Does he remember any of the titles of the plays?"

Danny admitted he'd forgotten, but the performances consisted of a number of short plays.

Chi told us he played the son of a Chinese military hero of the twelfth century. Danny almost jumped from his seat and exclaimed that this was beyond belief; he now remembered the costumes and simple sets of that play.

Danny told Chi about an incident during one of the performances.

At one of the joint open-air shows the victorious Allied troops put on to entertain each other and the local citizens, the American troops had been seated in the best place just in front of the stage. Their commanding officer arrived after dining with his Chinese guests and became quite upset.

"The Chinese troops are our guests," he barked. "We can't let our guests sit on the sides while we the hosts sit in the center." The American troops were ordered to rise, about face, and march out of the grounds.

Then the U.S. officer asked the surprised Chinese commander to move his men into the vacated area and apologized for the insensitivity displayed by the organizers. The American troops returned after the guest troops had been reseated.

Danny admitted that incident taught him a lifelong lesson; even if his philosophy embraced the whole of mankind, he could be unconsciously self-important as many Americans are. "From then on," said he, "I've had a better understanding of the principle of regarding people of all races as brothers, and today I've found a new one."

Danny and Chi remained on the best of terms until Danny's death years later.

The United States is a natural meeting place for people from different worlds. This is where I got to know my first South Korean, Romanian, Yugoslav, Bulgarian, Czech, and Indian acquaintances, as well as all kinds of Americans, all as equals.

A WITCH DRIVES ME HOME

It was Halloween at Stony Brook when I went by bus from SUNY campus to a large mall. I had noticed a magnificent plush dog there and was determined to get it for my niece.

A torrential rain was falling when I caught a homebound bus, and I chose this day of all days to get off a stop earlier to walk home from a new direction. Darkness fell as I floundered up the narrow roads. Unable to find any street sign, I couldn't even tell whether I was headed in the right direction.

I decided against stopping one of the few motorists; it was too dangerous to stand in their path in the blinding rain. I walked up and down the road a few times until I was convinced I had lost my way. My only comfort was that the plush dog was dry and cozy in the big shopping bag where I also kept my purse.

I tried to go back to the bus stop and find my way to the one where I used to get off. At least I'd be able to orient myself. Suddenly, I came upon an intersection called Twinkle Lights.

I walked across the well-lit street and stopped in front of a home with lights on its porch and in its windows. Maintaining a distance from the porch, I called out to the people inside that this was neither treat nor trick, that I was lost.

A child called his grandma, saying "Someone's lost!" The grandmother came to the screen door. After sizing me up she told me to wait; perhaps her daughter could see me back home.

I stammered words of gratitude and kept saying I knew this neighborhood but got confused in the dark and rain. Presently, a woman dressed as a witch came out onto the porch; after all it was Halloween. Despite my protests, she asked my address, stepped into her car, and motioned me to get in.

"It'll only take a few minutes to get you home, so why should I let you walk in the dark and rain?" she said. "I was about to leave for the Halloween party anyway. I'm a teacher, and I'll turn back to take my son to my school's party."

I looked at her in her witch's costume, complete with a mask. "With you behind that mask, I can hardly thank you to your face," I said. "I can only tell my housemates a witch drove me home." We laughed as she let me off in front of the garden gate.

I went to Twinkle Lights again that weekend, found my benefactors' house, and took down the street number. Later I sent an elaborate thank-you card to the grandmother, the mother, and the child. I explained who I was and why I happened to be here, and told them I would ever remember the night a witch drove me home.

IT HAPPENED IN BROOKLYN

I had a couple of satisfactory sojourns in Stony Brook on Long Island. The only drawback was the length of the island, which made getting to New York City and its surroundings a real pain.

I once planned a perfect round-trip: I'd go into Manhattan by train and stay with friends in Midtown. From there I would meet a young friend of my children's for lunch and he would escort me on the subway to Brooklyn to visit. Then I'd be picked up at a certain spot by a grad student who'd bring me back to Stony Brook.

Everything happened right on schedule, and fifteen minutes before the final rendezvous I was waiting on the southwest corner of a busy Brooklyn intersection. Then, without warning, my nose started to bleed. Not that it hadn't happened before, but I couldn't have thought of a worse time and place.

I was carrying my overnight bag and handbag, I had to tilt my head back, I had to keep an eye out for Joe's car, and I had to stop this goddamn bleeding. I fumbled for a couple of Clean Wipes I had with me, but they only made the bleeding worse. I suppose something in them irritated the membranes in my nose. Whatever the case, I have never had such a prolonged nosebleed in public.

I was attracting attention, and a few passersby stopped to ask if they could help. I peered down along my nose at them, tried to smile, and said it was an old problem of mine, the bleeding would stop by itself. A police car drew up and two officers inquired if they could take me to a hospital. I answered, again with my anguished smile, that I couldn't leave this corner because I was waiting for someone to meet me and drive me back mid-Island. "Well, we'll be cruisin' around. We'll keep an eye on ya!"

Suddenly I heard a warm, throaty voice at my shoulder: "Don't worry, honey, we'd have you all fixed up in a minute." I half-turned to see a middle-aged black lady holding a handful of napkins grabbed from a hot-dog stand close by. She drew my head down to her breast, as capacious as her heart, and crooned: "Don't talk, don't laugh, hold back your head and relax. We'll have the bleeding stopped right away. I heard you, I know you can't leave this corner 'cause you're waiting for your friend. Just let me hold you, honey."

I had never felt so safe, with my head resting on the bosom of that generously built lady. I muttered something to the effect that I knew I was in good hands. She chuckled, "You're darn right you're in good hands, sweetheart. I sure have stopped a few nosebleeds."

By the time my ride came, I was looking all right again, except for a few splatters of blood on my woolen scarf. The lady left with my profound thanks. I even managed to leave a dollar tip at the hot-dog stand for the stacks of napkins my rescuer had used on me.

The lady left me with a good feeling for Brooklyn. Whenever that district of New York is badmouthed, I don't jump on the bandwagon, for I can't forget the warmth of her arms and voice.

It Happened in Los Angeles

Amid all the talk of race, ethnicity, multiculturalism, and political correctness, I found myself in a long line at a West Los Angeles post office. There were three or four in front of me and a dozen behind.

A stout white woman in her sixties cut in at the head of the line in all readiness to be served next.

"Ma'am, can you get in line, please?" I said. She waved a dollar bill, indicating no doubt that her service needs would be simple, and then ignored me. I shook my head disapprovingly.

Then a voice boomed just behind me: "Miss," he said. "Here we line up. Go to the back, please." The older woman played deaf, and the young voice repeated "I mean you, miss. Please go to the back."

The woman moved past us, muttering. I caught a few words of Russian. Following her with my eyes, I noticed that the speaker behind me was a young black man in his late teens.

His gaze was on the woman as she tried to insert herself halfway down the line. "All the way," he said firmly. "All the way to the back. We all line up here." He turned his head and our eyes met for a second. We knew we had done a small thing that was right.

And so, in this city where the worlds meet, two so-called minorities—an African-American and I who could pass as an Asian-American—asked an ostensibly majority white woman to adhere to the norms of this society: "Stand in line and wait for your turn."

The woman's mutterings had clued me in to her origins; I wondered whether the young man knew. He had said, "Here we line up," in a way that made me think he did.

The Childless Ah Po

Ah Po became part of our extended family from the late 1950s until her passing away in 1986.

She was almost the same age as Mama and was born in the same province.

She had no children, but lived in a rather prosperous rural area until the out-break of the Sino-Japanese War. Her town was burned down by the invaders, and she and her husband fled on foot to nearby Shanghai. Ah Po was around thirty at the time and started to work as a domestic. Her husband went back to rebuild their home; he was the household's rice-winner, while she became the cash-winner.

The dozen or so years she spent as a nanny in Shanghai opened her eyes to urban life. She saw goodness, evil, generosity, and greed, as she was wont to tell us. And she would end up saying: "Maybe my income is small, but my eyes are not!" Meaning that she wasn't dazzled by luxury or lucre.

Ah Po's Shanghai employers brought her to the Beijing-Tianjin area. She stayed with them until political movements so reduced that family's circum-stances, that the mistress recommended her to our home. Ah Po's husband passed away around that time, and she stayed with our family for the next twenty-eight years.

I had already left home for college when she came and didn't become well acquainted with her until she and Mimi joined our small household, right after the Red Guards went on their rampage. From the way Mimi clung to her I could see their affection for each other. There's a saying one can't fool chil-dren and animals; they recognize good and bad people by instinct.

Ah Po, being a "proletarian" by classification, suffered no material damage during the Cultural Revolution. She stayed either in Beijing or Tianjin, wher-ever it was best for us, and refused to take her wages during our years of adversity, for she considered herself one of the family. When some of our money was returned to us, Mama gave her three thousand yuan as back salary, quite a large sum in those days.

I remember with gratitude how she lined up early in the mornings to buy cheap beef bones, with which to make a thick broth for me when I was preg-nant with Deedee and, later, breast-feeding him. She'd get two ounces of ground pork and somehow manage to serve up a meal for four. She was clever at making money stretch, and all benefited from her ingenuity. In later years, however, her money saving schemes became a fixation, and Toto, Bella, and I (the "millionaires") rebelled when she ordered us to haul back heaps of dirt-cheap *hsueh-li-hung*—the very same *brassica cernua* I composed an ode to in cadre school—for pickling. We could never have eaten that much *hsueh-li-hung* anyway! But to appease her, we paid an old handyman to do the hauling.

Ah Po was no feminist. She doted on my father, on Toto, on Deedee. She spoiled Deedee to the extent that she would buy cookies and crackers and leave them on the lower shelves of her storage cabinet for him to snitch. And when he did so, she'd make a fuss and once even rapped him on the head. I suspect, though, that this was only their private game of cops and robbers.

Ah Po was up early every day and had a strong voice until she reached her late seventies. By then, Toto's entire family had emigrated to the United States, my children and I were in Beijing, and the house in Tianjin was leased out. In its stead we got a temporary apartment in Beijing, and Ah Po was moved from Tianjin to this unit. Deedee lived with her. That apartment was not far from the one-room apartment we called home. I went on my second trip to the United States soon after that, in late 1985, and put Ah Po, her TV, and her transistor radio under the charge of my children.

On my return, I bought Ah Po a blood pressure kit as my homecoming gift. I'd been gone for five months and was puzzled when neither of my children were at the airport to meet me. My colleagues who came to meet the plane told me not to worry. They hadn't been able to come because the old lady wasn't well and they were taking turns looking after her.

"Oh, no! Not now!" I thought. Ah Po would be eighty in a few months.

Deedee was waiting at home to help carry my luggage up to the fourth floor. Mimi was at the hospital with Ah Po. What happened was that a new neighbor had talked Ah Po into having quite a few teeth pulled at one sitting, and the experience had been too much for her. She'd had a heart attack at about the time I was embarking on the flight home. My children were beside her at the time, and with the help of some friends got an ambulance and Ah Po was taken into intensive care.

Her condition had stabilized somewhat when I arrived in Beijing, but the doctors did not allow visitors. Since I was jet lagged and couldn't sleep anyway, I went to the hospital to see Mimi. It was late evening and I found the nurses and patients talking about our family and praising my children.

Apparently Mimi and Deedee had gotten hold of no less than six of their friends to help with Ah Po's hospitalization. One went to get some cash, another filled out the forms, and Mimi talked with Ah Po while the rest pestered the doctors with anxious questions. It was only after a while that the head nurse realized that the crowd escorting the old lady contained no "big people," as adults are called in China.

"Where are the big people in your family?" she asked.

"Oh, they're all in the United States," Mimi answered, thinking of Toto and me. "One is on her way back. The other lives there."

"Which of you are the old lady's grandchildren?"

Mimi pointed at Deedee and herself. By then, other patients in the crowded section were becoming interested. What well-bred children, some said. The old lady is lucky to have them.

Answering basic questions put to her by the hospital staff, Mimi happened to mention Ah Po had no children.

"Then who are you," exclaimed an astute patient, "if she's had no children?" Only then did it become clear that Ah Po had been a domestic servant of Mimi's grandparents and a nursemaid to both my children.

Ah Po was released to the common ward the next day, and I spent the night at her bedside. I noticed she was unusually spirited the next morning. I sought out an old nurse and asked her if Ah Po could be in what the Chinese call "the transient resurgence of the dying." She nodded, but predicted Ah Po would pass away without pain. "That's her good luck, you know."

Ah Po died peacefully in Mimi's arms the following day. I was notified, and the moment I got to the hospital, Mimi ran to me in tears. "Were you frightened?" I asked softly. Mimi was twenty-one. "No," she said. "I didn't feel afraid at all. But it's so sad. She's . . . dead."

Ah Po was cremated and, purely by chance, Toto and Bella returned to China from the United States that very day. Together, we sent Ah Po to her final resting place.

The savings account that she left came to three thousand yuan, exactly the amount Mama had paid her as back salary.

"Can you believe that?" I said to Toto. "She came to this world, she lived, she toiled, she had good and bad times, and when she left, she returned everything people had given her! As the ancient sages would say: She came and went with a free spirit."

"Oh! I Forgot About the Divorce . . ."

My marriage had petered out completely by the end of the Cultural Revolution. The tension between Fan and myself was so heavy we avoided being in the same room together. But we still had to share the one-room apartment, even though we never touched and seldom even looked at each other any longer.

In China, keeping up appearances is more important than what really goes on between husband and wife. Nobody, aside from Toto, Bella, and the omniscient Ah Po, knew our marriage was in trouble. One night in late 1975, at a time when Fan and I were the only occupants of our apartment, he was irritated by something I said when I gave him an account of how I happened to drop in at an old scientist's home, what we talked about, and what they had for dinner. Whatever it was, Fan worked up an enormous rage when I refused to be provoked into a quarrel with him.

Afraid that he might become violent, as he sometimes did, I said I'd leave for a while and talk when he cooled down.

I walked up to the open balcony, but it was a freezing winter's night, so I went down to the apartment occupied by old man Whiskers and his wife. It isn't unusual in China for neighbors simply to knock and drop in. We exchanged some small talk, then I said I had to tell them something for my own safety. In case Fan created a violent scene, Whiskers would best fill the post of mediator.

Mr. and Mrs. Whiskers, who were in their late sixties at the time, sat so still as I told them the secrets of my disintegrating marriage I felt my heart sink. Oh, dear, I thought, is telling others one's marriage has gone wrong just as reprehensible as letting the marriage get that way? They sat silently for another minute or two before Whiskers spoke:

"What you've said is like an underground blast. We know you both and like your company. I'm sorry things went wrong." He agreed to intervene on my behalf if Fan did anything drastic.

Fan had made up a bundle of clothes and bedding when I returned half an hour later, but he himself was nowhere in sight and did not come home until well past midnight. We didn't speak to each other until after a couple of days, when I offered to let him have within six months the divorce he seemed to want so much. The reason I wanted some time was that barely half a year had passed since I'd lost Mama so unexpectedly and my entire political and professional fate was still uncertain. To add a divorce to all that was more than I could handle at the time. I needed a few months to assess what lay ahead for me, and then I'd grant him a divorce if that was what he still wanted.

But then, in rapid succession, Zhou Enlai passed away, then the big earth-quake, Mao died, the Gang of Four fell soon after, and so the divorce issue was shelved for the time being.

Ostrichlike, I went on with life, pretending everything was normal. My professional life switched fields after decision was passed on my political fate, as related earlier; and first Mimi, then Deedee, came back to Beijing to live with us in that one large room. In spite of the strained non-relationship between the parents, we looked, outwardly at least, like one happy, healthy, and well-kept family.

Fan never mentioned our domestic troubles to Whiskers or his wife, and they remained discreet about my nocturnal disclosure.

One day, however, I needed to buy some tofu and sugar. These could only be obtained with a family ration booklet in which the sales clerk entered the amount one bought so that no family would exceed the monthly allowance. I looked high and low for that booklet, but in one of Fan's unisex handbags I came upon a letter without an envelope.

Words written on it in flowing handwriting jumped into my line of vision, and I immediately wished they hadn't. These words jerked my ostrich head out of its hole in the sand and set me on the final road to divorce. They read: "In a relationship such as ours, we have to be discreet." Yeah, I thought, by leaving the letter around without an envelope and the paper folded to show this line of all lines! I quickly scanned the letter, signed with a pet name and dated a month ago, telling Fan how the writer had arrived in Beijing and searched everywhere for him. In this letter she instructed him where she'd be waiting for him at a given time. I figured out who the writer was, and was again devastated by the realization that any of the women Fan presented to me as his friends, colleagues, or old comrades could very well be his mistresses at the same time.

But at that moment I was more conscience-stricken by the fact that I had read this letter. I had been brought up to refrain from reading other people's correspondence unless asked to (this principle of privacy happens to be very weak among most Chinese, and many are victimized by unofficial censor-ship). I trotted up and down the intervening staircases again to the Whiskers' apartment and asked them what I should do.

I kept saying I was sorry, I shouldn't have read the letter, but it was just lying there with that revelatory sentence in full sight. After about the fourth replay of my mea culpa, Whiskers blew up: "He should be the party to feel sorry. You're his wife and I think you have every right to read and keep this letter—I'll keep it for you if you're afraid to do so." Mrs. Whiskers then remarked, "Isn't it time you told her a thing or two?"

I learned quite a bit about what my neighbors had, on more than one occasion, heard or seen. Whiskers and all others had agreed not to tell me unless it became absolutely necessary, because they didn't want my children and me to be hurt.

I looked at the letter for a long time, then decided to return it to its original place until I found it in myself to confront Fan.

But as the sand dribbled away, this ostrich learned a lot more and finally raised her head to face realities. The truth is, I had felt I was also somewhat to blame for the cracking of our mirror, so to speak. I had been frosty after I found out his mistress was the cause of our political problems, and although Fan and I still met occasionally as man and wife in the next few years, my performance had been quite perfunctory. Since there was no trust or respect, there wasn't much inclination to love or make love. Indeed, such things came to a full stop in 1975.

To make this umpteen-year divorce story short, I didn't confront Fan with the letter I'd found until two years later. He didn't deny anything, but refused to talk. I did, however, for two hours.

We continued to maintain appearances and still went to my relatives for the Chinese New Year, but we'd hike over by different routes while the children took a bus. I finally divulged this state of affairs to a couple of my colleagues. One of them credited me on the spot with being the "best actress," for none of them had the slightest inkling of my absurd home situation.

That was in the early 1980s. Divorce, while no longer considered almost a misdemeanor, was regarded as a shame, a failure, a tragedy. Many marriages were kept going on account of the children, for the appendix "their parents are divorced" was still tagged on after introductions. I deferred the inevitable much too long.

Fan moved out in the meantime, because his *dan wei* had built some new housing and our family of four with two teen-age children of different gender was entitled to a three-room apartment. We sat down, all four of us, and agreed we would keep our big one-room apartment and that Fan would apply for an additional two-room apartment close to his *dan wei*. Fan would move out, while the children could decide where they wanted to live. They chose to make their home base with me because Deedee's school was in the vicinity and Mimi, now in college, did not want another move. Both children were given keys to Fan's apartment.

D-day (D as in divorce) was postponed year after year on account of my frequent trips to the United States and various business trips within China, until Mimi announced to me one day: "If you don't get the divorce done this year, I'm not coming home for New Year's Eve!" I still didn't, however, and the final severance took place in early spring of 1987.

I finally went to file our case at the divorce office. I did some investigation; I even enlisted a neighbor to find out when the office would be the least likely to have visitors.

But the timing couldn't have been worse! The office building was being repainted that day. I knocked on the door of the two-occupant office and stepped in to see nine women, all crammed in with their desks brought here from the "rooms-in-painting." I panicked and was on the verge of backing out. But my zealous neighbor, with my consent, had given the person in charge all necessary information about my never-ending divorce along with a detailed description of myself.

"Comrade Chen," the woman at the other end of the room waved cheerily. "Come over! We're a bit crowded today, but your case is simple and won't take any time."

Darn! I thought, I'll be the main course today for the appetites of gossipy minds. But I knew I was trapped, so I sat down and explained to the woman this would be a divorce by mutual agreement, and that both children were over eighteen. She insisted, however, on having in writing who would be in charge of them.

"I'll be in charge," I replied. "There will be no financial complications."

"What about assets?" she asked.

"We each have our own. There are no common savings and haven't been any financial ties between us for the past five years."

"I mean TVs, refrigerators, bicycles, and so forth," she persisted, apparently with the best of intentions.

The room was so quiet a pin would have dropped with an audible clunk. I could have kicked myself for choosing this day!

However, I had to do it, one way or another.

"You must realize this has been an umpteen-year divorce," I said. "I have no idea where and how he lives. He'll give you his address when he comes to sign."

The woman said: "We understand the strain this is putting on you, but regulations require you write down a list of all your property."

I held my breath and my tongue. Using imagination and snippets of conversation I'd overheard between the children, I put down what I thought Fan might have acquired over these last years: TV, fridge, VCR, bike, laundrette. I was granted a minor reprieve when I asked, rather ingenuously, "I don't have to guess at the brand names, do I?" The woman said no, that wasn't necessary.

We set the date for signing the document, which I'd tell the children to pass on to Fan. I then ran the gauntlet, without turning my head, back through the two rows of desks temporarily set up in that office.

I told my divorce story to a young British friend of mine then residing in Beijing. Together we laughed off my indignation regarding the crowded office. I also mentioned the date set for signing the papers.

A few days later, Fan and I met at the office (now cleared of the temporary desks and staff). I hadn't seen him for about three years, and we found nothing at all to talk about. We both read and signed the prepared documents, then we walked out of the building and politely said good-bye.

A trendy expression today in the United States is to "put it behind you and get on with life." I did just that. I penciled a checkmark in front of "divorce" on my list of to do things and went back to work on the article at hand.

My phone rang at around ten that evening. It was Barry, my British friend

"How are things?" he asked in Chinese.

"You mean the tapes?" I answered in English. "I gave them to so-and-so. He should be taking them to you tomorrow."

"No, I mean . . . " he faltered.

"You mean that magazine? I'll give it to you in a few days."

Exasperated, Barry blurted: "I mean your divorce!"

"Oh!" I exclaimed. "I forgot!"

"What!" My reply surprised him into English. "You forgot to go for the divorce!"

"No. I did it this morning. There've been so many things after that I'd forgotten about it."

Lost and Found Among the Bookshelves, IV

English-reading Chinese had a busy time in the 1970s and 1980s, collecting books and exchanging them with one another. As I have recounted, English books, which had already been hard to obtain in the 1950s, went completely underground and in hiding—those that weren't destroyed—during those ten uncultured years of the "Cultural Revolution." And when reading in English became legal and even fashionable sometime after the mid-1970s, I busily rode around town borrowing and returning books scrounged up by the local English readership.

Even with the relatively open atmosphere, however, there still were restrictions. Many library books were lent out only on presentation of special permits, and censorship was freely practiced by the Chinese Customs. An old friend was once called to his local post office to talk about an English book sent to him from overseas. The title was *Borrowed Husband,* and the postal clerk showed my friend the translation of that title as done by some customs officer who probably had no more than a smattering of English. The clerk very well-meaningly urged my friend to advise the sender to choose his gifts more carefully so as not to send books that had problems of ideology and content. My friend could have the book, for Customs had checked his reputation, but he had to promise not to lend it out to others who would thus run the risk of being contaminated. My friend, an elderly gentleman, huffed and puffed and left without the book.

I've mentioned way back that we shipped many books back to China in 1949. Among them was one 1948 volume of *Reader's Digest* condensed books, which carried an abridged version of *Our Hearts Were Young and Gay.* As a result, I've always wanted to read the complete version of that book.

When I came to the United States to teach, I'd decided that the only material things I would take back to China were books I wanted, not necessarily classics. Aware of the little money I'd have left after expenses, I asked to be taken to used-book stores instead of regular ones. When I scanned the shelves of a store in Hollywood, something that looked like *Our Hearts . . .* set my heart aflutter. I took another look, clapped my head, pointed at the bookshelf, and flopped down on my knees in the narrow aisle. The Chinese friend who took me there had something of a shock; she thought I'd succumbed to a heart attack. I found it hard to explain to her why I was so elated at finding a rather insignificant yet humorous book no one in any English Department in China had ever heard of.

By my third trip to the United States in five years, my first item of research on arriving in Madison in 1988 was to compile a list of used-book stores. My hosts, being even bigger bookworms than myself, gave me a list of five such stores on the spot. They even knew the street numbers by heart.

Toward December, I got a break when one of the stores had a clearance sale. Starting from 50 percent off the marked prices, the books were to be sold at 60 percent, 70 percent, and 80 percent off in successive weeks until the week before Christmas.

I went during the 50 percent off week and fine-combed the shelves with the help of a step ladder. In the "O" section near the ceiling, I came upon two thick and heavy books, *The Complete Works of O'Henry*, volumes I and II. I remembered the day Mama tore pages from "The Four Millions" to light our stove, and her conviction that if we lived through those hellish times, we would have the books again. Now here they were, the complete set waiting for me ten thousand miles away from home—and, affordably, at 50 percent discount!

I clambered down the ladder with the weighty volumes. I paid a total of, uh, six dollars for these precious books and hugged them all the way home.

Chinese scholars have a saying: "In books one finds houses of gold and faces like jade." I've lost a lot in life, but have found much more among bookshelves. I sometimes joke that I have an enduring lover named Books, who comes in many splendors, and with whom I am never lonesome.

The Last Time I Saw Beijing

Beijing is my birthplace and a place I've kept returning to during my peregrinations. I returned to it at the end of 1945 after my family's forced wartime emigration, and again from the United States in late 1949 at the end of a round-the-world journey. After my family had moved to Tianjin in 1953, I went back when my college relocated to Beijing in 1959. Following a long period of residence there as a young woman and mother, I was sent to the countryside between 1969 and 1975, and China came out of its long night-mare less than a year after I went back. And in the 1980s, I returned to Beijing from academic trips to the United States. To me, Beijing was home, the place I knew and loved, and I kept going back to it. I sort of hoped I'd stay with the later pattern—teaching trips to the United States and then home to Beijing. But it wasn't to be . . .

I've seen many changes in Beijing, both in its external appearance and its inhabitants, for better or for worse. The old city wall has been taken down, and a second and third (and now a fourth) ring road encircles the expanding metropolis. Matchboxlike apartment blocks and medium-height high rises have mushroomed everywhere, replacing the decaying residential courtyard houses, some built three hundred years ago and crowding the old palaces and temples. With a few showpiece exceptions, before the end of the Cultural Revolution the new buildings were unimaginative, shoddy, and utilitarian affairs.

Some of the newer construction, however, is worth mentioning as an illus-tration of the Chinese leaders' mentality—the kind that gave rise to the *ying pi*, the wall inside a gate.

When a twenty-two-story wing was added to the old Peking Hotel in the early 1970s, security officials discovered that guests staying in suites above the nineteenth floor on the west side could look directly across the Forbidden City into Zhongnanhai at about three miles distance, the place with the *ying pi* at the front gate where China's leaders live and work.

Their immediate reaction was to seal off to foreigners all rooms and suites above the nineteenth floor on the west side. The second thing they did was to convene a group of politically reliable architects to discuss the dilemma. The solution, a clever one in their judgment, was to build two similar towers on top of one of the east and west gates respectively of the five-hundred-year-old Forbidden City. The one on the east gate blocked the line of vision of anyone with the audacity to spy upon the Great Leader, and the twin on the west gate served no other purpose than to maintain the symmetry of the Forbidden City's layout. These eyesores were okayed by none other than the usually rational Zhou Enlai. "Don't they realize that the world has advanced into the satellite era?" a friend of mine remarked, "and that walls and towers can no longer hide things from foreign snoopers?"

The two flat towers, consisting of little more than two walls and some purely ornamental windows were correctly called "concealment towers" by the residents of the city, and remain as a puzzle to those who don't know the reason for their existence.

Another modification made to Beijing's ancient landmarks are the two rows of spiked iron fences replacing the original marble balustrades on the majestic bridge in front of North Sea Park—the place where Papa was dropped off to find his way home the night he was released from confinement in the early 1950s. The cause of this architectural obscenity is one of my cadre school comrades.

Du, a skilled maker of musical instruments, was in my cadre school company. Personal troubles had left him in a state of mental depression, and while quite friendly and harmless, he could also be quite unpredictable. He was unmarried, and once, when he left cadre school on his quarterly vacation, he failed to return on time. After he finally did come back, he was more subdued than usual. Moreover, a guard was assigned to accompany him wherever he went.

It was during one of our snacks at eight that Confu told us what had happened.

"Guess where he went to?" said Confu. "He went to visit Chairman Mao!"

Du apparently had a question or two concerning Mao's writings and decided to use his vacation to clarify them. He observed the operations of the guards patrolling the bridge that forms the border between North Sea Park and Zhongnanhai (Central-south Sea), and when both guards had walked to opposite ends of the pedestrian walkway, he jumped into the lake and swam toward the inhabited area. He wasn't fired upon because a crowd gathered to watch what was thought to be a suicide. A small boat pulled out from one bank and Du was dragged aboard. He repeatedly told his captors he wished to pay a visit to his beloved Chairman Mao to discuss one of Mao's classically written articles. The sentries finally realized they had a mental case on their hands and not a political one. Yet it was several weeks before he was released.

The news that someone hadn't been hurt or imprisoned after invading the sanctum got around and encouraged half a dozen other people to jump over the marble balustrade—people who wished to seek redress for unjust persecution during the Cultural Revolution or other reasons. So the authorities replaced the balustrades with iron railings high enough to ensure that no human being can vault over them.

The era of economic reforms began in the late 1970s, set off construction booms in Beijing. Instead of putting up bank buildings as in American cities, the boom consisted primarily of grand hotels at major crossroads, which gave Beijing a semblance of modernization even if the service in them left much to be desired.

Some of the superficial aspects of Beijing had improved drastically when I last saw it, but the combination of Communist doctrine and dogma and the mindless anarchism of the Cultural Revolution almost totally destroyed the better values Chinese civilization has produced. The Communist regime threw out the old courtesies and ethics cherished by old Beijing residents, and the architects of the Cultural Revolution condemned the basic tenets and norms of normal social behavior. This left young people to grow up in con-fusion and with little guidance from teachers, parents, or society. They have been so much exposed to rude, uncouth behavior that many don't know how to respond to a simple "thank you."

At one time service in stores, public institutions, and even hospitals got so bad that the authorities decreed one month of each year as a "Civilization and Politeness Month." March, I believe it was. Salesgirls in state-run stores are almost always chatting and laughing with each other, and customers who want service often have to call them half a dozen times—at the risk of being rebuffed with a sharp "Can't you see we're busy!"

But we were treated civilly one blessed month a year and whenever some national or Party conferences were taking place. Residents tried to do their major shopping then, because after the month or the conference was over, the mandatory smiles were once more replaced by indifferent stares.

My personal life, however, was tranquil and fairly fulfilling after my second teaching trip to the United States. My career grew in proportion to my hard work and self-confidence, and although I faced the same jealousies and intrigues encountered by most professional women, East or West, I preferred to overlook such things; my marriage-in-name had finally dissolved and I felt at peace, and I was finally very well off, not so much from the family money in my bank account as from my writing and translation fees. I became, in fact, a sort of bank to my close friends, always ready to provide a cash loan. And I finally got the long-awaited telephone, for which I had queued up three years because I refused to work through connections. It cost me 1,500 yuan to install, equivalent to a full year of my then not-so-low salary. The installation fee remains the equivalent of a full year's salary, going up proportionately with inflation.

In 1988 a five-month Rockefeller Fellowship was offered in the United States to film scholars. I applied, and my acceptance as a candidate opened up a whole new world for me.

The notification reached me at my office address, and was brought upstairs by a colleague who chose to have her lunch in my office. I skipped lunch, as usual. I opened the letter and sat down immediately. I couldn't believe it had actually happened. "I must tell Mama!" was my first thought. Then I realized she was not there to listen to me. How she would have enjoyed hearing this news! Because of the war, she had never been able to use the fellowship given her in 1937, but now her daughter had obtained an even more prestigious one, the Rockefeller.

For several minutes I sat oblivious of the chattering and laughter around me. I was with my parents, wherever they were.

A few days later, I received a call from the United States saying there would be an additional five months, if I'd agree to that. It was so unexpected I said I'd ask my children about it and reply in forty-eight hours. I got hold of Deedee first on the phone and asked if it would be okay if I stayed away for ten months.

"Why do you ask?" he replied immediately. "You must be crazy not to say yes right away." That's what one gets for raising independent children.

I laid some groundwork by having a few strong and persuasive conversations with various bosses, and when I formally handed in my request for a very long leave of absence, it was granted without much hassle. I got all the red tape wrapped up before they got too wise to what a *"Lo-ke-fei-le,"*—as Rockefeller is transliterated into Chinese—was. . . .

One of my buddies called on me a week before I left. "I've checked the files at a social sciences institute," he said, "and it seems you're the first Rockefeller Fellow from China, or at least the first woman. Let me do a little bragging for the benefit of those who'd prefer you didn't go."

We amused ourselves by thinking up some wisecracks and verbal digs. But after a while I said, "Stay low-key. Nothing is accomplished before all is done and over with. Save the fun for when I come back to report and celebrate."

I left my children and my friends, and set out for what was to be a year-long program of research. I have never returned.

Till the Tanks Roll By

I was somewhat uneasy when I left China, not only because this trip would be much longer than any previous one, but also because I had no idea how the rising inflation would affect the life of my children. Without any "big people" around, would they be able to manage their incomes and stock up on basic necessities?

"In any case, you still have your Pa around," I had finally conceded, realizing I wasn't their only parent. They laughed off my concern, for they considered themselves very much grown up and capable of coping with life with or without their Old Ma. Deedee was in college at the time while Mimi had become a journalist after obtaining her B.A.

The day I left for the United States, in August 1988, a San Francisco–area high school basketball team was returning on the same flight. They were quite conspicuous in their light blue team color and occupied the entire back section of the plane. As the long night receded and the American coastline came in sight in the sunlight, I heard a soft refrain sung in their young voices: "Oh beautiful for spacious skies, for amber waves of grain . . . "

My eyes tingled with tears at the sound of the familiar melody.

I have sung this song in English, I've sung the Soviet national hymn in Russian, and I sang that of the Republic of China as a child and that of the People's Republic of China in my youth. I am familiar with the sentiments conveyed by these songs and the pride they express. But in the 1980s we Chinese were no longer singing our song; the inspiring sentiments were gone, and mouthing a hymn to a country one no longer has confidence in is stupid, even ridiculous. I was touched by those American kids and their song, because as long as it's sung, there is hope.

I spent several days in Los Angeles touching base with friends before proceeding to my research site, Madison, Wisconsin, in the heartland. There, I was met and driven across the city, and I saw the moon reflected on water. I smiled, and my hosts asked me why. "Because," I answered. "Whoever I asked about Madison always said, `I must start with the five lakes.' Now I know why."

I passed the academically most fulfilling months of my career in the libraries and among archives, made more friends, and found time to visit New York, Ohio, Iowa, and Los Angeles while devoting myself to a full work schedule of eight hours daily.

In April 1989, the demonstrations on Tiananmen Square came to the attention of the world. In fact, political tension had been high for the past several months, and joint declarations and statements were being issued one after the other by dissident Chinese at home and abroad. I was called upon to join a couple of signings, but I declined; not that I disagreed, but because I wanted whatever I said to be in my own words alone. Little did I guess that I'd be doing just that in a few months' time.

The reasons for the dissatisfaction were economic and social, and protest was fueled by expected and unexpected political events, which culminated in the tragedy on Tiananmen Square.

One primary reason for the collapse of the KMT government on mainland China in 1949 had been economic. The regime was doomed by rampant corruption among all ranks of its officials and their indifference to the fate of the ordinary people who had undergone long and bitter wars. The forces of the Chinese Communist Party profited from this situation, and with the support of almost 90 percent of the then Chinese population—workers, poor peasants, and destitute city residents—swept across China. Their rallying cry was the establishment of a "new democracy," not socialism or communism.

The new CCP administration managed to stabilize the mainland Chinese economy to some extent in the 1950s. The officials of that period were relatively free from corruption, not only by contrast with the KMT's officials, but because they had been well disciplined. With the passage of time, however, as their power (one of the two *quan li* I've mentioned in the episode on *pinyin*) grew, their wants and desires increased. Yet the spartan lifestyle of the early years of the People's Republic did not provide room for much greed; there wasn't much to be greedy about anyway in an indigent and egalitarian society.

But by the mid-1980s, the Chinese were again facing institutional corruption, and the worst offenders were the offspring of high-ranking leaders as well as many of the officials themselves.

These offspring of Communist leaders who once fought against the KMT have now became symbols of corruption. Some controlled military aircraft and vessels and were known to use these to smuggle in luxury goods, which they listed as military supplies to escape customs inspection. Others took advantage of their parents' power and connections to grab fantastic profits through speculation and profiteering activities. These "princelings," as they are called by irate citizens, were well on the way to owning the nation.

While such things were happening and giving rise to popular demands that some sort of democratic controls be instituted to check the abuses, the Chinese media kept silent on the issue. But by the mid-1980s, any informed citizen could tell a dozen first- or secondhand stories about cases of bribery and embezzlement involving high officials. Corruption was so widespread even doctors, drivers, and salespersons expected to be bribed. Something was bound to break.

The winter of discontent erupted into a spring of unrest in 1989. Sporadic demonstrations—the Chinese Constitution nominally guarantees the citizen's freedom to demonstrate, assemble, and form unions—were fueled by an unexpected event: the untimely death of Hu Yaobang, a former CCP Secretary General. Hu was quick-thinking and direct; he was a short man, and so was his temper. Deng had handpicked Hu, but had the latter ousted when he became displeased with Hu's outspokenness. This action, taken in 1987, once more showed Deng's relentlessness and ruthlessness, though many realized this too late.

Young students were upset by Hu's death—it was rumored Hu tripped and fell while angrily denouncing the rampant corruption, and failed to survive despite medical efforts. Many were also finding their former idol Deng not so ideal after all. The scattered demonstrations converged, and naturally headed for Tiananmen Square in the heart of the city.

I have often wondered if those who approved the original blueprint for the Square ever regretted expanding it to its current size; it is larger than Moscow's Red Square. Many streets and buildings were demolished in its construction. It's almost like having a Disneyland parking lot smack in the middle of downtown Beijing. No other square could have accommodated the millions of demonstrators in 1976, and in 1989.

I have also speculated that if Deng hadn't hung on to power to consummate his historical handshake with Gorbachev, the situation might not have developed to such an extent. Because of that anticipated Sino-Soviet handshake, the world media was in China in full strength and with full permission to record the event; instead, they witnessed the demonstration that robbed Deng of his moment of glory in history and sent him down in ignominy.

If it hadn't been for the presence of the world media, would the demonstrations have blazed so fiercely? And if the regime hadn't lost face before the world audience, would it have resorted to such drastic measures? Sometimes loss of face is more devastating than loss of life. The thing is, whose life?

Tension continued to rise in Beijing during the last two months of my research. There was little fear felt on our side—the side of the ordinary Chinese people. All we wanted was for the leaders to take a better look at themselves and do something about the corruption that lay at the root of social unrest. Someone, hopefully, would listen to the ideas and suggestions raised by the people. I had hoped the administration and the ordinary people could at least establish some sort of rapport, as they had after the downfall of the Gang of Four.

I had gone to an end-of-semester party for faculty and grad students of the department with which my research was affiliated. The TV was on, and channel after channel was broadcasting triumphant demonstrations in Beijing. In fact, no one present had their minds on food, small talk, or the desultory academic discussions. Everyone's eyes were glued to the set, taking in what was going on in my home town.

Many Chinese students in the United States were in raptures and declaring their readiness to go back and join in the history-making, to help build up the kind of modern China they envisioned. Even I felt a similar urge as I watched the scenes unfolding at places I knew so well. I remembered the commemorations of Zhou Enlai on the same square thirteen years ago. I had also felt the impulse then to bring my two young children from Tianjin to participate in a historical event. Now they were both there, while their mother looked on from thousands of miles away.

I was getting more information through the grapevine than my American acquaintances, especially about the city residents' support for the students. And about the peasants' support for city residents; country people living around Beijing blocked roads to keep military convoys from entering the city. Some said jokingly it was like in the war days when peasants kept lookouts in the trees to warn Communist guerrillas about Japanese or KMT troop movements—only now the people were joining to deter the advance of the People's Liberation Army.

Was any uneasiness felt on the people's side? Yes, of course. Almost all had contemplated the possibility of batons and water hoses being used against them, but nothing more than that. No guns had been fired at Beijing's residents since the Japanese occupation, and even the 1948–1949 siege of Beijing had been terminated without bloodshed.

Toto happened to go to Beijing on a short business trip toward the latter half of May. He told me that demonstrators occupying the Square day and night were mostly college students in their late teens, and some were afraid at night, like children. So young people in their twenties made it their business to go to the square after work to keep them company. Young stewards in the hotel Toto stayed at knocked on his door every evening before they left for the square. "We're going now, sir!" they'd say. "Remember us if we don't come back." It was not mock heroism; it was an arousal of commitment among China's young people.

The only words of caution Toto gave my children was to try to get out of the way if beatings and pushing around started a stampede.

Secure in the knowledge that my kids would have the common sense not to get hurt if they could help it, I went on with my research in Madison, prepared for the next stop on my trip, and followed the news closely.

When I went to bed as usual on a June night in Madison, I didn't suspect my life was reaching a turning point; and that many other lives would reach their end.

EPILOGUE

After the Tanks Roll By

I woke up late on the morning of June 3, 1989, United States date. It was a Saturday. I had a leisurely breakfast and, before beginning the day's schedule, turned on the CNN News at about 10:00 A.M., my time. My world exploded.

I instinctively called both numbers in Beijing; the one at our one-room apartment and the one Deedee used. There was no answer at either. It was late at night in Beijing and the killing had just started. I called Toto in California; it was still early morning Pacific time and they hadn't turned on the TV. We spoke briefly and I resumed my calls to Beijing at ten-minute intervals, but with no greater success.

Then my phone began to ring. For the next few days I was to receive calls from all over the United States, Long Island to Hawaii; from people in all walks of life, students to stars; and of all ages, grade school children to Hollywood blacklistees in their seventies. I learned that the last act of "The Flying Dutchman" Joris Ivens, the legendary documentary filmmaker who had embraced the Chinese revolution for half a century, had been to condemn the massacre before his death; and the last call made by a young student at UCLA to his professor was to cry in anguish over the killings. This young man died a few days later in a car accident.

No words could convey my shock, anger, and shame on learning about the brutal, cowardly, and cynical carnage visited upon unarmed citizens. There aren't words strong enough in any language to condemn that heinous act. I knew that those who were most angered were people who cared about the state of the world and who were aware of the Chinese as a people and a nation. The utter stupidity, not to mention the inhumanity, of the authorities' so-called "necessary measures" shattered links of trust as well as the allegiance of many loyal hearts. It was an act which, as the Chinese say, pains one's own family and friends.

Before I got through to my kids, however, a friend called and asked if I'd consent to do an interview for a local TV station that afternoon at her house. I agreed.

I went on calling both Beijing numbers with a sinking heart. Toto and I both tried. We were afraid that even if my children were as yet unharmed, both of them might rush out crying for redress and get hurt, or worse.

A devastating fear gripped me on that bright early summer day in Madison as I tried to dial into the violence-filled Beijing night. Phone in hand, eyes riveted on the CNN news, I dialed again and again, wondering whether my babies were dead or alive.

Deedee answered, finally, at about 2:00 A.M. Beijing time. In a tight voice, he said he was told there were bodies all around; he had just come home but had to go out again to assist the injured. No, he was not with Mimi that night and had no idea where she was. I pleaded with him to stay until he heard from his sister.

Then it was time for the interview at my friend's house, which was more spacious than my apartment. I condemned the killing in plain terms: "The first shot marked the beginning of the end of that regime . . ." I said what I thought, and did what I had to do and wanted to do. It was a strong program; it had to be.

My friend drove me back. I went straight to the phone and called Deedee in Beijing. He had just spoken with Mimi. She was safe at a friend's house and would stay there until daylight. It was still dark in Beijing and not six hours since the killing started, but the phone had already been bugged, as I could tell from a distinct echo in the receiver. With so much bloodshed going on, the powers there didn't forget to tap the phone lines!

Then I started to worry: Was Mimi really safe? Or had Deedee only told me she was, so that I wouldn't be too anxious? I didn't sleep much that night. At about 2 A.M., my time, the phone rang and it was Mimi. I cried out in relief. She said: "I knew I had to call you, since you can't reach me. I had to let you hear my voice. I'm staying with some friends. Don't worry about us. We've grown up." She sounded cautious, but I understood. I understood right away that not only had suppression taken place, but the repressive controls were once again setting in, less than twenty-four hours after the killing had started.

I sat in front of the TV most of Sunday, watching CNN rotating its program every thirty minutes. Late into the night, I suddenly came upon myself. My brief interview, broadcast at the Madison station on Saturday night, had been picked up as an individual program. Only then did I realize that freedom of speech in the United States would become, for me, proof of culpability in China. I had given brief thought to that when I agreed to the interview, but assumed the Chinese authorities were not likely to pick anything up from a local channel. I hadn't anticipated the possibility of the CNN broadcast, which would be seen in China, even if only by the foreign embassies and the powers-that-be.

I could only wait until morning to contact the local station and ask them to call CNN to have the interview pulled off. I do not know how many times it was aired that night, at any rate, once was enough to damn me. The local station passed on my request but the harm was done.

Less than ten days after the massacre, I called Beijing again just to check if my children were all right. Mimi remarked: "You said something over there, didn't you?" I was surprised; I hadn't told my kids about the interview. She named a few of my bosses and said: "They were summoned to some place at the top and informed what people from each *dan wei* were doing overseas. You are among them. One of your buddies passed on the news to me."

I was in anguish, not because I didn't expect to be identified sooner or later. But I'd done that interview only as an obscure fellow at a Midwestern university. Yet they'd identified me, profession, *dan wei* and all, in a matter of days. They'd nailed me even before they had attended to the identities of the victims, and before deciding what casualty figures to release to the world. Their first priority was to hunt down those whom they saw as the disloyal, most of them angry but inconsequential people like myself. I knew then that I had reached the point of no return.

I stayed glued to the TV set in the meantime, to see how the Beijing regime reacted to worldwide condemnation, to see the fury of people in Hong Kong and of Chinese in the West. The TV images from China became more and more revolting as the regime's leaders brazenly paraded their enormities. I saw the premier, Li Peng, reviewing the killer troops and greeting them with an arm raised at an undecided angle, halfway between a wave and a Nazi-style salute. I unplugged the set for the rest of my stay in Madison. I could no longer bear to watch.

The Chinese authorities tried to explain the killing by claiming the riot police and army troops were not equipped with rubber bullets, and therefore had to use real ones; they also said that they had been ordered to shoot at the ground so it was not their fault that people died. I was later told what happened: The killer troops, brought in from other provinces, had indeed been instructed to shoot low. But their bullets were of a type that shattered on impact with a hard surface, say a cement-paved city street. The fragments then ricocheted with such lethal effect that many victims died of horribly lacerated abdomens. This explained instances I'd heard about where surgeons couldn't find any unbroken pieces of flesh large enough to suture together.

I also learned that doctors in nearby hospitals had been treating the fatally, hopelessly injured as best they could, and then strongly advising their families in private to take the victim home at once. The death could then be registered at the family's local neighborhood committee instead of at the hospital, and the cause of death given as a sudden seizure or accident. This might at least help the living escape being branded "family members of a counter-revolutionary rioter."

I later learned the route of the killer troops and that most casualties were on Chang An Avenue—the Avenue of Everlasting Peace. So the Chinese authorities vehemently denied anyone had died on Tiananmen Square.

Mail censorship was as blatantly evident as phone line bugging, and not even considered an invasion of privacy by most Chinese, who are accustomed to that kind of thing. Important letters are often hand-carried and mailed outside China. I received one such letter from one of my cousins. She gave me an "ear-witness" account of how the killing started, at one spot at least:

"We were at home that night," she wrote. "We're both in our sixties, after all, and our grandson was ill.

"We had been to the Tiananmen Square a week earlier to show our support as veteran student demonstrators of some forty years ago. We'd even taken our three-year-old grandson along. Since the students on the Square wore headbands expressing their will to be 'resolute to the end,' I took two handkerchiefs from my purse and tied them together to make a headband for the child. The enthusiastic young demonstrators were delighted and called, 'Hey, this kid is on our side!' They even treated him to popsicles.

"But in the intervening week, the tensions and uncertainty had mounted and everyone, including the students, anticipated some sort of forceful reaction from the authorities. Many civilians gave handkerchiefs, surgical masks, and bottled water to the students to use in case of tear gas attacks. Nobody imagined that anything more lethal would be used.

"We had already gone to bed that night but were unable to sleep because of the noise and excitement, since we live very close to the western end of Chang An Avenue. We could hear the surflike sound produced by the thousands of people thronging the streets.

"Then we saw a flash of light against the sky, like that of a conflagration, followed by a momentary lull. Suddenly, burst after burst of what could only be machinegun fire ripped through the night. We were both startled, for we had never heard a machinegun fired in real life. Then, after a stunned silence, shouts and screams came through the open windows. The roaring of thousands of voices swept through the streets.

"Early the next day, we had to take our grandson to a hospital for an injection. Our whole family went together, not knowing what we might encounter. We saw bodies laid out on the pavement in front of the hospital, with army men standing guard to prevent anyone from going near. Wounded people were being treated in the hospital's emergency ward and while we were there, students came in to ask the doctors for casualty figures. As far as we know, these figures gathered by the students were never released.

"After our grandson got his injection, his mother took him home while my husband and I listened to a man describing what had happened the night before.

"According to him and a dozen others, one of the clashes later much publicized by the government occurred in the following manner: An army jeep carrying six soldiers was speeding down the street, when the driver, probably upset by the jeers and shouts of the hostile crowds on both sides, made a sharp turn and caused the jeep to overturn. There was an explosion as the jeep's gasoline or perhaps some explosives in the vehicle ignited. (That was the flash of light we saw.) Then, from several directions, machine guns started to rattle, killing and wounding many bystanders. That man indicated the angry crowd `took care of' anyone who was still alive in that overturned and burning jeep.

"The authorities later dubbed the dead soldiers `the Six Defenders of the Republic' and used them to justify the army's crackdown on the `rioters,' as the demonstrators and bystanders are now called."

That letter was hand-carried out of China and passed on to our numerous relatives now in the West. It was worn and dog-eared by the time it reached me.

I realized I had become a homeless drifter on the road of self-exile. And with my future abruptly uncertain, when I left Madison at the end of June, I packed up more than I really needed, keeping things I would normally have discarded, and I ended with three large suitcases and numerous carry-ons.

According to my original schedule, I was to have spent the rest of 1989 at SUNY at Stony Brook on Long Island as a Resident Fellow, then gone on to teach a seminar at University of Southern California in Los Angeles on my way back to China, ending my third academic stay in the United States in a matter of twenty-one months. That plan remained unchanged except that now it had an open end.

I went east in accordance with my schedule, then returned to the West Coast at the end of 1989. Heartsick, weary, and again at crossroads, I secured three more seminars and managed to get by on the little I made from them.

Toto was keeping a close eye on me, but we understood I'd have to stand on my own feet. I maintained as much contact as I could with Mimi and Deedee. For financial reasons I couldn't afford to have them come to the United States, and for political reasons I couldn't afford to return to China.

It was not until 1991, after I started another stage in my life, again among film professionals—this time Americans—that I saw Mimi again. She was in Canada on a student visa and came down to California to see both Toto's family and me. I did not see Deedee until 1995.

By tacit agreement Mimi and I refrained from talking about the biggest event since the last time we'd seen each other three years earlier. We shopped, gossiped, took pictures, discussed anything but . . . until we finally sat down to review that June night of 1989. I had just learned to drive and took her to the Santa Monica beach close by. We sat down at a table at my favorite open-air café overlooking the ocean. Now and then, as our conversation progressed, we would gaze with tear-filled eyes over the sparkling ocean or at the little black birds pecking for crumbs nearby.

Mimi told me both Deedee and herself were unhurt because they were in the east side of Beijing. They were lucky. If home had happened to be on the west side, they would have run right into the line of fire, as many victims did.

None of the demonstrators had any prior knowledge of the direction of the troop movements, of course; that was a top military secret. But I also learned the story of my lifelong friend from a common acquaintance: Lifelong had left the navy, and he looked older than his years. He had been standing on a street corner watching the milling throngs of protestors. Suddenly, he heard a barely audible but tension-filled voice: "Go home now, old man! My gun isn't loaded, but others will be. Go home!" My friend looked around and glimpsed an expressionless armed guard—a not-so-young military man of the local Beijing garrison—before the latter moved on.

Mimi enlightened me regarding the circumstances of my exposure in China:

A person from my old *dan wei* who happened to be in Hong Kong at the time saw the CNN news, a program not available to ordinary mainland Chinese inhabitants. The moment this person returned to our *dan wei* in Beijing, she gave overblown accounts of my interview. She of course used her tattling for her own career ends.

I also learned from others that excerpts from my interview were also integrated into a program produced by a Shanghai TV station, purporting to show local Chinese audiences how counterrevolutionaries overseas were vilifying our great motherland. So there I was again tagged with the familiar old label: "counterrevolutionary—*fan-ge-ming*."

To the best of my knowledge, censorious statements regarding my sinful behavior have not yet ceased, despite all the magnanimous official declarations welcoming prodigal scholars back to the fold.

I walked Mimi over to the bluff above the beach to watch the sun go home. "Why do you say that?" asked my daughter. "You know the sun doesn't go anywhere!" I told her about the ritual we had observed in the living room when the weather was fine, in the house on Scenic Avenue she was recently taken to by her uncle Toto. That was many, many years ago when the Chens decided to go back to a land we grew up in and could not forget. The seniors have passed away but the then-juniors are both on this side of the ocean again, by free choice or by force of circumstances.

My wanderings have ended in the City of Angels; my three battered suitcases have completed their service and gone to the garbage dump. I have gradually come to terms with my present life and, paradoxically, feel that I am home at last, here in the Golden State I had dreamed about in the dungeon, here where I yearned to find refuge from all horrors and persecution.

Mimi and I leaned against the railing and gazed at the sinking red orb as it flattened and melted into the horizon, leaving a glorious afterglow; and I seemed to hear Mama call again: "Come watch the sun go home!"

Acknowledgments

I cannot list and give adequate thanks to all who read my manuscript in various stages of its completion—all my friends and colleagues who gave me support and encouragement in many ways. The manuscript has been read by a wide range of Americans: white, black, and of Asian heritage. The oldest person is ninety-four and the youngest in her late teens. Allow me to list the names of some of them in alphabetical order:

Sanora Babb, Stacey Behlmer, Chris Berry, Leo Braudy, Wenhui Chen, Carol Cullen, Linda Davidson, Pat DeFazio, Russell Good, Gaby Jacobus-Baudier, Kristine Harris, Martin Hoffman, Dick Howard, Lisa Jackson, Paul Jarrico, Marjorie Johnson, E. Ann Kaplan, Beulah Quo, Janice Lance, Ring Lardner, Jr., Wayne Lee, Stephen Lesser, Ivy Lew, Janet Lorenz, Daniel Mann, David Marsh, Adam Mehr, Linda and Sheldon Mehr, John Michaan, Sally Morgan, Janet Neipris, Bill Nichols, Jennifer Nye, Robert Rioux, Robert Rosen, James Schwartz, Susan Sheehan, Leon Slawecki, Robert Smolkin, E-tu Zen Sun, Faye Thompson, George Wallach, Jack Young, and E-an Zen.

I give special thanks to Charles Champlin, Arts Editor Emeritus of the *Los Angeles Times*, who enlightened me midway during my voluminous writing by proposing that I should make most of the fact that I straddle two cultures, thus guiding me to significantly refocus my narrative; I also thank specifically Richard Walter, professor at UCLA, who for the past five years has made unremitting efforts to help find an agent for this new writer. His continuing faith in my project, my writing, and in my mules on the mountain road emboldened me to go on searching for a chance to publish.

And the chance came in the form of my friend Dr. Nira Gupta-Casale; she and her colleague Dr. Charles DeFanti at Kean College of New Jersey brought my manuscript to the attention of John Weber and Daniel O'Connor of Marlowe and Company. I wish to thank them and all who have been involved in this project at the publishing company.

I am fortunate in that the publishers assigned to me an uniquely astute editor, Mara Lurie. She very firmly but gently guided me through the last stage of preparing the manuscript for reader consumption. In fact, she got into the manuscript so thoroughly that she has almost become an expert on those numerous political movements in China. I give my thanks to Mara for the quality of the final version.

Without my collaborator, Ted King, the manuscript would hardly be as presentable as it is—my grammar studies in English never got beyond the "present perfect" tense. He patiently toiled with me for the four long years of writing while at the same time working to build a career of his own in his adopted country, the United States. Without Ted, this book could not have taken flight.

Last but not least, I thank my nearest and dearest, my brother "Toto" and his family, and my children "Mimi" and "Deedee," for allowing me to poke fun at their childhood escapades. And especially to Toto for his understanding, and for sharing the agony caused by our memories, many written and more too painful to be written. I am grateful and thankful that I have had my family with me every step of the way.